Reading St La
Churchwardens' .
1498-1570

Part I
Introduction and
Accounts 1498-1536

Reading St Laurence Churchwardens' Accounts 1498-1570

Part I
Introduction and Accounts 1498-1536

Edited by Joan Dils

Berkshire Record Society
Volume 19
2013

Published by the
Berkshire Record Society
c/o Berkshire Record Office
9 Coley Avenue, Reading
Berkshire
RG1 6AF

Printed by Berforts
23-25 Gunnels Wood Park
Gunnels Wood Road
Stevenage, Hertfordshire
SG1 2BH

ISBN 978-0-9573937-0-7

Contents

Cover illustration: the opening page of the accounts for 1514-15
(Berkshire Record Office D/P97/5/2, p. 100)

Acknowledgements

Many people have been of immense help in preparing this volume. Two of them, whom I cannot thank personally, have been particularly important as will be seen from many footnotes: a former vicar of St Laurence, the Revd Charles Kerry, whose book on the parish has much useful information, and the late Dr Jeanette Martin whose doctoral thesis has important detail and comment on the role of leading parishioners during the Reformation period and on the problem of providing for the cure of souls after 1550. I am also indebted to Professor Ralph Houlbrooke who read an original draft of the Introduction and saved me from numerous errors, and Dr Alan Crosby whose comments on a later draft improved it immensely. Ms Lisa Spurrier checked the transcript of the accounts with me, correcting a number of uncertain readings and Fr Geoffrey Scott, Abbot of Douai solved the problem of divided Latin words in the inventories. Dr Peter Durrant, General Editor of the Berkshire Record Society, has been unfailingly helpful and patient with my many queries. All remaining errors are my own.

Joan Dils
August 2013

Introduction

1. The parish of St Laurence, Reading and its churchwardens' accounts[1]

i. The parish and the borough.

Reading in the early sixteenth century was the most populous and richest town in Berkshire. It lay on the important east-west road from London to Bristol, a comfortable day's journey from Windsor; this possibly influenced Henry I in choosing it as the site of Reading Abbey, his major monastic foundation in 1121. The road from Oxford to Southampton crossed the River Thames north of Reading before proceeding south over the smaller, many-streamed River Kennet which flowed through the town. The confluence of Kennet and Thames at Kennet Mouth less than a mile to the east of the Market Place allowed Reading's merchants to export agricultural produce from its hinterland to London and import a range of goods including the capital's specialist manufactures and foreign luxuries for local sale. However its wealth was based primarily on the production of high quality woollen cloth for which the Kennet provided an ample water supply. It was ranked tenth richest town in England according to its assessment for the lay subsidy of 1524-5.[2] The total tax paid in the two years was £422 14s 0d, the amount, and so the wealth, unevenly distributed among the town's three parishes. St Laurence, the richest parish, paid £265 9s 8d, almost 63 per cent of the total; it also housed almost half the taxpayers. St Giles, south of the Kennet, was the poorest and smallest. Even St Mary, the most ancient parish, paid less than a quarter of the total. A few very wealthy men were responsible for much of St Laurence's large contribution, among them William Wattis, Thomas Everard and Richard Turner who together contributed about £46 in 1524; at the other end of the scale were the wage-earners of the parish, 58 per cent of whom paid at the lowest rates.[3]

The parishes were also distinctive in area and population. The number of 'houseling people' recorded in the Chantry Certificates of 1547 was 1,000 in St Laurence (the smallest in area), 500 in St Mary, the largest, and 500 in St Giles.[4] They have one feature in common: early churchwardens' accounts

---

1. The modern spelling of the parish name is Laurence. In Charles Kerry, *A History of the Municipal Church of St. Lawrence, Reading* (Reading, 1883) the author used the contemporary spelling. In the sixteenth century there was no definitive form. Kerry was curate of St Laurence from 1880-83. He took a keen interest in the local history of all the parishes he served. *Crockford's Clerical Directory* (1890), 731.
2. Alan Dyer, *Decline and Growth in English Towns, 1400-1600* (1991) 70.
3. TNA, Lay Subsidy Returns for Reading, 1524-5, E/179/13,135,138,139. The 1524 return for St Laurence is incomplete with only 212 names compared with 245 in 1525. See also J. Sheail edited by R. W. Hoyle, *The regional distribution of wealth in England as indicated in the 1524/25 Lay Subsidy Returns* (List and Index Society Special Series xxviii, 2 vols, 1998), ii, 17.
4. *Chantry Certificates for Berkshire*, ed. N. E. Fox (privately published 1994), 38. The population total is calculated by assuming that houseling people (communicants and those over

survive for all three but only that for St Laurence has never been published.[1]

St Laurence's parish was established by Reading Abbey soon after its foundation in 1121. The town and manor of Reading and its parishes, formerly royal possessions were part of the king's endowment of the abbey which became lord of the borough, and rector and patron of all three parishes. The church of St Laurence was founded by the abbey first as a chapel by its Main Gate as an oratory for pilgrims. By the beginning of the thirteenth century it was referred to as a church. It became the parish church of a community which grew up near the abbey where a new market place and the pilgrim traffic attracted by the abbey's relics provided good economic prospects. Wholly within the borough boundary, it occupied the north-eastern part of the built-up area but extended as far as Kennet Mouth to the east. Like the other Reading parishes St Laurence's was a vicarage though it was a corrody vicarage without any glebe; nearly two-thirds of its income came from the abbey.[2]

ii. The office of churchwarden and churchwardens' accounts.

In England the appointment of churchwardens was first required by a canon of the Council of London 1127; thereafter it became accepted practice and was firmly established by the fourteenth century by which time the laity had responsibility for certain aspects of parochial life.[3] Most parishes had two wardens though some like Basingstoke and Wellingborough had four; large parishes in Lancashire with several townships had six or more. They were sometimes known by other titles such as guardians or church-reeves, and as befitted this important office, they were usually chosen from the more substantial parishioners.[4] Traditionally they were elected annually at a parish meeting, later called a vestry.

The primary responsibilities of churchwardens were to make adequate provision for worship in the church: upkeep of the fabric (excluding the chancel which was in the rector's charge) and of the churchyard; purchase, maintenance and safe-keeping of bells, service books, sacred vessels and

sixteen years old) comprised between two-thirds and three-fifths of the population. Calculations based on total taxpayers in 1524-5 produce an estimated total of 3452, Alan Dyer, *Decline and Growth in English Towns 1400-1600* (1991), 72.

1. Those for St Giles date from 1518, BRO D/P96/5/1, part of which was published as *The Church-Wardens' Account Book for the Parish of St. Giles, Reading, part 1 1518-46*, ed. W. L. Nash (Reading, 1881); and St Mary from 1555, *The Churchwardens' Accounts of the Parish of St Mary's, Reading*, ed. F. and A. Garry (Reading, 1893).
2. Brian Kemp, 'Reading Abbey and the Medieval Town' in *The Growth of Reading*, ed. Malcolm Petyt (Stroud, 1993), 46; Jeanette Martin, 'Leadership and Priorities in Reading during the Reformation' in *The Reformation in English Towns 1500-1640*, eds. Patrick Collinson and John Craig (Basingstoke, 1998), 116.
3. J. Charles Cox, *Churchwardens' Accounts from the fourteenth to the close of the seventeenth century* (1913), 1; David Dymond, *Churchwardens' Accounts*, Historical Association Short Guides to Records 25, (1995), 1. This pamphlet is an excellent short introduction to the subject.
4. Cox, *Churchwardens' Accounts*, 5; Dymond, *Churchwardens' Accounts*, 2. For the information on Lancashire I am indebted to Dr Alan Crosby.

vestments, and the provision of such items as a parish bier. In addition they were expected to inform the bishop or archdeacon at their visitations of any moral backsliding by either clergy or people.[1] During the sixteenth century, central government burdened them and other parish officials with many extra responsibilities towards the state.

Income to meet the expense of fulfilling these duties came from renting out parish property (which the churchwardens had to keep in good repair), parochial collections, parish entertainments such as church ales, festivals and plays, and fees for ringing bells at funerals and commemorations and for burials in church. If these sources were insufficient, the churchwardens were responsible for raising funds, usually by voluntary donations or assessed rates. Keeping a record of parish finances was enjoined by the Statute of Exeter, 1287; the survival of some churchwardens' accounts from *c.*1350 indicates how soon the practice became the accepted means whereby the parish was informed about its financial state, the churchwardens were exonerated from any suspicion of financial irregularities, and could be reimbursed for any personal debts they had incurred on parish business.[2]

How far such accounts reflect the totality of parish life is doubtful. 'Strictly speaking, the term churchwardens' accounts is misleading: the transaction which produced these Records was .....[that] of the corporate body of Parishioners ..... assembled together .... in order to receive their common property, the "Church Stock" from the hands of those to whom it had been entrusted, to receive an account of their income and expenditure, to elect new churchwardens and hand over the "parish stock" to them.' In essence the accounts are 'only incidental to a record of an annual Audit and Election'.[3] As such, the accounts are neat copies compiled from various bills and invoices (now lost) collected by the wardens during the year, a point repeated by Burgess who also warns against assuming that they are comprehensive. They include payments only for goods and activities for which the churchwardens were responsible, or for those purposes where collections failed to meet the whole cost.[4]

iii. St Laurence's churchwardens.

For the most part the churchwardens of St Laurence were the more substantial parishioners, a necessary attribute since they might have to loan

---

1. Berkshire churchwardens, including those from Reading, attended the archdeacon of Berkshire's visitations in 1560-2, BRO, Archdeacon's Records: Visitation Books, 1560-2 D/A2/e5. Individuals and organisations in the parish could and did donate extra church goods and provide extra services. C. Burgess, 'Pre-Reformation Churchwardens' Accounts and Parish Government: Lessons from London and Bristol', *English Historical Review*, cxvii (2002), 312.
2. Charles Drew, *Early Parochial Organisation in England.* (St Anthony's Hall Publications, vii, York, 1954), 7, 24.
3. *Lambeth Churchwardens' Accounts 1504-1645 and Vestry Book 1610* ed. Charles Drew (2 vols. Surrey Record Society, xviii and xx, London 1941 and 1950), i, xii-xiii.
4. Burgess, 'Pre-Reformation Churchwardens' Accounts ', 312-4.

money to the parish if the accounts were in deficit.[1] The wealth of wardens serving during the earlier years of the century can be judged from their assessment for a lay subsidy ordered by Henry VIII. This was a comprehensive, graduated tax collected in two halves in 1524 and 1525 and levied on either income from land or the capital value of goods, or wages if the taxpayer had no land or goods above the taxable limit. In 1524 fourteen men of the seventy-nine who had served or would serve as churchwardens between 1498 and 1570 can be traced. All were assessed on goods, one over £300, one at £200, two at £100 and the rest at £10 or more, levels which place them among the richest men in the borough.[2] They and many of the other wardens played a leading role in the economic life of the town; the occupations of thirty-five of them are known.[3]

Many were also significant players in urban politics. About two-thirds of the churchwardens between 1498 and 1560 were either already burgesses on election to the office or subsequently became so. Throughout the middle ages the title of burgess was given to members of the Gild Merchant, the leading men of the town. After 1560 when Reading became an incorporated borough by the great charter of Elizabeth I, the term burgess denoted the more elevated status of membership of the Corporation or Council as alderman, capital or secondary burgess; between 1560 and 1570, five of ten churchwardens were burgesses. Nineteen served as mayor before 1577, some on several occasions: Richard Turner six times, Edward Butler five and Thomas Turner three. William Edmunds and John Bell in addition to being chosen mayors served as MPs for the borough, Edmunds in 1523 and Bell in 1553, 1555 and 1558.[4] Other churchwardens served as cofferers (treasurers) of the gild, constables or wardens of the High Ward.[5] Successful service as churchwarden, it has been claimed, was a 'rung on the ladder en route to a position among the parish governors'.[6] In Reading men moved from civic to parish office and vice versa, often holding both simultaneously.

iv. St Laurence's churchwardens and the parish meeting.
There were normally two churchwardens, called *sacristi* in the 1430s, wardens in 1498, proctors from 1501-1516 and wardens thereafter.[7] They were elected at the annual parish meeting after the previous year's accounts

---

1. See St Laurence's churchwardens' accounts (hereafter Accounts) for 1513-15.
2. TNA, Lay Subsidy Returns, 1524-5, E/179/73/139.
3. Most information on occupations comes from wills, of which there is a limited number, either at The National Archives or the Berkshire Record Office. For more details see Appendix 1.
4. *Reading Gild Accounts, 1357-1516*, ed. Cecil Slade (Berkshire Record Society, vi, 2002) part 1, xiii; *Diary of the Corporation,* i, passim; Aspinall, *Parliament,* 105, 106.
5. *Diary of the Corporation*, i, *passim*. Reading was divided into five wards; the High Ward included St Laurence parish. The warden was responsible for the good order of his ward.
6. Burgess, 'Pre-Reformation Churchwardens' Accounts', 322.

7. BRO, St Laurence churchwardens' accounts, 1433-4, D/97/5/1; St Laurence churchwardens' accounts 1498-1626, D/P97/5/2, pp. 116, 113 and *passim*.

had been presented by the retiring wardens. The phrase most often used was 'chosen' or occasionally in the early sixteenth century 'electe' though there are no details of the process.

It is not clear in St Laurence or elsewhere how churchwardens' duties were defined and how far their accounts reflect truly parochial decisions. The size and composition of the parish meeting is never stated but almost certainly excluded the majority, especially labourers and women. In 1525-6 it was agreed the accounts would be presented to 'the parysheners assembled & gathered to gether in the seid parysh Church', but this agreement was made 'by thassent & concent of all the worshipfulles of this parresh', a select number.[1] Such groups frequently took the lead in parish business; St Laurence, where a small coterie of mayors and former mayors exerted a powerful influence, was no exception, a factor of great significance during the Reformation period.[2]

The composition of this elite was most clearly displayed on two occasions. The first was the parish meeting in 1533 when, after the accounts were agreed, a decision was made about the custody of a bridal cup. The second was an extraordinary meeting on 18 April 1547 to discuss aspects of parish finance. It was not the annual meeting, held at this period soon after Michaelmas; no accounts were presented and no new wardens elected. Both meetings were presided over by the current mayor and those present included former mayors. Also present in 1547 were the churchwardens and seven other men, five of whom had been or would later be wardens, as well as 'diverce others inhabitants' of the parish.[3]

Between 1501 and 1555 with a few exceptions wardens served for two years, first as the second-named, effectively the junior partner, then as the first or senior, so ensuring continuity. This practice was also followed at All Saints, Bristol and in several Hampshire parishes.[4] From 1559 to 1570 wardens served for two years, alternating the positions of 'senior' and 'junior' warden, and retired together. Serving wardens were not usually re-elected, the exception being during the uneasy years between 1557 and 1561 when Leonard Andrews served for four consecutive terms, in 1558-9 acting alone. In 1563-4 he was again elected as the sole office holder.[5] The only other

1. Accounts, p. 162.
3. Burgess, 'Pre-Reformation Churchwardens' Accounts', 322. J. Martin, 'The People of Reading', 184-5.
3. Accounts, pp. 190, 244. Martin states that the Mayor always presided over the parish meeting and certainly mayors played an important role there. It may be that if the mayor were a parishioner, he presided at parish meetings but that his presence was recorded only if it was incidental to a decision which was minuted. The only other occasion when the mayor certainly attended the parish meeting was in 1507 when the 'hole parysshyns' agreed to elect two 'cheffe Wardens'. Accounts, p. 32.
4. *The Pre-Reformation Records of All Saints Church, Bristol, part 2 The Churchwardens' Accounts*, ed. C. Burgess (Bristol Record Society, liii, 2000), 15; *The Early Churchwardens' Accounts of Hampshire*, ed. John Foster Williams (Winchester and London, 1913), xii.
5. Leonard Andrews never held important civic office and was not very wealthy. Others with

example of a single warden was in 1548-9 when the 'junior' warden, Nicholas Niclas, died in office and his fellow, John Poyntz, served the remainder of the year and presented his account alone.   In contrast, when in 1556-7 Thomas Sentman died in post, he was replaced by Richard Constable; the election procedure is not recorded.[1]

How the churchwardens divided their work is not stated though sometimes it is clear that one of the wardens took responsibility for the cash surplus. Among them was William Duddelsol, the senior warden in 1563, who in that year claimed that the balance of 10s 2½d was 'in his handes'; John Gatelye had acted in the same way two years previously. If there were a deficit, one warden bore the burden.[2]

v. Method of accounting.
From 1498 to 1516 the accounting year began and ended at the feast of the Annunciation, 25 March. As with other communities the parish meeting took place about Easter time; it was held on Good Friday in 1508.   In 1516 accounts were drawn up for half a year, from 25 March to 29 September, the feast of St Michael or Michaelmas Day, the parish having decided to move the accounting year to Michaelmas where it remained throughout the rest of the period covered by this volume.   The parish meeting was held shortly after, on the feast of Sts Simon and Jude, 28 October. In 1526 the date was moved to St Matthew's Day, 21 September and in 1553 to the Sunday after All Hallows Day (All Saints' Day, 1 November).[3]

The sheer number of entries in the accounts suggest that the wardens kept notes during the year, including bills for goods or labour supplied; they refer to one such, a bill for 'dyvers necessaryes for the churche' in 1538-9. As was suggested above, it was from these rough notes that the accounts as we have them were drawn up. For some aspects of the finances such as income from rents and a collection for the quire (the chancel) separate accounts were evidently kept; there is a reference to a rent roll in 1556-8 and 'them that gatheryd the quyer mony' in 1557-8.[4] The costs of some major alterations to the church at the Reformation such as those to the chancel in 1549 were also recorded separately but none of these specific accounts has survived. Sometimes they made or had made and preserved lists of donors for special projects such as building a church wall in 1556 and recasting the Kelsall bell eleven years later.[5]

The fair copy of the annual accounts for presentation to the parish was made by a professional scrivener. He was normally paid two shillings but

---

more to lose might have deemed it wise to avoid being legally responsible for parish business in these dangerous times. For more about him see Appendix 2.
1. Accounts, *passim*.
2. Accounts, pp. 308, 302.
3. Accounts, pp. 38, 108-112,162, 269.
4. Accounts, pp. 214, 284, 292, 290.
5. Accounts, pp. 261, 278, 323-6.

after 1556-7 when there were fewer entries his fee was halved. The writer is not named, except in 1564-6 when it was William Jeffery, churchwarden from 1566-8.

At the parish meeting, any goods or funds in hand were publicly handed over by the old wardens to the new. Sometimes this was specifically noted: in 1508 one of the outgoing wardens, Richard Brussh 'delivered ... to the handes of William Lessham & Richard Aman' 15½ pounds of wax, and lathes worth 8s 2½d. In 1548 it was cash, the very large sum of £30 13s 4d 'whiche money was delyvered to John poyntz [senior warden the following year] in presence of the parisshe'.[1]

There was a deficit in six years between 1498 and 1536; in such situations one of the wardens loaned money to the parish. Modest debts were repaid to the retired warden in the next year's accounts so no-one was burdened for too long. However from 1512-16 the accounts showed a deficit of over two pounds for three consecutive years, partly due to a reduced contribution from the two parish gilds. The accounts also showed a negative balance in five of the eight financial years between 1536 and 1544, a period when the churchwardens were 'seemingly complacent' about the state of the parish finances.[2] The largest shortfall was £9 19s 2d in 1543-4; the cost of a bell for the clock and other repairs increased outgoings while income was reduced because the two parish gilds failed to make their usual offering.[3] In two instances a warden wrote off the debt: in 1507-8 Richard Brussh was allowed 'his horse gresse [grazing] in the Chirchyerd' in return for not claiming 23s 5½d. In 1554 John Radley, warden in 1553-4, agreed to forego 6s 6d of the 39s 10d he was owed; the balance was repaid by 1555.[4] Between 1540 and 1570 only five accounts ended in deficit. Sales of highly priced church plate allowed the parish to balance the accounts for many of the turbulent years of the 1540s and 1550s. The enormous sums raised between 1547 and 1549 provided a temporary cushion against the unrelenting financial costs of complying with royal injunctions and parliamentary statutes concerning worship and devotional practices. For the most part the churchwardens balanced the accounts - there were deficits in only three years, 1552-4 and 1564-5 - although, unlike the wardens of St Giles, they had very little income from property to fall back on once the money from sales was spent and income from gatherings, traditional festivities and some bell ringing ceased.[5]

1. Accounts, pp. 38, 254.
2. J. Martin, 'The People of Reading', 353.
6. Accounts, p. 234.
4. Accounts, pp. 37, 274.
5. Accounts, pp. 250, 255; J. Martin, 'The People of Reading', 491; the finances of Ashburton, Devon, were 'at their lowest ebb' in Edward's reign for similar reasons, *Churchwardens' Accounts of Ashburton, 1479-1580*, ed. Alison Hanham (Devon & Cornwall Record Society, new series xv, 1970).

vi. The form of the document.

The earliest survivals are six membranes catalogued as BRO D/P97/5/1 containing accounts in Latin for six years between 1432-3 (Michaelmas 11-12 Henry VI) and 1458-9 (37-38 Henry VI). They are difficult, and in some places impossible to read partly because of poor repairs in the nineteenth century. They were more legible in Kerry's lifetime; he refers to them as 'rolls' and published extracts from them. They have not been included in this volume.[1]

From 1498 the accounts were entered into a parchment-bound volume measuring thirteen inches by nine (33.5 x 23 cm), catalogued as D/P97/5/2, and are then, except for part of two years detailed below, complete throughout the last flowering of traditional religion and the turbulent years of the English Reformation. Not only this, the volume is one of only eighteen such accounts from anywhere in England and Wales with detailed entries throughout the Tudor period, making it invaluable both for a study of the strength of late medieval Catholicism in an urban parish and of the reaction of a local community to religious change imposed from above.[2]

At some date a sheet comprising pages 1 and 2 covering income for the accounting year 25 March 1498 to 24 March 1499 became separated and is now catalogued as D/P97/5/2A. The volume catalogued as D/P97/5/2 begins on page 3 with the expenses for 1498-9; these are incomplete. The whole of the accounts for 1499-1500 is missing as are the receipts and most of the expenses for 1500-1501. From 1501-2 the accounts are complete except for 1542-3 and 1543-4; some of the expenses and the balance of the former year and the names of the wardens for the latter are missing.

The existing pagination is modern, probably by Kerry. It follows the arrangement of the volume after it was rebound at an earlier date, probably in the seventeenth century.[3] In that process some pages were cropped at the top and some misplaced; the accounts for 1554-5 break off on page 274 and continue on page 277. In this edition pages 275 and 276 have been ascribed to the accounting year 1555-6 following the opinion of Kerry, noted in his hand on page 279, and of Jeanette Martin.[4] This recreates the original

1. Charles Kerry, 'Six Ancient Rolls of Church Wardens' Accounts', *Berkshire Archaeological and Architectural Society Transactions,* i (1880-81), 1-8.
2. Ronald Hutton, 'The local impact of the Tudor reformations' in Peter Marshall ed., *The Impact of the English Reformation 1500-1640* (1997).
3. Kerry's numbering of the first three pages has caused confusion. All sheets in the volume are numbered consecutively front to back, for example pages 1 and 2 on the first sheet and pages 3 and 4 on the second. These cover the year 1498-9. Four sheets were torn out after page 4 before Kerry's time. Nevertheless he numbered the next sheet page 5 which contains accounts, not those of 1498-9 but of 1500-01. The evidence for this is the appearance of the annual obit for benefactors on pages 4 and 5 which must then refer to different years, and the change of hand on page 5. The reverse of page 5 is page 6 where the accounts for 1501-2 undoubtedly begin. The balance transferred to the wardens itemised on page 6 is identical with that given on page 5 which therefore refers to 1500-01.
4. Jeanette Martin produced a transcript of the accounts from 1519 in the course of writing her thesis. She died in 2000. I discovered her work after I had begun my own transcript. I used and

sequence of pages, making the text more accessible while keeping Kerry's pagination.   In addition, the inventories of church goods made in the early sixteenth century which were bound between pages 41-73 of the accounts have been placed at the end in this edition. Some of the material used in the seventeenth-century rebinding shows through at page 284 and pages 312-3. It appears to be from an obsolete copy of the Book of Common Prayer which was substantially revised in 1662; if so, this would confirm the suggested date of the rebinding.

For the most part, the preamble to each year's accounts dates them correctly, but occasionally they were wrongly annotated by a contemporary, for example in several years after 1522. Major confusion arose in 1542-3 when the accounts were not presented until 7 November 1543 and were attributed to the wrong regnal year by the new scribe. Additional dating, almost certainly in an attempt by Kerry to assist his understanding of the document, sometimes helps to clarify the situation but occasionally creates further confusion.

vii. The layout of the accounts.
Each accounting year begins with a preamble giving the names of the churchwardens, the feast day (Annunciation or Michaelmas) when the accounts begin and end, the calendar dates and after 1516, the regnal years. The accounts follow a regular pattern. The first financial entry was normally the surplus or deficit from the previous year. There follows the income, beginning with the money from gatherings, itemised as 'Receipts'. After 1508 these are listed under various headings such as rents, fees for burials and seats.[1] These headings are in the left-hand margin until 1556-7 when some are centred; in this edition they have all been centred for ease of reading. The total sum of the receipts follows. This edition has centred this no matter how it was recorded in the text.

Expenses are normally listed without subdivisions though occasionally there are sub-headings such as 'wages'. At the end, the total expended is given, usually centred. It has always been centred in this edition. Finally the balance for which the churchwardens were accountable, either surplus or deficit is stated. When there were still moneys owing to the churchwardens, these are listed after the balance, usually as 'Dettes owyng' or '*Super*' and sometimes a new balance is quoted. This has also been centred. Many outstanding debts especially in the 1540s and 1550s were paid off very slowly over a number of years, recurring in several accounts. Finally every year between 1502-3 and 1555, except in years 1538-40, the names of the new warden(s) were recorded at the end of the accounts.

Despite some minor irregularities, the overall interpretation of the

amended her version from 1519-1570.
1. Though there is a regular pattern, the accounts do not omit details of income and expenditure; they are not summaries until the 1550s.

accounts is for the most part straightforward. Receipts, expenses and balances are recorded with care and in great detail until 1558. Thereafter entries are much shorter: neither the names of tenants nor the parish properties they occupied are given and income from ringing knells and the use of the pall is entered as a single total with no individual names. From 1556, as the number of transactions dropped, entries are more spaced out on the page. Over a hundred entries were made in the accounts for 1528-9 and only fifty-eight forty years later when the simpler ritual of the Church of England required less expenditure on liturgical items and all income from social activities ceased. The names of the wardens elected in 1557 were not entered at the end of the accounts in the customary way, nor was the practice resumed thereafter. Nevertheless they were invariably recorded as usual in the following year's preamble. In 1559-60 the scrivener was paid for writing three years' accounts; either his pay was seriously in arrears or he wrote all three at the later date

The language used in the accounts changes significantly over the period. As late as the 1530s, the symbols, thorn for 'th' and yoch for 'gh' or 'y', are common. The Germanic form of plural nouns, for example 'gravn' for 'graves' on page 26, is very occasionally used; elision of vowels, 'thorgans' for 'the organs', is more common. Overall the accounts are in very legible hands with some initial letters highly decorated but not coloured.

viii. The parish and higher authorities.

In addition to their intra-parochial responsibilities, the churchwardens had to deal with external religious and secular authorities, the closest physically, temporally and spiritually being Reading Abbey. As has already been stated, until 1539 the abbey was rector and patron of the parish and its landlord; the quit rents paid to the abbey for properties the parish held in the borough amounting to 3s 6d a year may have been allotted to the almoner, the monk in charge of the abbey's charitable giving. Abbot Hugh Faringdon paid for a seat for his mother in the church.[1] After the dissolution of the abbey the Crown became the parish's landlord; the churchwardens paid the quit rents for parish property to a royal agent.

Reading was in the deanery of the same name, one of four in the archdeaconry of Berkshire, itself within the diocese of Salisbury. The bishop of Salisbury and the archdeacon of Berkshire ensured that the provision of church fabric and furniture was fitting for divine service, imposed adherence to church teaching on faith and morals and exercised jurisdiction over many other matters such as matrimonial disputes and probate. The bishop held a visitation every three years and the archdeacon twice a year in a large church in the deanery. Churchwardens were obliged to attend to present their answers to questions previously sent to them on such matters as the state of

---

1. Accounts, pp. 136, 181; J. B. Hurry, *Reading Abbey* (1901), 69, 90; B. Kemp, *Reading Abbey 2: an introduction to the history of the abbey* (Reading, 1968), 53, 49.

the church fabric, the provision of vessels, books and other necessities for church services and any deviance from orthodoxy in belief or practice on the part of the clergy or parishioners. The archdeacon often acted through other clerics, his Official or 'Register'. The parish also paid its peter pence or smoke farthings to the diocese, an annual tax to the Pope until 1534. The amount, based on the number of parishioners, was usually 3s 6d in St Laurence in the early sixteenth century. After the break with Rome when the levy was appropriated by the Crown, the alternative name of pentecostals ('pentecost stawles' in the accounts of 1536-7) was used and the rate dropped; it was 2s 1d in the 1560s.[1]

Relations with the borough were close and of great significance during the Reformation years. Many churchwardens had been, were or would be involved in urban administration. The Mayor and his wife had seats of honour, presumably when a parishioner held that office; similar provision was made at St Mary's.[2] As another mark of his standing in the community the mayor or a former mayor from the parish was entrusted with a gilt cup, given to the parish as a bridal cup. In October 1546 during a period when the borough had insufficient resources to meet its obligations, the churchwardens made it a loan of £6, repayable at 10s a year. Parish and borough records agree that the debt was discharged or remitted in the same financial year. In Mary's reign the parish became the borough's landlord when the acquisition of a new churchyard made the parish's 'old procession way' redundant. It had led into the abbey precinct under a gateway over which stood the former abbey prison, the Compter, first renamed the Grate and later the Counter. From 1557-8 the borough rented it for the same purpose; in 1560 the Crown gave the Counter buildings to the borough but the prison remained parish property.[3]

Of the parish's relationships with authorities beyond its boundaries, those with the Crown were arguably the most important but the least frequent. Twice, in 1515-16 when it paid a shilling and in 1546-7 when the amount tripled, the parish was assessed to the subsidy, a tax granted to the Crown by parliament. The power of the sovereign was most evident during royal visits which punctuate the accounts. At the very least bells were rung on his or her arrival, and sometimes on departure. Failure to do so incurred the royal displeasure, even when in 1528-9 the personage offended was Henry VIII's neglected queen, Catherine of Aragon. Some payments on these occasions

1. Accounts, pp. 80, 94, 206, 309; P. Durrant, 'The Archdeaconry of Berkshire', in *An Historical Atlas of Berkshire*, ed. J. Dils and M. Yates (2nd edition, Reading, 2012), 10; Ralph Houlbrooke, *Church Courts and the People during the English Reformation, 1520-1570* (Oxford, 1979), 6-7.
2. Payment 'for dressinge the seate which Mr. Mayor sittith in'. *The Churchwardens' Accounts of the Parish of St Mary's, Reading*, ed. F. and A. Garry (Reading, 1893), 46.
3. Accounts, pp. 85, 190, 244, 289; *Diary of the Corporation*, i, 199; *Reading Charters, Acts and Orders*, ed. C. F. Pritchard (1913), Charter of 2 Elizabeth, 32.

suggest that the sovereign visited the church: it was swept in preparation for Henry VIII's visit in 1525-6.[1]

ix. Churchwardens' accounts and the historian.

This volume is of inestimable value to both national and local historians. It is one of a very few such survivals from 9000 or so English parishes in that it is almost complete. In addition it is extremely detailed, remarkably consistent in its recording of large and small items of income and expenditure and in very good condition.[2]

Its most obvious value is the information it provides the historian of the English Reformation about the timing and extent of one parish's response to government orders, albeit a parish in a town whose lord was the Crown and where royal officials were important property owners. The timing cannot be too finely judged since entries were not usually dated. However the volume's great importance lies in allowing the historian a detailed insight into the local impact of and reaction to the cataclysmic events of the mid-sixteenth century. It has already contributed to several Reformation studies and will undoubtedly continue to do so.

The accounts also have a value for the social historian. Abundant references to popular culture expressed in drama and annual rituals appear in the pre-Reformation years; evidence of a social and economic hierarchy is apparent from the privileged seats for some women in church, and from the differential between the salaries of parish officials and the day wages of craftsmen, their journeymen and labourers.

In the absence of a parish register before 1605, the number of knells rung and graves opened in church provide a clue to the incidence of epidemics in Reading which can be substantiated from other sources such as the registers of the other two parishes and probate records. Burials in church were those of wealthier parishioners only, the deceased frequently referred to as Master, Mistress or Goodman; knells were probably rung for some lower in the social scale. Even so, the numbers are far too low to account for all the deaths in a parish of this size. However they follow the trends evident in better records, notably in the very large number of knells in 1557-9, years which saw a national epidemic of influenza and other ailments and high mortality in other Berkshire parishes.[3]

The spread of epidemics from the capital was one of the negative aspects of Reading's close and otherwise valuable connections with London based on trade and the court; several royal servants were parishioners. The churchwardens often used the services of London merchants and craftsmen: sea coals, a new organ, an expensive cope. These and many other references

1. Accounts, pp. 106, 248, 174, 161.
2. A total of 200 surviving for the period 1500-1549 is claimed, though 'long and continuous accounts are rare'. Burgess, 'Pre-Reformation Churchwardens' Accounts', 307.
3. J. Dils, 'Disease, death and doctoring ' in *An Historical Atlas of Berkshire*, ed. J. Dils and M. Yates (2nd edition, Reading, 2012), 80-81.

help to expand our knowledge of the all-important interplay between the capital and provincial towns in Tudor England.

Having considered the background to the accounts and their general form and structure, we can now consider in more detail their content and the evidence they provide for historical research and analysis.

2. Income.

Each year, after noting any surplus or arrears from the previous twelve months, the accounts began with the sources producing income, called receipts. The amount varied considerably over time, and falls into two distinct periods, before and after the reign of Edward VI (1547-53). Until the later 1540s annual income was usually between £15 and £23; the highest was £46 4s 9d in 1518-9 and the lowest £7 12s 1½d in 1501-2. The sale of church plate in 1547-9 resulted in a very high income over the short term but thereafter the level fell to under £10 in every year but three.

Other churchwardens' accounts show that the balance between different sources of revenue varied from parish to parish. Boxford, a cloth-making town in Suffolk, derived a small income from rents and dues, but most came from profits made at entertainments. Parishes in large towns such as All Saints, Bristol and St Michael, York depended mainly on rent from property in the pre-Reformation period.[1] In contrast, in the first half of the sixteenth century, St Laurence's wardens relied on three main sources: rents from church property; 'gatherings' or collections on major church feast days (All Saints, Christmas and Easter) and income from entertainments on various festivals. In most years before 1530 rents and gatherings brought in approximately equal amounts, an average of almost 60s and 68s a year respectively. Together they amounted to about three-quarters of parish income. When rents fell substantially in the 1530s and 40s, it was money from gatherings, amounting to £3 more or less before 1545, which provided a greater proportion of parish income, usually twice as much as from rents. Between 1547 and 1552 the balance changed again with a drop of about 50 per cent from gatherings. They increased just as dramatically in the early years of Mary's reign returning to the level of the 1520s and 1530s before declining from 1555-6; Easter 1559 saw the last traditional gathering which raised a mere 17s 6d.[2]

---

1. *Boxford Churchwardens' Accounts, 1530-1561*, ed. Peter Northeast (Suffolk Record Society, xxiii, 1982), xiii; *The Pre-Reformation Records of All Saints' Church, Bristol, Part 2, The Churchwardens' Accounts*, ed. C. Burgess (Bristol Record Society, liii, 2000), 17; quoted in *The Churchwardens' Book of Bassingbourn, Cambridgeshire 1496-c.1540*, ed. David Dymond, (Cambridge Records Society, xvii, 2004), xxxv.

2. Jeanette Martin attributed these variations to the changing numbers receiving the sacrament at Easter during the period of the Edwardian Reformation and the Marian Restoration. J. Martin, 'The People of Reading', 488-9. She also contrasted St Laurence's inadequate income from property with the better provision of the other two parishes, *ibid*, 491.

Until they ceased in 1546-7 (with a short-lived revival in three years between 1552-8), income from parochial festivities was about 44s a year on average, but varied from 20s to 50s, rising to over £4 or £5 some years such as 1512-13 and 1540-43 when the King Game was particularly profitable. In addition between 1512 and 1543 the churchwardens received a total of 66s 8d a year from the two parish gilds. Other income came from such dues as fees for burials, ringing knells and seats for some women in church; this varied in amount from year to year.

After 1558, with no income from festivities or gatherings, the parish relied mainly on property rents; these ranged from 30 per cent of the total in 1563-4, when high mortality increased the profits from knells and burials, to 64 per cent in 1564-5; the more usual was between 45 and 50 per cent. Even so they were a poor substitute for the traditional revenue providers, rarely managing to raise parochial income above £6 or £7.

i. Rents.

Collecting rents from parish property was a secular rather than a religious duty but one which was essential. It is not clear how property first came into the possession of the parish though possibly it was from bequests by former parishioners. The rents were set out under a separate heading after 1508 though the names of tenants were given from the beginning until 1556. Most of the rental income, which was not substantial, came from several tenements, two on the north and two on the south sides of New Street (sometimes called Friar Street). One, leased by John Barfote from 1517 to his death in 1546-7, was sub-let for most of the period. A shop in the Market Place, rented by John Fletcher from 1521 to 1524 was for some years afterwards called 'the Fletchers shoppe'. This was later known as the corner tenement by the Common Well. There was a property in Gutter Lane (now Cross Street) called a hog sty in 1505-6 and a stable from 1523-4. Smaller sums came from two gardens in Lurkmer Lane (later Hosier Street) and one in Gutter Lane. There were minor changes in the property portfolio: in 1523-4 Henry Moore bought the property he occupied on the south side of New Street, paying for it in seven annual instalments of 20s.[1] The other property on this side of the street was subdivided, described as two tenements 'under one roufe ' in 1567-8. The accounts of 1551-2 indicate that a property on the north side had been similarly altered, described as two 'tenementes lying together'; a survey made in 1552 calls it two tenements and gardens. A third property on the same side, which had disappeared from the accounts in 1528-9, reappeared at the same time.[2]

From 1523-4 all the above were referred to as 'rentes at farm' or

---

1. The accounts do not give a reason for the sale, nor explain why, not having paid the full rent of 12s for the two previous years, he decided to buy. He had a bargain since the purchase price of property was normally twenty times the annual rent.
2. Accounts, pp. 171, 327, 264; TNA, Survey of Reading by Roger Amyce, 1552, Misc. Bks. Land Rev. vol 187 ff. 36.

occasionally in the 1540s as 'rents at will'; they ranged from 6s 8d, to 10s and even 12s a year for tenements in New Street to 4d for the garden in Gutter Lane. Long-term leases would seem to have been common since many rents remained stable for lengthy periods, though only one, for a tenement on the north side of New Street, remained unchanged from 1498 to 1569-70 when it doubled. Some rents certainly rose when newly leased; that of the third property on the north of New Street rose in 1550-1 from 6s 8d to 10s and those on the south from 13s 4d to 16s. Others fell and rose again: the property in the Market Place was let at 10s until 1520, a figure it did not reach again until 1542 where it then remained. The stable in Gutter Lane followed a very similar pattern. As a result the total income from rents also fluctuated, being in excess of 60s a year before 1520, occasionally reaching a similar amount during the next decade, falling to a little over half this until 1545. Despite the high inflation of the period, rental income remained at just under 60s a year until 1568, almost 10 per cent lower than the peak of 1509-20. An increased rent on one property in 1568 finally resulted in a total higher than that of 1498. From this evidence, there does not appear to have been any great pressure on housing in the parish, perhaps a reflection of the troubled state of the borough's economy in the mid-sixteenth century.[1]

In addition the wardens collected quit rents, often called rents of assize in the accounts, from three tenements, one each in New Street, the Market Place and the High Street but owed these to the abbey. The only parish property outside the borough was half an acre of meadow in the parish of Burghfield for which the quit rent remained at 13d throughout the period; a lease for forty years copied into the accounts of 1534-5 refers to it as Aston Mede.[2] Rents at farm were due on 24 June, Midsummer Day, and so were entered as paid in the same accounting year; rents of assize were due at Michaelmas and were entered as paid at the beginning of the next financial year which for most of the period began on the same date.[3]

ii. Feast day collections, funerals, church seats and religious gilds.
Income from various activities connected with the cycle of the liturgical year and from the normal round of church services was more variable than that from rents. Before the Reformation there were collections called 'gatherings' at special feasts. The Easter gathering was variously described as 'for the Pascall' or 'in paschal money' and was a donation from communicants. In 1535 Thomas Everard bequeathed 6s 8d to the churchwardens of all three parishes in Reading to allow the poorest parishioners to 'take ther sacraments

1. N. R. Goose, 'Decay and Regeneration in Seventeenth Century Reading: A study in a changing economy', *Southern History*, vi (1984), 56.
2. Accounts, p. 199; it is variously described as Aston Mead, in or by Langley or Langney. Burghfield is about four miles south-west of Reading.
3. For example, in the accounts from Michaelmas 1541 to Michaelmas 1542 rents at farm due at 24 June 1542 were entered in that year's accounts as were the rents of assize due at Michaelmas 1541.

withall.' At All Saints' Day and Christmas the gathering was for the rood light or lights.[1] The amount raised at Easter was normally more than that at the other two feasts put together; in a fairly typical year, 1529-30, the totals were 37s 8d in paschal money, 12s at All Saints and 12s 8d at Christmas. For just two years, 1509-11, there was also a parish gathering to pay the sexton's wages; these raised 25s 8d a year.

Though funerals obviously took place frequently, no dates are given. Income came only from tolling the passing bell and ringing knells, and from those able to pay for burial in the church as opposed to the churchyard. At a total cost of 7s 4d (6s 8d for making the grave, presumably opening up part of the floor of the church, and 8d for closing it), this was a privilege limited to the well-to-do. Similarly, based on a parish agreement of 1515-16, the wardens charged 12d for ringing a knell on the Great Bell, probably a passing bell, but only 4d when the ringers tolled the bell summoning people to a funeral or a month's mind.[2] In 1557-8 when other income had fallen, these prices rose to 20d and 10d respectively; cheaper knells on the fourth bell called Our Lady Bell, including those for children, cost just 6d. Most people were buried in a shroud and temporarily placed in the parish coffin. This was not a very elaborate affair since 2s 4d sufficed both to make a new one and to mend the parish bier in 1517-18; no fee for their use appears in the accounts. Wealthier parishioners had their own coffins. The parish also provided a pall placed over the coffin during the funeral service though payment for its use does not appear until extra sources of income were needed in the decades after about 1550; the wardens charged 4d for the best pall in the 1550s. During the dirge and funeral Mass before the Reformation large candles called torches stood around the bier; mourners paid for the amount of wax used when the candles were lit, called in the accounts the waste of torches.[3] How many parishioners could afford to hire the pall and torches is unclear since, unlike the cost of burials and bell ringing where deceased is named in each instance, the accounts give only annual totals of receipts from these sources. It was possibly only a few. Though the number of payments for burials, commemorations and their associated rituals varied

1. Accounts, pp. 88, 195; TNA, Will of Thomas Everard, chandler, 10 April 1535, PROB 11/29/4. The Easter collection at St Laurence was not paid to the vicar. It differs from the 'statutory offering' which was made when a parishioner received the sacrament on Easter Sundays as described in Eamon Duffy, *The Stripping of the Altars: Traditional Religion in England, 1400-1580* (Yale University Press (1992), 93. Gatherings for parish funds occurred elsewhere, for example at St John the Baptist, Peterborough, which held four gathering days for repairs to the church, Christmas, Easter, 24 June and All Saints, W. T. Mellows: *Peterborough Local Administration and Parochial Government before the Reformation* (Northamptonshire Record Society, ix, 1939), xxxi.
2. Accounts, p. 108. The Great Bell was sometimes called the Kelsall Bell after its donor, Henry Kelsall, founder of the gild of the Mass of Jesus. The choice of burial place made by five testators 1515-41 confirms that churchyard burials did not attract a fee to the churchwardens: BRO D/A1/1/ 23, 134; D/A1/2/ 177, 265; D/A1/3/ 38.
3. Accounts, *passim*; David Cressy, *Birth, Marriage & Death: Ritual, Religion and the Life-cycle in Tudor and Stuart England* (Oxford, 1997), 421-424 and 430.

from year to year they do not reflect the total deaths in the parish, relating as they do to the wealthy few. How few it is impossible to determine but there must have been a far greater mortality in this large parish than the accounts would suggest.

What is certain is that a small number of men purchased another privilege as did those of other Reading parishes: a seat for their wives in church. There is only one reference to men's seats and no indication that they were paid for. The normal practice in English churches was for men and women to sit separately and, these accounts imply, hierarchically.[1] A seating plan of the church in 1607 shows payment for both men's and women's seats; the men occupied the front rows.[2] For most of the period there were two classes of seats costing 6d and 4d respectively; in 1545-6 two at 8d appear, in 1557-8 two at 12d and one at 10d, increasing to five in 1560-1. Under a parish agreement in 1515-6 'any seate' in the church was to cost 6d; cheaper seats at 4d were situated 'in the mydle range & the north range be neth the font'. From time to time new seats were installed at the cheaper rate: 'before our lady' in 1521-2 when the old font was removed and in 1541-2 'next the store howsse'. Some seats seem to have been enclosed, perhaps resembling box pews, since in 1554-5 three 'dores for seates' were made. How individual seats were allotted is not clear though St Mary's accounts for the early seventeenth century indicate the churchwardens had the final say.[3] The more expensive seats were occupied by the wives or sometimes the daughters of the richer and more influential men of the parish - burgesses, wealthy mercers, past and future mayors; the list of payments for seats in 1560-1 makes this clear. All those listed had a title: 'mistress' used for a gentlewoman (one of the 'better sort') whose seat cost 10d, or 'goodwife' (one of the 'middling sort' married to a respectable craftsman) who made do with a seat at 6d or 4d.[4] Women below these ranks would have been called by their Christian names: there was none such in the list. The social significance of church seating is further emphasised by a reference to the Mayor's seat in 1510-11 and such ordinances as that of 1545-6: that wives of present and former members of the gild of the Mass of Jesus were to have 'the highest seates or pewes next unto the Mayours wifes seate towardes the pulpitt'. In contrast, two men bought places for their maid servants in the cheaper range.[5] The income from seats varied considerably and the names of purchasers very rarely recur, making an annual seat rent unlikely. It seems that the right to occupy a seat for life was a one-off investment by husbands

---

1. Duffy, *The Stripping of the Altars,* 171.
2. BRO Seating plan of St Laurence Church, 1607, D/P97/5/3. Only 350 names appear on the list.
3. *The Churchwardens' Accounts of the Parish of St Mary's, Reading*, ed. F. and A. Garry (Reading, 1893), 105-7.
4. Accounts, pp. 108, 141, 225, 274, 301.
5. Among the names which occur are Richard Aman, Edward Butler and William Buriton, future mayors and Richard Turner a mercer; Accounts, pp. 244, 85, 169.

to display their own social status through their wives.[1] It is a pity that the absence of parish registers makes an attempt to link the few repeated names with second marriages hazardous though one example makes it an enticing possibility. Robert Dodson, dyer, bought such a seat in1503-4; the wife of this Robert was buried in church in 1508-9 and ten years later he again bought a seat for his then wife.[2] It is not clear where the many women without reserved seats sat or stood, though the presumption must be that it was in the humbler areas further back.[3]

For many years there was also a dependable income from the two religious gilds in the parish. From 1512 to 1543 both gilds, the Mass of Jesus and Our Lady Mass (see below) contributed 33s 4d a year, a total of five marks, towards the sexton's wages.[4] There is no explanation for this in the accounts. In the changing religious conditions of the mid-century, this source began to dry up. In 1543-4 only a proportion of the amount was forthcoming, and none at all the following two years. In April 1547 the Mayor of Reading, the churchwardens and other parishioners agreed that the gilds should continue to support the sexton, ironically since in that year an Act to dissolve the chantries and gilds and confiscate their property to the Crown was passed by Edward VI's first parliament.[5] St Laurence's gilds ceased to exist, the fate of all parish gilds in England.

iii. Occasional income.

Some major projects which could not be funded from normal income necessitated special collections. These took various forms: in 1518-9 collections for repairs to the church were made every Sunday from 1 January to 29 September raising £21 2s 1d which was supplemented by a further £6 13s 4d from various unnamed benefactors. The cost of new seats installed in 1522-3 was met by forty-six people who contributed sums ranging from 12d to 10s. In 1526-7 'divers persones' whose names are not given contributed £4 13s 1d for painting and gilding a representation of the Transfiguration over the High Altar. A much more costly undertaking, recasting the great bell called the Kelsall Bell in 1567, was met by contributions amounting to £12 5s 9d from 130 named parishioners and others from the borough and beyond.[6]

---

1. A life-time occupancy was the custom at Lambeth. *Lambeth Churchwardens' Accounts 1504-1645 and Vestry Book 1610* ed. Charles Drew (2 vols, Surrey Record Society, xviii and xx, 1941 and 1950), i, lii.

2. Accounts, pp. 15, 40, 125.

3. It is likely that the whole of the church did not have seats or pews. P S Barnwell, 'The Use of the Church: Blisworth, Northamptonshire, on the Eve of the Reformation', *Ecclesiology Today*, xxxv (2005), 47.

4. In 1514-15 there was no contribution from Our Lady Mass Gild and the following year a reduced amount from both gilds

5. Duffy, *The Stripping of the Altars*, 454-5; G R Elton, *The Tudor Constitution: documents and commentary* (Cambridge, 1965), 382-5. Jeanette Martin suggested the agreement was 'probably a defensive ploy to establish officially in parochial records the economic necessity of fraternity endowments' for the good of the parish and its liturgy. J. Martin, 'The People of Reading', 455-6.

6. Accounts, pp. 123, 146-7, 164, 323-6.

When repairs were complete there were often scrap materials which could be sold making a useful addition to church funds. Lead from the old font realised 7s in 1521-2, old timber and the old harness from the statue of St George raised 3s in 1534-5. The great organs should have brought in £10 from the Friars of Oxford but 50s of this was still outstanding when the friaries were dissolved.[1] Of a different order of magnitude was the sale in 1537-8 of candlesticks, cruets and other vessels of silver and silver gilt worth £20 11s 11d. This does not seem to be connected with any Reformation changes but was more likely prompted by the need to pay off some debts: 46s 8d to Richard Dodgeson, £6 13s 4d to the gild of Jesus Mass and £3 to that of Our Lady Mass. However news of the passing of the Act for the dissolution of the lesser monasteries in 1536 may have raised fears for the safety of parish valuables.

Small amounts sometimes came from bequests, more usually in the form of money: 3s 4d from Raphe White, 6s 8d from Master Carpenter and 20s from Master Justice, all in 1520-21. Very occasionally there were gifts in kind such as a twenty-rung ladder or the cow which the churchwardens sold for 8s in 1509-10.[2]

iv. Parish social activities.[3]

Before the Reformation, fund-raising at various festivities, most of them closely connected to the liturgical calendar, played an important role in parish finances as well as in parishioners' social lives. One event which occurred every year was at Hocktide (the week following the Sunday after Easter Sunday). The accounts refer to events merely as 'gatherings' i.e. collections: 18s 5d was received 'of the women for the gatheryng at hockmonday above all charges' in 1521-2. The men's gathering 'on hoktewisday' the same year produced 6s 6d. In 1516-17 and every year thereafter both days' collections are consolidated: 'Of the men and women for the gatheryng at hocktyde'. It may be that on Monday the women and on Tuesday the men took forfeits from visitors of the opposite sex as occurred in many English parishes, though there are no details of exactly what happened at Reading. However the women, often referred to as 'wives' and occasionally including maidens, always collected more than the men. Sometimes the accounts show that some of the collection was paid out by the churchwardens for a supper: 22d from the 24s gathered in 1506-7 laid out for the 'wymensoper a hokmunday' and in 1503-4 one for the wives and one for 'bachelers'.[4]

---

1. Accounts, pp. 139, 197, 183, 185, 209. The accounts do not say which order of friars bought the organs; all four were in Oxford at this date.
2. Accounts, pp. 134, 33, 78.
3. Some expenses incurred in the provision of social activities have been included in this section.
4. Accounts, pp. 39, 100, 109, 29-31, 16; Hutton, *The Rise and Fall of Merry England, 59-60*; *The Churchwardens' Book of Bassingbourn, Cambridgeshire, 1496-c.1540*, ed. David Dymond

Another very widespread parish celebration was the church ale, also called a king ale, an occasion for drinking, eating and dancing but also a money-spinner though some expenditure was necessary. It was usually held at Whitsuntide. The accounts do not suggest it was an annual event in Reading as it was in many rural parishes, and neither did the parish rely on it for income. There certainly was one in 1505 when the churchwardens collected wheat and malt, paid for meat, spices, ale and baking pasties and for 'makyng clene of the church agaynst the day of drynking'. This clearly suggests that such social events were held in the church though there is an isolated reference in 1506-7 to a 'church house' on which the parish paid quit rent. There are other references in the accounts to payments for bread and ale for church ales, the earliest in 1503-4. In 1513-4 a kilderkin (a cask of sixteen to eighteen gallons) of beer, a dozen of good ale and three gallons of penny ale were bought 'a geynst wytsontyde'. The presence of a taborer suggests there was dancing as well as feasting. In Reading as in some other villages and towns, church ales briefly returned in Mary's reign after disappearing from the accounts in Edward's. The last one, in 1557, was described as the 'gatheringe at the kynge ale in the whytsontyde at the churche ale suppars'. It raised 48s from which the wardens paid 14s for three barrels of beer and bread.[1]

The King Play or King Game, as distinct from a king ale, was always held at Whitsuntide. It occurred in several years in the early part of the century and annually between 1527 and 1533. It was the preserve of the young men and was usually profitable; it raised 45s in 1502-3 and £3 8s 7d in 1512-13. It is possible that such occasions were akin to the revel days in rural communities when a Summer King and a Summer Lady, chosen from among the young people, presided over youthful festivities including a feast, and that the 'king' referred to is such a king. There was usually a pole or tree erected in the market place, akin to a maypole. In 1531 morris dancers were an added attraction. Between 1504 and 1516-17 there were other 'gatherings' of young men and women of the parish: of the maids by a tree at the church door at Whitsun and of the young men on May Day, sometimes referred to as Fair Day. The churchwardens sometimes provided refreshments as they did for a dinner and supper on May Day 1504 at a cost of 1s 6½d from the 10s 7½d the young men had collected.[2]

Of equal significance financially and perhaps socially for St Laurence's parishioners were the entertainments and plays sometimes performed on May Day, Whitsuntide and the feast of Corpus Christi especially when troupes of

(Cambridge Record Society, xvii, 2004), lviii.

1. Accounts, pp. 24, 25, 19, 30, 16, 98, 285-6; *The Churchwardens' Book of Bassingbourn*, lviii-lx; Hutton has discovered similar restorations in other parishes in England. Hutton, *The Rise and Fall of Merry England*, 99.

2. Accounts, pp. 9, 19, 21, 92, 167, 171, 179; Hutton, *The Rise and Fall of Merry England*, 30. For a Whitsuntide revel day at Milton, Berkshire see BRO, Berkshire Archdeaconry Records: deposition book 1590-94, D/A2 c.154, 13.

performers from outside the town provided an added attraction.[1] May Day (1 May) was one of the borough's fair days which drew in many visitors who doubtless swelled the audience and consequently the parish coffers. In the early years of the sixteenth century these occasions were particularly profitable; the 'gaderyng of Robyn hod' yielded 49s in 1503-4. Unfortunately such lucrative events did not last and in any event do not appear annually in the accounts. In Reading as elsewhere Robin Hood lost his popularity early in the century; there is no mention of a play about him after 1507-8 though the profit the previous year was a creditable £5 10s 5d and the churchwardens paid 1s 5½d for a 'cote' for Maid Marion as late as 1529-30. There is no surviving script for the Robin Hood play and though it was performed on feast days, it had more in common with traditional folklore than with religious festivals. A maypole, morris dancers, and ringing of the church bells were also a feature of the entertainment. The maypole was called the 'sommer pole' in 1556-7 and in 1530-1 the old one was used to make a ladder.[2]

However there were occasions when religious dramas were performed though it does not seem that Reading had a cycle of plays as at Wakefield and York. Three can confidently be identified in the accounts, all appearing just once, perhaps the only occasions when expenditure was called for. On May Day 1499 horses appeared in a play of 'the kynges of colen', probably enacting the Epiphany story. In 1506-7 the churchwardens paid for 'cress cloth' to make costumes for Adam and Eve, and canvas for thirteen caps 'with the heres ther to longyng', a reference either to wigs or to ears for animal costumes. 'Caymes pageant' in 1515 may have been about Cain and Abel.[3] Others pose some problems of interpretation. On Easter Monday 1507 and 1508 a 'pageaunt of the passion' was performed in the church; no collection was made suggesting that it was intended as a religious service, not an entertainment. It does not recur in the accounts but in 1538 two unidentified plays in Easter week appear, obviously different in character from the pageant since collections at the performances raised a total of 34s 4d. Whether these are the resurrection play which Mr Laborne 'reformed' in 1533-4 and for which a 'boke' of the same play was purchased from him two years later is impossible to say with any certainty.[4] Some performances were staged in the Market Place and others in the Forbury, the outer precinct of the

1. The feast of Corpus Christi (Body of Christ) falls on the Thursday after Trinity Sunday. Players from Henley, Oxfordshire and Finchampstead, Berkshire enacted a Robin Hood play in 1504-6.
2. Accounts, pp. 14, 33, 24, 178, 181.
3. Accounts, pp. 3, 31, 106.
4. Accounts, pp. 208, 194, 202, 227. Miri Rubin said there were four, including the Resurrection Play. Miri Rubin, *Corpus Christi: the Eucharist in Late Medieval Culture* (Cambridge, 1991), 279. Costs incurred in these productions are considered below. For a discussion of these plays see Hutton, *The Rise and Fall of Merry England,* 30-33 and 66-7 and, *The Churchwardens' Book of Bassingbourn,* ed. David Dymond, (Cambridge Record Society, xvii, 2004), lx-lxvii.

abbey. In 1506 a platform was erected and barrels of beer taken into the Forbury for an unnamed play in August at which 23s 8d was collected; in 1541-2 after the Dissolution there was again a play, date and title unknown, in 'thabbay'.[1] Processions were also a feature of these feast days, particularly at Corpus Christi though Rogation Day processions or 'beating the bounds', a common feature of urban parish life, appear only in 1506 and not at all in St Giles'. They probably occurred more frequently but are not in the accounts because they neither produced income nor required expenditure.[2]

3. Expenditure

i. Officials and workmen

The many and onerous duties of the churchwardens necessitated the employment of a number of officials and workmen. Officials tended to be contracted for several years and paid an annual fee either half-yearly or quarterly; workmen were employed at piece-work rates for a specific task and presumably paid on its completion. When wages paid on quarter days are so recorded they can throw some light on the pattern of expenses throughout the year. One particularly clear example occurs in 1512-3 when the accounting year began on 25 March.[3] From 1525-6 to 1541-2 parish officials are listed in order beginning with the sexton with their remuneration given as an annual amount. This makes it possible to trace the continuity of an official in post in those years when only the occupant's name is given.

The one official who can be traced throughout the period is the sexton; the accounts show that he undertook a range of tasks including looking after the clock, caring for vestments and, since he was provided with a surplice, taking part in services. Before 1547 only five sextons are named. The first was Richard Walker, sexton from 1504-12; one of his duties, the care of the clock, was undertaken by John Cokkes from 1500-1503 whose office was not stated but who may have been sexton at this earlier date. In 1508 the parish agreed the salary for the office should be 26s 8d a year paid quarterly plus 6s 8d for looking after the clock. This was seemingly inadequate because for the next two years a collection, first of the parish and then of 'certayn men' raised enough to increase it to 53s 4d. An agreement begun in 1512-3 by which the two parish gilds should each contribute 33s 4d annually towards the sexton's salary allowed the churchwardens to pay Harry Water, newly appointed that year, £5 6s 8d in quarterly instalments. He stayed only two years, being replaced first by Nicholas Wood in 1514-15 and then by

1. Accounts, pp. 28, 30, 227.
2. Both Drew and Burgess say that churchwardens' accounts will only include those payments for activities or services for which they were responsible. *Lambeth Churchwardens' Accounts 1504-1645 and Vestry Book 1610* ed. Charles Drew, (2 vols, Surrey Record Society, xviii and xx, 1941 and 1950), i, xv. Drew also says that if a collection was entirely spent on an activity, neither the collection nor the activity will appear in the accounts.
3. Accounts, pp. 93-5.

William Myllyng from 1515 to 1518.[1] From this date to 1523-4 continuity in the post was lost; two individuals served for short periods but neither stayed a full year. In 1523-4 John Darlington was appointed at a salary which quickly rose to £5 9s 4d, presumably as sexton, though he is never called this in the accounts; he continued to receive the same sum until 1543-4. No other sexton is named in the accounts during these years except in 1534-5 and again in 1537-8 when two payments were made, the usual one to Darlington and one to 'the Sexton'. These seem to be mistakes as it is clear from the position of the entries in the list of officials that the term 'under-sexton' was intended. In 1544-5 a new sexton, Richard Tuyng or Tewin, appeared, paid only 21s 8d for the year; Darlington remained on the pay roll, albeit receiving a mere 20s. This situation continued until Michaelmas 1546. New arrangements for paying salaries were made in April 1547: the Jesus gild would pay the sexton; the churchwardens would pay the clerk and Darlington, and provide the latter with a house; they did this for that year. Darlington was paid 21s 3d for a short period of service in 1546-7 and then disappeared from the accounts. If the supposition that Darlington had been sexton all those years is correct, it is possible the churchwardens were giving a faithful official some small payment as a reward for long service, or finding him work he found acceptable in the changed situation of the late 1540s.[2]

Small additional sums had been paid to the sexton for extra work in early years of the century. Under the agreement of 1547 these now became part of his official duties and included looking after the clock, tolling the bell for gild services and cleaning the candlesticks. In return the Mass of Jesus gild agreed to pay his wages of £3 5s 8d, less than the amount the two gilds together had previously contributed which explains why the new sexton's wages were lower. John Darker, the sexton that year, also sang in the choir for extra pay. Even at this lower level the post provided a reasonable income although less than that of a craftsman with a year's contract. After the dissolution of the gilds under the Chantries Act of 1547 and the consequent disappearance of their contribution to parish finances, the sexton, Robert Tewin, was very rarely paid even this salary in full. Faced with the financial burdens of the following two decades the churchwardens sometimes paid him in arrears and often paid him only part of his salary. For three years, 1560-3, neither he nor the office of sexton appear in the accounts. In 1563-4 Darker, not called sexton in the accounts until 1566-7, was paid 20s; in the latter year his wages for keeping the clock, singing in the choir and ringing the bells every morning amounted to 27s 6d.[3]

From 1507 to 1562 there was usually an under-sexton in the parish. During the first few years of the accounts when no under-sexton is recorded, various tasks such as tending the rood lights, scouring the candlesticks before

---

1. Accounts, pp. 37, 83, 87, 88, 94, 102, 107; Our Lady's gild failed to contribute in 1514-5 and the next year both gilds paid less than agreed. Accounts, pp. 100, 103.
2. Accounts, pp. 154, 143, 148, 197, 210, 239, 243, 244, 247.
3. Accounts, pp. 99, 244, 322.

major feasts and cleaning the gutters were undertaken by one Makrell, and rewarded separately; in 1507-8 William Poo, under-sexton, swept the church, brought boards there for the pageant of the Passion and rang the bell at the *Corpus Christi* day procession. He also had the right to the nettles in the churchyard in return for cutting them down. Thereafter there is no reference to the under-sexton's duties though they may well have included similar occasional work. The wages were so low as to suggest it must have been a part-time occupation; William Long who was paid 5s a year from 1510 to 1517, plus a few pence more for odd jobs, rented a property in New Street with a rent more than twice this amount. Richard Andrews, who replaced him during the year 1517-18, was paid considerably more: 12s annually from 1518-9 to 1534-5 for which he added care of the clock to his duties. After Andrews' long years in office, various men occupied the post until 1545-6 being paid at rates ranging from 10s to 40s a year. One was Norrres, named as under-sexton in 1543-4; for many years previously he had been paid for various odd jobs including 'blowing' (working the bellows of) the organs. Matters were more settled after Richard Loryman was appointed in 1545; he was paid 13s 4d for the first few years, briefly rising to double this amount and settling at 20s from 1553 to 1561. He doubtless earned it since he was in post for periods when there was apparently no sexton.   In its straitened financial situation of these years the parish could not afford two salaries: when Darker became sexton in 1563 there was no under-sexton and neither was there again in the period discussed here.

Apart from a payment of 20d in 1508-9 to a man called Horn to come from Winchester 'For to a byn Clerk here of the Churche' there are no references to a salary for a parish clerk in the volume of the accounts until 1537-8. The role of the clerk was important; he assisted the priest in several ways such as serving at Mass; in 1433-4 a surplice was made for him and sleeves set into 'the Clerkes rochet' in 1504-5.[1] One explanation for the absence of a salaried clerk in the accounts is that in some parishes before the Reformation he was sometimes a teenager who was expected to enter the priesthood later. He received small fees for performing certain duties but was not usually paid, so would not appear in the accounts. No payment for either Richard Abyndon, parish clerk, who witnessed a parishioner's will in 1520 or Andrew Wright is recorded ; in 1537-8 Norris was paid 6s 8d for work done in the absence of Wright, called 'clerk'. After the Reformation parishes began providing clerks with a regular income once their fees ceased.[2] This could have been the case at St Laurence. However a more likely explanation is that, as with the provision of other parish needs, the accounts record only those for which the churchwardens were responsible, or where they had to supplement

---

1. Charles Kerry, 'Six Ancient Rolls of Church Wardens' Accounts', *Berkshire Archaeological and Architectural Society Transactions,* i (1880-81), 6-7. No salary for him is quoted. Accounts, pp. 17, 23. It is not clear whether the clerk from Newbury in 1503-4 was a parish clerk.
2. Accounts, pp. 75, 210. Nicholas Orme, *Medieval Children* (Yale 2001), 228-231.

parish donations.[1] One such was a bequest of 3s 4d to the parish clerk by John Hale in 1461. In 1540-41 the churchwardens received 59s 8d 'towardes the clerkes wages in Colleccion of honest men', with an additional 33s 4d from Master Turner.[2] The next two years, 1541-3 when similar collections raised £3 4s and 34s 6d respectively, the churchwardens again provided clothing, bedding and fuel, this time for 'the Clerk'. They made arrangements for his washing to be done and paid him 12d at Christmas and Easter. The clerk was named in 1544-5 as Sayntmore; he was paid 40s 'over & besydes the gatheryng in the parisshe' for playing the organs. The parish ordinance of 1547 quoted above stated that the clerk's salary would be 20s paid by the churchwardens, which is the amount Sayntmore's successor, Dixson, received from 1548-9. There is no explanation as to why his salary and that of future clerks was so much lower except that the simpler services of the Prayer Book reduced his liturgical duties and none of them was an organist.[3]

Whereas the churchwardens usually employed only three officials in any one year, they needed far more craftsmen, labourers and even a few professionals; a scrivener almost always wrote the accounts and in 1516-7 William Edmunds who had legal skills was paid for 'sortyng of evydences of the church'.[4] The skills or the brute strength needed for these tasks were mostly available within the borough: building craftsmen of all kinds, metal workers, plumbers, joiners, bakers, brewers and even a bell founder, as well as very skilled tailors to make and mend vestments and silversmiths to repair sacred vessels.When they were not, it was possible to find a craftsman elsewhere - an organ maker, an image maker or a singer.[5] The accounts describe these employees in different ways, mostly just names and the work done or the goods provided; in such cases their occupation can often be deduced. In rare instances the early accounts state both the workman's name and his occupation: Miller the joiner and Pasteler the carpenter. In many instances, especially in later years, there is the briefest of descriptions,

1. *The Churchwardens' Accounts of Ashburton*, ed. Alison Hanham,(Devon and Cornwall Record Society, new series xv, 1970) xvii. Hanham found no reference to a clerk between 1479 and 1511. Drew said that if parish collections entirely paid his wages, the clerk would not appear in the accounts.

2. BRO Calendar of Reading medieval deeds: copy of the will of John Hale 1461 R/AT1/202. A reference on page 17 to 'Everard the clerke' from Newbury does not seem to refer to a parish clerk. Thomas Carpenter's will made 20 August 1520 was witnessed by Richard Abyndon, parish clerk. TNA Will of Thomas Carpenter, 1520 PROB 11/20/3. A bequest to the churchwardens of £10 by Thomas Everard in 1535 to 'the waiges of Clarkes' may refer to parish clerks but is more likely to mean parish clergy. TNA Will of Thomas Everard, chandler, 1535 PROB 11/29/4. The wardens also made a number of payments to and for a certain 'lewes': for his indentures, thirty-seven weeks' board and lodging and several items of clothing, a total of £9 19s 0½d. He is never called clerk but it is possible he was one of the young clerks Orme has found.

3. Accounts, pp. 154, 220, 222-3, 227, 228-230, 239, 243, 247, 257, 261; the accounts for 1542-3 are defective. For the duties of the clerk see J. H. Bettey, *Church and Parish: an introduction for local historians* (1987), 50, 164.

4. Accounts, p. 116. For further details about William Edmunds see Appendix 2.

5. Accounts, pp. 89, 133, 286.

usually just the work done and the cost with no named craftsman. Though the amount they were paid is always stated, daily wage rates were recorded very infrequently. However in the first few years of the accounts, a carpenter and a mason are recorded as paid 6d and a tiler 7d a day. The cost of meat and drink for the tiler and his man for seven days was an additional 2s 10d. The rates paid to many men engaged on the major building work in the church of 1518-19 confirm those paid in other years: tilers on 7d a day, joiners 6d. Whereas a craftsman might earn 6d a day, his 'man', a journeyman employed by him, received only 5d and another 'man' just 4d. Labourers earned 5d at most. Wages had increased by the 1550s when a mason and his man were paid 17d a day between them, a total of 5s 8d for four days' work, a tiler with his man 3s 4d for three days, about 13d daily and two workmen making the Easter sepulchre 10d a day each.[1] Some idea of the purchasing power of wages can be gauged from the clothes provided for a certain 'Lewes' in the early 1540s. Shoes cost 9d a pair, a shirt 2s and a fustian doublet 5s 10d.[2]

Women were usually employed to wash church linen, sew vestments and church ornaments and sometimes to provide bread for parish feasts. More skilled were John Paynter's wife paid 3s 4d in 1524-5 for gilding part of St Vincent's statue and Dame Taylor who made a pillow of cloth of gold (probably to support a service book) in 1508-9. They are among the rare exceptions in an essentially male world.

ii. Church fabric, furniture and churchyard

Repairs and additions to church fabric and furniture swallowed up a very large proportion of the parish income, more so in years when major projects were undertaken. The church was the focus of parish life; the expenditure recorded in the accounts show the great care and devotion, not to mention large sums of money, lavished on it during the years before the Reformation. The church stood at the north end of the Market Place. Its brick-walled churchyard was a distance away within the abbey precinct on the north side of the abbey church but its upkeep was a charge on the parish. The churchyard had a distinctly rural appearance with grass and nettles through which there were paths; access was either by the gate, normally kept locked, or a stile. In 1556 when much of the abbey was in ruins, a new churchyard was created by a grant of Crown lands next to the church. Seventeen parishioners contributed a total of £9 5s 6d for a wall 159 yards long to surround it.[3] Apart from this outlay, the churchyard made few calls on the

1. Accounts, pp. 3, 17, 126, 223, 272, 283. These amounts are comparable with those paid to craftsmen and labourers employed to demolish the abbey in 1549, Arthur E. Preston, ed., 'The Demolition of Reading Abbey', reprinted from *Berkshire Archaeological Journal* xxxix, No. 2 (1935), 19, 20.
2. Accounts, pp. 222, 230. By the 1540s there was significant price inflation.
3. Accounts, pp. 7, 86, 94, 35, 22, 174, 278. The position of the churchyard is given by Kerry, 201 as on the north side of the Abbey church; Cecil Slade, *The Town of Reading and its Abbey 1121-1997* (Reading 2001), 29.

parish's resources.

Most of the workmen employed by the churchwardens were engaged on repairs or alterations to the fabric of the church itself. The parish was responsible for the whole building apart from the chancel, the upkeep of which belonged to the rector, Reading Abbey until 1539 and thereafter the Crown. There were always minor problems to deal with: providing new locks, clearing gutters, repairing the clock, but more substantial though mercifully infrequent works necessitated major expenditure. That this was discussed and agreed at parish meetings seems to be the meaning of the phrase 'by thassent of the parisshe' which occurs in the accounts from time to time.

The period between 1513 and 1525 saw some new installations and major changes in the appearance of the church. Improvements to St John's Chancel also called St John's Chapel in 1513-14 included laying new floor tiles, installing seats and closing the door from the chapel to the main chancel, replacing it with a parclose or screen. Most important was the construction of an altar made by removing the front of the High Altar and setting it up in the chapel. St John's altar and the reconstructed or new High Altar were consecrated the following year. The total cost of the work was 11s 6½d.[1]

The works undertaken in 1518-21 were of a different order of magnitude. The purchase in 1518-19 of 5,400 bricks, 1,200 laths, 3,000 tiles, 5,422 lbs of lead, quantities of lime and loads of stones and sand were the prelude to a major building project. In that year substantial alterations to the chancel included re-glazing the three lancet windows at the east end with eighty-two feet of glass, inserting dormer windows and retiling that part of the roof and re-plastering the walls. The High Altar was reset on an elevated platform and new tabernacles made and gilded. Some of the materials may have been used for the raising of the arches between the nave and the north aisle which was not undertaken until 1521-2, after which part of the north aisle was re-paved. Two problems are thrown up by the accounts for these years: the whereabouts of a vestry and a new chapel which have left no traces in the existing building. For the first and only time a vestry is recorded in the accounts; in 1518-9 small sums of 6d each were paid for an altar and windows there and the following year 'Colis occupied in the vestrie' cost 4d. Miller 'the Carver' made a 'parclose in the newe chapell' in 1518-9 and was eventually paid £4 6s 8d for this and 'the newe lofte' which he constructed in the following year. The exact nature of these structures is as problematic as their location.[2]

The town could not supply all the workmen needed: at least a hundred

1. Accounts, pp. 97-99, 101.
2. Accounts, pp. 125-8, 131-132, 141. Kerry believed that the new vestry was a identical with the new loft and was a 'wooden chamber' with a flat roof 'forming a sort of small gallery' which seems unlikely since the new loft was built after the vestry windows and altar were in place. For this and his comments on the old views of the church showing some of the dormer windows see Kerry, *A History*, 13-15, 46. There is now no evidence of this vestry.

man-days' work in 1518-19 and 167 days tiling and labouring the following year. Harry Horthorne was paid £7 0s 4d by the churchwardens for 'bowrdyng of men as apperith by his billes'.[1] Such enormous costs could not be met even from the collection made in the parish every Sunday for nine months that year though a few wealthy parishioners stumped up an extra £6 3s 4d. The sale of more than 212 cwt of old lead, 525 lbs of surplus new lead and a silver salt given by William Staunford raised £8 1s 8½d ensuring that the accounts ended the year in surplus. Not so in 1561-2 when major repairs to a gutter prompted the purchase of timber, tiles and large amounts of lead which with the labour totalled £7 8s 4½d; together they contributed to the large deficit in that year's finances.[2]

Besides repairs to the structure, essential church furniture needed repair or replacement from time to time. Preaching played a growing part in forming lay spirituality in the late middle ages. Over 200 pulpits survive, most from the fifteenth century, and though St Laurence's is not listed among them the accounts show that one existed by the 1530s. It is mentioned twice: in 1537-8 when a 'wall' was constructed 'about the pulpett' and in 1547 when the 'highest seates or pewes' were said to be 'towardes the pulpitt'. It continued in use after the Reformation.[3]

Another essential feature of a church, the font, was replaced in 1520-21. The overseer of one of Cardinal Wolsey's building projects was given a small gift to allow Chayney, a mason there, to undertake the work, evidence of the importance placed upon it.[4] The next year the lead lining of the old font was sold for 7s and the year after that Chayney was paid 31s 8d, presumably when the work was complete.[5] The net cost, including the overseer's gift, the cost of bringing Chayney and making the font was a mere 32s 4d.

The completion of this project was quick and easy in comparison with the making, repair and replacement of the great organ, a saga which troubled the churchwardens for much of the early sixteenth century. Until 1505-6 it stood on the rood loft but was then moved. In 1510-11 Robert Barkby, an organ maker from London, received an advance of £4 for making a new organ. This was installed in the following year when he was given a further £6 1s 6d at various times and a 'Master Wod' brought from Windsor to 'se' the new organs, though whether this was to tune them, try them out or give his seal of approval is not clear.[6] The new instrument seemingly stood in a new organ loft, lit by a new glazed window. Wainscot panels enclosed it and an 'arch' or

1. Accounts, pp. 126, 131-2.
2. Accounts, pp. 123, 128-9, 305.
3. Accounts, pp. 210, 244. See Duffy, *The Stripping of the Altars, 57-8*
4. The building could well have been Hampton Court which was constructed for Wolsey between 1515 and 1526. Simon Thurley, *The Royal Palaces of Tudor England: architecture and court life 1460-1547* (1993), 41-2.
5. Accounts, pp. 137, 139, 150. The font now stands in the south-west corner of the nave.
6. This was Richard a Wood, organist of St George's Chapel, Windsor. Kerry, 60; Magnus Williamson, 'Liturgical music in the late-medieval parish', in *The Parish in Late Medieval England*, eds. Clive Burgess and Eamon Duffy (2006), 194.

vault of brick and tile was constructed, possibly under it, to house the bellows, necessitating a breach in a wall. Locks were made for the organ loft, the organ stops and the keyboard.[1]

The old organ was still in place, the bellows being repaired in the same year. Barkby's new organ was called the 'great organs'. He was summoned back to Reading on several occasions over the next few years to sort out problems. Eventually the lead pipes of the great organs were sold to 'Segemond, the organmaker', who was later paid £6 1s 8d for 'transposyng' the organ and 13s 4d for further work on the instrument. His work was not to the satisfaction of the parish which began a suit against him in 1522-3. Two years later another new organ was carried 'from the water to the church' which suggests it may have come from London via the Thames and Kennet to the town wharf; this may have been the little organ mentioned in 1525-6.[2] In 1531-2 the great organ was sold to one of the orders of friars from Oxford for £10 of which 50s remained unpaid at the dissolution of the monasteries and friaries.[3]

Whereas the organ looms large in the accounts for a period, minor repairs to the bells are a recurrent feature with two major replacements being necessary. Four bells hung in the tower, called in the accounts a steeple, the usual late medieval term. There is a reference to five bells in 1510-11 but it is likely that the fifth was the sanctus or sacring bell, normally set externally and rung at the elevation of the host during the Mass. The tenor, variously called the Great Bell, Harry or the Kelsall Bell was newly cast in the 1490s following a bequest in Henry Kelsall's will of 1493. (There was an earlier great bell for which a rope was bought in 1433-4.) The Kelsall Bell was consecrated by the suffragan and hung in 1500-1501 with three parishioner 'godparents'.[4] Being in frequent use for ringing knells, it often needed repair and occasional extra support; in 1526 it was given four iron clamps. In 1567 it required a complete recasting. Its weight (over 34 cwt. when it was taken down for repair in 1594) made this a costly undertaking, financed by contributions from parishioners of St Laurence and the other two urban parishes as well as from the countryside around. The work was entrusted to a Reading bellfounder, William Knight, and the new bell re-hung by taking out the south window in the tower. The total cost of the project was £11 7s 5d; the collection raised £12 5s 9d, so leaving the parish a small profit. The fourth or Lady Bell weighing 125 lbs, also used at funerals, was recast in 1515-16. The cost of recasting and hanging was a mere 21s 3½d, only 18 lbs

1. Accounts, pp. 25, 86, 88-90, 93, 94. The accounts refer to the instrument in the plural, a 'pair of organs' but this means a single instrument. Kerry gives an account of events from 1506-33, including the possiblity that the organ was removed from the rood loft in 1506. Kerry, *A History, 59-62.*
2. Accounts, pp. 129, 138, 142, 158, 161.
3. Accounts, p. 183. Kerry believed that the amount was £12 10s of which £10 was paid but he appears to be mistaken. Kerry, *A History,* 62.
4. Accounts, pp. 3, 85. The will does not state the amount of the bequest. Kerry, *A History,* 84-96 gives a detailed account of the bells and of various parishioners associated with them.

of new metal being used.[1] The other bells are merely described as second or third bells. All were in constant use: as well as ringing for funerals, they were heard during processions, at festivals such as May Day and Whitsuntide, during royal visits and for national celebrations. Ten ringers were paid and supplied with drink when the king left Reading in 1509-10, others were given two gallons of ale in 1513 when an English army captured the French city of Tournai and the King of Scotland, James IV, was killed at the battle of Flodden.[2] As a result they needed constant attention, some parts more than others.

Bells were heavy. To secure them they were attached to a wooden 'yoke' set in a wooden frame or stock. In time they became loose and needed to be secured more tightly. This 'trussing' was carried out several times, in 1503-4 on the fourth and the great bell, in 1530-1 on the great bell and in 1533-4 on all the bells. In the latter year a 'Man of Crendon' was paid 20d 'for trussyng & serchyng the belles'. The wooden wheels (to which the bell-yokes were attached and which swung the bells) also needed repair or replacement: a new wheel for the second bell in 1530-31 and 'compass boards' for all the bells in 1507-8. The metal parts of the bells, especially the clappers, often became worn; in 1521-2 a new one weighing 119 lbs was made for the great bell and that of the second bell was repaired. The clapper had a loop at the top, the 'eye'. Baldrics, straps of white leather threaded through the 'eye', attached the clapper to the bell. In 1508-9 Thomas Smith made a new 'eye' for the clapper of the third bell and in 1530-31 the eye of the fore bell clapper was 'turned', probably to reduce the wear. Some less robust parts of the bells wore out very quickly: the heavy bell ropes weighing 13lbs or more were replaced or repaired almost every year though the ropes for the sanctus bell lasted longer. The provision of lines to toll the great and fourth bell may have been an attempt to reduce the wear on their ropes from frequent use at funerals.[3]

Another mechanism, a clock, was a further drain on the churchwardens' resources though to a lesser extent than the bells. There is a reference to a clock in 1433-4 but information on its appearance occurs only in the bound volume of accounts. It was probably inside the church; in 1500-01 it was attached to two pieces of wood set into a wall. It may have been a simple mechanism with a rod, weighted at each end and fixed to an axis which could pivot, allowing small rods to engage with the teeth of a wheel. The wheel was rotated by a cord attached by a wire to a weight (the peise). As it did so, 'pallets' or small rods engaged with a tooth, the rod stopped and the rod

1. Accounts, pp. 323-6 and 106; BRO, Will and inventory of William Knight, 1587, D/A1/ 89/ 9.
2. Accounts, pp. 80, 98, 177, 182.
3. Kerry, *A History*, 87; Accounts, pp. 17, 181, 194, 182, 36, 143, 75, 182. For a comprehensive description of bells and their upkeep see *The Churchwardens' Book of Bassingbourn, Cambridgeshire, 1496-c.1540*, ed. David Dymond (Cambridge Record Society, xvii, 2004) xliii-xlv. I have relied heavily on this in interpreting the St Laurence evidence.

swung in the opposite direction. St Laurence's clock was made of iron with a wheel, a weight and a considerable amount of wire. The purchase of a little rope 'for the watch of the clock' weighing 8lbs and mending the clock pulley are also evidence of the winding mechanism. There was a figure which perhaps rang the hours: in 1500-01 the churchwardens paid for 'the settyng of Jack with the hangyng of his bell & mendyng of his hond' but there is no later evidence of this feature. Other costs were incurred: in 1506-7 the Mayor as well as the parish witnessed Thomas Quedyndon's agreement to maintain the clock for twelve years; the parish meeting of 1510-11 requested the repair of the clock which cost 26s 10d.[1]

In 1520-21 the parish commissioned a new clock at a cost of £5 though another entry the following year gives it as £6 10s; in both cases only a part payment was made. In 1522-3 a further payment of 30s 8d for making the clock was made to one, Garret. No receipts for the sale of parts of the old clock are recorded. The new clock in its 'clockhouse' had a wooden dial and was erected in the tower under a window. In 1543-4 it was given a bell at a cost of £4 5s.[2]

At intervals, other church furniture was either installed or repaired including several items for storage: an 'almery' (aumbry or chest) with a lock for service books, a chest to keep torches, also locked, and one for copes. The latter was expensive, costing 10s 10d. It was probably in the shape of a large semi-circle since copes were (and still are) stored flat. The locked aumbry in the chancel was probably used to store church plate or the holy oils. The provision of two locks and keys to the 'churche wardens Coffar for the churche bookes & evydences' in 1556-7 was probably what came to be called the parish chest. There had certainly been a chest before this to preserve leases, deeds and possibly service books. However, included in the legislation of 1538 ordering parishes to keep a register of baptisms, marriages and burials was a clause that 'a sure coffer' with two locks, one each for the incumbent and the wardens, be provided. Other objects and places were also locked: the covered font to prevent the superstitious use of blessed water, the entrance to the tower and the doorway from the church to the procession way.[3]

iii. Repairs to church property
Maintenance of the houses, shops and other buildings owned by the parish was a constant drain on its finances though less so than the upkeep of the

---

1. Accounts, pp. 4, 98, 99, 32, 85. Kerry stated that a John Tyler was clock keeper from 1433-4. He mistakenly attributed the setting up of the figure to 1498-9. Kerry, *A History*, 97.

2. Accounts, pp. 137, 138, 141, 150, 142, 143, 232, 234; Kerry, *A History*, 97-8.

3. Accounts, pp. 116, 35, 99, 286, 35, 98; Duffy, *The Stripping of the Altars*, 280; *Documents of the English Reformation*, ed. G. Bray (Cambridge, 1994), 182; W. E. Tate, *The Parish Chest: A Study of the Records of Parochial Administration in England* (Cambridge, 1960), 44. It is possible that Richard Turner sold the parish a book for the parish register in 1538. J. Martin, 'The People of Reading,' 423.

church fabric. Most repairs were minor and relatively cheap and generally covered by the rents. The cost of wood, planks and nails for the barn that John Punsar rented in Gutter Lane and building a hog sty there in 1501-2 came to little more than two years' rent; no further work was needed. A few pence was all it cost to repair the tiles in Jenyns' wife's property in 1501-2, to construct a hatch in a house in New Street in 1507-8 or provide a plank for a shop in the Market Place thirty years later.[1] Most repairs were of this order.

4. Parish worship and religious change

The pre-Reformation Church

The pre-Reformation church was at the heart of the spiritual life of the parish; the cost of repairs and alterations to its structure and fittings recorded in the accounts can help to explain its appearance, the services and devotions which took place there and the beliefs which they expressed. The most important part of the church was the chancel or choir,[2] lit from the east end by a triple lancet window; on the wall below was a representation of the Transfiguration, painted and richly gilded. Against the wall, raised above the rest of the chancel, stood the High Altar behind which on a low platform were statues of the twelve apostles in niches called tabernacles, forming a reredos. Hanging in front of the altar was a frontal of exotic fabric embroidered with images.[3] Above it was a velvet canopy attached to a wooden frame supported by four staves. It was probably from this frame that a consecrated host in a silver-gilt pyx was hung, covered with a canopy.[4] Somewhere in the chancel a light or lights 'before the sacrament' were suspended from a beam. At the High Altar the priest celebrated daily Mass for the parishioners, and High Mass on Sundays and major feast days. The most solemn part of the service was the consecration of the bread and wine followed immediately by the elevation when the celebrant held up the host and chalice for the people's adoration. At this 'sakeryng of Masse' a black cloth was drawn across the back of the altar to make the host more visible. Another curtain, the Lenten veil or 'lent cloth' stretched across the chancel in Lent obscuring the High Altar. St. Laurence's was expensive: it cost 4s 4d in 1510-11. On either side of the chancel were stools and desks for the 'rectors' (cantors), probably in front of choir stalls. As was fitting for this sacred space, the bosses in the painted roof were gilded. From the chancel roof

---

1. Accounts, pp. 7, 8, 36, 207.
2. 'Choir' can also be written 'quire'. Since the word 'choir' can also mean singers, the area containing the High Altar will be called the chancel in this introduction.
3. Accounts, pp. 164, 127, 75, 79, 210, 127. For a discussion of the place of the Mass in medieval religion see Duffy, *The Stripping of the Altars,* chapter 5 especially 95-6 and 111. The Transfiguration was the occasion when Christ appeared to some apostles as a divine apparition. The painting was discovered in 1848 - see Kerry, *A History,* 71-3. See the inventories for altar frontals.
4. This canopy may have been a square pyx cloth of fine fabric with a hole in the centre for the chain holding the pyx. There was an example in the church of St Ethelbert, Hessett, Suffolk.

suspended on a pulley hung a trendal, a painted wooden wheel which was used as a chandelier.[1]

On the north side of the chancel stood the Easter Sepulchre which played a central role in the Holy Week liturgy when Christ's Passion and Resurrection were celebrated. The Sepulchre, which every church was obliged to have or to make, had for some time been the focus of lay devotion throughout England. At St. Laurence it seems to have been a wooden structure consisting of a table-like base surmounted by a frame onto which the sepulchre light and other candles could be set. The sepulchre has not survived - it was sold in 1549-50 - but the few examples from the same period which still exist suggest that it could have been a fine piece of carpentry. Its cost would certainly suggest this since £4 13s 10d was paid for its construction in 1512-13 and extra for the frame. It seems to have been a permanent structure although examples of movable sepulchres are known.[2]

The chancel was separated from the nave by a rood screen, above which was the rood loft, so called because it supported a rood or crucifix flanked by gilded statues of the Virgin Mary and St John. Nothing about the appearance of the screen itself can be gathered from the accounts but the rood loft with its images is well documented; remains of the stairway leading to it can still be seen. At either end were substantial iron structures supporting the rood light; this seems to have been a number of lights either candles or oil in latten bowls suspended from the screen rather than a single flame. Five pendents 'for the Rode lyghtes' were purchased in 1523-4. Six bowls were added in 1500-01 and by 1547-8 there were twenty. The rood light was financed by specific parish collections; 19 lbs and 31lbs of wax were provided at Christmas and All Saints' Day in 1508-9. During Lent the rood was covered with a hanging, the rood cloth. Many English churches had a representation of the Last Judgement, a Doom, painted above the rood screen but there is no mention of this in these accounts.[3]

Neither is there much information about other wall paintings and decoration, but given that this wealthy parish owned many magnificent vestments, books and sacred vessels, it is highly likely that the church was ablaze with colour on walls, pillars and windows but the accounts are silent about the location and form of most of them. A few remnants were uncovered in the nineteenth century including the representation of the Transfiguration referred to above. Though some of the church was white-limed it would be unusual if no other wall paintings had existed, particularly images of saints who were revered not only as exemplars of the good

---

1. Accounts, pp. 16, 85, 99, 210, 127, 158, 86, 12; Duffy, *The Stripping of the Altars*, 96, 111, 13.
2. Accounts, pp. 259, 89, 91. For an example of such a sepulchre see R. Marks & P. Williamson eds., *Gothic: Art for England 1400-1547* (V & A publications, 2003), 388, and for stone structures, Duffy, *The Stripping of the Altars,* plates 7 and 8.
3. Accounts, pp. 25, 3, 4, 154, 127, 37, 250, 76, 75. See Duffy, *The Stripping of the Altars*, 112, 157, 548.

Christian life but as powerful intercessors in Heaven for the welfare of souls on earth. Individuals had their favourite saints, crafts, religious gilds and parishes their patrons. Every year before the Reformation St Laurence's churchwardens organised a parish 'gathering' to renew the rood light for All Saints' Day, an important feast which commemorated all known and unknown deceased faithful Christians.   Whatever representations of saints did adorn the walls the only reference in the accounts is to an image of St Christopher. This was created by Mylys, a painter, for a fee of 8s 4d suggesting it may have been large as images of this saint often were.

A much smaller fee of 20d was all John 'paynter' received in 1521 for completing the statue of St Leonard 'left by the wyffes unpayntyd'. This was probably a wooden image but whether the others mentioned in the accounts were made of wood or stone is unclear.[1] They stood either in niches or under wooden canopies called tabernacles. In 1518-19 some of these were brought by barge probably from London; which images they contained is not known. Two tabernacles, gilded at the enormous cost of £14 13s 4d, and therefore at least two statues, stood in the chancel. Four images are mentioned by name: St Clement's had a light before it; a new image of St Michael was brought from London in 1519; St Vincent's statue received a gilded tabernacle in 1524 and Mary Magdalen's 'cote' of cloth of gold is found in the inventory of 1517.[2]

We can be reasonably confident about the location of images associated with an altar. St John's stood in a chapel of the same name discussed above. Here too was St Catherine's statue, for whose light 12d of wax was bought in 1433-4 according to the accounts of that year.   Other altars, dedicated to the saint whose statue stood there including St Clement, were in the north aisle and the nave. St Thomas's and St George's altars were constructed in 1501-2 at the entrance to St John's Chapel; when the altars were re-consecrated in Mary's reign, that of St Thomas was said in the accounts to be 'in the North side' of the nave. The statue of St George and its altar stood on a loft, a northward continuation of the rood loft over the east end of the north aisle. In 1534-5 the image was completely renovated - a 'cote', girdle, sword and dagger for the saint, calf and horse skins to make his steed, roses and bells to adorn it. Since John Paynter was again employed at a cost of 45s, the effigy was painted and possibly gilded. The most important images, apart from those of Christ and the Virgin, were those of the church's patron saint. There were three statues of St Laurence, one erected in 1520-21 on the exterior east wall of the chancel under a pentice and another, possibly the one with the gilded gridiron, the instrument of the saint's martyrdom, at the north side of the High Altar, called in 1557 'the high awter of Saynt Laurence'. A third once stood in a niche at the west end of the church; Kerry said that in his day

1. Accounts, pp. 17, 142.
2. Accounts, pp. 127, 131, 116, 133, 157. For details about all the saints mentioned here see David Hugh Farmer, *The Oxford Book of Saints* (Oxford, 1978).

it was in the vicarage garden 'in a sadly mutilated condition'.[1]

Between 1433 and 1524 no fewer than twelve altars are mentioned in the inventories or churchwardens'accounts but two appear just once, that of St Blaise in 1433 and St Nicholas in 1538-9. The one at the Easter Sepulchre was used only at Eastertide; the exact locations of the vestry altar, the marble altar of the Trinity and St Clement's altar are unknown.[2] Two altars occupied very prominent positions at the east end of the nave or 'in body of the churche' and so nearer to the people than the High Altar.' One was the Lady Altar; the other was described in 1557 as the 'Myddell alter called Jh[es]us alter'; earlier a pew and a desk, perhaps a prie-dieu stood before it.[3]

The 'characteristically English' devotion to the Holy Name of Jesus became very popular in the late fifteenth century when a Proper of the Mass and Office for the feast of the Holy Name was written; the St Laurence accounts refer to a 'gret priksong boke' belonging to the gild with music for the liturgy, and a parchment copy of the Mass. As was the case in other parishes the altar, vestments and service books belonging to it were for the use of members of the gild or 'brotherhood of Jesus Mass' whose members were some of the richest and most influential men in the borough, John Barfote, William Edmonds and Richard Turner. William Kelsall who had endowed the great bell had also founded the gild and left it money and plate. The high status of its members is confirmed by an ordinance of 1547: the wives of former and present gildsmen should occupy seats next to the Mayor's wife 'towardes the pulpitt'.[4]

These were not craft but social and religious gilds such as could be found in every urban and many rural parishes. The purpose of such organisations was mutual support through charity, fellowship, and religious devotion in this life and prayers for deceased members in the next. There was a weekly Mass at each gild altar (one of the duties of the sexton was tolling 'to Jh[esu]c Masse' and 'to our lady Masse') and perhaps an annual requiem Mass, an obit, for deceased members. This is the possible meaning of the 'terment for the brethern of Jhesus Masse' in 1537-8, it being a traditional duty to attend both the burial of a gildsman and the annual gild obit.[5] Each gild had its own chaplain, essentially a chantry priest, who celebrated its Masses. These were primarily for the select few, though in practice other parishioners might and probably did attend. In this way the gilds provided the parish with additional

1. Accounts, pp. 259, 8, 276, 198, 137, 161, 276; Kerry, *A History*, 36, 40, 67, 17, 175. A vicar, Richard Bedowe, asked to be buried in the chancel before the image of St. Laurence 'at the aulters end'. *Ibid.*, 175.

2. Kerry, *A History*, 26-40. In his will made 8 March 1527/8 Thomas Everard, junior left 2d each to six altars: Jesus, Our Lady, St Thomas, St John, the Trinity and the Sepulchre. TNA Will of Thomas Everard 1527/8 PROB 11/22/32.S

3. Accounts, pp. 226, 227, 276. 276.

4. Accounts, pp. 37, 98, 244; Kerry, *A History*, 33, 169-70. Kerry places the Jesus altar on the north pier of the chancel arch, *ibid.* 31; wills made by St Laurence parishioners frequently left money to the Jesus or Mary gild or altar.

5. Accounts, p. 209

opportunities to hear Mass as well as the extra clergy needed for solemn High Mass when a celebrant, deacon and sub-deacon were required.

The names of several gild chaplains are known including two buried in the parish, Sir John Richemond in 1519-20 and Sir William Wryght in 1527-8. When the traditional liturgy was restored by Mary Tudor but the gilds were no more, a former gild priest, Sir William Webbe, was paid a salary for celebrating the 'morrow Mass' at dawn attended by devout parishioners before beginning work.[1]

On the south side of the nave was 'one alter called our ladye awter of the Nativitie'. This was maintained by a second gild, the 'brotherhood of our lady' or Our Lady Mass though there are fewer references to it in the accounts. Devotion to the Virgin was a well-established feature of medieval spirituality and grew in importance in the later middle ages; in life believers prayed to her to intercede with God for them, and near to death they often left goods or money for a light to burn before her image.[2] The wardens of this gild were also substantial townsmen, William Edmonds, warden in 1512-13, John Barfote in 1513-4 and others who also served as churchwardens. The basis of its funds is unclear. Whereas the properties of the Jesus Mass after its dissolution can be traced in later documents - tenements in New Street, Gutter Lane and the Market Place - none which can be attributed to Our Lady Mass is recorded. However, like the Jesus Mass, it was wealthy enough to contribute to the sexton's salary and to lend substantial sums to the parish from time to time.[3]

Among the reasons to found a gild was to support a light or lights before an altar or an image; the Lady Altar had its own great candlesticks and a beam from which to suspend a light to burn before the statue of the Virgin. The church was also illuminated by many candles, tapers and torches such as burned in all medieval churches: on the rood screen, round the coffin at funerals and at least two on the altar lit during Mass. In the list of plate sold in 1547-8 were four little candlesticks, six 'greate' ones, a 'branche' with seven candlesticks and a 'beame' with ten. All these were made of latten which when 'scoured' by the sexton in preparation for feast days resembled silver. Two great candlesticks in the chancel are mentioned in 1513-14 and eighteen in total in 1508-9. There were more precious candlesticks of silver or silver gilt such as the two sold in 1537-8.

Maintaining lights burning before altars and images was, as Duffy puts it, 'the single most popular expression of piety' and a 'sort of proxy for the

1. Accounts, pp. 244,130, 168, 292; Duffy, *The Stripping of the Altars*, 115, 140. The other two Reading parishes also had gilds. 'Sir' was a title given to a non-graduate priest.
2. Accounts, p. 276. A marble fragment of the visit of the Magi which may have been the reredos of the Lady Altar is now inserted in the south wall of the nave; Duffy, *The Stripping of the Altars*, 45, 113-6, 141; some will evidence suggests devotion to the Virgin was less fervent in this parish immediately before the Reformation. J. Martin, 'The People of Reading', 591-2.
3. *Chantry Certificates for Berkshire*, ed. N. E. Fox (privately published, 1994), 37; *Reading Charters, Acts and Orders*, ed. C. F. Pritchard (1913), Charter of 2 Elizabeth, 48.

adoring presence of the donor' whether an individual who had bequeathed money for the purpose, or an organisation such as a gild.[1] Several images and altars had their own lights, though only those mentioned in the accounts are verifiable; these include St Catherine in 1433-4 and St Clement in 1516-17.[2] An enigmatic entry in 1539-40 suggests that perhaps other groups besides the two religious gilds maintained a light before the image of a favourite saint: the shoemakers paid 5s for wax for their lights in 1539-40. Most shoemakers in the borough lived in Shoemaker Row, just to the south of the church, and so were St Laurence's parishioners.[3]

Apart from the support of lights before images, other pious practices can be recognised from income or expenditure in the accounts. Inside the west door stood a lead-lined stoup containing holy water with which parishioners blessed themselves as they entered the church; a battered remnant of what may be its stone base survives. Banners carried in procession at Whitsuntide and other feasts, were made or occasionally repaired. When the sacrament, enclosed in a monstrance, was carried in procession as on the feast of Corpus Christi, a canopy was held over it. The 'procession way' probably surrounded the church and since processions punctuated the liturgical year, cleaning it regularly cost the parish a few pence. After 1557-8 when the parish had been given a churchyard adjoining the church, the Abbey precincts having acquired new owners following the dissolution, the churchwardens received rent from the borough for 'a pece of tholde processyon waye wyth the chamber over it, and som more buyldinge new therunto sett now used for the gayle called the grate'.[4] The former procession way had become the route from the Market Place to the Forbury, the name used for the former abbey and its grounds.

Pre-Reformation worship and the liturgical year

The costs of providing for church services reveal further details of pre-Reformation liturgy and popular devotion. The sacred objects which parishes were required to own and maintain are listed in the inventories but their purchase, repair and eventual sale are also found in the accounts. Frequent washing, mending and occasional new making of surplices, albs and girdles hint at the numbers of acolytes required for the ceremonial surrounding the Mass and other services. The new 'stok' costing 2s 6d in 1507-8 was possibly used in the frequent blessing of people and objects by sprinkling with holy water. The purchase in 1517-8 of a pax, a small object decorated with a religious picture or emblem, highlights another aspect of lay participation in the Mass. It was probably one of two owned by the parish and made of copper and enamel since the cost, 16d, was insufficient to purchase the one

1. Duffy, *The Stripping of the Altars*, 96, 134, 146. Accounts, pp. 250, 99, 77.
2. Accounts, pp. 250, 99, 77, 209, 26, 116, 215; Kerry, *A History*, 34.
3. BRO, Reading Court Leet Rolls, 1584, R/JL1/10, f. 1a. Transcript by C. Slade in the editor's possession.
4. Accounts, pp. 227, 174, 289

of silver gilt in the inventory of 1517. Kissed by the priest just before his communion, it was then passed round for the people to do likewise. Intended to induce peace in the community, it sometimes provoked quarrels over social precedence.[1] At the end of Mass a loaf provided by one of the parishioners was blessed, broken into fragments, placed in a basket and distributed to the congregation, a ceremony which Duffy sees, like kissing the pax, as a substitute for communion which the laity received once only in the year. In 1553-4 the churchwardens paid 6d for 'a basket to bere holy brede' once the ceremony had been restored under Mary Tudor.[2]

Music was an integral part of most services, especially at the Sunday High Mass and on great feasts. The expenses of providing and maintaining the organ have already been discussed but in addition there were extra payments as in 1534-5 when 9s was paid to one organist, Thomas Alyn, for seven weeks and 12s to another from 21 December to three weeks after Candlemas (2 February). William Norres was paid 6s 8d annually for working the bellows in the 1530s. Sometimes the clerk played the organ. Additional costs for the choir frequently occur, especially for albs and surplices. It was composed of men (possibly including the parish clerk and the chantry priests) and boys, often referred to as singing boys or children. By an agreement of 1547 the gild of Our Lady Mass was to pay wages of 40s a year to John Barker, a singing man while the churchwardens paid 53s 4d to another, Dixson. These men could well have been cantors, each leading one side of the choir in antiphonal chants; the accounts refer to them as 'rectors'.[3] Two stools were provided for them in 1510-11, perhaps replaced by those bequeathed by Richard Bedow in 1533.[4]

Some singers were brought in from outside the borough, among them a 'syngyng man' from Rickmansworth, another who boarded with the currier's wife for a short time and a 'syngyng child' from Binfield. Various payments to bass singers were recorded: 2d to 'new basses in reward' in 1541-2, 8d each to eight 'basses for the quere' in 1545-6, and 3s 6d to a bass from Westminster who boarded in the town in 1556-7. From the small amount involved, it seems that they came to reinforce and extend the range of the choir on great feasts when they possibly sang polyphony, music written for several voices. The special collections made in 1555-7 were partly to meet the costs of the choir.[5]

---

1. Accounts, pp. 37, 121. Inventories, pp. 46, 47, 57, 61.
2. Accounts, p. 272; Duffy, *The Stripping of the Altars*, 133, 125.
3. Accounts, pp.197, 244; Dixson was paid 36s 8d in 1546-7 and only 28s 4d the next year. In 1548-50 a certain Dixson was paid twenty shillings a year as the clerk. For a valuable discussion of music in parish liturgies, see Magnus Williamson, 'Liturgical music in the late-medieval parish', in *The Parish in Late Medieval England*, eds, Clive Burgess and Eamon Duffy, (2006), 177-242 which includes evidence from two Reading parishes.
4. Accounts, p. 86; Kerry, *A History*, 176.
5. Accounts, pp. 198, 194, 189, 227, 243, 285, 286, 291. Special collections were made in 1555-7 partly to meet the costs of the choir but since the word 'quire'is used for the chancel and the musicians, this could have been for the former.

There were specific volumes of music for different services. The inventories show that the parish owned all of them: missals with the priest's words and music for the Mass; several processionals with chants for use in processions on great feasts; at least six grails or graduals containing the choir parts for the Mass (in 1517-8 the churchwardens bought a new printed gradual costing 10s 4d); and antiphonals with music for Divine Office such as Matins. They would have contained both the Latin words and musical settings for the ordinary (unchanging) and proper (specific to each feast) parts of the Mass and Office. The Jesus gild had its own 'gret priksong boke of Jhesu Masse'. The books, some very large like the great Eton Songbook, were most probably for the cantors, the deacon and the celebrant. If so, they would have been placed on the lectern for several singers to share. It is likely that the boys sang by heart. Most if not all the music was Gregorian chant or plainsong which could be sung unaccompanied or with the organ; it is possible the organ sometimes played solos.[1]

Provision for the celebration of two of the seven sacraments, essential elements of traditional religion has already been discussed: baptism was celebrated at the font and the Eucharist, the Mass, at an altar. Only one other involving expenditure appears very briefly in the accounts, matrimony. The parish was given a bridal cup to be carried before all brides married in the church; it became a communion cup after the Reformation. At the fictional Jack of Newbury's wedding, a 'fair bride cup of silver and gilt' was carried before the bride as she was led into church for her wedding.[2] For a short time between 1556-7 and 1561-2 the churchwardens received 6s 8d a year for the hire of 'bride pastes', headdresses worn by brides.[3]

The duties of the churchwardens regarding funerals - providing a coffin, bier, pall and torches - and the income they derived from knells, tolling and grave digging have already been discussed. One other custom concerning the dead occurs in the accounts every year until the Reformation: the holding of an obit or memorial Mass for the deceased benefactors of the parish. In some years the accounts are clear that it was held on the Monday in Holy Week but this may not always have been the case. That prayers for the dead were conducive to their salvation was a fundamental belief before the Reformation, and to pray for the dead a Christian duty; the feast of All Souls' Day, 2 November, was specifically instituted with this in mind. Additionally, since few were wealthy enough to belong to one of the gilds or to leave a bequest for Masses for their souls, the annual parish obit gave assurance that no-one would be forgotten.

1. Accounts, pp. 121, 37; Margaret Bent, 'Music seen and music heard: music in England c.1400-1547' in R. Marks & P. Williamson eds, *Gothic: Art for England 1400-1547*, (V&A Publications, 2003) 121, 126.
2. David Cressy, *Birth, Marriage and Death: ritual, religion and the life-cycle in Tudor and Stuart England*, (OUP paperback edition 1999), 356.
3. Accounts, pp. 190, 284, 291, 295, 299, 300, 304; the OED defines 'paste' as 'headdress worn by women'.

The liturgical year with its round of feasts and fasts provided the structure for the churchwardens' expenditure, chief among the feasts being Holy Week from Palm Sunday to Easter Day, and Christmas. Seasonal purchases for the latter celebration reflect popular traditions as much as religious practice: 'a holly Bossche For the churche' was one of many references to greenery bought for decoration, though ivy appears just once. The holly bush seems to have acted as a Christmas tree, inside in 1506 when it was set up before the rood screen and adorned with wax tapers but outside in 1557 when a yew tree stood at the church door. In other years there was something resembling a nativity scene: in 1524-5 a frame for the angels on Christmas Day cost 4d and the following year a pound of tapers was provided for them.[1]

The rood light was always renewed for Christmas, paid for by a parish gathering; 28 lbs of wax was used in 1509. The tallow candles purchased in the same year 'to sett in the church on Crystmas Daye' would have dispelled some of the winter gloom, especially for the first Mass of Christmas said *in gallicantu* (at cockcrow) though the light may have extended only to the chancel; in 1506 the tapers were 'for the quyre'. Clouds of incense would have spread further; 'a quatern' costing 3d bought for Christmas would have sufficed for other feasts and Sundays though in 1507-8 another was needed by Twelfth Night Eve.[2]

Holy Week, beginning with Palm Sunday and ending with Easter Day, included the most important religious and liturgical feasts of the Christian year; they involved the churchwardens in considerable expenditure. Occuring year after year, these items make it clear that the parishioners of St Laurence took some part in the highly symbolic ritual for the feasts according to the Sarum Use, observed in its most elaborate form by many urban parishes throughout England. During the forty days of Lent a veil hid the rood screen and its images and the celebrants wore 'Lent' vestments, one of which was white.

The mood changed on Palm Sunday when red vestments were used. The ritual began with a procession (the church and procession way were regularly cleaned in anticipation) recalling Christ's entry into Jerusalem. Both congregation and clergy took part in the procession in which we should presume that green fronds were carried though since these were easily gathered from gardens, no purchases appear in the accounts. At one of the 'stations' in the procession a clerk or clerks dressed as prophets sang one of the Old Testament prophecies; in 1541-2 and 1545-6 Loreman was paid a few pence 'for playng the prophete on palme sonday'.[3] The purchase of 'wafers' and 'singing bread' in 1541-2 suggests that another part of the ritual,

1. Accounts, pp. 81, 102, 31, 157, 161, 286.
2. Accounts, pp. 81, 31, 37.
3. This was specified in the Sarum rite. Alexandra F Johnston, 'Parish playmaking before the Reformation' in *The Parish in Late Medieval England*, eds. Clive Burgess and Eamon Duffy, (2006) 335.

the scattering of unconsecrated Mass wafers before the sacrament in the procession, also took place in the parish. Following a return to the church, the cloth covering the rood was drawn up revealing the crucifix. Mass was sung during which the narrative of the Christ's sufferings as related in St Matthew's gospel was read or sung; at St Laurence as in some other churches, three clerks sang the Passion from the rood loft; in 1524-5 the singers were supplied with 'drynk in the roode loft uppon palme sonday'. The Sarum Use required three differently-pitched singers, *media vox* (tenor) as Evangelist or narrator, *bassa vox* (bass) as Christ, *alta vox* (treble) as other characters and the crowd though Duffy gives the last role to a male alto, a possible option at Reading. The accounts annually record the purchase of ale, beer or wine for the singers of the passion.[1] The parish may have celebrated *Tenebrae* on three days from Wednesday in this week;[2] the accounts are silent since no expenditure was incurred until Maundy (Holy) Thursday when the bells may have been rung.[3]

Next day, Good Friday, the priest wore red vestments; the inventories include a chasuble for this day with a narrow cross embroidered on the back. There was a service but no Mass. The last part of the liturgy was a procession from the High Altar to the sepulchre. In the procession a host, contained in a pyx, was carried by the priest and with a crucifix placed in the sepulchre, symbolising the death and burial of Christ on Good Friday.[4] Some of the parishioners kept continuous vigil until the first Mass on Easter Sunday, more evidence of lay piety and of the opportunities for the people to share in the liturgy, though a more prosaic reason may have been to prevent the theft of the valuable pyx. The churchwardens normally paid a few pence for 'watching' the sepulchre, sometimes providing ale to fortify the watchers and ensure a continuous vigil. Lights burned during the vigil and during other services for several days after on a wooden frame and after 1516 in a loft built for the sepulchre light. The 1503 inventory includes a 'sepulcre Cloth of right crymson Saten' four yards long embroidered with images and two cloths of lawn [fine linen] for the sepulchre' given by Mr Richard Smith, an example of what Duffy describes as a widespread desire to be associated

1. Accounts, pp. 174, 226, 242, 181, 157. That the parish used the Sarum Rite is clear from the list of service books in the inventories. Duffy, *The Stripping of the Altars,* 22-37 describes the ceremonial of Holy Week in great detail; Magnus Williamson, 'Liturgical music in the late-medieval parish', in *The Parish in Late Medieval England,* eds. Clive Burgess and Eamon Duffy, (2006) 211-2.
2. Thomas Everard referred in his will to 'Tenebrae Wensdaye', TNA Will of Thomas Everard, chandler, 10 April 1535 PROB 11/29/4. In 1556-7 the rural parish of Stanford in the Vale, Berkshire, held the office of *Tenebrae* from Wednesday to Friday in Holy Week. *Stanford in the Vale Churchwardens' Accounts 1552-1725* transcribed by Violet M Howse (privately published, 1987) 38.
3. Holy Thursday may refer to Ascension Day, in which case bell ringing took place then.
4. In modern Roman Catholic liturgy this ritual takes place on Maundy Thursday, the sacrament being placed in a specially constructed Altar of Repose. Three hosts were consecrated on Maundy Thursday, one consumed at that Mass by the celebrant, the second at the Good Friday service. The third was placed in the sepulchre.

with the parochial celebration of the Easter mysteries. Such a cloth, covering or hung before the sepulchre, symbolised the pall placed over a coffin, the linen cloths the winding cloths wrapping the body of Christ. St Laurence's church had whip cords and 'peces' to hang the cloth and incurred extra costs in most years for nails or other materials to adorn or repair the structure. The dramatic rituals of Good Friday emphasised for the medieval worshipper, in Reading as elsewhere, the past reality and the present saving effects of Christ's death and burial.[1]

Holy Saturday, Easter Eve, ushered in the most important feast in the liturgical calendar. Every year the accounts record payments to ensure the church looked its best, the building cleaned and its plate, especially the candlesticks, 'scoured'. The richest vestments would be laid out, perhaps the white damask chasuble with gold embroidered branches, a gift of Abbot John Thorne recorded in the inventories. The dramatic ceremonies began with kindling and blessing the new fire.[2] The churchwardens purchased charcoal for the fire; in 1513 they 'payd Nicholas hyde for ij bushelles off Colys to make the halowyd fyre on Ester yeve'. From this special bonfire first the paschal candle, symbol of the light of the Risen Christ, and then all the lights in the church were lit. The large paschal candle, placed in a painted candlestick, called a Judas to make it look even taller, stood in a basin in the chancel; in 1507 it weighed 14lbs. Sometimes it had green wax decorations, or perhaps flowers which would not appear in the accounts. A candle which stood by the font, called the font taper, was also newly made at Easter, the blessing of the water in the font being another part of the Easter Eve liturgy.

As for the rest of the ceremonies on Saturday and those surrounding the celebration of Mass on Easter Sunday, the accounts are silent, no further purchases being needed. However if the parish observed tradition the day would have begun with the 'opening of the sepulchre' very early on Easter Sunday morning. The host was taken from the sepulchre, carried in procession and returned to its usual place in the hanging pyx. This may have been part of what in other churches is described as a 'Resurrection play', a dramatic representation of the Resurrection narrative as an extension of the Easter liturgy: in 1506-7 the churchwardens paid 2½d for nails for the sepulchre and 'rosyn' for the resurrection play. 'Rosyn' (resin) could have produced a flash of light at the height of the drama. However two entries in the accounts suggest the Resurrection play was a theatrical performance about Easter time rather than part of the liturgy: a text for the 'play' was 'reformed' at a cost of 8s 4d in 1533-4 and two years later a bound 'boke of

---

1. Accounts, pp. 106, 116, 97; Duffy, *The Stripping of the Altars,* 32; Hutton, *The Rise and Fall of Merry England,* 22-23.
2. In the early middle ages the Easter Vigil took place at night, a practice which the Roman Church revived in 1951. Over time it was celebrated earlier and earlier so that by the late middle ages it was a morning service resulting in anomalies in the text and rites. J. D. Crichton, 'Paschal Vigil' in J.G.Davies, ed., *A Dictionary of Liturgical Worship* (London, 1972), 309.

the resurreccion play' was bought for the large sum of 9s 10d.[1] Whatever the case, once the 'tomb' was opened, the parishioners attended High Mass and received communion; only at Eastertide did the laity receive the sacrament.

iii. The impact of religious changes 1534-1553

This religious scene completely changed in the space of a few years: Henry VIII repudiated papal supremacy and had himself declared Supreme Head of the Church of England by statute in 1534. He subsequently authorised some religious changes by means of statute and royal injunction while retaining most Catholic beliefs and observances; it was the government of his son Edward (1547-53) which imposed the reformed religion. Mary I's reign (1553-58), reversing the Protestant innovations of Edward VI, separated the earlier Reformation from that of Elizabeth I. Some historians now refer to these as the English Reformations, an evolving rather than a once-for-all comprehensive change.[2] The experience and pressures of conforming with one change after another are reflected in the accounts of churchwardens in Reading as elsewhere, as are the increased surveillance of the bishop and occasional visits by royal commissioners to satisfy the authorities that the parish was complying with the law.

Worship

Change, especially as seen from the viewpoint of the parish, was moderate at first.[3] Since items in the accounts are not dated, it is not possible to judge the rate at which government orders were obeyed at Reading or most other places beyond judging that they occurred within an accounting year. That said, St Laurence's churchwardens seem to have been among the more compliant. Some prominent parishioners sympathised with the reformers, added to which the king was now the lord of the town and several royal officials owned property here. Henry VIII's Injunctions of 1538, the work of Thomas Cromwell, ordered all churches to have a Great Bible in English by Easter, 6 April 1539, the cost to be divided equally between the parish and the parson. It was to be placed in church where all could read it, a reflection of the reformers' belief in the primacy of Scripture. The accounts record that in the accounting year ending at Michaelmas 1539 the churchwardens duly paid nine shillings 'towards the newe byble'.[4]

Despite the King's general adherence to traditional belief and forms of worship, some use of the vernacular was authorised early in 1544. This was

---

1. Accounts, pp. 97, 34,85, 4, 29, 194, 202; Duffy, *The Stripping of the Altars,* 23, claimed that the ceremonies of Easter Eve 'attracted no lay interest' and took place in the day, but compare Hutton, *The Rise and Fall of Merry England, 24-5.*
2. C. Haigh, *English Reformations: Religion, Politics and Society under the Tudors* (Oxford, 1993), 14.
3. *Ibid,* 16, 18-19.
4. Accounts, p. 214; *Documents of the English Reformation,* ed. G. Bray (Cambridge 1994), 179, 250. J. Martin, 'The People of Reading', 432-3. This was probably the Great Bible published in 1539. W. J. Sheils, *The English Reformation 1530-70* (1989), 34.

Thomas Cranmer's English version of part of the *Processionale* known as the Litany. Outside London and the larger towns interest in the use of English in worship was limited, so the churchwardens' purchase in 1543-4 of seven 'processionalles' shows that some influential men in the parish shared this interest.[1]

Much more radical changes in religious practice were introduced by Edward VI's councillors. The Injunctions of 1547 ordered each church to purchase within three months a 'whole Bible of the largest volume' in English and within a year a Book of Homilies and a copy of *The Paraphrases on the Gospels,* a scriptural commentary by the humanist scholar, Erasmus. The churchwardens obeyed, paying 10s 4d in 1547-8 for the *Paraphrases* only; their existing Bible seems to have been acceptable until 1549-50 when they bought a new chained Bible costing 12s 8d, a psalm book and a Book of Homilies.[2] In 1547-8 the parish acquired nine books of psalms, probably to enable the ministers and choristers to use Cranmer's English version. Other payments during the same year indicate that St Laurence quickly adopted new musical settings of the English Order of Communion. Some were possibly by John Merbeck, organist at the royal chapel, Windsor, who was one of the first to set the new English liturgy to music: two gild chaplains, Sir William Webbe and Sir Richard Deane, were paid for buying 'certayne songes for the Churche' and for 'Riding to wyndesore for the service in Englisshe' respectively, while paper and ink were bought for 'prickyng [notating] the songes in Englisshe' which implies the parish was eager to have copies.[3]

Some traditions survived a little longer: on Palm Sunday 1549 the usual quart of wine was provided for the readers, not singers, of the Passion presumably proclaimed in English since the vernacular Bible was to be used for all readings. St Laurence was one of only two English parishes with surviving records to maintain this tradition.[4] By this date or shortly after the parish purchased, and by law was obliged to use on and after Whit Sunday, the 'boke of the newe service' imposed by the Act of Uniformity of that year. The 'boke' was the First Book of Common Prayer, containing the order of service for Matins, Evensong, the Lord's Supper and the sacraments. They bought another copy the same year as well as six psalters, and also paid for the 'prickyng of certayne newe songes' in London. In 1549-50 more 'songes'

---

1. Accounts, p. 233; Hutton, 'The local impact', 145-6. The processional service known as the Litany was published in May 1544. It was a translation of the Sarum Rite *Processionale* but excluding all references to the saints except Mary. D. MacCulloch, *Thomas Cranmer: A Life* (1996), 328. I owe this reference to Prof. Ralph Houlbrooke.
2. Accounts, p. 233; The Book of Homilies was a collection of twelve sermons, some by Cranmer. D. MacCulloch, *Cranmer,* 272-5.
3. Accounts, pp. 254, 261, 254. By September 1548 the complete English service was being used at the Chapel Royal, Westminster. Shield suggests that the same order of service may have been sung at the Chapel Royal, Windsor and that copies of their service books made by Deane were in use in Reading by the end of the year. Shield, thesis, 111.
4. Hutton, 'The local impact', 149.

were copied at the same time as existing books in the choir were defaced to render them unusable for the Latin Mass and the Catholic rites of the sacraments.[1] The publication of the revised Second Book of Common Prayer and its imposition by the Act of Uniformity of 1552 caused the wardens to buy two 'bokes of the Comunyon' sometime after September that year. Communion under both kinds (reception of both bread and wine) was introduced by statute in 1547 and presumably was practised in the parish. Evidence from the accounts in the form of purchases of bread and wine is lacking before 1552. An agreement was made in that year, probably at the parish meeting, that every tenement which had formerly provided the holy loaf should now contribute to the cost of the elements, which may be how the costs had been met from 1549 to 1552. At Easter 1553, the last of Edward's reign, the churchwardens paid 10s 5½d for wine.[2]

Well before Edward's death in July 1553 traditional Catholic ritual had been comprehensively replaced by a Protestant form of worship. The accounts from 1553-4 show churchwardens making provision for services from the Book of Common Prayer until the summer of 1553; then between Mary's accession in July and the end of September they bought a 'boke called an Emanuell', a manual of rubrics for celebrating Catholic sacraments.[3]

Furnishing and appearance of the church

The new services of the reformed liturgy needed fewer vestments and sacred vessels. However the first substantial sale of church plate by St Laurence churchwardens occurred in 1537-8, a decade before the government imposed any major reforms. The primary motivation was probably to raise money to pay off debts to the two gilds but the attack on religious houses which began in Reading with the dissolution of the Franciscan priory in 1538 must have raised fears for the safety of church property; 'the country as a whole had become alerted to the threat (or promise) of royal iconoclasm'. Whatever the motive, the sale of silver candlesticks, a pax, a silver gilt cup and other things raised £20 11s 11d, a huge sum.[4]

Another significant sale of plate including a censer, an incense boat and a chrismatory in 1544-5 brought in an even larger sum, £25 14s 4½d. Such sales were not unusual and in St Laurence's case the reasons for them are not

1. This was in response to the proclamation in 1549 ordering the destruction of old service books. *Tudor Royal Proclamations,* eds. P. L. Hughes and J. F. Larkin (3 vols, Newhaven and London, 1964-9), i. 485-6.
2. Accounts, p. 267. This was in accordance with an instruction in the Book of Common Prayer that the former rota for households to provide the holy loaf should now pay for the communion bread and wine. Duffy, *The Stripping of the Altars,* 125, 464; Hutton, 'The local impact', 147.
3. Accounts, pp. 261, 257, 269. Wine for Easter was bought in 1553-4 and in subsequent years despite the return of the Mass. For a brief discussion of changes in the communion service 1549-52 see W. J. Sheils, *The English Reformation 1530-70* (1989), 44-6, 93-4.
4. Accounts, p. 209; M Aston, 'Iconoclasm in England: official and clandestine' in *The Impact of the English Reformation 1500-1640,* ed. Peter Marshall (1997), 173.

hard to see.[1] In 1539 the abbey was dissolved, its abbot executed and everything of value seized. Suspicions of possible attacks on church goods may have prompting their sale to forestall confiscation. Fears would have been further heightened by the proclamation in 1545 of the Act Dissolving the Chantries though it was not yet implemented. In 1545-6 the churchwardens paid 16d for wine for the Commissioners appointed by the Chantries Act to survey the property of all such foundations but the Act lapsed with Henry's death in January 1547.[2] The churchwardens, legally responsible for the safety of parish property, may also have hoped to protect themselves and the community from prosecution by showing they had acted for 'the good and profit of the parish'.[3]

Henry's legislation was replaced by a new statute in the first year of Edward's reign empowering the Crown to seize all endowments for the support of obits, lamps or lights in church or to maintain a priest to say Masses for the dead. This included the property of parish gilds intended for the same purposes. Commissions were set up to survey all the possessions of the chantries and orders given to bishops that inventories of parish goods should be compiled. The commissioners were active in the summer of 1548 but it does not seem that they required another inventory from St Laurence; they presumably used the earlier document to draw up the chantry certificate which listed the goods and property of the parish gilds. Nevertheless it is clear that the gilds were dissolved, their land and goods confiscated and the Jesus altar removed.[4]

In the same year royal commissioners distributed copies of the Royal Injunctions of that year, commands with a radical agenda including the destruction of images which had lights before them (altered later that year to all images) and an end to many traditional ceremonies. They also brought articles of enquiry about the existing state of affairs. In 1547-8 the churchwardens appeared before commissioners at Windsor and Wallingford; the parish implemented the Injunctions very shortly after. Images and the tabernacles enclosing them were removed in 1547-8 by two carpenters and sold to local men along with a number of 'coffins' or chests and hundreds of tiles. No wonder that, probably believing that the Crown intended to confiscate those items of church plate thought by the reformers to be superfluous for Protestant ritual, the churchwardens indulged in an orgy of sales. Three small images, latten goods including at least twenty candlesticks

1. Accounts, p. 236; Hutton, The local impact', 147.
2. Accounts, p. 243. The accounts for 1543-4 include a payment of 20d for 'wrytyng of the certificat to the Commissioners uppon the Chanteris' p. 235. This is too early to apply to the Act of 1545. It may have been 'an exploratory survey' for which prototype chantry certificates were made. J. Martin, 'The People of Reading ', 355.
3. Jeanette Martin, 'Leadership and Priorities in Reading during the Reformation' in *The Reformation in English Towns 1500-1640* eds. Patrick Collinson and John Craig (1998), 127-8.
4. *Documents Illustrative of English Church History,* eds. H. Gee and W. J. Hardy (1914), 328-57; *Chantry Certificates for Berkshire,* ed. N E Fox, (privately published, 1994), 37. The chantry certificate for St Laurence parish records only one gild, the Jesus Chantry.

great and small and twenty bowls which had held the rood light were bought by a former churchwarden for £7 13s. A silver-gilt chalice, a monstrance, a cross and other silver vessels with a total weight of over 150 ounces were purchased by Nicholas Bull, a London goldsmith, for the considerable sum £47 18s.[1] Compared with this bounty, the amount raised by the sale of lead from the holy water stoup, the images with their tabernacles and hundreds of tiles was very modest and did not in any way reflect the cost of their original installation. However, it provided the churchwardens a cash reserve to meet the expenses of buying new service books and converting the church to conform to the new dispensation. For the parishioners these sales marked the beginning of the end of the familiar, time-honoured and possibly well-loved character of their parish church.

In 1548-9, the parish meeting agreed to give £13 6s 8d to the Mayor of Reading 'towardes the pavynges of the stretes', a tactic adopted by other English parishes to ensure that some proceeds from the sale of parish goods benefitted the local community. A further £7 13s 4d, proceeds of the sale of three chalices, was given for the same purpose. The sale of the chalices was prompted by the knowledge that the Crown had ordered inventories of church goods to be drawn up by sheriffs and J.P.s and that no further church goods were to be alienated except with the permission of the Privy Council, a prelude to possible confiscation.[2] The churchwardens did indeed pay for inventories of church goods for the commissioners 'at ij times' in that year. The total income from sales over the years 1546-8 was over £113. The only church goods the parish needed to retain were those for the services according to the rites of the reformed Church of England. The 1552 Prayer Book stipulated that the minister should wear a surplice only at all services yet there are remarkably few references to the sale of the many vestments and altar furnishings listed in the churchwardens' inventories. Some church goods were possibly taken by parishioners in hope of a return to traditional practices. If so, this is in contrast with the situation at St Mary's where, with the consent of leading men of the parish, vestments, copes and altar cloths were sold at the same time as church plate.[3]

In 1549 Edward's ministers ordered the removal of any church furnishings associated with traditional liturgy and beliefs. The parish was one of a small number which was quick to respond. In 1549-50 the altars were pulled

1. Accounts, pp. 249, 257, 250; Duffy, *The Stripping of the Altars, 453-6; Documents Illustrative of the History of the English Church,* eds. H. Gee and W. J. Hardy (1914), 328; Frere and Kennedy, *Visitation Articles,* ii, 103-113. Nicholas Bull lived in Southwark. TNA Will of Nicholas Bull of Southwark, 1581 PROB 11/63/33.

2. Accounts, pp. 256, 257; J. Martin, 'The People of Reading ', 469-70.

3. Accounts, p. 257; Duffy, *The Stripping of the Altars,* 474, 567; *The Churchwardens' Accounts of the Parish of St Mary's, Reading,* ed. F. and A. Garry (Reading, 1893), 1-3. These entries were dated by the editor to 1550-53. An unnamed clergyman from 'Rednege' [sic] was summoned in April 1553 by the Privy Council accused of counselling the retention of church plate; his parish is not given. *Acts of the Privy Council of England, New Series iv, 1552-1554* (HMSO, 1892) 252.

down and sold, mostly to former churchwardens: St John's, St Thomas', St Clement's, the marble Trinity Altar, the Jesus' and the High Altar, and the Easter Sepulchre; there is no mention of the sale of the Lady Altar.[1] On the other hand, unlike more radical parishes, St Laurence retained the structure of the rood screen but what happened to the images on it is unclear.

An enigmatic statement, afterwards deleted, 'to remember what was done with all the old glasse of the wyndows in the Churche' must refer to the removal of the stained glass windows, presumably containing images. The wording implies that it was not sold. A total of 777 feet of glass was purchased for £15 10s 5d to replace it. St George's loft, no longer supporting its image, was dismantled. Any damage to the walls in the course of taking down the statues was repaired, and wall paintings so thoroughly covered with white lime that it took two men twenty-three days to complete. The statues themselves, 'being defaced' were sold for a mere 18d and their tabernacles with 'other thynges' for 2s 6d.[2]

The chancel was reorganised once the High Altar and the Easter Sepulchre had been dismantled. The wages of carpenters and masons plus the materials for 'the newe Quere' amounted to £6 15s 1d, an indication of just how thorough the alteration was. The churchwardens recorded no details though they listed them in a 'boke of the parcelles therof' which they had 'examyned'. Unfortunately the 'boke' has not survived though the work must have included the provision of a communion table and possibly benches for communicants.[3]

The impact on popular culture

Alongside the religious changes came the end of those parochial festivities closely related to the liturgical year. The King Play or Game was revived in 1541 and the two following years but the connection between this resumption and a parish recovery from the loss of the abbey should not be overstated; no King Game was recorded between 1534 and 1540 and, with two exceptions, none after 1543.[4] The last merry-makings were at Hocktide, May Day and Whitsuntide in 1547, their absence depriving the churchwardens of a vital source of income. For parishioners it was a cultural loss no less profound than the religious one, but welcomed perhaps by civic authorities as removing potential occasions of disorder and by reformers in the parish as a further weakening of traditional religion and progress towards a reform of morals. Some hope of restoration or survival remained; the parish meeting of 1553 noted that John Saunders, churchwarden in 1546-7, still had

---

1. Accounts, p. 259; Hutton, 'The local impact', 151, 164; Frere and Kennedy, *Visitation Articles,* ii. 242 n, iii, 61.
2. Accounts, pp. 250, 252, 261, 253.
3. Accounts, p. 261.
4. Accounts passim; Alexandra F Johnston and Sally-Beth Maclean, 'Reformation and resistance in Thames/Severn parishes: the dramatic witness', in *The Parish in English Life 1400-1600,* eds. K. L. French, Gary G. Gibbs and Beat Kumin (1997), 187.

the bells and costume belonging to the morris dancers.[1]

iv. The Marian Restoration

Edward VI died on 6 July 1553, so the churchwardens' accounts for 1552-3
reflect both conformity with the demands of the reformers up to that date and
the speedy return to tradition during the few months ending at Michaelmas of
that year. Mary I intended, as soon as was practicable, to restore the status
quo of 1529. The first step, the Act of Repeal in late 1553, cancelled many of
Edward's statutes: from 20 December church services were to be conducted
as in the last year of Henry's reign. This order was enlarged and reinforced
by Royal Injunctions in March 1554; commissioners travelled the country to
ensure conformity. In 1555-6 the churchwardens paid for a copy of 'tharticles
sett out by the Commyssioners and 'for a boke of the returne of the same
Articles'.[2]

Long before this, they had shown little hesitation in restoring the
traditional rites, facilitated by the return of goods and furniture sold to
parishioners in Edward's reign. By the end of September 1553 (the
accounting year 1552-3) the High Altar had been reinstated at a cost of 12s.
Four essential service books were bought: a manual for 5s, and for 22s 8d
three others, an antiphonal, a processional and a small mass book were
procured by a parishioner, John Radley. At Easter 1554, the first of the new
reign, the ceremonies of the holy fire, the font taper and paschal candle (with
its Judas), and the distribution of 'houselyng bread' all returned though the
candles were rather smaller than in earlier times and the sepulchre a
makeshift affair made from a 'whope' costing just two pence.[3]

By Michaelmas 1554 the appearance of the church and patterns of
worship had resumed much of their ancient form. A 'greate Masse boke' was
bought for 13s; vestments were repaired or bought back. The sepulchre was
rebuilt at great expense by two men working for ten days and enquiries made
as to who had the sepulchre curtain 'in kepyng'. John Saunders sold back a
cross and a pair of candlesticks, possibly intended for one of the altars.
Almost all of the costs were met by the churchwardens but at least one
donation came from a parishioner: Robert Persey in January 1554/5 left 40s
to buy 'a grayle or Antiphoner to singe gods devyne service'. During the next
few years four more altars were restored: those of St John, St Thomas, Jesus
and Mary though the gilds were not revived. On 2 May 1557 these and the
High Altar were re-consecrated by William Finch, suffragan bishop of Bath
and Wells.[4] In that year the morrow mass was again said. The absence of
evidence that the rood loft was restored in accordance with the Queen's

1. Accounts, p. 269.
2. Accounts, p. 283; Frere and Kennedy, *Visitation Articles*, ii, 322-9.
3. Accounts, pp. 269, 271-2. St Laurence was one of the first parishes to restore the Catholic
liturgy (Shield, thesis, 132). For more about Radley see Appendix 2.
4. A bishop consecrated an altar by pouring chrism oil onto five crosses cut into its surface and
placing relics into a cavity on or under it. This had to precede any celebration of Mass.

orders is not significant; there is no indication in the accounts that the rood had been taken down in Edward's reign and it certainly did exist in the early years of Elizabeth. That no statues were purchased is puzzling as the accounts stated that all the images had been 'defaced' and sold in 1547-8. However the wall behind the image of St Vincent was plastered in 1556-7, suggesting it may have been restored or returned. It is possible others were returned and that the payment of 10s 6d to a painter in 1557-8 was an attempt to regain some of their former splendour. Mary's Injunctions specifically ordered the restoration of an image of the church's patron as a minimum; a parish conforming in so much else was hardly likely to do otherwise in this respect. Whether some deficiencies resulted from a shortage of cash or lack of will is difficult to infer from the accounts alone, though the expenses of restoring the Catholic liturgy were high and the parish short of funds. It is also possible that some church goods had been notionally 'sold' in Edward's reign and were now returned. Whatever the case, some of the old certainties had been weakened. Parishioners' wills proved in the archdeaconry court during the reign support the view that for the most part they were as lukewarm about devotion to the Virgin, the saints and prayers for the dead as were many others in England. With one exception no will maker requested prayers for his/her soul though some relatives paid for a month's or year's mind mass.[1] Significantly the annual obit for deceased benefactors of the parish was not celebrated.

Simply restoring the essentials required considerable resources, some of which came from parish gatherings. In 1554 and 1555 those at Easter and Christmas realised similar amounts as in the early 1530s though the gathering for lights at All Hallows (All Saints) was made only in 1553. At Easter 1556 the collection fell by about fifty per cent, never to return to the previous level.[2] Special collections were needed in 1556-7 for the choir and the morrow Mass and the next year for the choir, organs and clock raising £5 6s 2d and £4 10s respectively. Parish festivities which had once been a fruitful source of revenue and a major aspect of parish life did not regain their earlier vitality. Hocktide, last held in the first year of Edward's reign was not revived until Easter 1555. The King Play was again held in summer 1553, a very early revival. No other summer celebrations appear until 1556 when there were gatherings for young folks on May Day and Whitsuntide but neither made a profit. However at Whitsuntide the same year the wardens received 48s from the King Ale and the church ale. Hocktide at Easter 1558 raised 23s 4d, the highest amount of the reign, ironically since it proved to be the end of

---

1. Accounts, pp. 271-2, 283, 276, 291, 286, 306; Hutton, 'The local impact', 155-6; BRO, Will of Robert Persey D/A1/7/101. The one exception was William Webbe, former chantry priest who left money for a dirge and masses. Of eleven wills 1553-8, two invoked the intercession of the Virgin and four the company of saints.

2. This decrease in the collection has been attributed to a reduction in the number of parishioners receiving the sacrament at Easter, suggesting they lacked a firm belief in Catholic teaching. J. Martin, 'The People of Reading ', 541-2.

the tradition of parochial merry-making in St Laurence. In the county and
the country such customs lasted a little longer but over most of England a
whole tradition of popular culture was eradicated by 1600.[1] The early
disappearance of parish drama and celebrations in Reading has been
attributed to the influence of Sir Francis Knollys of Rotherfield Greys, a
fervent Protestant who acquired land in the town and its locality, and whose
family dominated the borough's parliamentary representation from 1563.[2]

v. The Elizabethan Reformation

In November 1558 Mary died, and was succeeded by Elizabeth I, heralding
another phase of the English Reformation. Elizabeth's chief advisers took as
their starting point the state religion as Edward VI had left it, but his
'settlement' of 1552-3 was slightly modified in a conservative direction as a
result of Elizabeth's own preferences, and possibly in order to lessen Catholic
opposition. Militant Protestants looked forward to further reforms, but
Elizabeth was adamantly opposed to any but minor innovations. As in earlier
reigns, changes in doctrine and worship were introduced both by
parliamentary statute and royal injunction. Two statutes of April 1559
restored the royal supremacy and Protestant worship; Injunctions with further
commands about the provision of books and the conduct of services were
issued in July. By this date the accounting year of the churchwardens,
beginning at Michaelmas 1558, was well underway, resulting in entries
showing conformity with the traditional and the reformed religion. Relatives
of several deceased parishioners continued to request a month's mind, and a
gathering for the paschal was made at Easter 1559 though it raised a mere
17s 6d.[3] Purchases of a Bible, four psalters and a Book of Common Prayer
show the parish making ready for the return of the reformed liturgy in
English when its use became compulsory from 24 June 1559. More service
books, books of metric psalms and a Book of Homilies were purchased in
1559-60. The absence of payments for removing images suggests that very
few had been restored in the previous reign and that these were taken by
parishioners in hope of another about turn in religion.[4]

The altars were taken down in summer 1559 in accordance with the
Injunctions enforced during the royal visitation, but not sold. Next year the
walls and floors damaged in the process were repaired and a communion

1. Accounts, pp. 285, 291, 273, 270, 285, 295; the last church ale in Childrey, Berkshire, was in
1594 (BRO, Childrey churchwardens' accounts 1568-1688 D/P35/5/1); for the survival and
disappearance of customs elsewhere in Berkshire see Alexandra F. Johnston and Sally-Beth
Maclean, 'Reformation and resistance in Thames/Severn parishes: the dramatic witness', in *The
Parish in English Life, 1400-1600*, eds. K. L. French, Gary G. Gibbs and Beat Kumin (1997),
191-3; for England see Hutton, *The Rise and Fall of Merry England,* chapter 4.
2. A. F. Johnston and S. Maclean, 'Reformation and resistance', 189; Aspinall, *Parliament,* 40-
41.
3. Accounts, p. 295.
4. Accounts, p. 298.

table and seats set up.[1] The wood from the Easter Sepulchre was sold in 1560-61 though it may have been taken down earlier. It fetched 26s 8d, confirming that it was a substantial structure. The frame holding the sepulchre light survived until the following year.[2] Royal Orders of October 1561 commanded that rood lofts above the beam should be dismantled, leaving only the base to serve as a division between nave and chancel, and that a table of the Ten Commandments should be erected above the communion table. The churchwardens were again prompt to obey after they received the orders on 15 November 1561; they paid a mere 2s in 1561-2 for the loft to be removed but sold the wood for considerably more. However it was not until 1567-8 that two 'tables' of commandments were erected, a royal visit possibly providing the necessary stimulus.

Meeting the expenses of this third set of alterations was difficult, more so given the huge reduction in parochial income. The lucrative gatherings at two of the great feasts virtually ceased; only at Christmas 1568 and All Saints 1569 were tiny sums donated. However the Easter gathering survived under different names. There was no collection for the paschal after 1559 but in 1563 Easter donations appeared in the accounts as £3 3s 10d 'receaved at Easter for the hed pence'. Two years with no collection were followed by 'Easter bread & wyne monye' in 1567 and 'the odd pence at the Communyon all things discharged' in 1568. The 'easter booke' made in 1562-3 probably recorded these donations; in 1569 and 1570 the income was specifically credited 'for the Ester booke'.[3]

The amount recorded as 'hed pence' in 1563 is almost exactly the same as the £3 3s 2½d collected 'of the parishioners at Ester' in the last year of Mary's reign though later collections were smaller. Only on one occasion, Easter 1553, was money given for the holy loaf. Thereafter no income specifically for this purpose is recorded despite an agreement made by the parish in 1552 that the cost of bread and wine at Easter would be met by those households formerly providing the holy loaf, with any profit going to the churchwardens as instructed in the Book of Common Prayer.[4] The churchwardens met the cost of the 'houselyng brede' consecrated at the first Easter Mass of Mary's reign and under Elizabeth they paid for the bread and wine. This seems to confirm that the donations recorded in St Laurence's Easter book continued the tradition of contributions from Easter communicants, formerly attributed to the paschal; they were used as before for parish expenses.

1. In 1568-9 these were replaced by a joined table and benches with mats for communicants.
2. Accounts, pp. 295, 298, 332, 301, 306.
3. David Hey, ed., *The Oxford Companion to Local and Family History*, (1996), 142 describes the Easter book as a list of householders in parishes liable to pay personal tithes and other dues to the incumbent at Easter but St Laurence's churchwardens seemingly used it for parish expenses. In any event until 1565 the parish did not have a permanent vicar. The book has not survived.
4. Accounts, pp. 267, 268, 271; a detailed account of how the custom of providing holy bread operated in one Berkshire parish can be found in *Stanford in the Vale Churchwardens' Accounts 1552-1725*, transcribed by Violet M. Howse (privately published, 1987), 23-6; Duffy, *The Stripping of the Altars*, 464. See glossary for houseling bread and holy loaf.

The Bishop of Salisbury during these years (1560-71) was John Jewel, a fervent reformer and apologist for the Church of England and 'an exemplary bishop' who took great pains to ensure his diocese conformed to the new dispensation.[1] He held two visitations of the diocese during the 1560s though he had more frequent contacts with the parish. The first visitation of the Reading deanery was held in St Laurence church in 1560; the parish paid 4d to the bell ringers summoning people to the visitation sermon, 5s to the preacher and 2s in unspecified expenses. On 17 March 1562 the churchwardens paid a shilling for writing their presentments to the bishop's court (answers to questions about the state of the parish) and 2s for a gallon of sack for the bishop. During his second visitation of the diocese in 1565 the parish paid the bishop's clerk 8d in for making a 'bill' and the bishop sent the parish two service books for which the churchwardens paid. In 1568-9 the churchwardens were summoned to Salisbury by the apparitor on the bishop's orders, again taking their presentments.[2] The archdeacon of Berkshire exercised authority on behalf of the bishop, both at his court and during his own visitations. A 'presentment of all the parryshoners' was taken to this court at Oxford in 1562-3 and another was made two years later.[3] The parish and the diocese were obviously being kept under close scrutiny during these years of religious change and political uncertainty.

vi. The parochial clergy 1547-1564
To all the confusion caused by the religious changes was added the problem of providing sufficient clergy to serve the parish once the gilds were dissolved. Despite the admission by the chantry commissioners that the parish needed more than one priest, no financial provision was made for additional clergy. Yet, until the religious changes of 1549, many traditional forms of worship required more than one priest. The gild chaplains, Richard a Deane and William Webbe, were still in the parish but the confiscation of the gilds' assets left them with a reduced income. They might leave to seek paid employment so it was perhaps to keep them in the parish that the wardens paid Richard a Deane and another priest, Sir John Harper, a former Reading monk, 10s wages in 1547-8. From 1548 to 1550 these priests and William Webbe were paid 20s in addition to the provision of rent-free

---

1. *Oxford Dictionary of National Biography* (Oxford, 2004).
2. Accounts, pp. 298, 306, 315, 333; the visitation presumably took place in Reading since the churchwardens did not claim expenses for going to it. For an account of episcopal administration at this period see Ralph Houlbrooke, *Church Courts and the People during the English Reformation, 1520-1570* (Oxford, 1979), chapter 2. Records of another Berkshire parish confirm the visitation in 1562 and 1564-5 but record that of 1560 as a visitation by the 'bisshope of Cantorburye'. They also include expenses for the 'bysshope of Sarum weke' in 1561-2. *Stanford in the Vale Churchwardens' Accounts, 1552-1725*, transcribed by Violet M Howae (privately published, 1987) 45, 47, 53, 58.
3. Accounts, pp. 309, 315. Archdeaconry courts were often held near Folly Bridge, just on the Berkshire side of the River Thames, Peter Durrant, 'The Archdeaconry of Berkshire' in *An Historical Atlas of Berkshire*, ed. J. Dils and M Yates (2nd edition, Reading,2012) 10.

houses.[1] Their inadequate salaries were supplemented on several occasions in 1549-50: Richard a Deane was loaned four pounds by the assent of the parish. He and William Webbe undertook other work; William was paid 3s 4d for 'makyng and prykkyng of songes'. Thereafter apart from John Harper, paid 40s wages in 1551-2, and two small payments to others the following year, no former priests were employed until 1555-6. In that year William Webbe was paid 6s 8d for 'the prestes noble'. He continued saying the morrow Mass until late summer of 1558 receiving £4 6s 8d a year in 1556-7 and £5 6s 8d in 1557-8. The chantry certificate had given his age as fifty-two, describing him as 'decrepit'. Richard a Deane was better placed. Aged only thirty-nine in 1547 and with other assets, he was judged able to serve another cure; he last appeared in the accounts in 1558 still owing 2s 6d from his loan.[2]

After the dissolution of the abbey, the right of presentation to the living belonged to the Crown. The poverty of the benefice and frequent religious changes made it difficult to attract and keep a clergyman.[3] John Maynesforth, vicar from 1534, was buried before Michaelmas 1550; his will is dated 17 August. An unnamed curate was present by December 1551.[4] The accounts help to explain how the parish was served over the following two decades. In 1552-3 two priests were paid small sums, one specifically for help at Easter, and a 'Mr Vicar' paid 30s 'at the request of the parrisshe'. This latter was Thomas Thackam or Thackham; an entry in the accounts in the same year subsequently deleted refers to him as 'beyng Vicar'. He was formerly master of Reading school and married.[5] Thackham was removed as a result of the Marian Injunctions of March 1554 which restored clerical celibacy and deprived married clergy unless they put away their wives. On 12 September 1554 Thomas Greneway, bachelor of theology, and for a short time a canon of Christ Church Oxford, was presented by the Crown to the living, 'void by the deprivation of Thomas Thackam, clerk' but he refused to serve.[6]

After Thackham's departure, the churchwardens resorted to paying clergy, former chantry priests to serve or help to serve the cure. The last such

1. Accounts, pp. 254, 256, 257. Richard a Deane was chaplain of the Jesus gild; William Webbe is not assigned to a gild but to a separate, unnamed foundation by Thomas Justice; *Chantry Certificates for Berkshire*, ed. N. E.Fox (privately published, 1994), 37.
2. Accounts, pp. 261, 264, 266, 269, 289, 290, 277, 281, 286, 292, 287. For more about William Webbe and Richard a Deane see Appendix 2.
3. J. Martin, 'The People of Reading', 285-6.
4. BRO, Will of John Maynesforth, 1550, D/A1/5/113; accounts, p. 260; the Warden of the Fleet prison was ordered to bring John Poyntz, a former churchwarden and the curate to the Privy Council, *Acts of the Privy Council of England, New Series, vol iii* (HMSO 1891), 445.
5. In 1553-4 he paid sixpence for his wife's seat in the church. For more about Thomas Thackham see Appendix 2.
6. Accounts, pp. 269, 271, 296; *Narratives of the Days of the Reformation*, ed. J. G. Nichols (Camden Society, 1859), 131; *Calendar of Patent Rolls, Philip and Mary, vol ii, 1554-1555*, (HMSO, 1936), 202. For Greneway see J. Martin, 'The People of Reading', 511.

payment was to William Webbe for two whole years between 1556 and 1558. After his death in 1558 the accounts refer to clergy as curates or ministers. A succession of such were hired by the parish; a curate, Richard Cam, received 13s 4d for a fortnight's service in 1559-60, the following year another curate receiving 40s. Some of the 17s 3d paid to a minister, Mr Croft, for five weeks in 1562-3 was raised by a parish 'gathering'; he was also paid 46s 8d for serving the parish at Whitsuntide and two months after. Another minister received 12s the following year.[1]

Throughout the 1560s the parish had been attempting to have the value of the benefice increased, much of the work undertaken by John Radley, a successful baker who had been active in the parish for many years, first appearing in the accounts in 1551-2. He was involved in the parish's suit to the Crown for a new churchyard and other matters during the 1550s but in a more significant way from the early 1560s. During this period he seems to have remained a traditionalist in religion.[2]

In 1561-2 the churchwardens paid him a total of 60s 'to followe the same suyte of our benyfice'; and 3s 4d for making 'supplicacyons unto the Queenes maiestie for the benefyce'. In April 1562 Radley and one churchwarden, William Lendoll, rode to London to sue yet again. The churchwardens were cited by the archdeacon to appear at his court at Oxford about the benefice in 1564-5 and again the following year, each time by John Radley's 'procurement'. On the second occasion he was described as 'vyckar'.[3] He was presented to the vicarage of St Laurence by the Queen on 21 November 1565, having been ordained just seven months before; inexplicably he was called Sir John in the accounts of 1563-4, the title given to a non-graduate priest, though he was a layman at that date. His presentation to the vicarage following the removal of a religious extremist, Mr Fyttes, marked the success of the religious conservatives in a struggle with radicals within the town's elite. Radley was vicar until 1574 when he resigned.[4]

vii. New administrative duties

The parish complied with many other parliamentary statutes and royal injunctions which punctuated the middle years of the sixteenth century including those concerning poor relief. Gifts to the poor had always been commended by the Church as charitable acts; wills from Reading and elsewhere show that many testators followed this exhortation. From an early date St Laurence's parish had a church box, most likely a poor box, for which

1. Accounts, pp. 299, 304, 308, 313.
2. Accounts, pp 315, 264, 268, 270, 271, 274, 283; Radley was said to be one of those who 'left no means unpractised to catch and persecute the members of Christ i.e. reformers. *Narrative of the Days of the of the Reformation*, ed. J. G. Nichols (Camden Society, 1859), 110 and note. For more about Radley see Appendix 2.
3. Accounts, pp. 304, 306, 308, 315, 319.
4. Accounts, pp. 313, 333; *Calendar of Patent Rolls, Elizabeth I, vol iii, 1563-66* (HMSO, 1960), No. 2955; *Calendar of Patent Rolls, Elizabeth I, vol iv, 1572-75,*(HMSO, 1973), No. 190. J. Martin, 'The People of Reading', 233, 533-7.

the wardens provided a key in 1502-3. An Act of 1536 requiring parishes to collect voluntary alms for the poor in a poor-box did not result in such a purchase by the churchwardens which perhaps suggests that the existing box sufficed. However a new poor box was made in 1547-8 with iron work and locks at a total cost of five shillings; a separate entry recorded fitting two new locks and mending the existing one, thereby obeying the Injunction of 1547 that a poor box to be set up near the altar with three locks, one each for the parson and churchwardens or those charged with the care of poor. Another 'poore folkes box' was set up in 1560-1. By a law of 1552 the parish was required to keep an account of weekly collections for the poor; the purchase of a 'regester booke for the collectyon of the poor' in 1562-3 was presumably for this purpose.[1] The same year the churchwardens bought a book in which to record baptisms, marriages and burials; until this date they probably used the book sold to the parish by Richard Turner.[2] No register for the Tudor period survives.

5. Conclusion

The picture of pre-Reformation St Laurence's painted by these accounts is of a well-endowed, conscientiously administered parish where all the practices of traditional religion were provided for. Lay participation both in religious and secular activities is very evident. In these respects it conforms to the situation found in other urban parishes though some had more elaborate furnishings, richer gilds and bigger dramatic performances.[3] During the period of religious change in the mid-century, the churchwardens promptly obeyed parliamentary statutes and royal injunctions which changed the state religion; while not as radical as some urban parishes, it was not as conservative as some rural ones. In the process, the appearance of the church interior, the pattern of parochial worship and the experience of community festivities were utterly transformed. For a number of years parish finances were severely strained; the lack of an endowment for the vicarage served to exacerbate the problem. The leaders of the parish were divided over religious change but determined that both parish and borough would survive it. How the majority of parishioners reacted appears uncertainly through the problematic evidence of the few surviving wills but undoubtedly the whole community of St Laurence's was troubled for several decades.

---

1. Accounts, pp. 11, 252, 253, 302, 309; *Documents of the English Reformation*, ed. G. Bray (Cambridge, 1994), 255; Paul Slack, *The English Poor Law 1531-1782* (1990), 59; Duffy, *The Stripping of the Altars*, 510.
2. Accounts, pp. 106, 248, 161, 80, 197, 329, 174, 309. The parish was not assessed for any other Tudor subsidy; for the keeping of parish registers see David Hey, ed., *The Oxford Companion to Local and Family History*, (1996), 341-2.
3. *The Early Churchwardens' Accounts of Hampshire*, ed. John Foster Williams (Winchester and London, 1913); *Churchwardens' Accounts of Pilton*, ed. Bishop Hobhouse (Somerset Record Society, iv, 1890).

Editorial note

Spelling and punctuation.

Commas and full stops have been retained. In the accounts / and //
have been transcribed as commas and full stops respectively but have
been retained in the inventories. The same letter shape and size was
almost invariably used by scribes in the early sixteenth century for
lower and upper case 'A', 'S' and 'M'. They have been transcribed in
lower case except for proper nouns and where it is seems likely that
upper case was intended. Where the text has a lower case initial for a
proper name, this has been retained. In the 1550s and 1560s upper
case 'L' and 'T' frequently occur where modern usage would require
lower case; the upper case has been retained. Symbols for 'th' (thorn)
and 'g'/'gh' (yoch) have been written as 'th' and 'g' or 'gh'. Where 'y'
was used instead of 'yoch', for example 'ayenst'; this has been
transcribed as 'agenst'. In some instances 'yoch' was used for the sound
'y' as in 'willyam'. 'Ye', 'ys ' and 'yt' have been transcribed as 'the', this'
and 'that' except where 'yt obviously means 'it'. In some instances 'ye'
and 'the' were used indiscriminately; both have been transcribed as
'the'. The letters 'u' and 'v' were interchangeable and have been
transcribed as modern spelling demands.

Proper names

All proper names are spelt as in the document. Those abbreviated
have been silently extended, for example 'Willm' to 'William'.

Abbreviations

All abbreviations including tilds have been silently extended. Mr and
Mter meaning Master and Mres meaning Mistress or Maistres have
been extended. Contractions for 'er' have been silently extended to 'er'
or 'ar', and 'ir' to 'ir' or 'er' as required by the context. Where it is not
clear at the end of a word that a contraction was intended, a single
inverted comma has been used e.g. It'. 'Jhc' has been extended to
'Jh[esu]s' except where the letters 'J h c' were embroidered on
vestments. 'Xp' and 'X', the Greek letters for 'Chr' and 'Ch', have been
extended, e.g. 'Xpi' to 'Christi' and 'Xpofer' to 'Christofer'. Superscripts
in Latin words have been retained except for li (£), s (shillings) d
(pence) and a[nn]o (year). Superscript xx after a number indicates
twenty or a score, making iiij^{xx} equal to four score or eighty.
Superscript 'tie' after a number indicates the pronunciation e.g. xxv^{tie}

is pronounced 'five and twenty'. Latin phrases in the inventories have been put into italics.

Deletions, insertions and omissions

Deletions in the original are noted thus: {mynde}and insertions thus: <burying>. Missing letters have been inserted in square brackets e.g. S[um]ma.

Editorial comment and headings

Editorial comments are written as [*new hand*]. Headings in the left hand margin e.g. 'Seates' have been centred at the beginning of the section to which they refer; headings centred in the manuscript have been retained in this position.   Other marginal comments have normally been centred. Marginal comments in later hands have been noted except those from the nineteenth century which have been omitted unless they add important information.

Pagination

 Originally the document was not paginated. Kerry added page numbers in pencil sequentially from the beginning, so continuing the incorrect placing of some pages. The numbers used here are his.

Dating

No attempt has been made to begin each accounting year on a new page as in most of the original text. Instead, a date e.g. **1515-16** has been inserted before the prologue to each new account. Most were dated by the regnal years of the sovereign though the early ones also gave the year of the Christian calendar. For example the accounts for September 1520-September1521 were also dated 12-13 Henry VIII. Some relevant dates are:

13 Henry VII	22 August 1497 to 21 August 1498
1 Henry VIII	22 April 1509 to 21 April 1510
1 Edward VI	28 January 1547 to 27 January 1548
1 Mary	6 July 1553 to 5 July 1554;
1 Philip and Mary	25 July 1554 to 5 July 1555; 2 & 3 were 25 July 1555 to 5 July 1556
1 Elizabeth	17 November 1558 to 16 November 1559

Value of money and weights

The abbreviation 'li' for *libra* (pound) was used for £ sterling and lb avoirdupois. A £ sterling was a unit of account made up of twenty shillings (20s); each shilling was worth twelve pennies or pence (12d). None of these abbreviations has been extended nor has 'ob' meaning *obolus*, a half penny. A quarter of a penny, a farthing, usually written in an abbreviated form has been extended to 'quarter'. Three farthings was written 'ob quarter'.

A mark, another unit of account, was worth 13s 4d making three marks worth £2. Annual or bi-annual payments for wages were often in multiples or fractions of a mark.

A pound troy was made up of 16 ounces, often written as oz.; a pound troy was also written as li.

A bushel was a measure of volume, not weight, with eight bushels to a quarter; a stone weighed 14 lbs.

Short titles

Aspinall, *Parliament*
A. Aspinall, Barbara Dodwell, M. D. Lambert, C. F. Slade, E. A. Smith, *Parliament through Seven Centuries: Reading and its MPs* (1962)

Burgess, 'Pre-Reformation Churchwardens' Accounts'
J. C. Burgess, 'Pre-Reformation Churchwardens' Accounts and Parish Government: Lessons from London and Bristol', *English Historical Review,* cxvii (2002)

Diary of the Corporation
Reading Records: Diary of the Corporation, 1431-1654, ed. J. M. Guilding (4 vols, Reading and London, 1892-6)

Duffy, *The Stripping of the Altars*
Eamon Duffy, *The Stripping of the Altars: Traditional Religion in England, 1400-1580 (Yale University Press, 1992)*

Frere and Kennedy, *Visitation Articles*
Visitation Articles and Injunctions of the Period of the Reformation eds. W. H. Frere and W. M. Kennedy (3 vols, 1910)

Hutton, *The Rise and Fall of Merry England*
R. Hutton, *The Rise and Fall of Merry England: the Ritual Year 1400-1700* (Oxford, 1994)

Hutton, 'The local impact'
Ronald Hutton, 'The local impact of the Tudor reformations', in *The Impact of the English Reformation 1500-1640,* ed. Peter Marshall (1997)

Kerry, *A History*
Charles Kerry, *A History of the Municipal Church of St. Lawrence, Reading* (Reading, 1883)

J. Martin, 'The People of Reading'
Jeanette Martin, 'The People of Reading and the Reformation 1520-1570', (unpublished PhD thesis, University of Reading, 1987)

Shield, thesis
I. T. Shield, 'The Reformation in the Diocese of Salisbury 1547-62', (unpublished B. Litt thesis, University of Oxford, 1960)

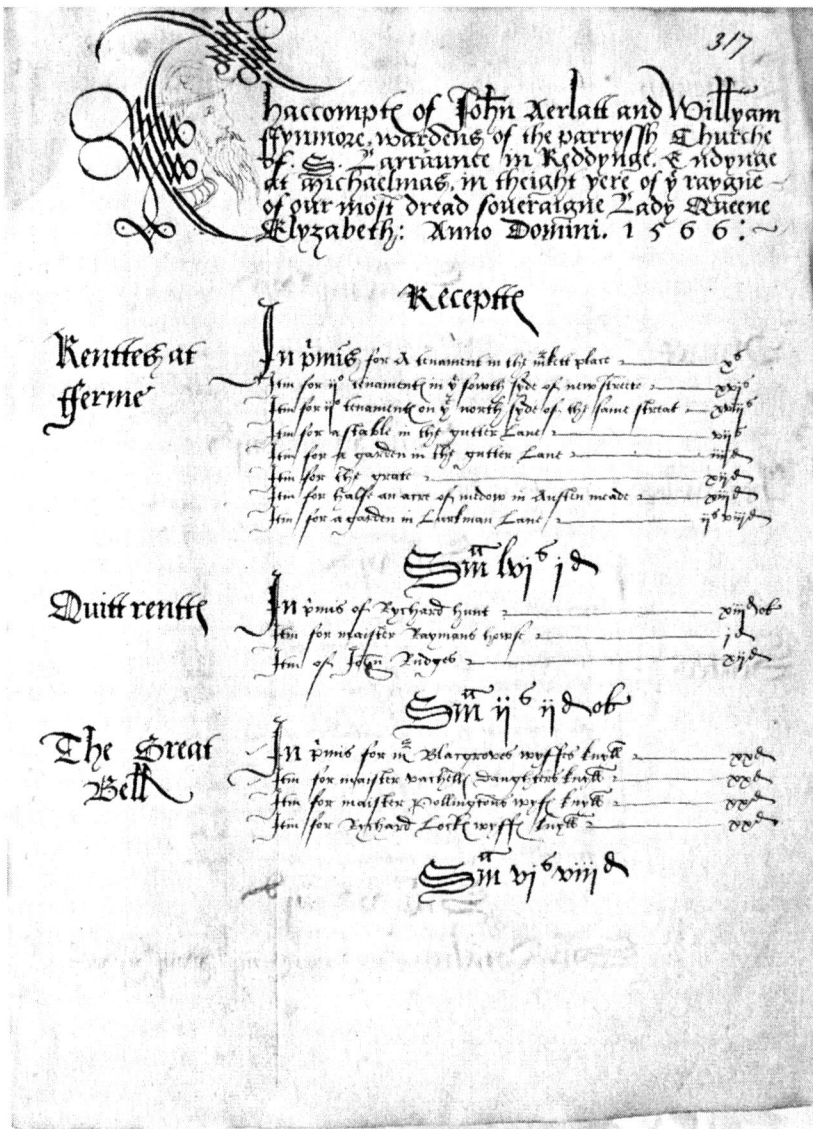

The first page of the accounts for 1565-66
(Berkshire Record Office, D/P97/5/2, p.317)

The opening of the 1517 inventory
(Berkshire Record Office, D/P97/5/2, p. 47)

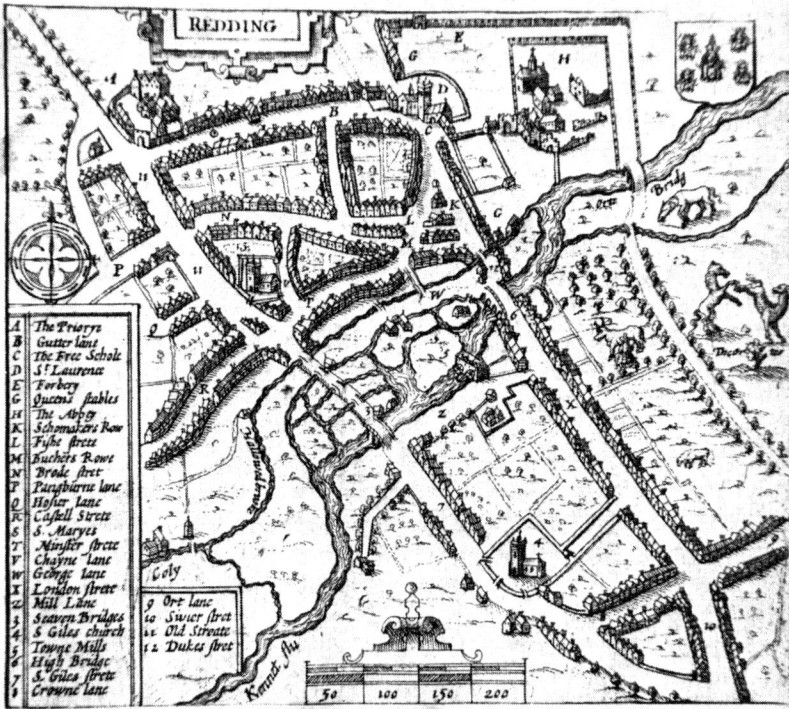

Speed's map of Reading, 1611
(St Laurence's Church (D) is at the top (north) of the map)

St Laurence's Church from the west in 1941, before the bomb damage
suffered in 1943 (Berkshire Record Office, D/EX1028/106E/E42)

Churchwardens' Accounts of
St Laurence, Reading

1498-9

[*p 1*] **Comptus of Nicholas Hyde and William Lendall wardens of the church off Seynt Laurence in Redyng Fro the Fest of Thannunciacion of our lady In the yer of oure lorde god M CCCC XC VIIJ in the <xiiijth> yer of Kyng Harry the vijth unto the same Fest In the yer of our lorde god M^o CCCC XCIX and in the xiiijth yer of our sayd soverayn lorde kyng Harry the vijth 1499**

Recytes

In primis rec' of William Wattes and Philypp Kysby as it apperith in the fote of their accompte	vj s. iij d.
Item rec' at Estur for the Pascall[1]	xxxvij s.
It'rec' of hok money gaderyd of women	xx s.
It' rec' of hok money gaderid of men	iiij s.
It' rec' of the gaderyng of Robyn hod	xix s.
It' rec' of the gaderyng of a stage play	xij s.
It' rec' of the gaderyng of the paristh by Raphe Myllington and William Netter for di' yer [2]	xliij s. iiij d.
It' rec' of the gaderyng of the parisch by John Punsar and William Whight for a quarter of a yer	xxiiij s. iij d.
It' rec' at Alhalow tyde for a rode lyght	x s. iiij d.
It' rec' at Cristmas for the <same> Rode lyght	xiij s. iiij d.
It' rec' of Sir William Symmys parish prest of his gyfte to the church[3]	iij s. iiij d.
It' rec' of the bequest of Alyce More	xx d.
It' rec' of the gyft of William Trew	iij s. iiij d.
It' rec' of John Punsar for a tapyr boll of laten in the rode loft	xvj d.
It' rec' at the fayer for a stondyng at the church porch	iiij d.

S[um]ma   x li. iiij s. vj d.

Item rec' of di' an acre of mede lying in Langley in the parish of Tylehurst	xiij d.
It' rec' of John Wattes for the rent of one yer of his tenement in the market place	x s.

---

1. The offering made by communicants at Easter.
2. Di' is the abbreviated form of *dimidium*, the Latin for half.
3. The vicar at this time was Thomas Hill. It would seem that William Simms was a gild chaplain, his title indicating that he was a non-graduate. He was buried in the church in 1502-3. See below.

It' rec' of Harry Sutton for the rent of a tenemente lying in th'e new streete for a yer	x s.
It' rec' of Robard Cavy for a rent of a tenement in Guttar Lane for v yer by the yer - vij s. S[um]ma	xxv s.
It' rec' of Genyn for the rent of a tenement th[a]t he he holdyth lying in New strete for a yer	x s.
It' rec' of William Rawlyn for rent of a tenement in the same stret for a yer	iiij s.
It' rec' of William Kene for rent of a grownde lying in Guttar lane for yer	iiij d.
It' rec' of Harry Sutton for rent of ij gardens lying in Lurkmer lane for a yer	xviij d.
It' rec' of William Hunte Joyner for <quit> rent of a ten[emen]t set in the hye strete for a yer	xiij d. ob.
It' rec' of Thomas Harte for the tenement late of William Blewet besyde the market for a yer	xij d.

S[um]ma iij li. xiiij s. ob.

It' rec' for the sepulcre of Thomas Butler	vj s. viij d.
It' rec' for wast of Torchys at the burying of the same Thomas	ij s. j d.
It' rec' for wast of torchis at the burying of Webbys wyfe	iiijd.
It' rec' for the grete bell at the burying of Henburyes wyfe of Caversham	vj d.
It' rec' for the sepulcre of Alysaundre Prentyse wyfe	vj s. viij d.
It' rec' for wast of torchis at the burying of the same wyfe	ij s.
It' rec' for the grete bell at the burying of the forseid Thomas Butler	vj d.
[p 2] Item rec' for wast of torchis at the burying of Thomas Payne	viij d.
Item rec' for the grete bell at the burying and the moneth mynde of the same Thomas	xij d.
Item rec' for wast of torchis at the burying of boldys moder	iiij d.
Item rec' for wast of torchis at the burying of Richard Ades	iiij d.
Item rec' for the sepulcre of Thomas Carpynters wyfe is moder	vj s. viij d.
Item rec' for wast of torchis at the same tyme	iiij d.
Item rec' for the grete bell at the burying of Plecyes wyfe	vj d.
Item rec' for the sepulcre of Alysaundre Prentyce	vj s. viij d.
Item rec' for wast of torchis at the same tyme	xiiij d.
Item rec' for wast of torchis at the burying of Hudsons wyfe	iiij d.
Item rec' for the grete bell at the burying of John Fullars wife	vj d.
Item rec' for wast of torchis at the same tyme	viij d.

Item rec' for the sepulcre of Robard Caryes wyfe	vj s. viij d.
Item rec' for wast of torchis at the same tyme	xx d.

S[um]ma xlvj s. iij d.

[The next seven lines are bracketed together]

Item rec' of the wyfe of Thomas Smyth for a sete	vj d.
Item rec' of the wyfe of Hudson bocher for a sete	vj d.
Item rec' of the wyfe of John Carpynter for removyng her sete	iiij d.
Item rec' of the moder of Agnes Quedainton for a sete	vj d.
It rec' of the wyfe of William Hasylwood for a sete	vj d.
Item rec' of the wyfe of John Fauxbye for a sete[1]	vj d.
Item rec' of the wyfe of William Wattes for a sete	vj d.

S[um]ma of this with the parcell underwritten vj s. vj d.

S[um]ma to[ta]lis xvj li. xj s. iij d. ob.

{Expenses }

Item rec' of the wyfe <of> William Jonson for a sete	vj d.
Item rec' of the wyfe of Bartylmew Capper for sete	vj d.
Item rec' of the wyfe of Robard Dyer for a sete	vj d.
Item rec' of the wyfe of John Darling for a sete	vj d.
Item rec' of the wyfe of William Dayntre for a sete	vj d.
Item rec' of the wyfe of Mathew [*blank*] for a sete	vj d.
Item rec' of the wyfe of Nicholas Goldsmyth for a sete	vj d.

[*p 3*]   Expenses[2]

In primis payed for makyng of the sepulcer	viij d.
Item payed for a li of encens	xij d.
Item payed for colys	j d.
Item payed for the Pascall and the Fonte taper to Mr Smyth	iiij s.
Item payed to John kyng for beryng of bokys	xij d.
Item payed for wasshyng of divers ornamentes of the church	iij s.
Item payed for horsemete to the horssys for the kynges of colen on may day[3]	vj d.

[*in margin in another hand*] nota quid licet nota valet

---

1. The name is written Fawsby elsewhere.
2. The bound volume begins here. The top of the letter E of Expenses is missing because the page was cropped when the volume was rebound. This occurs on later pages but will not always be noted. The first letter I of Inprimis is elaborate and decorated with a picture of a face.
3. A reference to a play including the Three Kings or the Magi. They were revered by some people as saints; in her will made 21 July 1500, Margaret Twynyhoo included them with the Virgin, St George and other saints whose protection she sought. (TNA Will of Margaret Twynhoo, 1500, PROB 11/13/15).

Item payed to mynstrelles the same day	xij d.
Item payed to John Turner for makyng of iiij bawdrykes	ij s.
Item payed for a box to put in the evydens of the church	j d.
Item payed for whipcord to draw the cloth at the hy auter	j d.
Item payed for mendyng of the blak cope	iiij d.
Item payed for mendyng of Poppams vestment	ij d.
Item payed for mendyng of the beer	ij d.
Item payed for an hynge of a dore in Jenyns howse	iij d.
Item payed for a lok with ij° keyes on the bell howse dore	viij d.
Item payed for staynyng of a dex cloth	x d.
Item payed for hallowyng of the grete bell namyd harey	vj s. viij d.

[*in right-hand margin*]The gret bell [*na*]med Harrie a[*nd*]
Christened[1]
And ovir that Sir William Symmes Richard Clech and
Maistres Smyth beyng god faders and god moder at the
consecracyon of the same bell and beryng al other costes to
the ssuffrygan [*sic*]

Item payed for staples to the grete bell waying ij li. and an di' and to John Turner for settyng of the same	xij d.
Item payed for ij torchys weying lxj li. pric le li. ij d. ob.	xij s. viij d. ob.
Item payed for a rope to the grete bell wewying xvj li. pric le li. ob. with cariag	ij s. iiij d.
Item payed to the officiall for petur pens	iij s. vj d. ob.

[*In the margin in another hand*] peter pence

Item payed for garnysshyng of the same paras of a vestment of the vij sciences[2]	iiij d.
Item payed for pavyng of iij gravys in the church	xij d.
Item payed for xviij d. elles of cloth to iij albys and iij amys at v d. the ell S[um]ma	vij s. vj d
Item payed for makyng of the same albys and amys	xviij d.
Item payed for xliij li. of Irewarke on the sowth end of the rode loft to stay the lyght pric the li. ij d. S[um]ma	vij s. ij d.
Item payed for xxvj li. of Irewarke on the north syde or end of the same rode loft to stay the same lyght pric the li. ij d. S[um]ma	iiij s. iiij d.
Item payed for turnyd pynnys to the said lyght	vj d.
Item payed for scowryng of the laten bolls in the seid loft	iiij d.
Item payed to Strawford for bragettes to fastyn the crestes in the same loft	vj d.
Item payed for nayles to set the same bragettes	j d.
Item payed for lyne to draw the curtens in the same loft	iij d.

1. Part of this marginal note in another hand was lost when the page was cropped. This bell was donated by Henry Kelsall. See Appendix 2. The naming of a bell was often referred to as a christening, with godparents attending as at a child's baptism.
2. These are possibly the seven liberal arts of the university curriculum: grammar, logic, rhetoric, arithmetic, music, geometry and astronomy.

Item payed for tymbre to the steple windows with sawyng of the same	ij s. j d.
Item payed for ij C borde to the same	v s.
Item payed for ij C nayles at v d. the C S[um]ma	xvj d.
[*in margin at the bottom of the page*] iij li. xiiij s. x d.	
[*p 4*] It payed for an C of laths to the same wyndows	v d.
Item payed for vij d. C lath nayle with ij d. to mende the grete bell whele	vij d. ob.
Item payed to <ij°> Carpynters for vij dayes takyng vj d. a day	vij s.
Item payed for makyng fast of the cloke howse with ij peces of Tymbre set in to the wall with a mason	viij d.
Item payed for makyng clene of ij° loftes in the steple with the gutter on the church	vj d.
Item payed to Strawford for settyng of a pece of tymbre at the clok hammer with nayles	iij d. ob.
Item payed for the settyng of Jak with the hangyng of his bell & mendyng h[i]s hond	iiij d.
Item payed for vj latten bolles on the north syde of the rode lofte	viij s.
Item payed for the settyng of the same bolles on stokkes of tymbre & pynys to the same	vj d.
Item payed for mendyng of the Cloke	xiij s. iiij d.
Item payed for wyer to the same Clok	xj d. ob.
Item payed for makyng of a sete with stuff to the same	xiiij d.
Item payed for led to make the payce of the Clok	v s. vj d.
Item payed to John Cokkes at mychaelmas by the handes of John Punsar & Whight	v s.
Item payed to the same Cokkes for di' yer endyd at mydsomer by Mr Raphe and Netter	x s.
Item payed to Stevyn Squyer for takyng up of the bell frame	vj s. viij d.
Item payed for castyng of the payce	iiij d.
Item payed for torchys waying xlviij d. li. at ij d. ob. S[um]ma	x s.
Item payed to Robard Cavy for dettes of the church	iiij li.
Item payed for a boke to make in the church accompte	xx d.
Item payed for a rope to the grete bell	ij s. vj d.
Item payed to Cavy for makyng of the iiij[th] bell Clapper	v s.
Item payed to Mr Smyth for wex by all the yer	xxj s. viij d.
Item payed for mendyng of vestmentes & settyng on of paras on albys	viij d.
Item payed for a dosseyn of tukkyng gyrdels	viij d.
Item payed for mendyng of Darbyes vestment	iiij d.
Item payed for vj elles of cloth to an awbe and an amys at v d. the ell S[um]ma	ij s. vj d.
Item payed for makyng of the same	vj d.

Item payed for stuff to make the paras stole and fanon, and a yerd of blew bocram	vj d.
Item payed for a yerd and an di' of bustyan	xij d.
Item payed for iij yerdes of blake bocram to lyne the vestmentes	xij d.
Item payed for canvas to lyne the paras & stole	iij d.
Item payed for xij yerdes of ryband to the same	vj d.
Item payed for making of the seid vestment paras stole & fanon	ij s. iiij d.
Item payed for a yerd of red say to make the cros on the same vestment	x d.
Item payed for makyng of paras to the red vestment with a stole	xij d.
Item payed for stuf & makyng of paras for iij albys & amys to the ray sewte	iiij s.
Item payed for the pascall bason and the hangyng of the same	xviij s.
Item payed for vij pendauntes for the same bason and the caryage fro london	iij s.
Item payed for kepyng of the Obyt of the benefactours of seynt laurens church on palme sonday	ij s. x d.
Item payed for makyng lenger of Mr Smythis molde with a Judas to the pascall[1]	vj d.

[Between the sheet numbered pages 4 and 5 four sheets have been torn out. They probably contained the end of the accounts for 1498-9, the whole of 1499-1500 and most of that for 1500-01. When the volume was paginated, probably by Kerry, no account was taken of this. Pages 5 and 6 are on the front and back of the same sheet, the one now following page 4.

[p 5] [This is the last section of the missing account for 1500-01. The balance matches that itemised as received by the wardens in 1501-2 which begins on page 6.]

It' payed for mendyng of the bere	xvj d.
It' payed for scowryng of the candylstykkes at the hy awter	xij d.
It' payed to John Troll for a bz of lyme	ij d.
It' payed to the same John for pavyng {in} <of> dyverse gravis	xiiij d.
It' payed to John Knyght for makyng of a bawdryk	vj d.
It' payed for an C. lathis to the tenement in gutter lane	v d.
It' payed for naylys. lyme. & evyslath to the same	xvj d. ob.

---

1. The rest of this account is missing. The total expenses listed here amount to £14 18s 4½ d.

It' payed for carying of . ij°. lodes of erth to the same — ij d.

It' payed for tyle pynnys — j d. ob.

It' payed for pale borde . rayles . nayles . ij° dur postes and workmanshipp of the same tenement — ij s. viij d.

It' payed to John Tylor of Seynt Mary parish for his labor in grete at the seid tenement — iij s. iiij d.

It' payed for the durge & massys for the benefactours of the church[1] — ij s. iij d.

It' payed for makyng of an hegge at the tenement that Puntydon dwellyd in — v d.

It' payed for a pece of tymber to dub the bell frame — xvj d.

It' payed for an hynge — ij d.

It' payed to Thomas wiche for yron warke to the grete bell — xij d.

It' payed to William Trew for quyte rent — iij s. vj d.

It' payed to John Cokkes for wrytyng of this accompte — ij s.

S[um]ma to[ta]lis xvj li. iij s. viij d. ob.[2]

And so remaynyth clerely to the seid church vij s. viij d.

Dettes owyng to the seid church

In primis of Robard Cary and diverse other as it apperith by parcelles written in <this boke at> thend of the accompte of Nicholas hyde and the forseid Richard Byrch

Also ther remaynyth in the hondes of William Sutton a yere rent endyd att the fest of <seynt> michaell anno r[egni] r[egis] henrici vij [blank] for the tenement that the same William holdyth of the church by Indenture set in the sowth syde of the newe strete — x s.

---

1. This is another reason to attribute these accounts to 1500-01 since an obit had already been paid for in the 1498-9 accounts on page 4; there was only one such obit a year.
2. This is not the correct total for the entries on pages 3-5. The total for the entries on p. 5 is £1 2s 11d. The total for entries on pages 3, 4 and 5 is £16 0s 3½d, another argument against the entries belonging to the same year.

1501-2

[p 6] **Comptus of Henry Horthorn[1] and Nicholas Kent proctours of the church of of [sic] Seynt Laurence in Redyng fro the fest of thAnnunciacion of our lady In the yer of our lorde god a M⁰. CCCCC and I. unto the same Fest In the yer of our lord god a M⁰. CCCCC and ij⁰.**

Rec'

Inprimis rec' {of old} as it apperith in the fote of the last accompte	vij s. viij d.
Inprimis receyvid at the fest of Ester for the pascall	xxxvij s. iiij d.
It' rec' of the gaderyng of wymen at hoktyde in mony	xvij s. vj d.
It' rec' of the gaderyng of men at the same tyme in money	v s. iiij d.
It' rec' of the may play of callyd Robyn hod on the fayre day	vj s.
It' rec' of wast of torchis at the beryng of Sir John Hide vicar of Sonnyng[2]	ij s. vj d.
It' rec' of William Tru for his wyvis grave	vj s. viij d.
It' rec' of the same William for v li. wast of torchis at the same tyme	xx d.
It' rec' of gaderyng of the parissh at Alhalowen tyde	x s.
It' rec' of gaderyng of the seid parissh at Crystmas	x s.
It' rec' of Gylmyns wyfe for her sete	vj d.
It' rec' of Dausons wyfe for her sete	vj d.
It' rec' of John Parkers wyfe for her sete	vj d.
It' rec' of Robert Wylshiers wyfe for her sete	vj d.
It' rec' of John Skynners wyfe for her sete	vj d.
It' rec' of Thomas Charnockes wyfe for her sete	vj d.
It' rec' of John Bysshoppes wyfe for her sete	vj d.
It' rec' of William Trappes wyfe for her sete	vj d.
It' rec' of Robert Fawces wyfe for her sete	vj d.
It' rec' of John Wattes {for} Cobber for a yer rent <endid> at michaelmas	x s.
It' rec' of Jenyns wife for a yers rent endid at the same tyme	x s.
It' rec' of Noreys for a yers rent at the same tyme	vj s. viij d.
It' rec' of William Stayner for di' yer rent endyd at the same tyme	vj s.
It' rec' of Thomas Harte for quyte rent of his tenement	xij d.
It' rec' of Corderay of Tylehurst for di' an acre of mede in langney	xij d.

1. For more about Henry Horthorne see Introduction and Appendix 2.
2. Sir John Hyde requested to be buried in the chancel of Sonning church. Since there is no payment for his grave in these accounts, it is possible the torches were used at a dirge not a burial in St Laurence. Several men of this surname lived in Reading. (TNA Will of Sir John Hyde, 1501, PROB 11/12/16). Sonnyng, modern spelling Sonning, is a village on the Thames about two miles east of Reading.

It' rec' of Harry Sutton for ij° gardens in lurkmer lane   xviij d.
[*In another hand*]<hoser lane>
It' rec' of kene Bocher for a yer rent of an hog sty in gutter   iiij d.
lane
It' rec' of William Joyner for quyte rent of his howse   xiij d. ob.
It' rec' of John Punsar for di' yer rent of a barne in gutter   iij s. vj d.
lane ended at mychaelmas
It' rec' of Roger Jonson for tyles   x d.
It' rec' of the be quest of Isabell the wife of Robert Sadler   xij d.

S[um]ma totalis vij li. {<xij s.> v d. ob.} xij s. j d. ob.

[*p 7*]   Expenses
In primis payed for wacchyng of the sepulcre   viij d.
It' payed for j li. of sens a genst Ester   viij d.
It' payed for colys and naylis to the sepulcre   ij d.
It' payed to Fuelles wyfe for wasshyng   iij s.
It' payed to Mr Smyth for ij° torchis waying xlvij li. pric le li.   x s. viij d.
iiij d. S[um]ma
It' payed to Robard Cavy for makyng of the yghe[1] &   iiij s.
mendyng of the boll of the iiij[th] bell clapper
It' payed to mynstrelles at the chosyng of Robyn hod   vj d.
[*In the margin in another hand*] Nota quod licet nota valet
It' payed to William Stayner for ij C liverays   viij d.
It' payed for iij quarters of stone lyme pric le quarter   iij s. vj d.
xiiij d. S[um]ma
It' payed to Thomas Hendy of Caversham for ij° M & an di'   xij s. vj d.
of bryk
It' payed to John Tyler for tyling & mendyng of the wallys of   xx d.
the howse that John Wattes Cobler dwellyth in
It' payed for lathis & naylis to the same   viij d.
It' payed for an C fote & an di' of borde to the barne in gutter   iij s.
lane
It' payed for di' C of plankes to the same. for iiij   ij s. iiij d.
peces of tymber. for ij hokes & nayles to the same barne
It' payed to Skydmore For makyng of an hogsty in the ten'   ij s. vij d.
that John Punser holdyth in gutter lane & for naylis to the
same
It' payed for carying of a lode of flynt & tylesherd to the   ij d.
church
It' payed for carying away of ij° lodes of donge fro the   ij d.
foreseid barne
It' payed for a rope to the grate bell   xvj d.
It' payed for mendyng of the hamer of the clok   ij d.

---

1. The eye of the bell. See Introduction.

It' payed to Payfote for iiij° lodes of way sond | xviij d.

It' payed to William May for dressyng up of the same sond | j d.

It' payed for iij quarters of stone lyme pric le quarter xiiij d. S[um]ma | iij s. vj d.

It' payed to John Stone for ij° bz of stone lyme | iiij d.

It' payed for di' M of bryk | ij s. vj d.

It' payed for voyding away of rubbell & makyng clene of the procession way | iiij d.

It' payed to John Troll for makyng of ij botras in the north of the church | x s.

It' payed for mendyng of the church yerd wall | x d.

It' payed to the officiall for peter pens | iij s. vj d. ob.

It' payed to ij° men laboryng ij° dayes in settyng up of ij° {ba} yron barres on seynt Georges lofte for boxyng of the grete bell. for takyng out of a brokyn goyon out of the ij^de bell & settyng on of a new | ij s.

It' payed for a quarter of ston lyme | xiiij d.

It' payed for a vij C tyle | iij s. vj d.

It' payed for a lanterne | vj d.

It' payed to Thomas Which for iiij^xx & iiij li. of Iron to seynt Georges loft pric le li. – ij d. S[um]ma | xiiij s.

St George chappell

[p 8] It' payed to the same Thomas for a new goyon to the ij^de bell weyng vij li. | xij d.

It' payed for the makyng of Seynte Thomas awter. Seynt Georges awter for settyng of Seynt George in to the loft. & for leyng of the gownsell at the ssowth [sic] dore of the church & bordyng of the same | viij s. viij d.

It' payed for makyng of ij setes for chyldern in the quere | vj d.

It' payed for a quyte rent of the church for a yere | iij s. vj d.

It' payed to the Glasyer for mendyng of dyvers wyndows in the church | xij d.

It' payed for skowryng of the grete candylstykkes in the quere | vj d.

It' payed for summonymg of William Geffrey to the Chaptour for xv s. and the church box which he holdeth for the church | ij d.

It' payed to Thomas Nicols for ij° dayes in tylyng of the church & the tenement that Jenyns wyfe dwelleth in. to hymself and his man | xx d.

It' payed to William Netter for a rope to the first bell | xiiij d.

It' payed to the same William for a rope to the Sanctus bell | viij d.

It' payed to Mr Smyth for <xiiij li. & di' of> wex & makyng a gayn Estar. Alhalow tyde & Cristmas | ix s. viij d.

It' payed to John a Wyght for ryngyng at the month mynd of Maistres Twyneho[1]	xvj d.
It' payed to Thomas Mascell for clensyng of the church gutter	ij d.
It' payed for the dirige & masses of the benefactours of the church	ij s. j d.
It' payed for kepyng of the clok for a yer endyd at michaelmas	viij s. viij d.
It' payed for settyng on of paras on the feriall vestment	j d.
It' payed for beryng of the <church> bokes in to the towne for a yer	xij d.
It' payed for wrytyng of this accomptus	ij d.
It' payed to William Stayner for makyng up of the maydens baner cloth	viij d.

S[um]ma totalis vj li. xix s. viij d.

And so remaynyth clerely to the Church {iiij s. ix d. xij s. v d.} <xiiij s.>

1502-3

[p 9] [*The initial letter C is decorated*]

Comptus of Nicholas Kent and Water Parson proctors of Seynt Laurens church in Redyng Fro the fest of the Annunciacion of our lady In the yer of our lorde god . M^l.CCCCC. and .ij°. unto the Fest that shall be in the yere of oure lord .M^l.CCCCC. iij^e.

Rec'

In primis the seid Proctors recyvyd as it apperyth in the fote of the late accompte	xiiij s.
It' rec' at Estur for the Pascall	xl s.
It' rec' of the gaderyng of men & wymmen at hoktyd	xxiij s. v d.
It' rec' of the kyng play	xlv s.
It' rec' of the parissh in gaderyng at Alhalow tyde	ix s. ix d.
It' rec' of the parissh at Crystmas	x s. iij d.
It' rec' of Robert Prow at the byryng of Harry his sone for the grete bell & for wex	xx d.
It' For the grave of Laurence morton gentyllman	x s.
It' rec' for the wast of torchis <at> the same byrying	xx d.
It' rec' for the grete bell the same tyme	xij d.

---

1. Margaret Twynyhoo was buried in the Franciscan Church, Greyfriars. She belonged to the Jesus Gild of St Laurence parish to which she bequeathed forty shillings. TNA Will of Margaret Twynyhoo, 1500, PROB 11/13/15.

It' rec' for the grave of Roger Jonsons wyfe & for pavyng of the same	vij s. ij d.
It' rec' for the grave of John Crewse & for pavyng of the same	vij s. ij d.
It' rec' for the grete bell at the burying of the same John	xij d.
It' rec' for wast of torchis the same tyme	viij d.
It' rec' for the grave of Thomas Plattes and for coveryng of the same	vij s. ij d.
It' rec' for the grete bell at the burying of the seid Thomas	ij s.
It' rec' for wast of torchis the same tyme	xij d.
It' rec' for the rode lyght the same tyme	xx d.
It' rec' at the burying of Sir John Pymber[1]	ij s. iiij d.
It' rec' for wast of torchys at the byrying of John Long maister of the gramer scole[2]	xx d.
It' rec' of the bequest of my lorde Wod[3]	vj s. viij d.
It' rec' of maistres Smyth for j li. of wex	viij d.
It' rec' for the grave of Thomas Rede and for pavyng of the same	vij s. ij d.
It' rec' for the grete bell at the burying of Elizabeth the wyfe of Harry Prow	xij d.
It' rec' for the wast of torchis at the same tyme	xvj d.
It' rec' for wast of torchis of William Hyll	vj d.
It' rec' of William Typpynges wyf for her sete	vj d.
It' rec' of Edward Taylers wyf for her sete	vj d.
It' rec' of John Haws wyf for her sete	vj d.
It' rec' of William Dodsons wyf for her sete	vj d.
It' rec' of John Sharpes wyf for her sete	vj d.
[p 10] It rec' of Richard Thornleys wyf for her sete	vj d.
It' rec' of Thomas Smythis wyf for her sete	vj d.
It' rec' of Ricardus Colyars wyf for her sete	vj d.
It' rec' of Nicholas Vos wyf for her sete	iiij d.
It' rec' of John Andrews wyf for her sete	vj d.
It' rec' of Isabel Balam for her sete	v d.
It' rec' of Thomas Nores for a yer rent endyd at mychaelmas	vj s. viij d.
It' rec' of William Stayner for a yer rent endyd at the same tyme	xij d.
It' rec' of John Wattes for a yer rent endyd at the same tyme	x s.
It' rec' of Jenyns wyf for a yer rent at the same tyme	x s.

1. He is identifiable by his title as a non-graduate priest, possibly a gild chaplain or chantry priest.
2. The most recent history of Reading School suggests it was a medieval foundation refounded as a free grammar school in 1486 and that John Long is the 'earliest identifiable' master of this free school. M. Naxton, *The History of Reading School* (Reading, 1986), 9-12.
3. Identity unknown. He was not the abbot.

It' rec' of John Punsar and Richard Coursey for a yer rent at the same tyme of a barne and a garden in {Lucke} Gutter lane	vij s.
It' rec' of kene Bocher for a yer rent the same tyme of an hog sty in Gutter lane	iiij d.
It' rec' of William Joyner other wyse called Hunt for quyte rent of his tenement at the same tyme	xiij d. ob.
It' rec' of Harry Sutton for a yer rent the same tyme of ij gardens in luckmer lane [*in another hand*] <now Hoser lane>	xviij d.
It' rec' of di' an acre mede lying in langney by the yer	xiij d.
It' rec' of William Justyce for quyte rent of the tenement that Thoms Harte inhabiteth by the yere	xij d.
It' rec' for the grave of Sir William Symmys	x s.
It' rec' for the grete bell & for the wast of torchis the same tyme	iiij s.
It' rec' for the grave of William Dodson	vj s. viij d.
It' rec' for wast of torchis the same tyme	viij d.
It' rec' of William Wattes for the grete bell	xij d.
It' rec' of at the burying of William Harebotell for the grete bell	xij d.
It' rec' of William Hasylwood for his wyfe is grave	vj s viij d.
It' rec' of the same William for wast of torchis & for the gret bell the same tyme	vj s.
It' rec' of Margaret Plattes for a stone to cover her husbandes grave	xx s.

S[um]ma to[ta]lis xv li. xvij s. xj d.	
of which the seid Proctors ax to be allowed for di' yere rent endyd at michaelmas of the tenement that William Stayner dwellid in for nothing was ther to strayn[1]	vj s.
It' the seid proctors askyth to be allowyd of ix s. viij d. being in the hondes of Margaret Plattes in parte {for} of the stone that coveryth her husband Thomas Plattes	

[*p 11*] Expenses	
In primis payed for wachyng of the Sepulcre	viij d.
It' payed for nayles to the Sepulcre	j d.
It' payed for colys	ij d.
It' payed for wasshyng of divers ornamentes of the church	iij s.
It' payed for a li of ensens	viij d.
It' payed for an hyde of white lethre	xx d.
It' payed for a bawdryk to the {grete} <iiij[th]> bell	iiij d.
It' payed for trussing of the same bell	xx d.

---

1. Distrain, i.e. to seize in lieu of unpaid rent.

It' payed for makyng clene of the aley & the gutter & for drawyng up of the wyndow of the stepyll	iij d.
It' payed for bred & ale on hok Monday and tewsday	ij s. iiij d.
It' payed for flessh & spyces at the same time	xiiij d.
It' payed for a Capon	vj d.
It' payed for a lyne to draw the curteyne in the rode loft	ij d.
It' payed for coveryng & pavyng of William Trewis wifes grave	iij d.
It' payed for a kay to the church box	ij d.
It' payed for flessh for the wymmen soper	vj d. ob.
It' payed for entryng of an accion in the spirituall court & to the Somner for his labor to ascyte[1] Sir Geffrey	vj d.
It' payed for payed for mendyng of the beer	ij d.
It' payed for iij quarters of lyme	iiij d.
It' payed to the tyler for tylyng at Noreys place	xij d.
It' payed for makyng of ij bawdrykkes	vj d.
It' payed for colis to the plommer	iij d.
It' payed for sope for wasshyng of corporas	j d.
It' payed for ij° payre of crewettes	xiij d.
It' payed to the plommer for his labor	xij d.
It' payed for xvij li. of Sawdyr	v s. viij d.
It' payed for castyng of led	xvj d.
It' payed to John Cokkes for kepyng of the clok at michaelmas	iij s. iiij d.
It' payed for ij° rochettes & for the makyng	v s. x d.
It' payed for ij° clampys of Iron for the gutter	vj d.
It' payed for viij C tylys	iiij s.
It' payed to Thomas Smyth for makyng of the grete bell claper	x s.
It' payed for j lode of sand	vj d.
It' payed for skowryng of the candylstykkes in the quere	iiij d.
It' payed to William Cone for his labor to set on the trayles in seynt John chauncel	xj s. viij d.
It' payed for makyng of the bere	xviij d.
It' payed for a rope to the grete bell	xv d.
It' payed for mendyng of setes for wymmen	xij d.
It' payed for to John Trall for ij° dayes & an di' in tylyng at	ij s. ij d.
[p12] It payed for ij° evys bordes	viij d.
It' payed for carying of ij° lodes of dunge	ij d.
It' payed for guttar tyle	iij d.
It' payed for nayles & laths	ij d.
It' payed in parte of full payment of ij torchis	ij s. iiij d.
It' payed to John Turner for makyng of the trendyll	ij s.
It' payed for corde to the same trendyll	vj d.
It' payed for vij C & an di' of tylys	iij s. ix d.

---

1. To cite, to summon to a court.

It' payed for tymber to make the trendyll whele	ij d.
It' payed for colors to the same trendyll	ix d.
It' payed for payntyng of the same trendyll	ix d.
It' payed for tyle pynnys	ij d.
It' payed to Thomas Smyth for lokes staples & haspys	ij d.
It' payed for iiij torchis waying iij^{xx} li & v[1]	xx s. iiij d.
It' payed for wast of pascall taper	ij s. viij d.
It' payed for the vaut taper	xvj d.
It' payed to John Troll for vij dayes in tylyng of the church	v s. x d.
It' payed for iij crestes	j d. ob.
It' payed for a lode of sand	v d.
It' payed to the Officyall for peter pens	iij s. vj d. ob.
It' payed to William Cone for makyng of iij lectors	xvj d.
It' payed for grownsyll to the tenement in the market that	vj d.
John Wattes dwelled in	
It' payed for hokes & hynges to the same tenement	viij d.
It' payed to the carpynter for his wages	vj d.
It' payed to William Cone for a diner	x d.
It' payed for lathis to the church	ij d.
It' payed for nayles to the church	iij d.
It' payed for iiij crestes & an hoke	iiij d.
It' payed for iiij torchis waying iiij^{xx} li pric le li. ij d. ob.	xvj s. viij d.
Sum[ma]	
[In the left-hand margin a pointing finger]	
It' payed byndyng & new coveryng of the grete antyphoner	xvij s.
& for makyng of & puttyng in of Festes of the visytacion.	
transfyguracion of jhesu[2]	
It' payed for carying of the same boke	ix d.
It' payed for mendyng of the coper Sencer & the latyn cros	xij d.
It' payed to William Cone for makyng of a trayle & mendyng	xij d.
of iij bell whelys	
It' payed for a surplys to Richard Barn	v s.
It' payed to Thomas Smyth for makyng of ij wegges of yron	x d.
& for a key to the grete bell	
It' payed to John Cokkes for kepyng the clok at michaelmas	iij s. iiij d.
[p 13] It' payed for mendyng of awbys & supplyces	vj d.
It' payed to Maistres Smyth for the trendyll	xiij s. iiij d.
It' payed for wax agayn alhalown day & Crystmas	xj s. iiij d.
It' payed to Robert Cavy for a bell rope	xviij d.
It' payed for ij lodes of erth	x d.
It' payed for a bolte & a swevyll to the trendyll	vj d.
It' payed a lode of thornys	xij d.

1. The total is 65 lbs. An xx above the line indicates twenty. Three x twenty = sixty + five.
2. These feasts, on 2 July and 6 August, commemorate respectively the visit of the Virgin to her cousin, Elizabeth, and the Transfiguration of Jesus before three of his followers.

It' payed for puttyng a way of dong fro the pale besyde \<church\>	ij d.
It' payed for a lode of sand	vj d.
It' payed for mendyng of the bere	vj d.
It' payed \< to macrell\> for makyng clene of the gutter & the church aley[1]	iij d.
It' payed to the same macrell for makyng clene of the setes in the church \<&\> for swepyng of the church {walles} \<rofe\>	xj d.
It' payed for polys to John Turn\<er\> for the trendyll	ij d.
It' payed for pavying of iiij gravis	xij d.
It' payed to John Kyvet for mendyng of the setes annext the store house	iij d.
It' payed to William Cone for removyng of the store howse	viij d.
It' payed for iij old dores & a wyndow to the tenement in the market	xx d.
It' payed to By for carying away of the dust of the church	v d.
It' payed for dirige & masse for the benefactors of the church	ij s. iij d. ob.
It' payed to John Troll for this labor in grete of whitlymyng the church & saynt Johnes chauncell & for syse & glew to the same	vij s. vj d. ob.
It' payed to William Cone for mendyng of the iiij bell whele & settyng on of a borde under the loft for the ryngers	ix d.
It' payed to William Tru For quyte rent	iij s. vj d.
It' payed for wrytyng of this accompte	ij s.

S[um]ma to[ta]lis vere expensorum xj li. xiij s. vj d. ob.

And so it remaynyth clerely to the church iiij li. iij s. vj d. ob.
And upon Thomas Plattes wyfe ix s. viij d.

Et sic dimissus est predictus Nicholus et in loco suo electus
est Johannes Darlyng junior

And upon the wyfe of William Dodson for the grete bell	vj d.

---

1. These jobs were performed in later accounts by the under-sexton, a post Macrell may have held.

1503-4

[*p 14*] [*The first letter C is decorated*]
Comptus of Water Parson and John Darlyn the yonger proctors of the church of seynt Laurence in Redyng {In the} fro the Fest of thannunciacion of our lady In the yer of our lord god .M^l .CCCCC and iii^c. unto the same fest that shal be in the yer of our lord god .M^l .CCCCC and iiij^{or}.

In primis the seid proctors receyvid as it apperith in the fote of the last accompte	iiij li. iij s. vj d. ob.
Also rec' for the pascall at Ester	xxxviij s. iiij d.
Also rec' of the wymmen at hoktyde	xx s. iiij d.
It' rec' of the men at hok tyde	vj s. viij d.
It' rec' of the maydens at the same tyme	iiij s. vij d.
It' rec' of Isabell late the wife of William Dodson for covering of the grave of the same William	vj d.
It' rec' of the same Isabell for wast of torchis at the month mynde of the seid William	vj d.
It' rec' of Nicholas kent for the grete bell at the berying of Johane his wife	xij d.
It' rec' of Elizabeth mayho for ryngyng of the grete bell at the ij^o yeres mynde of William Hyll Fyssher late her husbond	vj s. viij d.
It' rec' of Thomas myryman for wast of torchis at the berying of his wife	iiij d.
It' rec' of Thomas Tanner for wast of torchis at the berying of his wyfe	iiij d.
It' rec' Isabell Dodson for the grete bel at the month mynd of William Dodson late her husband	xij d.
It' rec' of Alice Sharp for the grave of Florence Rede and for coveryng of the same	vij s. ij d.
It' rec' for wast of torchis at the berying of the same Florence	viij d.
It' rec' of Nicholas kent for his wyvis grave	viij s. viij d.
It' rec' of Johane Hyll for wast of torchis at the month mynd of William Hyll late her husband	xij d.
It' rec' of the gaderyng of Robyn hod x busshelles of malt pric	v s.
It' rec' of the gaderyng of the same Robyn hod j bz of whete pric	xij d.
It' rec' of the gaderyng of the said Robyn hod in mony	xlix s.
It' rec' of Margaret late the wife of Thomas Plattes for a ful contentacion of the marbyll stone upon the seid Thomas grave	ix s. viij d.
It' rec' of the same Margaret for wast of torchis at the yer mynd of the same Thomas	xij d.

[*A pointing finger in the margin*]

It' rec' at Alhalow tyde of the gadering of the parissh	xiij s.
It' rec' of Agnes Elynger late the wife of Thomas Bale for the grete bell & for wast of torchis at the yer mynd of the seid Thomas	xx d.

[*A pointing finger in the margin*]

It' rec' of Randall Kelsall for the wast of torchis at the yer mynd of Harry kelsall[1]	x d.
It' rec' of the bequest of John Hygsons wife toward the bying of a Corporas	viij d.
It' rec' of the gaderng of the parissh at cristmas	xij s. xd.
[*p 15*] It' rec' of Thomas Barbor for his wifes sete	vj d.
It' rec' of John Pastler for his wifes sete	vj d.
It' rec' of John Semper for his wyfes sete	vj d.
It' rec' of Thomas Poynt for his wyfes sete	vj d.
It' rec' of Robert Dodson dyer for his wyfes sete	vj d.
It' rec' of Harry Sadler for his wyfes sete	vj d.
It' rec' of Richard Coursey for his wyfes sete	vj d.
It' rec' of John Body for his wyfes sete	vj d.
It' rec' of John Kyvet for his wyfes sete	vj d.
It' rec' of Jenyns wife & of John Nycols Chapman for a yer rent endyd at michaelmas	x s.
It' rec' of Thomas Noreys for a yer rent at the same tyme	vj s. viij d.
It' rec' of William Trapp for ij quarters & an di' of rent at the same tym	viij s. ix d.
It' rec' of John Web Skynner for a yer rent at the s. tyme	x s.
It' rec' of Richard Coursee for a yer rent at the s. tyme of a tenement in Gutter lane	vij s. v d.
It' rec' of William Justice Merchaunt for a yer <quit> rent of the tenement that Thomas Harte dwellyth in	xij d.
It' rec' of Harry Sutton for ij° gardens in lurkmer lane for a yer the same tym	xviij d.
It' rec' of Thomas Cordrey for di' an acr of mede in langney for a yer	xiij d.
It' rec' of William Joyner for quyte rent of his hows	xiij d. ob.
It' rec' of William kene for rent of an hog sty in gutter lane	iiij d.

S[um]ma to[ta]lis xvj li. v s. vij d.

[*p 16*] In primis payed for nayles to the sepulcre	j d.
It' payed for colys on Ester evyn	ij d.
It' payed for j li. of frankensens	viij d.
It' payed for wacchyng of the sepulcre	viij d.

---

1. In his will made in November 1493 Henry Kelsall left land to the gild for a yearly obit in perpetuity. See Appendix 2.

It' payed to snellys wyfe for wasshyng of the church gere for a yere — iij s.

It' payed to John Cokkes for a yer endyd at michaelmas in kepyng of the cloke — vj s. viij d.

It' payed for a new rope to the grete payce — xviij d.

It' payed for a yerd of wyer to the same clok — j d.

It' payed to Thomas Macrell for lyghting of the trendyll & strekyng of the church — vj d.

It' payed to the same Macrell for lyghting of the rode lyght for a yer — xvj d.

It' payed to the same Macrell for lyghting of the rode lyght & clensyng of the church goter at michaelmas — ij s. iiij d.

It' payed to the same Macrell for bering away of the rubbell at the church dore — j d.

It' to the same Macrell at cristmas for the rode lyght and for the holy bowze — iij d.

It' payed to the same Macrell for castyng out of snow of the church gutter — viij d.

It' payed to an harper on the church holyday — iiij d.

It' payed for bred & ale to Robyn hod & hys company the same day — iiij d.

It' payed for a cote to Robyn hod — v s. iiij d.

It' payed for lyvereys — xij d.

It' payed to a Taberer on Philips day & Jacob for his wages mete & drynk & bed — viij d.

It' payed for mete & drynk to Robyn & his company — xvj d.

It' payed for mete & drynk at hoktyde to the wyvis soper — xviij d.

It' payed for mete & drynk the same tyme to the bachelers soper — xij d.

It' payed for mendyng of the sylver sencer — ij d.

It' payed to Thomas Smyth for yron hopes to stay the baners — iij d.

It' payed to Thomas Nicols for pavyng of ij° gravis — viij d.

It' payed for makyng of ij albys of old cloth for chydern — iiij d.

It' payed for mendyng of the parissh surplys — iij d.

It' payed for bryk to cover the grave of Florens Rede — j d.

It' payed for whipcord to draw the blak cloth at sakeryng of masse — j d.

It' payed for lettyng hyer the coveryng of the font — ob.

It' payed for ij° yerdes & an di' of wyer to the auter in seynt Georges loft & for dressyng of the same Auter — iij d. ob.

It' payed for poyntes to the canapy & for tukkyng gyrdyls for the chyldern awbys — j d.

It' payed for bred & ale spent to the use of the church at Witsontyd — ij s. vjd. ob.

It' payed for wyne at the same tyme — xiiij d.

It' payed for fellyng & bryngyng home of the bow <set> in the marcat place for settyng up of the same mete & drynk	viij d.
[*p 17*] It' payed to Thomas Taberrer for his labur in grete[1] for fornyght	iij s. iiij d.
It' payed for bed & borde to the same Thomas by the meane tyme	ij s. iiij d.
It' payed for M[l] tyle	v s.
It' payed for a quarter of stone lyme	xvj d.
It' payed for trussyng of the iiij[th] bell & the gret bell	iij s. iiij d.
It' payed for new casting of the brasis for the iiij[th] bel & for more metal to the same	ij s.
It' payed for mendyng of the iiij[th] bell whele	iiij d.
It' payed for settyng on of the paras of the feriall vestment[2]	ij d.
It' payed for a rope to the iij[de] bell	xvj d.
It' payed for a bawdryyk to the same bell	v d.
It' payed for iiij[or] wegges for the gogyns of the iiij[th] bell	vj d.
It' payed for frankensens	ij d.
It' for a new whele to the first bell	ij s. viij d.
It' payed to Mylys paynter for paynting of seynt Christofer	viij s. iiij d.
It' payed for a payer of grete candylstykkes before seynt Thomas Alter	xl s.
It' payed for nayles to set on the first bel whele	j d.
It' payed for mendyng of the iiij[th] bel clapyr	iij s. iiij d.
It' payed for mendyng of the bawdryk for the iiij[th] bell	iiij d.
It' payed for frankensens	ij d.
It' payed for nayles to mend the iij[de] bel whele	iij d.
It' payed for whipcord & for settyng on of paras	vj d.
It' payed for ij lodes of sand	x d.
It' payed for a new led to the torch cofer	x d.
It' payed for xij[li] & an di' of Sowdyr	iiij s. ij d.
It' payed to a plummer for this labor & for fyer	xvj d.
It' payed for coveryng of Nicholas Kentes wyves grave	iij d.
It' payed for new pargetyng of the wal whers' Christofer is payntid	vj d.
[*In the right-hand margin in a later hand*] or Peter's pence	
It' payed to the Officiall for smok farthynges	iij s. vjd. ob.
It' payed for a rope to the first bell	xvj d.
It' for di' li. of franensens at Alhalow tyde	iiij d.
It' payed to a clarke dwellyng at hendley to a reward	xij d.
It' payed for a lyne to draw the curten before the rode lofte	iiij d.
It' payed to mylam for vij. dayes tylyng	iij s. vjd.
It' payed for mete & drynke by al the seid tym to the s' tyler & his man	ij s. x d.

1. The Oxford English Dictionary gives 'by the great' as work done 'by the task or piece' as opposed to a daily wage.
2. These are vestments for daily use as distinct from those for feast days.

It' payed for iij li. sowder to a gutter at the tenement in the market place	xiij d.
It' payed for a lode of erth & nayles for the tenement that Jenyn late held	vij d.
It' payed for a new lover[1] at the tenement that William Trap holdyth	viij d.
It' payed to John wylcox for iij torchis weying iij^{xx} & iiij li. pric le li. iij d. S[um]ma	xxj s. iiij d.
It' payed for mendyng of a chesyble & for ryband to the same	vj d.
It' payed mendyng of the iiijth bell whele	vj d.
It' payed for a lok to the torch cofer	iiij d.
It' payed the hyer of an hors for iij dayes to set Thomas Everard and the clerke fro Newbury	xij d.
It' payed for mete & drynk to the s' Thomas for ij° dayes before he was a myttid[2]	iiij d.
[p 18] It' payed Sir Thomas parissh preste of Seynt Maryes for his labor in ryding to Newbury for the seid clerk	xij d.
It' payed to Maister Smyth[3] for lvij li. of torch wex pric le li. iiij d. S[um]ma	xix s.
It' payed to the s' Mr Smyth for iiij li. wex wastyd of the pascall at Ester & for ij^{li} to the font tapyr	iiij s.
It' payed to the same Mr Smyth for viij li. & di' of wex to the rode lyght	v s. viij d.
It' payed to the same Mr Smyth for a li of sysis	viij d.
It' payed to Hew goldsmyth for mendyng of the pyx	vj d.
It' payed to Thomas Nicols for mendyng of the stapper at the church dore	vj d.
It' payed to John Kyvet for iij holy water stykkes	vj d.
It' payed to William Pastler for makyng of a cape wyndow in the north syde of the body of the church	x s.
It' payed for a lode & an di' of Sand	ix d.
It' payed for lath nayle & tyle pynnys	xj d.
It' payed for xx^{ti} gutter tyle to William Netter	x d.
It' payed for dirige & masses for the benefactours of the church	ij s. v d.
It' payed for vij busshells of stone lyme	xiiij d.
It' payed for streytes	ij d.
It' payed for a lode of erth	v d.
It' payed for l C of nayle	j d.
It' payed for wrytyng of thys accompte	ij s.

---

1. Probably a louvre window.
2. It is not clear what business took Everard to Newbury. He was a chandler and a future churchwarden who left ten pounds in his will for the parish clerk's wages. TNA Will of Thomas Everard, 1535, PROB 11/29/4.
3. This was probably Richard Smith. See Appendix 2.

[*In the right-hand margin in another hand*] x li. x s. x d.	
It' payed for mending of the white cope	ij d.
It' payed for tyling of the cape wyndow in myddys of the body of the north syde of the church & for mendyng of the walles	iij s. viij d.

S[um]ma x li. xiij s. xj d.

And so remaynyth clere to the seid church v li. xj s. viij d. ob.

And so hath ben left the seid Water & in his place hath ben chosyn William Stamford

1504-5

[*p 19*] [*first letter C decorated*]

Comptus of John Darlyng and William Stamford proctours of thechurch of seynt Laurence in Redyng fro the fest of thannunciacion of our Lady unto the same fest of thannunciacion In the yer of our lorde god. M^l. D. V. yer.

In primis the seid proctours receyveid as it apperith in the fote of the last accompte	v li. xj s. viij d. ob.
It' receyvid of the pascall at Ester	xxxix s.
It' rec' of John Wylcox at the burying of Mr Richard his son for the grete bell	xij d.
It' for the wast of torchis the same tyme	ij s.
It' rec' of the gaderyng of wyvis at hoktyde	xvj s.
It' rec' of the gaderyng of maydens the same tyme	ij s. xj d.
It' rec' of of the maydens gaderyng at Witsontyde by the tre at church dore clerly	ij s. xj d.
It' rec' of the gaderyng of the church men the same tyme[1]	vij s. ij d. ob.
It' rec' of the gaderyng of the bachelors {the} at may tyde	x s. vij d.
It' rec' of John Wilcox at the month mynde of Mr Ric' his son for the grete bell	xij d.
It' rec' of Laurence Hyll at the burying of Agnes his wyfe for wast of torchis	iiij d.
It' rec' of the gaderyng of the church men at wytson tyde	v s. vj d.
It' rec' the same tyme v busshelles of malte pric	iij s. iiij d.
It' rec' one bushell of whete pric	xiij d.
It' rec' of the gadering of Robyn hod	xviij s. xj d. ob.
It' rec' of Margaret Nassh at the burying of her husband for wast of torchis	viij d.

---

1. This was probably money collected by the churchwardens (churchmen) at the church ale. There is a second reference three entries below to similar collection at Whitsuntide and gifts of malt and wheat for the festivities.

It' rec' of William Trew that was found in the church   j d.
It' rec' of the same William at the burying of Alyce Adene   xvj d.
for wast of torchis
It' rec' for the sepulcre of the same Alice   vj s. viij d.
It' rec' of Richard Warren for the tre at the church dore   iij d.
{It rec' of the gaderyng of the maydens at wytson tyde}   [*blank*]
It' rec' of Randall kelsall <for wast of torchis> at the mynde   viij d.
of Harry kelsall
It' rec' of John Sharpe for the sepulcre of Agnes his wyfe   vj s. viij d.
It' rec' of the same John at the same tyme for wast of torchis   xij d.
It' for the grete bell the same tyme   xij d.
It' for {wast of torchis } <the grete bell> at the month mynd   xij d.
of the same Agnes
It' for coveryng the grave of the seyde Agnes   iiij d.
It' rec' of Symond Lambe at the burying of Thomas Buntyng   xiij d.
for wast of torchis
It' rec' at Alhalow tyde for the rode light   xiij s. v d. ob.
It' rec' at Crystmas for the rode light   xiiij s.
It' rec' of Harry Wylcox for his wyfes sete   vj d.
It' rec' of William Rawlyns for his wyfes sete   vj d.
It' rec' of Robard Myryell for his wyfes sete   vj d.
It' rec' of Richard Torner for his wyfes sete   vj d.
It' rec' of Robard Clerke for his wyfes sete   iiij d.
It' rec' of John Wy for his wyfes sete   vj d.
It' rec' of [*blank*] for his wyfes sete   vj d.
It' rec' of Harry Blanksten for his wyfes sete   iiij d.
[*p 20*] It' rec' of John Webb Skynnerer for the tenement in   x s.
the market place for one hole yere endyd at michaelmas in
the yer a bov expressyd
It' rec' of Richard Arnold Bocher for a yer rent at the same   x s.
Fest < of a tenement at New strete>
It' rec' of John Nicols Spycer for a yer rent at the same tyme   x s.
in the Newe strete
It' rec' of Thomas Noreys for a yer rent att the same tyme in   vj s. viij d.
the same strete
It' rec' of John Haw for a yer rent of a tenement in gutter lane   vij s.
the same tyme
It' rec' of William Kene for a yer rent of an hogsty in the seid   iiij d.
lane the same tyme
It' rec' of Harry Sutton for a yer rent of ij° gardens in   xviij d.
luckemer lane the same tyme
It' rec' of Nicholas Hyde for a yer rent of di' an acre of mede   xij d.
in Langney the same tyme
It' rec' of William Justice for a quyte rent of his tenement   xij d.
that Thomas Harte inhabitith in

It' rec' of William Hunte Joyner for the quyte rent of his tenement which he dwellyth in	xiij d. ob.
It' rec' for {makyng of } the grave of John Darling thelder my fader[1]	vj s. viij d.
It' rec' for the grete bell at the same tyme	xij d.
It' rec' for the grete bell at the month mynde of the seid John	xij d.
It' rec' for the Sepultur of Anne Darlyng my moder	vj s. viij d.
It' rec' for the grete bell the same tyme	xij d.
It' rec' of William Wattes at the mynde of Agnes his Wyfe for the grete bell	xij d.
It' rec' of Nicholas Kent at the mynd of Johane his wife for the wast of torchis	xvj d.
It' rec' of Richard Frankleyn for his wyfes sete	vj d.
It' rec' of Richard Bryce for his wyfes sete	vj d.
It' rec' of Roger Grave for his wifes sete	vj d.
It' rec' for the grete bell at the mynd of T. Plattes for the grete bell	xij d.
It' rec' of the gyfte of John Greke toward a payr of gret candylstykkes in seynt Johnes chauncell	iij s. iiij d.
It' rec' of John Powncer to the same candylstykkes	iij s. iiij d.
It' rec' of Richard Eve to the same	{xvj d.} <viij d.>
It' rec' of John Cokkes to the same	iiij d.
It' rec' of Ric' Frankleyn to the same	viij d.
It' rec' of Robert Pruw for this wifes gave	vj s. viij d.
It" rec' of the same Robert at the same tyme for iiij li. wast of torchis	xvj d.
It' rec' of the bequest of John Love by the handes of William White executor of the same John to the church[2]	vj s. viij d.

S[um]ma to[ta]lis xviij li. viij s. iiij d.

[p 21] Expenses	
In primis payed for naylis for the sepulcre	ob.
It' for Colys on ester evyn to be Halowyd	ij d.
It' for j li. of Frankensens the same tyme	viij d.
It' for Wacchyng of the sepulcre	viij d.
It' payed to Macrell for makyng clene of the seetes in the church a gayn Ester	viij d.
It' payed for Wasshyng of the ornamentes of the seid Church for the yer past a fore	iij s.
It' payed for settyng of the paras	iiij d.
It' payed to Macrell for scowring of the grete candylstykkes a gayn Estyr	vj d.

1. John Darling was one of the churchwardens, hence the more personal reference.
2. By his will made 9 August 1503 John Love left 20s to St Mary's church where he was probably buried, and 6s 8d to St Laurence. TNA Will of John Love, 1503, PROB 11/13/26.

It' payed to Maistres Smyth for wast of the pascall   ij s.

It' payed to the same Maistres for wax & makyng to renew   vj d.
the old fonte tapyr

It' payed to Robart Bye for carying away of iij loodes of   iiij d.
dong fro the seid church a gaynst Ester

It' payed for goyng to Twyford to arrest the stuff of [*blank*]   iij d.
for di' yer rent of the church tenement in the new street

It' payed to William Cone for makyng of a lectern to stond   viij d.
on the stalles in the quere

It' payed for ij gyrdyls for the ij Sencer caces   iiij d.

It' payed for the Bachelers dyner & for soper on the May day   xviij d.

It' payed to Macrell for the mendyng of the grete bell rope   j d.

<It payed to Pastler Carpynter in a recompens for makyng   <ij s.>
largyr of the cape window>

It' payed to William Stamford for iij li. & di' sowdyr to the   vij d.
new cape wyndow in the north syde of the church

It' payed to Thomas Wich Smythe for makyng of the yron   viij d.
barrys for the same wyndow

It' payed for naylis to the same wyndow   ij d.

It' payed to William Netter for ij tablis & an di' of glas for   ij s.
the same wyndow

It' payed to the Glasyer for glasyng of xxx^{ti} fote & ix ynchis   v s.
of the same wyndow pric le fote ij d. S[um]ma

It' payed to William Cone for celyng of the same wyndow   iij s.

It' payed to Maister Clech for Robyn hoddes cote & his   vj s. vij d.
hosyn

It' payed for lyvereys   xj d.

It' payed for pynnys   j d.

It' payed to Crystan Bryll by the hondes of William Stamford   ij s.
for wyne to Robyn hod of hendley & his company

It' payed to the Taberer   vj s.

It' payed for li. of Frankensens   viij d.

[*p 22*] It' payed for di' an hyde of whit leder to mend the bell   ix d.
ropes & bawdrikes

It' payed for a lok to the torch cofer   iiij d.

It' payed to Macrell for tendyng of the rode lyght. for   iiij s. viij d.
makyng clene of the rode loft & for shottyng of the organs
for a yer endyd at Mychaelmas

It' payed to {the} Richard Walker <Sexton> for kepyng of   vj s. viij d.
the cloke for the yere

It' payed for naylis to the grete bell whele   j d.

It' payed for mendyng of the red sute & for makyng largyr of   iij s. vj d.
the vestment slevis of the same sute

It' payed for the whit leder to the belys of thorgans [*This is*   iij d.
repeated in margin in a later hand.]

It' payed for j li. of glew to the same   iij d.

It' payed for mendyng of the same belys	iiij d.
It' payed to Macrell for pavyng of the aleys of the church yerd for beryng away of the same paving	ij s.
It' payed to the Offyciall for smokefarthynges	iij s. vj d. ob.
[*In the margin in later hand*] or peter pence	
It' payed to William Tru for quyte rent of the tenementes perteynyng to the same church	iij s. vj d.
It' payed to Robert Haywod for trussyng of the iiij[th] bell & mendyng of all the belles	xx d.
It' payed for mendyng of the ij° Sencers of sylver & for makyng of a new pan of yron for the bottum of the one sencer	xij d.
It' payed for broke sylver to the same	v d.
It' payed to Thomas Smyth for makyng of yre wark to the belles	ix d.
It' payed for a key to the tenement in gutter lane	ij d.
It' payed for a lode of erth to the same tenement	v d.
It' payed for scowrying of all the laten bolles in the rode loft	iiij d.
It' payed for makyng of the rodelyght at Alhalown tyde	viij s. viij d.
It' payed to Harry Horethorn for a beme in the bell loft for weryyng of the ropes agayn the wall	xiiij d.
It' payed to William Cone toward the selyng of the north syde of the church	iij s. iiij d.
It' payed for iiij gravis coveryng	xx d.
It' payed for mendyng of the blew sute	xxj d.
It' payed for ij° holy water stykkes	iiij d.
It' payed for ij° chaynys to hang them by	vj d.
It' payed for ij° staplis to the same	j d.
It' payed to Makrell for the holy busshes a gaynst cristmas	ij d.
It' payed to the same Macrell for lytyng of the trendyll	ij d.
It' payed {to the} for makyng of the rode lyght at cristmas	iij s. ij d.
It' payed for j li of sysis at the same tyme	vj d.
It' payed for vj torchis waying iiij[xx] & xvj li. pric le li. – iiij d. S[um]ma	xxxij s.
It' payed to Maister Wodcok {the kynges} Collector for cessyng of the church lyvelode[1]	iiij s.
[*p 23*] It' for a li. of frankensens	iiij d.
It' payed for mendyng of the cloke	v d.
It' for Wyer to draw the vayle in the quere	ij d.
It' payed to macrell for clensyng of the gutter & for {ma}havyng out of the snow in the church the xx[th] day of February	xij d.

1. 'Lyvelode ' means wealth. This was assessed for the benevolence, theoretically a voluntary payment but in practice a national tax. It was also paid by Reading's Merchant Gild. See Slade, *Gild Accounts,* i. xcviii; ii. 202.

It' payed to a Carpynter for mendyng of the stalles in the   xiiij d.
quere. for mendyng of the flore in the bell loft & for
mendyng of the setes in the church

It' payed for naylis to the same   vj d. ob.

It' payed for xxviij d. li. wex <for a stoke> to the pascall &   xj s. viij d.
to the font tapyr & for to renew the rode lyght pric le li. v d.
S[um]ma

{It' for j li of syses for the judas lyght   vj d.}

It' payed for makyng & settyng on of ij slevys on the Clerkes   iiij d.
rochet

It' payed to John Cokkes for notyng of the storeys of Seynt   xij d.
Osmond the transfiguracion of Jhesu the visitacion of our
lady and part of the comyn in the portoos bought of J
Turner[1]

It' payed to the Clerkes for syngyng of the passion in palme   j d.
sonday in ale

It' payed to the dyrige massis for the benefactours of the   iij s. {vj d.} ix d.
church

It' payed for a payre of gret candylstykkes in seynt Johnes   lj s. vj d.
Chauncell weying v^{xx} & iij li. pric le li. vj d. S[um]ma

It' for caryage of the same   xij d.

It' payed for writyng of this Accompte   ij s.

S[um]ma to[ta]lis x li. iiij s. v d. ob.

And so remaynyth clerely to the seid Church viij li. iij s. x d.
ob.

And at this Compte hath byn dysmyssid the foreseid John
derlyng and in his place hath byn electe William Jonson

---

1. St Osmund was Bishop of Salisbury 1078-1099. The comyn (Common) refers to those
prayers said at Mass on feasts of classes of saints e.g. martyrs, confessors, virgins for whom no
specific liturgy (a Proper) had been composed. 'Notyng' probably means adding musical
notation.

1505-6

[*p 24*] Comptus of {John Darlyng} William Stamford and William Jonson proctours of the church of seynt Laurence in Redyng fro the Fest of thannunciacion of our lady unto the same Fest of thannunciacion of our lady In the yere of our lord god .M.^{1} D^i. vj. yere

In primis the seid proctours receyvid as it apperith in the fote of the last Accompte	viij li. iij s. x d. ob.
It' rec' of the pascall at Estur	xl s. xj d.
It' rec' at hoktyde of the wymen gadering	xix s. v d.
It' rec' of the men gadering at the same tyme	vij s. vij d. ob.
It' rec' of the gadering by the church men at Witsontyde	iiij s. vij d.
It' rec' for iiij^{or} bz malte gaderid by the seid church men	ij s. viij d.
It' rec' for j bz & an di' of whete gaderid by the seid church men	xviij d.
It' rec' for the rode lyght at Alhalowtyde	xij s. v d. ob.
It' rec' for the rode lyght at cristmas	xij s. iiij d. ob.
It' rec' for di' an acre of mede in langney	xiij d.
It' rec' of [*blank*] for a tenement in the market place by the yer	x s.
It' rec' of [*blank*] for a tenement set in the southe part of the New strete	xj s.
It' rec' of Henry Sutton for ij^o gardens in luckmerlane	xviij d.
It' rec' of John Haw for a tenement in gutturlane	vij s.
It' rec' of John Spicer for a tenement in the new strete on the south side	vj s. viij d.
It' rec' of Thomas Nores for a tenement in the same strete on the northe side	vj s. viij d.
It' rec' of William Hunt Joyner for a quyte rent of his tenement in the hy strete	xiij d. ob.
It' rec' of Thomas Hart for quyte rent of the tenement in which he inhabit late bleweth	xij d.
It' rec' of William kene for an hogsty in guttur lane by the yere	iiij d.
It' rec' of John Derling at the month mynd of Agnes Derlyng his moder for the grete bell	xij d.
It' rec' of John Grffyn for wast of torchis at the moneth mynde of Helyn laughman	ij s.
It' rec' of John Derling at the yer mynde of his fader for the grete bell	xij d.
It' rec' of Margery Hall for the grete bell & for the grave of William Hall her husband at his burying	viij s. iiij d.
It' rec' of the gadering of Robyn Hod at Witsontyde	v li. x s. v d.
{It rec' of Thomas Dawsons wife for her sete}	{vj d.}
It' rec' of the parisch for the cape wyndow over the north dore	x s. vij d. ob.

It' rec' of Thomas Dawsons wife for her sete	vj d.
It' rec' of Randall Kelsalles wife for her sete	vj d.
It' rec' of Henry Carpenters wife for her sete	vj d.
It' rec' of Robert Westend wife for her sete	vj d.
It' rec' of John Kentes wife for her sete	vj d.
It' rec' of William Hasylwoddes wife for her sete	vj d.
It' rec' of John Nokes wife for her sete	vj d.
It' rec' of Thomas Symsons wife for her sete	v d.
It' rec' of Mr thomas Justice vicar for Helyn laughmans grave[1]	vj s. viij d.
{It' rec' of a man of tyllhyrst}	[blank]
[In a different hand] It resavyd of a man of tyllhyrst for the church	xij d.

Sum[ma] to[ta]lis xxiij li. j d.

[p 25] Expenses	
In primis payed for nayles for the sepulcre	j d. ob.
It' payed for colys to be halowed on ester evyn	ij d.
It' payed for a li. of Frankensens	xj d.
It' payed for wacchyng of the sepulcre	viij d.
It' payed to Maister Cleche for old det du to Jhesu masse[2]	iiij li.
It' payed for wasshyng of the church cloths by the yer	iij s.
It' payed to Makrell for tendyng of the rode lyght <& shutting of thorgans> by the yere	iiij s. viij d.
It' payed to the same macrell for skowring of the grete candylstykkes in the quer a gayn cristmas	vj d.
It' payed to Thomas Bye for carying away of ij° lode of dust fro the church dore	ij d.
It' payed to Thomas Taberer on the dedicacion day for his wages. mete & drynke	x d.
It' payed to John Knyght for mendyng of the poley ovir the hye Auter & for the belows of the organs	iiij d.
It' payed to William Netter for ij bell ropys	ij s. viij d.
It' payed for bred & Ale to the ryngers in the rogacion weke	ij d.
It' payed for lyvereys on our fayr day	xvj d.
It' payed for a supper to Robynhod & his company when he com from Fynchamsted	xviij d.
It' payed to Richard Walker Sexton for kepyng of the clok <by the yer>	vj s. viij d.
It' payed to Thomas Bye for carying of iij lode of dust fro the church	iiij d.

1. Thomas Justice was vicar from 1502 until his resignation in 1518. Kerry, *A History*, 218. There are frequent references in the accounts for someone to carry his book to church.
2. Probably Richard Cleche, a founder member of the Jesus Mass gild.

It' payed for v coples to the selyng above the rode loft   xvj s. viij d.

It' paied for a bell rope weying xxix li.   ij s. ij d.

It' payed for ale to Robynhod & his company   iij d.

It' payed for pavyng of helyn langams grave   iiij d.

It' paied for a skyn of white lether for bawdrykes   xvj d.

It' payed to Macrell for swepyng of the church wallys   iiij d.

It' payed for making of ij° bawdrykes   ix d.

It' payed to Macrell for makyng clene of the church agaynst the day of drynking in the seid Church   iiij d.

It' payed for flessh spyce & bakyng of pasteys a gaynst the said drynking   ij s. ix d. ob.

It' paied for ale at the same drynking   xviij d.

It' paied for mete and drynke to the Taberer   ix d.

It' paied to Henry Blanksten paynter for gyldyng of the rode mary & John in the rode loft   xiiij s.

[In the left-hand margin in a later hand]
the organ loft or the Rod loft where the Images used to stand

It' paied for the seling behynde the seid rode   vj s.

It' paied for settyng up of the <seid> Rode mary & john. for removing of thorgans & for making the sete for the pleyr of the same organs   xx d.

It' payed for making of a bawdryk   iiij d.

It' payed for an ell of <linnyn> cloth for a vestment   iiij d.

[p 26] It' paied for half a pownd of frankensens   vij d.

It' payed for xxx li. of led to the wyndow in the rode loft   xv d.

It' paied for vj li. of pewter to the same wyndow   xij d.

It' paied for tymber lyme & sond. tyle & evys borde & for the Warkmans Wages <of the wyndow in the rode loft>   iiij s. iiij d.

It' paied {for glasing} to Ric' Eve for glas to the same window   vij s. xj d.

It' paied for glasing of the same wyndow   iiij s. viij d.

It' paied to Thomas Wich Smyth for xxij barres & for naylis to the same window   ij s.

It' paied to a glasier for mending of dyverse windows in the church   vj s. viij d.

It' payed for paving of the gravn of Nicolas Kent & William Hall   viij d.

It' paied for making of a new cope <of crane colour> to Davith Thomas   ij s. iiij d.

It' paied for a bawdryk to the gret bell   v d.

It' paied for skowring of candylstykkes & taper bolles in the rode loft   viij d.

It' paied a lyne to draw the curtens in the rode loft   v d.

It' paied for mending of one of the grete candilstikkes be fore our lady   vj d.

It' paied to John Wylcox for iij coples to the selyng in the rode loft	x s.
It' paied to John Troll for mending of the tenement that John Spicer dwellith in	ij s. j d.
It' paied to Ric' Cave for makyng of ij gogyns	x s.
It' paied the same Ric' for oder yron warke	v s.
{It paied for sysis} It' payed for sysis to the holy bussh at cristmas	ix d.
It' paied to John Turner for mending of the grete bell and the ij^{de} bell	vij s. viij d.
It' paied for mending of the Wyer for the clothe before the rode	v d.
It' paied for mending of the dur going into seynt Johns chauncell	ij d.
It' payed {J} to Macrell for an holy bussh be fore the rode	ij d.
It' paied to John Darling for ryband to the new cope of crane color	xxiij d.
It' paied to Robert Glover for a skynne of Whit lether	xx d.
It' paied for making of a bawdrik to the grete bell	viij d.
It' paied for mending of ij° durres & setyng on of a lok at the ten[emen]t of the church in the which John Spicer inhabitith	xiij d.
It' paied to thOfficial for smoke farthynges	iij s. vj d. ob.
It' paied to Mr Smyth for making of the rode lyght & for ij° li. of new wex to the same	iij s. iiij d. ob.
It' payed to the same Mr Smyth for j li. & an di' of syses	ix d.
It' payed for the dirige & massis for the benefactors of the church	iij s. ij d.
It' paied to Thomas Wiche Smyth for making of a key to the gret cofer in the rode loft	v d.
It' payed for mendyng of the parish surplices for Sir Henry[1] & Ric' Walker Sexton	viij d.
It' paied to Nicholas Hide for vj yerdes of bocram to lyne the cope of crane color & for iij tukkyng girdils to the blak velwet sute	ij s. viij d. ob.
It' paied for lathis & nayle to the new cape wyndow over the north dore of the church	xvj d.
It' paied for sand & tyle pynnys to the same	v d.
It' paied for xxij gutter tyles & vij d. crestes	xix d.
It' paied to Henry Horthorn for makyng of the same wyndow	xij s.
[p 27] It' paied to {M}the coler maker for ij bawdrikkes to the gret bell	ix d.
It' payed to Maistres Smyth for wast of the pascall wax & makyng of the pascall and font taper	ij s. xj d.

1.　He was presumably one of the gild chaplains, a non-graduate priest.

<It' paied to the same Mr Smyth for wax & makyng to renew the old font taper>	[*blank*]
It' paied to Sandford Tyler {for tyling} & his man for iiij dayes in tyling	iij s. iiij d.
It' paied to John Gege joyner for selyng of CCCC <fote> & a quarter pric le C - xj s. S[um]ma	xlvj s. ix d.
It' payed to the same Gege for settyng up of the wier to draw the cloth before the rode in the rode loft	iij d.
It' paied for Writing of this accompte	ij s.

S[um]ma xxj li. xij s. v d. ob.

And so remayneth clere to the seid church xxvi s. vij d. ob.

And so hath byn dismissed the foreseid William Stamford
and in his place hath ben electe Richard Brussh

1506-7
[*p 28*] [*A different hand and a different script begin here.*]
**Comptus of William Jonson and Richardus Brosh
proctours of the church of seynt Laurence in Redyng fro
the fest of thannunciacion of our lady virgin to the same
Fest off thannunciacion of our lady In the yere of our
lord god .M. D. vij. yer**

In primis the seid proctours receyvyd as it apperyth in the fote of the last accompte	xxvij s. vij d. ob.
It' rec' of the pascal at Estur	xl s. ob.
It' rec' at hoktyde of the wymen gadering	xxxiiij s.
It' rec' of the menys gadering at the same tyme	vij s. vj d.
It' rec' of the yongmen gadering at Seynt Phylyppe day & Jacob[1]	v s. ij d.
It' rec' {of} the sonday a fore Bartylmastyde for the pley in the forbery[2]	xxiij s. viij d.
It' rec' for the rode lyght at all Holowtyd	xj s. x d. ob.
It' rec' for the rode lyght at cristmas	x s. ij d.
It' rec' for di' an acre of mede in Langney	xiij d.
It' rec' off [*blank*] for a tenement in the market place by the yere	x s.
It' rec' off Henry Sutton for ij° gardens in Lurkmer lane	xviij d.
It' rec' off John Haw for a tenement in guttur lane	vij s.

1. The feast of SS Philip and James (*Jacobus* in Latin) was 1 May, May Day.
2. This was the feast of St Bartholomew, 24 August. The Forbury, a name pre-dating the founding of the abbey, was an area to the west of the church occupied by the abbey's outer precinct.

It' rec' John Spicer for a tenement in the new strete on the south syde	x s.
It' rec' for a tenement in the same strete in the northsyde	iij s. iiij d.
It' rec' off William hunt Joyner for quyte rent off hys tenement yn the hy strete	xiij d. ob.
It' rec' off Thomas harte for quyte rent of the tenement in which he [blank] late blewettes	xij d.
It' rec' of William Kene for an hogsty in guttur lane by the yer	iiij d.
It' rec' of Sybell Derling for the berying off her housband and for the grete bell	vij s. {vj d.} viij d.
It' rec' off dancasters wyff for the berying of {hys wyff} her housband	viij s. viij d.
It' rec' off John Arnoldes wyff for the grett bell	xij d.
It' rec' {also} off dankcasters wyff for the grete bell	ij s.
It' rec' of William Stanford for vj bushell of lyme & for a corde	xiij d.
It' rec' for a bowe in the Merket place	iiij d.
It' rec' of John {Bar} barfote for hys wyf sete	vj d.
It' rec' of a wydwo [sic] that dwellyth by Roger hosier shop for her set	vj d.
It' rec' of Richard vysent for hys wyf sete	vj d.
It' rec' of William Wyett for hys wyf sete	vj d.
It' rec' for aldren polys left of the pley	v d.

Sum[ma] totalis xj li. vij d.

[p29] Expenses	
In primis paied to a Tyler an Estur Evyn	iiij d.
It' paied to the Sexton for thred for the sepulcre	j d.
It' payed for Colys to be halowd on Estur evyn	ij d.
It' paied for a li. off frankensens	xij d.
It' paied for wacching of the sepulcre	iiij d.
It' paied for wasshyng off the Church clothes by the yer	iij s. iiij d.
It' paied to Makrell for tendyng off the rode lyght & shutting off the yorgans by the yere	iij s. viij d.
It' paied to Makrell for skowring off the gret candylstykkes in the quyre a gayne estur	xij d.
It' paied to the seid Makrell for makyng clene off the church	viij d.
It' paied for the Wymensoper a hokmunday	xxij d.
It' paied to Richard Walker Sexton for kepyng of the Cloke	{xv d. ob.} vj s. viij d.
It' paied for a bel rope & a small rope for the clok	xv d. ob.
It' paied to makrell for havyng a waye of trash at the church dor	j d.
It' paied for Nayles for the rode lowghte	ij d.

It' paied for the mendyng of ropys for the belles & for a box	vj d.
It' paied for mendyng off a Stokke for the second bell	xviij d.
It' paied to Sybel Derling for Nayles for the sepulcre & for rosyn to the resurreccyon pley	ij d. ob.
It' paied to John Cokkes for wryting off the fest of Jhesu & for vj hoddes and bordes to the church	xviij d.
It' paied for the dirige & masses fore the benefactours of the church	iij s. v d
It' paied to the Coller Maker for mendyng of baudrykkes for the belles	vj d.
It' paied for the tenement that John haw holdeth for reparacyon	iij s. v d.
It' paied to Thomas Quyddynton for mendyng off the Clokk	iij s. iiij d.
It' paied to Mr Clech for Carying off wayneskotte that was gevyn to the church	vij s. ij d.
It' paied to the officiall for Smokefarthynges	iij s.vj d. ob.
It' paied for iij M^l Tyles	xvj s.
It' paied for Naylles to the Ladder & to the bere	ij d.
It' paied for boxys for the bellys	v d.
It' paied for nayllys for the boxys	iiij d.
It' paied for the makyng of a dublett of lethures & j peyr off hosyn off lethure a gaynst corpus Christi Daye	viij d.
It' paied for the legent	xij s.
[p 30] It' paied for a censer of Latyn	iiij s. viij d.
It' paied for a shepskyn for the yorgans	iij d.
It' paied for Mending off the Organs	v d.
It' paied to William Netter for a bell ropp	xv d.
It' paied to Richard Cave for makyng of a clapper for the iiijth bel	iiij s.
It' paied to Makrell for tendyng off the trendall	ij d.
It' paied to John Rey for mendyng of the gutters	x d.
It' paied to Roberd Glover for schepskynnys	xviij d.
It' paied for Lyme for the church	xv d.
It' paied for a lode of aldren polles	xij d.
It' paied for a Cart for carying off pypys & hogesheddes in to the forbury	ij d.
It' paied to the Laborer in the forbury for setting up off the polles for the schaphold	ix d.
{It' paied to the Ber Man for ber for the pley yn the forbury}	{x d.}
It' paied to Roberd Lynacre for havyng a wey off all maner off thinges owght off the forbury	vj d.
It' paied to Henry paynter for hys Labor the corpus Christi day	xx d.

It' paied to the goodman Cone for dressing of the Rodlowght[1]	ij s.
It' paied to the Smyth for Mendyng off the clok & ij° gymmows	viij d.
It' paied for the glasyng off the wyndow tharn wurke & peuter that longyth to hytt	ix s. ix d.
It' paied to William Trew for the quyte rent off the church howse	x s. vj d.
It' paied for bred ale & bere that longyd to the pley in the forbury	ij s. vj d.
It' paied for reparacyon off the Taylours hows in the market plac	x d.
It' paied the glacier for Mending of a wyndowe in the church	viij d.
It' paied to Christon for a Cophyn for the ber & other thinges	xx d.
It' paied for drink for the ringers a halow Thursday[2]	iiij d.
It' paied for the bere al maner of thynges perteynyng to hyt	x s. ix d.
It' for the repering off the legent paied for a hynd skyn	xx d.
It' {also} j li sysys at al halowtyde	vj d.
It' paied for ij° bokes of the fest of Jhesu & the vycytacyon of our lady	ij s. viij d.
[p 31] It' paied for a bagg for the whyghte sute[3]	v d.
It' paied for j {p} li. of syses for the quyre a gaynst cristmas	vj d.
It' paied to Roberd Davy for the carreag off the legent to london & home a gayn	iiij d.
It' paied for half a li. of sysys for the holy boussh	iij d.
It' paied for di' li. frankensenc a gaynst cristmas	vj d.
It' paied for di' yard cloth for an ames	v d.
It' paied for whyght threde deliverd to Ric' walker to sow the vestmentes wyth all	j d.
It' paied for mendyng of the lectern a fore the vicars	j d.
It' paied to Thomas Smyth	j d.
It' paied for viij d. elles di' holond for a corpeles & for the makyng off the corpeles	vij s. viij d.
It' paied for iiij M[l] D of lath nayle at {ix} <x>d the C	iiij s. j d.
It' paied for j ell quarter of crescloth for adam for to make j peyre of hosyn & j ell for a dowblettes	ix d.
It' paied for course canvas to mak xiij Cappes w[i]th the makyng & w[i]th the heres there to longyng[4]	ij s.
It' paied for ij° elles di' off crestcloth for to mak eve a cote	x d.

1. Rood light
2. Holy or Maundy Thursday, the Thursday before Easter Sunday.
3. A suit or set of vestments for Mass
4. 'Heres' could mean hairs (wigs), particularly since dyed flax was also used. The same word is used to mean wigs in other churchwardens' accounts of this date. J.C. Cox, *Churchwardens' Accounts from the Fourteenth to the Close of the Seventeenth Century* (1913), 254. It could also mean 'ears' attached to caps for actors portraying animals in the Creation drama.

It' paied for ij° qweyr of paper for the pagenttes	v d.
It' paied for dyed flex iiij li.	v d.
It' paied for j quarter off peymettes for the church	iij d.
It' paied for Tyles for the wyndow last made	xx d.
It' paied for pavying & tylying of the wyndow	xx d.
It' paied to Thomas Smyth for the repeyring of vj gogyns & v bondes for the whelles for the belles ij Reyn Nayls for the steroppys[1]	ij s. vj d.
It' paied for xlvi fote boorde for the wyndow yn to the gutter	x d.
It' paied for j C lathys - iiij d. ob. for naylis - v d. s[um]ma	ix d.
It' paied for vij crestes	iij d. ob.
It' paied for xiiij gutter tyle	vij d.
It' paied for xj fote of evys boorde	iij d. ob.
It' paied for a peke of tyle pynnis	ij d.
It' paied to Nicholas hyde for a xj peces of old timber for the gutter wyndow	vj d.
It' paied to Mr Smyth for the pascall & the font taper	iij s. vj d.
[p 32] It' paied for the repering of the jth bell the ij^{de} bell the iij^{de} bell the iiijth bell & the vth for the wurkmanschypp	iiij s. ij d.
It' paied for the makyng of the wyndow to the carpynter	iiij s.
It' paied for naylis	j d. ob.
It' paied to Mr Smyth for the rode lyght at al halow tyd	iiij s. viij d.
It' paied to Mr Smyth for the rode lyght at cristmas	iiij s.
It' paied for Naylis	iij d.
It' paied for lyning of furschen for the pelow of cloth a gold with seyng cawlt[2]	ix d. ob.
It' paied for rep[ar]acion of a tenement that loge dwelyth yn in the New stret on the sowght sed	xij d.
It' paied for writing of this accompte	ij s.
It' paied to Thomas quedynton for reparacion of the clok for the which iij s. iiij d. with other iij s. iiij d. to hym before paied as apperith yn thys accompte. he hath bownd hymself by for the Mayer & the paryssh to kepe al maner of rep[ar]acion of yarn warke to the same cloke be longyng by the space of xij yere at hys on cost & charg {fof}	iij s. iiij d.

S[um]ma ix li. xiiij s. iij d. ob.

And so remayneth clere to the seid church xxvj s. iiij d. ob.

And so hath byn dismissid the forseid William Jonson & yn
    hys plac hath byn elect William Lessham

1. See the description of the bells in the Introduction.
2. The cloth was fustian and cawlt was probably the thread for sewing it.

[The next few lines are in a different ink and hand.]
& the seyd Willyeme & Richard brusshe to be & occupy as
wardens & by the assent of Thomas Carpynter beyng mayre[1]
& the hol parysshyns they have electe & chosen Robert
benet & Worter Barten to be cheffe Wardens of the seyd
Churche to contynew so {all} as long as shall plese the seyd
parysshyns & yerly ij new Wardens to be ellecte to occupy
the busynesse of the seyd rowme

1507-8

[The original hand resumes here.]

**[*p 33*] Comptus of Richarde Brussh and William
Lassham of the church of Saynt Laurence in Redyng fro
the Fest of thannunciacion of our lady unto the same Fest
of thannunciacion then next folowing In the yere of our
lorde god. 1.50.8.**

Receytes

In primis the seid proctors have receyvid as it apperith in the fote of the last accompte	xxvj s. iiij d. ob.
It' rec' at Estur for the pascall	xl s. iiij d.
It' rec' on hok Monday of the gaderyng of Wymen <in halpens>[2]	vij d.
It' rec' hok tewsday of the gaderyng of {men} church men	vj s. j d. ob.
It' rec' of Raff Mylyngtons wyfe of hok money gaderyd of maydens	xij d.
<It' rec' of the gaderyng of Robyn hod play>	<xvij s. ix d.>
It' rec' of William Stamford fownde in his sete	ob.
It' rec' a gayne Wytsontyde iij busshelles <& di' > of malte pric le bz iiij d. S[um]ma	xiiij d.
It' rec' in gaderyng of money at the same tyme	ij s. iiij d.
It' rec' of Richard Vyncent for an C of tyle	vj d.
It' rec' for the bogh in the market place	iij d.
It' rec' of John Bysshopp for hyer of a payer of Fullers Sheres <late with Geffrey>	iij s.
It' rec' of the gyfte of Henry Herethern to the church of Seynt Laurence a ladder of xx ronges Som tyme of John Turner in the hystrete Turnor	
It' rec' at Alhalow tyde for the rode lyght	xj s.
It' rec' at Cristmas for the rode lyght	xiij s. ix d.
It' rec' of John Vyncent for the leying of a stone on the grave of maister symeon	iiij d.

1. Thomas Carpenter was mayor from Michaelmas 1506 to Michaelmas 1507. See the
Introduction for the role of the mayor in the parish meeting.
2. Half pence i.e. half of a penny.

It' rec' of William Cone for iiij C {& di' of a} tyle	ij s.
It' rec' of Thomas Walssh for wast of ij° torchis at the burying of h[i]s kynnysman	iiij d.
It' rec' {of} for John Wylcox grave <& for leying of the stone on the same grave>	vij s. vj d.
It' rec' of Maister Cleche for the grete bell at William Hethers mynde	viij d.
It' rec' of John Kent for the grete bell at his faders mynde	xij d.
It' rec' of Sybell Derlyng for the grete bell at her husbandes mynde	xij d.
It' rec' {of} for Thomas Hartes grave	vj s viij d.
It' rec' of John Puncer for the grete bel at the {mynde} <burying> of Sir John Styry	xij d.
<It' rec' of the same John for the grave of the same Sir John & the g[r]ete bell at the monyth mynde	vij s. viij d.
It' rec'of William Lenall for Robert Prows grave	vj s. viij d.

Setes

It' rec' of John Netter for his wyvis sete	vj d.
It' rec' of John Ely for his wyvis sete	vj d.
It' rec' of William Tyting for his wyvis sete	vj d.
It' rec' of Hew Smyth for his wyvis sete	vj d.
It' rec' of John Derby for his wyves sete	vj d.
It' rec' of Robert Goodlad for his wyves sete	vj d.
It' rec' of Roger Bocher for his wyves sete	vj d.
It' rec' of Gylberte Lyvynden for h[i]s wyvis sete	vj d.
It' rec' of Maister Pach moder for her sete	vj d.
It' rec' of William Edmundes for his wyvis sete	vj d.
[p 34] It' receyid of Richard White for his wyfes sete	vj d.
It' rec' of Thomas Wylkyns for his wyves sete	vj d.
It' rec' of Trystam Bowre for his wyves sete	vj d.
It' rec' of di' an acre of mede lying in langney in the parissh of Tylehurst	xiij d.
It' rec' of William Wodrose for a yere rent of a tenement in the market place	x s.
It' rec' of William lang & Alice Chamber for a yere rent of a tenement set in the south side of the Newe strete	xij d.
It' rec' of John Spicer for a yere rent of a tenement in the same strete & on the sam side	x s.
It' rec' of Richard Page for a yere rent of a tenement in the seid strete on the north syde late in the hold of Thomas Makrell	vj s. viij d.
It' rec' of henry Sutton for a yere rent of ij° gardens in lurkmer lane	xviij d.
It' rec' of John Haw for a yere rent of a tenement in gutter lane	vij s.

It' rec' of William Hunte for a quyte rent of his tenement in the hystrete by the yere	xiij d. ob.
It' rec' of William Justice for a quyte rent of his tenement set in the market place in whiche Isabell Hart Wyddow now inhabitith by the yere	xij d.
It' rec' of William kene for an hogsty in gutter lane by the yere	iiij d.
It' rec' of John Sponer for a tenement which he inhabitith in the new strete for a yere <at michaelmas>	v s.
It' rec' of Thomas Carpenter for iij⁰ peces of tymber	xx d.

[*Added in very small letters*] 58 s. 10 d. ob.

S[um]ma de omnibus receptes xj li. ij s. x d.

Expens

In primis payed to John Punsar on good Frydey by thassent of the parish for the rest of the best cope[1]	xiij s.
It' payed the same day to Water Barton for xx li. wex for a pascall pric le li. v d. Sum[ma]	viij s. iiij d.
It' payed to Maistres Smyth for making of xiiij li. wax to the same pascall	vj d.
It' payed to the same Maistres for a li. of wax to the same taper	vij d. ob.
It' payed to the same Maistres for j li. of grene Flowre to the forseid pascall	vj d.
It' payed for j li frankensens on Estur eve	xij d.
It' payed toWilliam Poo under Sexton for makyng clene of the church a genst [*p 35*] tyme of Estur	xiiij d.
It' {to}payed to the same William for carying & recarying of bordes to the church for the pageaunt of the passion on ester monday & for swepyng of the church at the same tyme	viij d.
It' payed to the same William for wacchyng of the Sepulcre	viij d.
It' payed to the same William for skowryng of xviij laten candylstykkes in the seid Church grete and smale & for makyng clene of the guttur	xiij d.
It' payed to Dame Taylor for making of the pyllow of cloth of gold of the gyft of Maister Richard Smyth	vj d.
[*in very small letters*] 28d ob.	
{It' payed to the reparacions of the Well bucket at the church dore}	{ij d.}
{It' payed for ij galons of ale for the ryngers on mayday} <dedycacion>	{iij d.}
It' payed for a stoklok & a key for the steple dur	ix d.

---

1. The term 'assent of the parish' which occurs frequently refers to a decision at the annual parish meeting.

It' payed to Mores son the harper	iiij d.
It' payed for xli li. waygth of Ropes for the belles	iij s. ij d.
It' payed for j li. & quarter of sowder to mend the church gutter in v places for warkmanshipp & colys to the same	iiij d. ob.
It' payed to John Bysshopps wyfe for wasshyng of thornamentes of the church	iij s. iiij d.
{It' payed to the ryngers on holy Thursday of coustom to ryng at procession}	{xiij d.}
It' payed for M¹ tyle fro Wokingham¹	v s.
It' payed for a quarter of lyme	xiij d.
It' payed to Richard Walker Sexton ther for keping of the clok for a yere <endyd at michaelmas>	vj s. viij d.
It' payed for carying of a bough for the king play at Whitsontyde	iij d.
It' payed to the taberer at Wyssontyde for his labor	iiij s. viij d.
It' payed to William poo subsexton for fellyng of the nettyls in the church yerd <wher the vicar hath gevyn the profyght therof for kepyng of the same>	iiij d.
{It' payed to the same William for Ryngyng on Corpus Ch[risti] day at procession}	{ij d.}
It' payed for vj li. & di' {of} wayght of smale corde for the sanctus bell & for to toll to Jhesu masse	vj d.
It' payed for xvj C of latthis pric	v s.
It' payed for ij° hynges & a borde to the church yerd gate	ix d.
It' payed for making of the same gate to the carpynter	iij d.
It' payed for ij bzs of Colys to the halowyd fyer	ij d.
[in the margin in a different hand] Hallowed fire	
It' payed to the Joyner for settyng on of a fyllet in a sete in seynt Johns chauncell with mendyng of the dore	ij d.
It' payed for a lok to the torche coffyn	ij d.
It' payed for v C xxv fote & di' of borde pric le C xx d. S[um]ma	viij s. ix d.
It' payed to for caryage of the same borde from Barkham² to Redyng	vj d.
It' payed to ij° men to have up the same borde & to ley it over the selyng in seynt Johns Chauncell & mete & drynk. And also to have <them> upp	vj d.
It' payed to hamond Caryntons wyfe for a dosseyn ale & bred	xxj d.
It' payed to By the caryer for a lode of sand	v d.
It' payed for x C latthis	iiij s. ij d.
It' payed for a padlok to the font	iij d.

---

1. Wokingham is a small market town about seven miles south-east of Reading.
2. Barkham is a village just over six miles south-east of Reading and south-west of Wokingham.

It' payed to mylam for tyling & sowdering of a tenement that William wedrof inhabitith & the ij° tenementes in the south parte of the newe strete <for mete & drynk by the space of v days>	iij s. x d.
[p 36] It' payed for the leying of the stone on Mr Symeons fader	iiij d.
It' payed to a plumer for ij li. & quartern of sowder & for his labor in mendyng of the church gutter	viij d.
It' payed to a Carpenter for makyng of an hach at the tenement in the {suth} <northe> parte of the newstrete in the holde of Ric' Page	iiij d.
It' payed for ij° hynges & nayles to the same hach	v d.
It' payed for blew bocram & rybond to the blak worsterd chesyble & for makyng	iiij s.
It' payed for vj tukkyng gyrdyls	vj d.
It' payed for a pece of tymber to make vij stoppes for the seller at William Wodrofes <tenement>	iiij d.
It' payed to a carpenter for iiij° dayes labor in makyng of diverse necessaryes at the same tenement	xvj d.
It' payed for xxvj fote of borde to the seid necessaryes	vij d.
It' payed for ij° payer of Jemews & nayles {at} to the same	viij d.
It' payed for a padlok to the church yerd gate	iij d.
It' payed for a yerd & di' of rybond to mend a cope	ij d.
It' payed for a lood of erth to repare the walles of the tenement in the southe parte of the newe strete that William long inhabitith & for makyng of the same & mete & drynk by the space of iij° dayes	xvj d.
It' payed to Stevyn March of Tylehurst for a M^l tyle	v s.
It' payed for A quartern of a li. of frankensens	iij d.
It' payed to Ric' Walker Sexton at Mychaelmas for a di' yer wages	viij s. iiij d.
It' payed to the same Ric' for the same day wages	v s.
It' payed to William Poo Subsexton at the same tyme for his wages	ij s. viij d.
It' payed for the new making of ij° chalesys as it apperith by a byll to the boke annexed	xxx s. ij d.
It' payed for iij unces {of Sylver} & viij d. penys wayght of sylver to the same Chalesis	x s. ij d.
It' payed for ij caces for the same Chalesis	viij d.
It' payed to Steven holy for smoke farthynges	iij s. vj d. ob.
It' payed for A quartern of an C of polen Wex	x s. vj d.
It' payed for ij° yron pynnys for ij° bawdrykkes	j d.
It' payed to John king for mendyng of an old grayle	xiij s. iiij d.

It' payed for the making of the rode lyght at Alholow tyde <xxx li.>[1]	xij d.
It' payed for 1 li of syses at the same tyde	vij d.
It' payed for mendyng of iiij° bawdrykes	ij d.
It' payed for a quartern of frankensens	iij d.
It' payed to a plummer on seynt Marten day for serchyng of the gutter for ij° li sowder & for his labor[2]	viij d.
It' payed to {John} Isabell Turner for ix compas bordes sawyd for the sydes of the bell whelys	vj d.
It' payed for making of the ferther style in the church yerd	viij d.
It' payed for lyvereye at Whitsontyde	x d.
It' payed for a quartern at[3] frankensens at Cristmas	iij d.

5 li. 5 s. 6d. ob.

[p 37] It' payed to Hew Goldsmyth for mendyng of the vyces in the sylver candylstykkes	xvj d.
It' payed to the same Hew for gyldyng & sowdryng of the fote of on sylver canstyk	iiij d.
It' payed for makyng of xviij li. of wex a gayn Cr[i]stmas	vij d.
It' payed for quyte rent to William Trew	iij s. vj d.
It' payed to Symond Alfy Joyner for repayryng of iij bell wheles & nayles to the same	iiij d.
It' payed for a quartern of frankencens on xij[th] evyn[4]	iij d.
It' payed to Richard Walker Sexton on Seynt Valentyne day for his di' yer wages payable at thannunciacion of our lady[5]	viij s. iiij d.
It' payed for carpynters lyne to draw the blak sarsenet before the Sacrament at the hy aulter	j d.
It' payed to a Stacyner for mendyng & bynddyng of an old grayle	viij s.
It' payed to John Cokkes for mendyng of the gret priksong boke of Jhesu masse	xx d.
It' payed to John Cokkes wyfe for mendyng of <surplis> vestmentes settyng of the paras for mendyng of Jhesu cope & for sowyng on of the aulter cloth to the {nether} frontell of Jhesu auter	x d.
It' payed to Hew Smyth for sowderyng & settyng in of the prik of a g[r]et candilstyk	viij d.
It' payed for j li & an di' of sowdyr to the same candilstyk	vj d.
It' payed for makyng of the pascall agayn ester	vj d.
It' payed for a squar pyn to put within the seid pascall[6]	iij d.

1. This insertion refers to the amount of wax bought to make or renew the light, ie 30 lb.
2. St Martin's feast day or Martinmas was 11 November.
3. This is a mistake. 'Of' is intended.
4. This was 5 January, the eve of Twelfth Night, the feast of the Epiphany.
5. St Valentine's feast day was 14 February and the Annunciation the 25 March.
6. This probably refers to a large square-headed pin. Five of these, each containing a grain of incense, were placed on the paschal candle during the Easter Vigil, signifying Christ's five wounds.

It' payed for makyng of the font taper	[blank]
It' payed to William Hasylwed for a new holy water stok of laton	ij s. viij d.
It' payed for the leyng of the marble stone on the grave of John Wylcox & for removing of a nother marble stone for the leyng of the same on Sir John Stypys grave	xx d.
It' payed to the tyler & his man for ij° dayes <di'> in tylyng <in the gutter>	xx d.
It' payed for making clene of the same gutter & beryng forth of therth fro the seid gravis & {fro} in bred & ale to the syngyng of the passion on palm sonday	iij d.
It' payed for ij° torchis <of wex> wayng xxx li pric	ix s. iij d.
It' payed to William Poo subsexton for di' yer wages at thannunciacion of our lady	ij s. viij d.
It' payed to William Stamford for {set} mendyng & settyng on of alyeu¹ upon a grete candylstyk before Seynt Thomas Aulter	iij d.
It' paid for smal lyne to draw the Rodecloth	iij d.
{It' payed} It allowyd to the seid Church men for a ten[ement] stonding vacant <by di' yere> in the which somtyme Thomas Macrell inhabit in the northe parte of the {same}<new> strete	iij s. iiij d.

S[um]ma to[ta]lis de omnibus {receptes} <expences>
xj li. iij s. xj d. ob.

{It' payed to Ric' Walker for di' yeres wages endyd at Michaelmas}	{[blank]}
{It' payed to the same for the other di' yer endyd at [word illegible]}	{[blank]}
It' payed to Richard Walker for a full contentacion of his wages endyd at thAnnunciacion of our lady {last past} at the makyng of this accompte for one hoole yere	v s.
It' payed to the same Ric' at the same day for a full contentacion of his wages in keping of the Cloke for a hoole yere	iij s. iiij d.
It' payed for wrytyng of this accompte	ij s.

S[um]ma to[ta]lis xij li. vj s. iij d. ob.

M[emoran]d[um] that it is grauntyd by all the parish that the sexton shall receyve of the church men for his yere wages to be payed quarterly vj s. viij d. S[um]ma xxvj s. viij d.

---

1. This is possibly alloy.

It' {I} for his wages in kepyng of the Clok payd di' yerly vj s.
viij d.

S[um]ma exspensorum   xij li. vj s. iij d. ob.

The Churche ys indettyd to the seyd Richard Brusshe in
xxiij s. v d. ob. therof to be aborted for his horse gresse in
the Chichyerd
[*p 38*] It' {more} ther remayneth to the church delyvered by the
forseyd Richard Brussh <at his dimission on good fryday> to
the handes of William Lassham & Richard Aman then proctors
of the seid Church in Pulleyn Wex xv li. & an di'
It' delyvered by the seid Ric' Brussh to the seid Proctors the   v s.
same day xvj C latthis pric
It' delyvered by the seid Ric' Brussh to the seid proctors the   iiij s. ij d.
same day x C latthis pric

1508-9

[*p 39*] **Compotus of William Lassham and Rychard
Aman proctors off the churche of Seynt laurence in
Redyng fro the Fest of thannunciacion of oure lady unto
the same Fest of the Annunciacion then next folowing in
the yere of oure lord god M^l CCCCC IX**[1]

Receytis

In primis the Seyd proctors have rec' at Estyr For the paskall   xl s. iij d.
Item rec' of the gathering on {goodfry} the Fayre dayr   vij s. iij d.
Item rec' of hok tewsday of the gathering of churchemen   vij s. ij d.
Item rec' in malte & in money ageynst Whytsontyd For the   iij s. vj d.
kynges play
Item rec' at the Fest of all seyntes For the Rode leygth   xij s. iiij d. ob.
Item rec' at the Fest of Creystis beyrth for the Rode leygth   xj s. ix d.

The receyttes of the Rentes

In primis rec' of John Wyleer of the <theell>[2] For di' acre of   xiij d.
mede in the pareshe of Tylehurst lying in langley
Item rec' of William Wodroff For the tenement in the   x s.
Market place

---

1. The C of Compotus and the I of In primis are decorated. Part of the binding is showing
between pp. 39-40 and seems to be a page from a Book of Common Prayer containing the liturgy
for Christmas Day. It reads 'Almighty God, which hath given us they onely begotten Sonne, to
take our nature uppon him, and this day to be borne of a pure Virgin. Grant that we being
regenerate'. At p. 74 the binding is again visible reading 'is one man and man is one Christ' and
at pp. 75-6.
2. Theale is a village about seven miles west of Reading.

Item rec' of William longe {For} <&> alycie Chambyr for a   xij s.
yere Rent For a ten' set in Sought[1] syde of the Newe strete

Item rec' of John Spycer for <a> yere rent of a ten' in the   x s.
same strete and on the same syde

Item rec' of Rychard page For a yere rent for a ten' in the   vj s. viij d.
seyd strete on the north {stre} syed late in the holde of
Thomas makrell

Item rec' of John Sponer For a yere rent for a ten' sett in the   x s.
seyd strete & on the north syed

Item rec' of harry Sutton for a yere rent of ij° gardens lying   xviij d.
in lurkmer lane

Item rec' of John Haw for a yere rent of a ten' in gutter lane   vij s.

Item rec' of William hunte for a quyt rent for his ten' in the   xiij d. ob.
hygh strete by yere

Item rec' of William Justice for a quyt rent for his ten' set in   xij d.
the market place by yere

Item rec' of Thomas Everode for a garden plote in gutter   iiij d.
lane the Whiche William Kene late held by yere

The greatt bell & gravys

Item rec' For the grete bell {of} For John Gryke   xij d.

Item rec' John vynsettes g<r>ave {ad} and for the kevering   viij s. viij d.
[covering] ther of and For the grete bell at the same tyme

[p 40] It rec' For William Nettar is grave & for kevering   vij s. iiij d.
therof

Item rec' For the grete bell at the bereyng of the same   xij d.
William

Item rec' For William myllis grave   vj s. viij d.

Item rec' of John Kent For his Wyffys grave & the kevering   vij s. ij d.

Item rec' of the same John For the grete bell at the bereyng   ij s.
of his Weyff and at hyr monyth is meynd[2]

Item rec' For the grete bell at the bereing of Robert Byrle is   xij d.
Weyff

Item rec' For the grete bell For Mr Rokys   xij d.

Item rec' of the same Mr Rokes for the Waste of ij° torchis   ij s. j d.
the Whiche was v li.

Item rec' of Vyncenttes Wyfe For hir husband is grave and   vij s. ij d.
the kevering ther of

Item rec' For the grete bell For Colyar   xij d.

Item rec' of Davys Weff For her husbond is grave   vj s. viij d.

1. South.
2. The 'is' indicates a possessive. In modern punctuation this would be expressed as hyr
monyth's meynd'. The same punctuation is used below at 'Robert Byrle is Weyff' and throughout
the text.

Item rec' of Robard Dobson For his Weffes grave & the kevering ther of	vij s. ij d.
Item rec' For Agnes Darling is grave and the kevering ther of	vij s. ij d.
Item rec' For the grete bell at the berying of the sayd Agnes	xij d.
Item rec' for Roger graneys grave <& for the keveryng ther of>	vij s. ij d.
Item rec' of Thomas hart is Weff For the grete bell	xij d.
Item rec' of John pownser For the grete bell at Sir John is meynd	xij d.

Setys

Item rec' of Byrge For his Weyff is seyt	vj d.
Item rec' of paytow For his Weyff is seyt	vj d.
Item rec' of John hosteler For his Weyff is seyt	vj d.
Item rec' of Syr Thomas Syster For her seyt	vj d.
Item rec' of Thomas Brygges For his Weyff is seyt	vj d.
Item rec' of Barfots his mother for her seyt	vj d.
Item rec' of Richard Barnys for his Weyff is seyt	vj d.
Item rec' of doe for is Weyff is seyt	vj d.
Item For the Waste of ij° Torchys of Banastyr is mother	ij d.
Item rec' of Mr mayr For xiij C lathis	iiij s. viij d.
Item rec' of Mr vycary For CC lathis	viij d.
Item rec' of John Semper for a C of lathys	iiij d.
Item rec' of Rychard Barons For CCCC lathys	xviij d.
Item rec' of the seyd Rychard For vj bz of lyme	ix d.
Item rec' of Rockys For j bz of lyme	ij d.
Item rec' For the tre in the market place	ij d.

[At this point the inventories from 1503 and 1517 are bound into the accounts which continue at page 74]

[p 74] [in a later hand at the top of the page] Anno 1509

It' Rec' of money found in the churche	j d.
Item rec' off the Taylor in the markett place an yernest peny For his house	j d.
Item rec' of the executors of Mr Bereman[1] that he bequest to the church	vj s. viij d.

S[um]ma[2] to[ta]lis Re[cey]te xij li. vj d.

Expenses

In primis payed For the Wacheyng of the Sepulkyr	viij d.
Item payed For i li. of ynsences	xij d.
Item payed For Colys on Estyr evyn to be holowed	ij d.

---

1. No will has been found for this donor.
2. The 'S' of S[um]ma and below the 'I' of Item are highly decorated.

Item payed For the Caryage of the Burdys For the pageant on Estyr Monday	j d.
Item payed to Bysshopis Weyff For Wesseyng of all suche ornamentes {asse} as perteyneth to the churche	iij s. iiij d.
Item payed For iiij baner pollis	v s. iiij d.
Item payed unto William a powell undyr Sexton for Skowrring of the kanstykes	viij d.
Item payed For CC lyveres & C pynnys agenst may daye	xj d.
Item payed unto John raye For the Reparacion of the gotter for the hole yere	vj s. viij d.
Item payed For the halowyng of ij Chalys	viij d.
[*In the margin in a later hand*] wages	
Item payed unto Rychard Walker Sexton	viij s. iij d.
Item payed unto a Tyler & his men For ij° dayes tyling of the churche	xviij d.
Item payed to William Sexton For the mendyng of a bawderike & for Carrying out of the Erthe of the gravys	vj d.
Item payed unto William powell undyr sexton for makyng clene of the Setys	xij d.
[*p 75*] Item payed For keveryng of William mylles grave with the Whyte stone that is brokyn	viij d.
Item payed For ij° quarters of lyme	ij s. ij d.
Item payed to a Tabyrat[1] at Whytsontyde	iiij s. viij d.
Item payed For the tymbyr & naylis and the werkemanship of the Frame For the Canopye and For Whyte lyre For to take the same canopy[2]	x d.
Item payed for xij Thredyn poyntys for to Faston the same Canopy to the Frame	j d.
Item payed For iij new stavys and for the peyntyng of the hole iiij stavys For to bere the seyd Canopy	xij d.
Item payed to Wone horne[3] that was causyd to come Froe Wynchestyr unto this Towne For to a byn a Clerke here of the Churche by the Assent of Mr smyth William Battes & phylyp Rysby	xx d.
Item payed unto broysshe[4] for the Dewtte that the churche owd hym at his a cownte	x s. j d.
Item payed For the mendyng of the gret bell in {Well} <Whele> & in naylles	v d.
Item payed For the mendyng of the Organs	j d.
Item payed to Rychard Walker Sexten	viij s. iiij d.

1. A taberer was a drummer.
2. This was the canopy over the altar.
3. 'One' i.e. a man whose surname was Horne. Refering to him as 'a clerk' suggests he was a clergyman rather than a parish clerk.
4. Richard Brush, churchwarden in 1507-8 when the accounts were in deficit. Accounts page 37.

Item payed For iij ston & iiij li. of {Rol} Ropys	iij s. x d.
Item payed to Thomas Smyth for makyng of a nye for the iij^{de} bell clapper	xx d.
Item payed For a quarter of li. ynsens	iij d.
Item payed For ij° Ropis on For the grete bell & a nother for the small bell conteynyng in Weygth ij° ston di' & iij li. di' s[um]ma	iij s. ij d.
Item payed for a quarter of li. ynsens	iij d.
Item payed to John Rysset kerver for the makyng of the drawyng of the sacrement[1]	xx d.
Item payed For the plowmet for the same & the lyne to drawe the same sacrement	v d.
Item payed to d[avi]d Taylour For the mendyng of the Canopy	iiij d.
Item payed for leyng of a stone a pon Netter[2]	viij d.
Item payed For a quarter of a li. of Insens	iij d.
Item payed For the makyng of XXXI^{ti} pownd wax For the Rode leygth a genst the Feest of all Seyntys	xiij d.
Item payed For ij° holy watyr styckys	iiij d.
Item payed For a quarter of a li. of Insens	iij d.
Item payed to Thomas palmer For v Gravys and mendyng of other Fawttes in the Churche And For the laying of a ston apon Agnes darling	iij s. iiij d.
Item payed unto John Kneygth For the mendyng of the organs	ij s. vj d.
[p 76] Item payed to a glasyer For v dayes werke and his stuffe For mending of dyvers wyndows in the churche	vj s. viij d.
Item payed unto Regestyr for Smoke Farthynges	iij s. vj d. ob.
Item payed <for> the makyng of xix li. wex for the Rode leygth a genst crystmas	viij d.
Item payed to Borne the Colour maker For a new bawdryk	xij d.
Item payed to the seyd Borne For the mendyng of iij bawdrykes	xiij d.
Item payed For the makyng of a li. of sysys agenst Haloutyde & krystmas	ij d.
[*A pointing finger in the right-hand margin.*]	
Item payed For iij li. of Talow Candylles that was sett on the pyllers in the churche	iij d. ob.
Item payed For a quarter of a li. of Insens	iij d.
Item payed to hew Smyth for j henge of a dore and the mendyng of a loke And also for the mendyng of a peyr of Jemowys & Stapylles to the house that William Wodroff Taylour late dwellyd in	vj d.

1. This entry and the next relate to the rope and the counterweight used to lower and raise the pyx containing the sacrament.
2. Netter was the name of the man on whose grave the gravestone was laid.

Item payed For ij⁰ Smale Bordys For to mend the wendows with naylys and with the werkemanshipp for the same house	iiij d.
Item payed For a man is labour For to mende the walles of the same house & For di' lode off Erthe to the same	vj d. ob.
Item payed For a aube For a cheyle and the makyng therof	xiiij d.
Item payed to Raby For the mendyng off a whele of the Cloke	viij d.
Item payed to Thomas Smythe For mendyng and Bowlling off the iiij^th bell Clapyr	v s.
Item payed For a quarter of Insens	iij d.
Item payed For ij⁰ bz of Tyle pynnys	{vj d.} <xij d.>
Item payed For a quarter of C wex	xj s. viij d.
Item payed unto William Godney goldsmyth of london For the makyng and gylding of a Fote of a chalys and for amelyng[1] of ij Cnappys the whiche stondeyth in the myddys of the same Chalys. Conteyning the weytt of the Fote vj unce & a quarter at xx d. le unce the Fasthenyng S[um]ma	x s.
Item payed unto the seyd Goldsmyth For j unce & iij quarter of Sylver {the} to Fulffyll the fote of the same Chalys price lez unce iij s. ij d. S[um]ma	v s. vj d. ob.
Item payed unto William Trewe For queytt rent	iij s. vj d.
Item payed For ij⁰ kasys For ij⁰ chalys	viij d.
Item payed to Mr Ayssepole For entering of a playnt in the Court For William Jaffrey	j d.
Item payed the same tyme unto John Sutton the under baylly[2]	j d.
Item payed For a quart[3] of Bastard for the Synggers of the passhyon on palme sondaye	iiij d.
[p 77] Item payed unto William Battes For the reparacions of a small grayle the whiche William leye owt For the Churche	iiij s.
Item payed For the Durges & masses off all benefactours of the same churche of seynt laurence	iij s. ij d.
Item payed For iiij Torchys conteynyng in weygth {iiij^xx li.} iiij^xx iij li. di at iij d. li. S[um]ma	xx s. x d. ob.
Item payed to William longe for scowring of xviij^th Candylstekes agenst the Fest of All Seyntes	vj d.
Item payed unto John vyntener Barbour For the peyntyng of a banar {clogth} <poll>	viij d.
Item payed unto William longe For ryngyng of the grete bell for Mr Bereman	xvj d.
Item payed For mendyng of ij Syrpleys	iij d.

1. Enamelling of two knobs.
2. The under bailiff was a lay official of the abbey.
3. In the text this word is written in the same way as 'quarter' but since bastard was a wine, 'quart' seems a more appropriate transcription.

Item payed unto Symond Asley For mendyng of the gret bell whele and the dexst in the quere	vj d.
Item payed unto a tyler for mendyng of John Spycer is house wallis	iiij d.
Item payed For di' lode of Erthe to the same	ij d. ob.
Item payed For the makyng of viij li. waxe For the paskcall & the Fonte tapyr	vj d.
Item payed For the makyng and Wryting off the same acowmpte	xij d.

id' S[um]ma alloc' & soluc' ix li. v s. ix d. ob.
[*In another hand*]
And so remayneth to the seyd Churche liiij s. viij d. ob. &
then was dismyssyd William lessome & in hys rowme was
chosen Richard Turner

1509-10

**[*p 78*] Compotus[1] Richard a mane & Richard Tornor
proctors off the Churche of Seynt laurence in Redyng
fro the Feest of thAnnuncyacion off oure lady unto the
same Feest of the Annuncyacion then next follyng in the
yere of oure lord god M[l] CCCCC X**

Receyttes

Inprimis rec' off William lesseham as hit apperyth in his Fote off a Cownte	liiij s. viij d. ob.
Item rec' on Estyr daye For the pascall	xxxix s. iij d. ob.
Item rec' on Mondaye gethered by the wyvys	xxvj s. x d. ob.
Item rec' on hocke tewsdaye getherd by the men	vj s. x d.
Item rec' For the getheryng on Maye daye	iiij s. viij d. ob.
Item rec' at the Fest of all Seyntes For the Rode leygth	xij s. vj d.
Item rec' at the Fest of Crystemas For the Rode leygth	x s. vij d.
Item rec' of Mr More For a kowe that was bequest to the Churche[2]	viij s.
Item rec' For the gethering for the Sexten of the pareshe	xxv s. viij d.

S[um]ma   ix li. xiiij s. ij d.[3]

Receytt of the rentes

Item rec' of John Sponer For a tenement in the new strete	x s.
Item rec' of John Spycer For a tenement in the New strete	x s.

1. The 'C' of Compotus, the 'I' of Item below and the 'S' of S[um]ma on p. 79 are highly decorated.
2. It was common practice for churchwardens to sell crops or livestock bequeathed to the parish. The donor is unknown.
3. The correct total is £9 9s 2d.

Item rec' of Thomas hart is Weyff For quyt rent	xij d.
Item rec' of William longe For a tenement lying in the New strete	xij s.
Item rec' of John hall for a tenement yn gutter lane by yere	vij s.
Item rec' of Thomas Taylour For a tenement in market place by yere	x s.
Item rec' of Thomas Evered For a garden plott in gutter lane by yere	iiij d.
Item rec' of William honte For a quytt rent For an Acre <mede> lyeing in langley	xiij d. ob.
Item rec' of harry Sutton For ij garden plottes lying in lukmer lane by yere	xviij d.
Item rec' of Rychard page For a tenement lying in the {Nef} Newe strete	vj s. viij d.
Item rec' of John welder For di' an acre of mede lying in langley by yere	xiij d.

S[um]ma lx s. viij d. ob.

The grett bell & gravys

Item rec' of Mester Bereman For Rynging of the grett bell	xij d.
Item rec' of Nettar is weyff For Rynging of the gret bell	xij d.
Item rec' of Edward of the kynges stabull for ringyng of the grett bell[1]	x d.
Item rec' of hasylwod is wayff For ringyng of the grett bell[2]	xij d.
Item rec' of Mays is weff For hir husbond is grave and Coveryng	vij s.
[p 79] Item rec' of Robard Dodson for his kynnes woman is grave & for Coveryng	vij s. ij d.
Item rec' of harry wylkokes for his Weyff his grave & for Coveryng of the same	vij s. ij d.
Item rec' of hasylwod is weff for hir husbond is grave & for coveryng of the same	vij s. ij d.

S[um]ma xxxij s. iiij d.

Setys

Item rec' of wyntener stayner For his weyff is sett	vj d.
Item rec' of lesatyr for his weyff is sett	vj d.
Item For a waynescott of the Churche	{vj d.} <viij d.>
Item rec' of harey Sparawke for his weyff is sett	vj d.

---

1. He is one of several royal servants mentioned in the accounts and inventories. His identity is not traceable since only his Christian name is given.
2. In his will made 8 March 1507 and proved 10 December 1509 William Hasylwood, bellfounder bequeathed 12d to the Mass of Jesus gild. TNA Will of William Hasylwood, 1507, PROB 11/16/23. He asked to be buried in the church.

Item rec' of Bocke for his weyff is sett	vj d.
Item rec' of Alys whytt for hyr sett	vj d.
Item rec' of william davy for his Wyff is sett	vj d.
Item rec' of Davy Taylor is weyff toward the makyng of hir sett	{vj d.} <iiij d.>
Item rec' of kokes weyff of the Abbey For hyr sett[1]	vj d.
Item rec' of Em Barton For hyr sett	vj d.
Item rec' of william Bocher for his weyff is sett	vj d.
Item rec' of Thomas Sowgth for his weff is sett	vj d.
Item rec' of Alys gorden for his weyff is sett[2]	vj d.
Item rec' of Symond Alse for his weyff is sett	vj d.
Item rec' of kockes toward the mending of a sett	ij d.
Item rec' of Mr vycary For j bz of lyme to whyte lyme the chaunsell	ij d.

S[um]ma vij s. iiij d.

S[um]ma totalis Re[cy]te xiiij li. xiiij s. vj d. ob.

Idem computat' in alloc'[3] In primis payed to William lesshame For wascheynge of the gere uppon good Frydaye	iij s. iiij d.
Item payed For Nayles to mend the Sepulker	ob.
Item payed For takkys for the Canope	ob.
Item payed For a small lyne to hange the kanope over the hey auter	j d.
Item For a li. of sence agenst Estyr	xij d.
Item payed For wacheyng of the Sepulcre	viij d.
[p 80] Item payed unto Rychard Sexton {For} <toward> his wages	xx s.
Item payed For ij bz of colys at the halowyng of the vaute	ij d.
Item For the mending of the whole of the grett bell & nayles	iiij d. ob.
[A pointing finger in the left-hand margin]	
Item payed for X Rynggers at the parting of the kyng & For drynke and to the sexton	ij s. ob.
Item payed For CC levers & {tyle} pynnis	xj d.
Item payed For mendyng of the gutters unto John Raye for the hole yere	vj s. viij d.
Item payed to william Roke For ij lode of sonde for the churche	xij d.
Item payed For CC of lathe naylis	ij d.
Item payed to william longe For his quarter is wagis at estyr	xij d.

---

1. She was the wife an employee called Cook. The abbey employed a number of household servants.
2. This appears to be an error. Alys [Alice] would have been Gordon's wife
3. The usual heading of 'expenses' is here replaced by a Latin phrase meaning 'calculated for allowances' i.e. what the churchwardens were allowed to claim against income.

Item payed For M^l of tyle	v s.
Item payed For iij quarters of lyme	iij s. vj d.
Item payed For makyng clene of the churche after the tyling	iiij d.
[*In the left-hand margin*] wagis	
Item payed to Rychard walker sexten For mydsomer quarter	viij s. iiij d.
Item payed to the tyler For tyling of the Churche	viij s.
Item payed to {m} william longe For midsomer quarter	xij d.
Item payed For kareyng of iiij paner pollis^1	iiij d.
Item payed to the geldesmyth For mendyng of the crosse with the selver	ix d.
Item payed For mendyng of the candylsteke that was brokyn in the churche	ij s. vj d.
Item payed for mending of the whele of the grett bell	ij d.
Item payed For bordys to mend the setys	vij d.
Item payed For a staffe For the crosse	j d.
Item payed For makyng of a New sett & mendyng the old setes	ij s.
Item payed the same tyme For Naylis	iiij d.
Item payed For makyng clene of the proshessing way & the setes in the churche	iij d.
Item payed For a loud of Sond	vj d.
Item payed for Coveryng of {kavye} <mays> grave	vj d.

Reparacions

Item payed For tyle pynnes	iiij d.
Item payed For lathes	viij d. ob.
Item payed For lathe Nayle	vij d.
Item payed For vj peny Nayle	j d.
Item payed to a tyler and his man workyng apon longe {l}is house ij dayes	xx d.
Item payed to a tyler For workyng on John Spyser is house iiij dayes and his man	iiij s. iiij d.
Item payed For a C tyle & a quarter	vij d. ob.
Item payed For iij Crestys	iij d.
Item payed For a lode of Erthe	vj d.
Item payed For C of lathes	v d.
Item payed For ij peny Nayle For the Canopy a genst all haloudaye	ob.
Item payed For a Rope a genst all haloudaye weying xlv li. price the li. j d. s[um]ma	iij s. ix d.
Item payed For the Carage of the same	iiij d.
[*p 81*] Item payed for mendyng of the rope of the grett bell when he was barst	iij d.
Item payed For a lode of Sonde	viij d.

1. This was probably intended to be banner poles.

Item payed to Richard Baker For the Canopye & the stoff that gosto hym	ij s. iiij d. ob.
Item payed to longe For mykealmas quarter For his wages	xij d.
Item payed For Covering of ij gravys	xij d.
Item payed to the Regestyr For smoke Farthynges	ij s. vj d. ob.
Item payed For a holly bossche For the churche	ij d.
Item payed For makyng of xxviij[ti] li.[1] of waxe For the rode leygth	xx d.
Item payed For iij li. of talow Candylles for to sett in the churche on Crystmas Daye	iij d. ob.
Item payed For quarter of sence	iij d.

[In the left-hand margin] wages

Item payed to Rychard sexten For halff a yere is wagis	xvj s. viij d.
Item payed to longe For Crystmas quarter is wages	xij d.
Item payed For making clene of the Candylstekes agenst Crystemas	viij d.
Item payed to Trowle For coveryng of a grave	vj d.
Item payed to Trowle For iij dayes & di' workyng uppon the churche werke {iij da} he and his man	ij s. xj d.
Item payed For a mantyll For the tenement in the markett place	xvj d.
Item payed For Nayles lathes & pynnes the same tyme	vij d. ob.
Item payed at the same tyme For iiij[xx] & vj of tyle[2]	v d. ob.
Item payed For hewyng & pargettyng off the syde awter	xiij d.
Item payed For Whyte lymyng of the Churche	vij s. viij d.
Item payed For a bz of glover sherdes	iij d.
Item payed For woode & besomys	ij d.
Item payed For ix bz of lyme pric	xviij d.
Item payed For mendyng of a locke of the churche & the key	viij d.
Item payed to kavy {wyffe Fo} is wyff For the dewty that was betwene the churche & hur husbond	xiij s. iiij d.

[In the left-hand margin] wages

Item payed unto Rychard Walker For a quarter is wages	viij s. iiij d.
Item payed for karyeng Wey of a lode of Doste oute of the churche	ij d.
Item payed unto longe For makyng clene of the churche & swepyng of the dost of the seyntes and breyng owt of the same[3]	viij d.
Item payed unto Alse kerver for setting up of ij settes & mendyng of a sett & for a bord & Nayles[4]	xvj d.

---

1. Superscript 'ti' is used because the number twenty-eight was pronounced 'eight and twenty'.
2. Superscript 'xx' indicates twenty, a score, hence the total is four score and six or eighty-six.
3. 'Seynts' refers to statues of the saints which had been cleaned.
4. Alse is probably a surname and 'kerver' (carver) his craft.

Item payed for a quart of weyn for the syngers on palme sondaye that songe the paschesyon	iiij d.
Item payed for kepyng of a meynd For all the benefactors of the churche of seynt laurence	iij s. v d.
Item payed a serpeles for kockes	vj s. vj d.
Item payed for the makyng of xiiij li. of wax for the paskall & the Fonte tapyr	vj d.

S[um]ma viij li. v s. vj d.

Idem comput' in alloc' redd' of a tenement in New strete the whiche late John Spyser held[1]	v s.
Item also For a tenement in the markett place that Thomas Taylor dwellyth yn	x d.
Item payed For the wassheyng of the Churche gere	iij s. iiij d.
Item payed For settyng on of the Albys and sowyng of the same for a hole yere	viij d.
Item payed For makyng of this a cowmpte	ij s.

S[um]ma xj s. x d.

[p 82]   S[um]ma Alloc' et Soluc' viij li. xvij s. iiij d.

And so remayneth of this a cowmpte to the Churche
C xvij s. ij d. ob.

And then was dysmyssid Rychard a man And in his Rome
was chosen John Skynner

[*The rest of this page is blank.*]

---

1. *Idem comput' in alloc' redd'* meaning 'also they calculate in allowance for rent'. The first two entries are for rents not received and the next three for extra payments made, a total of 11s 10d. The words, *alloc'* (allowed) and *soluc'* (paid) explain the final amount to be deducted from income.

1510-11

[*p 83*] **Comptus of Rychard Tourner and John Skynner proctours off the chyrche of Seynt Laurence in Redyng fro the Feest off thannuncyacion off our lady unto the Same Fest off thannuncyacion then next folowyng in the yer off our lord god M^l CCCCC xj**

Receytes

In primis Receyvyd off Rychard Aman as it apperythe in the fote of his accompte	v li. xviij s. ij d.
Item Receyvyd toward the making of the lent clothes made for the hygh awter	xxiij d.
Item Receyvyd at ester for the pascall	xlj s. v d.
Item Receyvyd on hocke Monday gaderyd by the wyves cler	xxij s. iiij d.
Item Receyvyd on hocke tewisday gaderyd by the men	x s. viij d.
Item Receyvyd on Seynt phylypp & Jacobes day for ij° stondynges at the chirch porch	vij d.
Item Receyvyd at the fest of all Seyntes for the roode lyght	xiij s. vj d.
Item Receyvyd at the fest of Crystmas for the rode lyght	xiiij s. vj d.
Item Receyvyd of the bequest of maistres Justis[1]	iij s. iiij d.
Item Receyvyd gatheryng for the Sextons wages of the paryssh	xxv s. viij d.

S[um]ma xij li. xj s. j d. ob.
[This is in a different ink and was inserted in front of the next entry.]

Receytes of the Rentes

Item Receyvyd off John Sponer for a tenement in the new stret for a yer	x s. <for iij quarter ix s.>
Item Rec' of John Carpenter for a tenement in the new strete	xij s.
Item Rec' of william long for a tenement in the new strete	xij s.
Item Rec' of John Page for a tenement in the new strete	vj s. viij d.
Item Rec' of the good wife hart for a quyte rent	xij d.
Item Rec' of woodrof is wife for a tenement in the mercat place	x s.
Item Rec' of John Halve for a stabull & a gardyne in the {sta} gutter lane	vij s.
Item Rec' of william Hunt Joynor for a quyte rent of a tenement in the hygh stret	xiij d. ob.
Item Rec' of John wilder for half an acre of mede lying in langley	xiij d.

---

1. No burial in the parish is recorded for Maistres Justice nor has her will been traced.

Item Rec' of Thomas everod for a gardeyn plot lying in the gutter lane	iiij d.
Item Rec' of Thomas Sowthe for ij° gardeyn plottes lying in luckmere lane for half a yere endyd at {mykelmas}<our lady day in lent>	ix d.
Item rec' of thomas Sowthe for {a hole yere {rest} <rent>} <haff yere at michalmasse> of the seyd gardeyns	{xviij d.} <ix d.>
Item rec' for the old canapye clothe without the crownes	iiij s. iiij d.

{S[um]ma iij li. vij s. ix d. ob.}
<S[um]ma iij li. iiij s. ob.>

[*p 84*] gravys the greate bell & the wast of torchis	
Item Rec' for the grave of nycholas ward[1] servant with the kyng {with the kyng}	vj s. viij d.
Item Rec' for Coveryng of the Same grave & for wast of torchis ther	xij d.
Item Rec' for the grave of Raufe mylyngton & for the Coveryng of the Same[2]	vij s. iiij d.
Item for wast of Torchys	viij d.
Item Rec' for the great bell at hys beryng & duryng the monethe and at the moneth mynde	v s. iiij d.
Item Rec' for the grave of william Cobbe & for the greate bell	viij s. viij d.
Item Rec' for the wast of torchys of John Semper at his wyfs berying	iiij d.
Item Rec' of Harry wylcox for Wast of tourchis	iiij d.
Item Rec' for the <greate> bell at hasylwodes mynd	xij d.
Item Rec' for the grave of rawlyns wyfe & for the Coveryng	vij s. ij d.
Item Rec' for the grave of the wyffe of John Tournor baker & Coveryng	vij s. ij d.
Item Rec' for the grave of Harry wylcox & for the Coveryng of the same	vij s. ij d.
Item Rec' for the great bell at the berying of the seyd John tournors wyfe & at her moneth mynd	ij s.
Item Rec' for the grave of Irelond's wyfe & for the Coveryng of the same	vij s. ij d.
Item for the greate bell ther	xij d.
Item Rec' for wast of torchis of the seyd Irelond	[*blank*]
Item Rec' for the grave of Sharpes wyfe & for the Coveryng of the same	vij s. ij d.

1. Nicholas Ward held several offices in the royal household including that of purveyor of various provisions. *Calendar of Patent Rolls Henry VII 1494-1509*, 203, 224, 288, 408.
2. Rauf or Ralph Mylyngton was one of the ten members of the gild of the Mass of Jesus named in Henry Kelsall's will 1493. His will was proved 24 August 1510. Kerry, *A History*, 169; TNA Will of Ralph Mylyngton, 1510, PROB11/16/30.

Item Rec' for the greate bell at the berying	xij d.
Item Rec' for lyme Solder to bryce	xxiij d.

S[um]ma iij li. xiiij s. j d.

Seates

Item Rec' of william Veld for a seate for hymself under the clock hows[1]	iiij d.
Item Rec' of Robert grene for his wifes seat	vj d.
Item Rec' of Sampson shomaker for his wyfes seat	vj d.
Item Rec' of whelar for his wyfes seate	vj d.
Item Rec' of John Twytt for his wyfes seate	vj d.
Item Rec' of William kene for his wyfes seate	vj d.
Item Rec' of maxfeld for his wyfes seate	vj d.
Item Rec' of George woddos for his wyfes seate	vj d.
Item Rec' of holyer for his wiffes seate	vj d.

S[um]ma iiij s. viij d.

Item Rec' of the gatheryng of Robyn hoode & all Costes alowyd	viij li. ij s. v d.
Item Rec' of Sir John tendall in money found in the church	ij d.

S[umma] viij li. ij s. vij d.

S[um]ma totalis xxvij li. xv s. vj d.

[p 85] Expenses	
Item payd for the lent Clothe made for the hygh awter	iiij s. iiij d.
Item payd for watchyng of the Sepulcre	viij d.
Item payd for a li. of Sence	x d.
Item payd for takkes for the Sepulcre ij boushelles of coles & for ale	iiij d.
Item payd for an awbe for a Chylde	xiiij d.
Item payd for tapys <for> Childernes amys	j d.
Item payd for Settyng on parours on the Childernes albis for a hole yere	viij d.
Item payd for a Surplyce for the Sexten that now Thomas werythe	vj s.
Item payd for nayles	ij d.
Item payd for Caryage of bourdes from the chirche on ester Monday	j d.
Item payd for clensyng of the Imagererye of the rode lofte at the request of the parisshe	ij s. viij d.

---

1.   This is a very unusual example of a man purchasing a seat.

Item payd to a taberer on may day	iij d.
Item payd to Cone for selyng & dressyng of the awter be Mr mayers set	ij s. iiij d.
Item payd to harry hawthorne for sawyng of waynscotes for the same awter	vj d.
Item payd for whytt lether & for repayryng of the bawdrykes to the v belles	iij s. iiij d.
Item payd to Rychard Cavye for shotyng of the iiijth bell clapper	xviij d.
Item payd for caryage of iij lode of dust from the Chyrche	vj d.
Item payd to Harry hawthorne for removyng and repayryng of iiij seates be fore our ladye awter for nayles bourdes & grownde pynnyng to the same seates	iij s. x d.
Item payd for wasshyng of the ornamentes of the Chyrche for a hole yere	iij s. iiij d.
Item payd for makyng clen of the candstickes & the basyn that the pascall stondythe in	x d.
Item payd for a M^{li} & di' of tyles	vij s. vj d.
Item payd for vij quarter v bowshelles of stone lyme	viij s. ix d.
Item I have alowed John Haw for a grownd syll leyd in hys stabull	viij d.
[*The cost of this item is included with the next*]	
Item payd for correctyng & byndyng of a grayle also for byndyng of a pystyll boke	
Item for settyng in queyrys in to an antyphoner and for claspis & pynnys for the seyd bokes at the request of the parysshe	xxij s.
Item payd for mendyng of iij° bell ropes	vj d.
Item payd to Troll & hys man for vj dayes tylyng, and for latthes & nayles over the new selyng	vj s.
Item payd to the Clocke maker for reparacion done to the Clocke first and last at the request of the paryssche	xxvj s. x d.
Item payd to John roye for reparacion done to the gutter <for a whole yere>	ij s.
Item payd for pavyng of viij gravys as it apperyth by ther names before rehersyd	ij s. viij d.
[*p 86*] Item payd for Coveryng & dressyng of the ij° stoles for the rectors	xix d.
Item payd for {C} Repayryng of the wall of the chirche yerd for sendstone bryckes & werkmanshypp	ij s. iiij d.
Item payd long for mowyng & makyng clene of the chirche yerd	vj d.
Item payd for mendynge of the greate orgaunce	xx d.
Item payd to <the> regester for smoke farthynges	iij s. vj d. ob.
Item payd for a rope for the greate bell	iij s. iiij d.

Item payd for {rome} renewyng of the rode lyght a genst Haloutyde	iiij s. iij d.
Item payd for a li. of syses	viij d.
Item payd for trussyng of the ij^d bell to hasylwoodes man	xij d.
Item payd to hughe Smyth for mendyng of the greate bell whele	vj d.
Item payd for Renewyng & dying of the Cope with whyt rosys	iij s. iiij d.
Item payd for dying & repayryng of an old Cope with yelow orpherus of saten of brydgis, with v yerdes & iij quarters of bokram for lynyng of the same Cope, thred rebend & the makyng of the same Cope	ix s. x d.
Item payd for mendyng of a Syrplyce	iiij d.
Item payd for Renewyng of the vj tapers in the rode on the north syde vj li. di' off Wax at vij d. a li. / A li. of Sysis for the makes of the same wax	v s. ij d. ob.
Item payd for iij li. of Talow candyls set in the roode lofte at crystmas	iij d.
Item payd for a quarter of sens	ij d. ob.
Item payd for a lode of sond	vj d.
Item payd for a bourd to be occupyed in the Chyrche	iij d.
Item payd for the obijt for the benefactours	iiij s. iiij d.
Item payd to a tyler & his man for ij dayes tylyng uppon longhows & for sond	xviij d.
Item payd to water Smythe for ij latchis of Iron for woodrofe hows	iiij d.
Item payd for a locke to the same hows	iiij d.
Item payd for skowryng of the Canstykes to long a genst Crystmas	{vj d.} <viij d.>
Item payd for Wrytyng of this Accompte	ij s.
Item payd to barkbye uppon a bargen of a peyr of orgaunce at the Instaunce of the parisshe at ij° tymes	iiij li.
Item payd for makyng of the pascall & the font taper & for iij li. of Wax for the same	ij s. vij d.
[p 87] Item payd to Rychard walker sexten for his whole yeres wages	liiij s. iiij d.
Item payed to Roberd that ran away the Syngar for {a} helpyng of the quyre for almost half a yer	iiij s. iiij d.
Item payd to lawardes wyfe for his bourd	xiiij d.
Item payd to long for his hole yeres wages iiij s. Item for mendyng of his wages	xij d. Summa v s.
Item [blank]	

S[um]ma xv li. iiij s. ij d. ob.

S[um]ma alocat' & solut' xv li. iiijs. ij d. ob. & remayneth of
thys accompte to the churche xij li. xj s. iij d. ob. & then
was dysmyssed Ric' Tornour & in hys Rowme ys chosen
{Ryc' Johnson} Symon lambe

1511-12
[*p 88*] **Compotus of John Rede al[ia]s Skynner &
Symond Lambe proctors of the church of Saynt
Laurence in Redyng fro the Fest of thAnnunciacion of
our lady unto the same Fest of thAnnunciacion of our
lady then next ensewing In the yere of our lord god
.1.5.12. /**

Inprimis the seid proctors have receyvid as it apperith in the fote of the last Accompte	xij li. xj s. iij d. ob.
It' rec' at ester for the Pascall	xl s. xj d.
It' rec' of Thomas Slythurst in ernyst for the ij° gardens in lurkemer lane	j d.
It' rec' for lyme	iiij d.
It' rec' for torchis at the burying of William Irelands wife	iiij d.
It' rec' in money garderid on Saynt Philipp & Jacob day	v s. v d.
It' rec' in money at hok tyde gaderid on the menys parte	x s.
It' rec' of Mr Cleche toward the new organs	vj s. viij d.
It' rec' of Mr White towards the same organs	xx s.
It' rec' in money at the play of kayne[1]	x s. vj d.
It' rec' for bryk & morter left at the makyng of the vowte & for the belys of the organs	xxj d.
It' rec' at All halowyn tyde for the rode lyghte	xiij s. vj d.
It' rec' at Cristmas for the rode lyght	xv s. j d.
It' rec' of certayn men to the augmentacion of the Sextens wages	xix s. ij d.

S[um]ma xix li. xv s. ob.

For the grete bell & gravis

It' rec' for the grave of John Pastler	vj s. viij d.
It' rec' for the grete bell at the monyth mynde of John Semper	xij d.
It' rec' for the grave of John Turner & for coveryng of the same	vij s. iiij d.
It' rec' for the grete bell at the burying of the same John & at the monyth mynde	ij s.

S[um]ma xvij s.

1. Probably a play about the killing of Abel by his brother, Cain.

For Seates

It' rec' of Nicolas Bocher for his wifes seate	vj d.
It' rec' of Thomas Bukland Skynner for his wifes seate	vj d.
It' rec' of Jamys Blewet for his wifes seate	vj d.
It' rec' of John Grene for his wifes seate	vj d.
It' rec' of Raphe Brown Fuller for his wifes seate	vj d.
It' rec' of William Taylor for his wifes seate	vj d.
It' rec' of John Grene for his wyfes seate	vj d.

S[um]ma iij s. vj d.

Receytes of rentes

Item Receyvid of William Carpenter for a tenement in the south [p 89] parte of the new strete for a yere	xij s.
It' Rec' of William Paslow for a tenement on the market place for a yere	x s.
It' Rec' of John Sponer for a tenement in the north parte of the new strete for a yere	x s.
It' Rec' of Thomas Myrthe for a stable & a garden in gutter lane for a yere	vij s.
It' Rec' of John Page for a tenement in the north parte of the new strete for a yere	vj s. viij d.
It' Rec' of William Long for a tenement in the south parte of the same strete for a yere	xij s.
It' Rec' of Thomas Everard for a garden plote in gutter lane for a yere	iiij d.
It' Rec' of Thomas South for ij° gardens in the south parte of lurkmer lane for a yere	xxj d. ob.
It' Rec' of Isabell Harte for quyte rent for the tenement that she dwellith in	xij d.
It' Rec' of William Huntes wyfe Joyner for quyte rent of a tenement that she inhabitith in the north parte of the hye strete for a yere	xiij d. ob.
It' Rec' of John Wylder of the Thele for half an acre mede lying in langley for a yer	xiij d.

S[um]ma iij li. iij s.

S[um]ma tot[al]es de omnibus Receptes xxiij li. xviij s.
<vj d.> ob.

Expenses

Inprimis payed to Harry Horethorn for carying a way of the swepyng of the church	j d.
It' payed for ij° busshelles of colys & drynke & naylis to the sepulcre	iiij d.
It' payed for wachchyng of the Sepulcre	viij d.
It' payed for a li. of frankensens	xij d.
It' payed for staplis and nayles for to set in the banner polys	vj d. ob.
It' payed for lyvereys to John knyght	v d.
It' payed for a rope to the iiij[th] bell	xiiij d.
It' payed to Hew Davas Smyth for mendyng of the best cros	viij d.
It' payed for an hors hyde to make bawdrykkes	xviij d.
It' payed for makyng of ij° bawdryckes to the grete bell & to the iiij[th] bell	xvj d.
It' payed to Water Barton to the new Sepulcur[1]	iiij li. xiij s. x d.
It' paied to Robert Barkbe Organ maker	xiij s. iiij d.
It' paied to William kene for iij° waynscottes	iij s.
It' payed to Mr white for waynscott that he bought to the new organs	xxxj s.
It' payed to Ric' Turner for such stuf as he delivered to the same organs	xv s. x d.
It' payed for currying of the leder to the belys of the same organs	ij s. ij d.
It' paied to Ric' Turner & John kent for the organ maker at one tyme	xxxj s. vj d.
It' payed for vj Waynscottes at london	xiiij s.
It' payed for carying of the same Waynscottes	xvj d.
It' payed to Ric' Turner & John kent for the organ maker at a nother tyme	l s.[2]
It' paied to Thomas Everard for Robert Barkbe	vj s. viij d.
It' paied to Ric' Turner at a nother tyme for the same Robert	xx s.
[p 90] Item payed to Robert Barkbe Organ maker before Mr Clecke	xiij s. iiij d.
It' payed for led to ley upon the {organs} belis of the organs	xj s. iiij d.
It' payed for a shepeskyn to mend the belis of the old organs & for a li. of glew	vij d.
It' payed for a lode of sand	vj d.
It' paied for a man and an horse to send for the clok maker	viij d.
It' paied to Robert Slan for wasting of the Taylors torchis on Corpus Ch[risti] day	iij d.
It' paied for ij lodes of sand	xiiij d.

1. For more information about Walter Barton see Appendix 2. This was the Easter Sepulchre, obviously lavishly built in view of the high cost of construction. The purchase of glue (below) indicates that it was wooden. Its building or rebuilding may have been necessitated by the building of a new organ.
2. This is fifty shillings in Roman numerals.

It' payed for a rydder & for naylis	j d. ob.
It' paied to a fre mason that shuld have made the arch for the belis of the new organs for iiij dayes & an di' / by the day vj d. S[um]ma	ij s. iij d.
It' payed to a laborer for the same arche for v dayes & an di'/ by the day v d. S[um]ma	ij s. iij d.
It' payed to Nicolas Hyde for latthis & nayles to the same Warke	ix d.
It' payed for a M^l & an di' of bryk to the same Warke	vij s. vj d.
It' payed for iij^e quarters of lyme for the same Warke	ij s.
It' payed for iij^e C tyle & for ij^o crestes to the same	xix d.
It' payed to Thomas Nycols for making of the same arch & for tyling of the same	viij s.
It' payed to John Roysor for mending of the church gutter	xx d.
It' payed to the Registre for smoke farthynges	iij s. vj d. ob.
It' payed to a Tylor for mending of ij tenementes of the same church	vj d.
It' payed for nayles & a borde to make a lover at the church tenement that John Page holdith	iiij d.
It' payed to Hew Smyth for Iron Warke in the new organ loft	x d.
It' paied for xl^{ti} tylis & a busshell of lyme	iiij d.
It' paied for making of the rode lyght a gayn All Halown tide	xv d.
It' payed for mending of the grete bell rope	j d.
It' paied for carying of <v lodes of> stonys fro the church to the church yerd	x d.
It' paied to a laborer for to bere the same stonys in the church yerd	iiij d.
It' paied to a laborer to breke up the wall to make the arch for iij^o dayes & an di'/ by the day iiij d. S[um]ma	xiiij d.
It' paied for making clene of the setes through the church	ij s. iiij d.
It' payed to William Long <under Sexten> for his yeres wages	v s.
It' payed for the scowring of the Candilstykkes & the pascall bacyn a gayn Ester	x d.
It' payed for scowring of the same agayn Cristmas	viij d.
It' payed to the under Sexten for settyng <to church> & bering home agayn of Sir Thomas antiphonar for di' yer[1]	iiij d.
It' payed for a rope to the lytle bell	xij d.
It' paied for coveryng of John Turners grave & for mending of a nother grave	vij d.
It' payed to Hew Davas Smyth for an yron pyn to the Clok	iij d.

1. Sir Thomas was probably one of the gild chaplains. The vicar was also Thomas Justice but he is usually referred to as Mr Thomas.

It' payed to William long for bering out of the rubell of the gravis aforeseid — j d.

It' payed for a quarter li. of frankensens — iij d.

It' payed for carying a way of ij° loodes of dust out of the church — iiij d.

It' payed for making of {the vj tapers} xiiij li. of old wax in the vj tapers in the Rode loft a gayn Cristmas & for iiij li. of new wax to the same — iij s. iij d.

It' payed to Mr Vicar for a li. of syses agayn All Halowtyde — viij d.

It' payed for iij li. of talow candyl a gayn Cristmas — iij d.

It' payed for the Holy bussh & for a di' a li. of sysis a gayn Cristmas — iiij d.

It' payed to Ric' Walker late sexten for his hole yer wages — liij s. iiij d.

It' payed for a lode of sand & for a lode of erth — xij d.

[p 91] It' payed for xiiij crest tylis — vij d.

It' payed for xliij gutter tylis — xxj d. ob.

It' payed for xvj busshelles of lyme — xvj d.

It' payed for {v} vj C of tyles — iij s.

It' payed to Harry Horethorn for a certayn stuf to the organ loft & for making of the skafold & takyng downe of the same with ij° evys latthis for the new wyndow for a ladder to the clok & for makyng of the frame for the sepulcre lyght — viij s.

It' payed for latthis naylis & tyle pynnys to the new wyndow — ij s. viij d.

It' payed to Thomas Nicols & his man for tyling & celyng of the new wyndow — iij s. vj d.

It' payed for wasshyng of the church gere — iij s. iiij d.

It' payed for settyng on of the paras on the awbys — viij d.

It' paied for mending of awbys — iiij d.

It' payed for di' a li. of sysis for Mr Vicar — iiij d.

It' payed for Ric' a Woodes costes when he come to se the organs — vij d.

It' payed for having in of {the} <ij°> lodes sand & erth into the church — ij d.

It' payed for the obyt of the benefactors of the church — iiij s. v d.

It' payed for Wryting of this accompte — ij s.

It' payed for carying a way of a lode of dust out of the church — ij d.

It' payed for xiiij li. of wax to the pascall & font taper & the makyng — viij s. ix d.

It' payed for a quarte of malmesy to the clerkes on palme sonday — iiij d.

{S[um]ma to[ta]lis de omnibus expenses}

It' payed for ij li. glew to the sepulcre — v d.

It' payed to William Trew for quyte rent of iij yeres endyd at   x s. vj d.
the Fest of thAnnunciacion of our lady anno iij° henr' octa' of
the tenementes of the church {yerely} by the yere iij s.
vj d. S[um]ma

  S[um]ma to[ta]lis de omnibus expenses xxiij li. xvjs. xj d.

          And so remayneth clerely xix d. ob.

And then hath byn dismyssid John Skynner & in his rome
was chosyn Richard Barnys

1512-13

[*p 92*] **Comptus of Simon Lambe and Richard Barons
Proctors of the church of Saynt Laurens in Redyng fro
the Fest of thannunciacion of our lady unto the same
Fest of thannunciacion then next folowing In the yere of
our lord god .1.5.13.**

In primis the seid Proctors have receyvid of as it apperith in   xix d. ob.
the fote of the last a Compte
It' rec' at Ester for the Paschall   xlij s.
It' rec' of money gaderid at hocktyd of the mennys parte   x s. j d. ob.
It' rec' of money gaderid at the same hocktyde of the   xxxj s. j d.
wymens parte
It' rec' of money gaderid at witsontyde of the kyng play   iij li. viij s.
remaynyng in the handes of Thomas Carpenter   viij d.
It' rec' of Hew Davas for ij quysshons of the bequest of Jone   xij d.
Jeffrey[1]
It' rec' for the rode lyght at Alhalowyn tyde   xiij s. ij d. ob.
It' rec' for the rode lyght at Crystmas   xiiij s. vij d.
It' rec' of John Punsar Warden of the Masse of Jh[es]u   xxxiij s.
toward the wages of Harry Waters Sexton for a yere endyd   iiij d.
at Crystmas
It' rec' of William Edmond Warden of our lady masse   xxxiij s.
toward the wages of the seid Sexton for a yere endid at the   iiij d.
seid Fest

     S[um]ma {xij li. ij d. ob} <xij li. viij s. xj d.ob.>

---

1. A will of Jone Jeffrey has not been found. The cushions may have been a life-time gift or, if
she died as a married woman, one made in the absence of a will.

For the grete bell & graves

It' rec' for the grete bell at the buryeing of John Andrews wyfe	xij d.
It' rec' for the grave & the coverynge of the same	vij s. ij d.
It' rec' of Richard Turner for the grete bell at his Faders yeres mynde	xij d.

S[um]ma ix s. ij d.

For Seates

It' rec' of Robert Elwold for his wyfes sete	vj d.
It' rec' of Thomas Bryce for his wifes sete	vj d.
It' rec' of Nicholas Browne for his wifes sete	vj d.
It' rec' of William Benaham for his wifes sete	vj d.
It' rec' of William Hoper for his wifes sete	iiij d.
It' rec' of John Jonson my lordes underporter for his wifes sete	vj d.
It' rec' of Christofer Spakeman for his wyfes sete	vj d.
It' rec' of John White for his wifes sete	vj d.
It' rec' of Robert lenthall for his wifes sete	vj d.
It' rec' of Henry lewse for his wifes sete	vj d.
It' rec' of John Andrew for <his> wifes sete	vj d.

S[um]ma vs. iiij d.

For rentes

It' Rec' of William Carpenter for a tenement in the south side of the New strete for a yer	xij s.
It' rec' of Roberte Cokcetor for a tenement in the north syde of the same strete for a yere	x s.
[p 93] It' rec' of Thomas Dodson for a tenement on the same syde of the strete late in the hold of John Page by the yer	vj s. viij d.
It' rec' of William longe for a tenement in the {north} south side of the same strete by the yer	xij s.
It' rec' of Thomas Myrthe for a stable in gutter lane by the yer	vij s.
It' rec' of Thomas Everard for a garden plot in the same lane by the yere	iiij d.
It' rec' of Thomas Slythurst for ij° gardens in the south side of Lurkmer mane[1] by the yer	ij s. viij d.
It' rec' of William Hunt of the hye strete Joyner for the quyte rent of the tenement that he inhabitith in by the yere	xiij d. ob.

---

1. This is a mistake. It should be 'lane'.

It' rec' of Isabell Harte for the quyte rent of the tenement of William Justice that she inhabitith in in the market place by the yere	xij d.
It' rec' of William Paslow for a tenement on the est syde of the market place by the yer	x s.
It' rec' of John Wylder of the Thele for half an acre of mede lying in langley by the yer	xiij d.

S[um]ma iij li. iij s. x d. ob.

{S[um]ma de omnibus receptes xj li. xvij s. vij d.} <xij li.>
S[um]ma de omnibus rec' xvj li. vij s. iiij d.

<Unde super Thomas Carpenter iij li. vj s. viij d. {& super
Ric' Turner xxj s. j d.} & super Robertus Lentall ij s.
S[um]ma iiij li. ix s. ix d. Et sic clare in manibus
Competentes xj li. xvij s. vij d.>[1]

Expenses

In primis payed for nayles to the Font & to the Sepulcre	{ij d.} ij d.
It' payed for the skowring of the pascall bason & the candylstykkes in the quere	x d.
It' payed for ij bushelles of colys on ester eve to make the halowid fyere	ij d.
It' payed for wachyng of the Sepulcre	viij d.
It' payed for mendyng of the grete bell whele	ij d.
It' payed for ale at the makyng of thaccompte un on[2] good fryday	j d.
It' payed to Harry water Sexten for a quarter wages of his salary at thAnnunciacion of our lady	xxvj s. viij d.
It' payed for mendyng of a bawdryk to the second bell	iiij d.
It' payed for tornyng of the claper of the same bell	vj d.
It' payed for a hope for the Joycoint[3] & for ale to the moreys dawncers on the dedicacion day	iij d.

1. This entry was inserted between the original income totals and the heading 'Expenses'. Such changes to the balance were more usually placed at the end of the year's accounts. The churchwardens first stated, then deleted, total receipts as £11 17s 7d, (money actually received less money owed). They inserted £12, still incorrect.They then correctly accounted for £16 7s 4d as itemised in their accounts. To explain the changes they had made, they listed as debits (*super*) money not yet received from three men, in total £4 9s 9d, but deleted Richard Turner's debt of £1 1s 1d. They repeated their original erased total of cash in hand of £11 17s 7d, still incorrect since they had not taken account of having deleted Turner's debt. The total in hand should have been £12 18s 8d.
2. Probably a mistake for 'up on' or a duplication of 'on'.
3. Kerry read 'joycoint' as 'joyaunt' (Kerry, *A History*, 226). This was an entertainer associated with morris dancers. The purchase of a hoop may indicate that he was dressed as a woman with a hoop to hold out his skirts but Kerry's reading would allow the presence of a giant figure.

It' payed for mending of ij ropes to the grete bell & the iij^{de} bell	ij d.
It' payed to the mynstrelles for iiij^{or} dayes	xxij d.
It' payed for lyvereys	xx d.
It' payed for the brekefast at the gadering on the Fayer day	iiij d.
It' payed for ryding to Wynsor to set Mr Wod to se the new organs	x d.
It' payed to the same Master for his costes at his comyng	vij s. x d.
It' payed for a lok to the organ loft dore & for Iron Warke to the same loft	xij d.
It' payed for ij^o lokkes to the same organs viz one for the stoppes & the other for the keyes	xj d.
It' payed to Roberte Barkbe Organ maker for a reward	v s. iij d.

S[um]ma xlix s. viij d.

[p 94] It' payed for a Jemew to the organ loft dore	j d. ob.
It' payed for ij^o yerdes of wyer for the Clok	j d.
It' payed for makyng of the Indenture of the tenement that William Longe holdith	iiij d.
It' payed to Harry Water Sexten for his salary at Mydsomer	xxvj s. viij d.
It' payed to William Glyatt for sand to the church yerd wall	iij s.
It' payed to William Roke for and to the same warke	iij s.
It' payed for xj quarters & iij busschelles of lyme to the same warke	xj s. ix d.
It' payed for xj quarters of tyle sherdes to the same warke	v s. vj d.
It' payed for makyng of the same church yerde wall	xxiij s. ij d.
It' payed to a laborer for viij dayes at the same wall by the day iiij d. S[um]ma	ij s. viij d.
It' payed for half a M^l of tyle	ij s. vj d.
It' payed to a tyler for a daye labor in tyling at the tenement that William long holdith	vj d.
It' payed to the same Tylers man for his labor the same day	iiij d.
It' payed to Thomas Nicollys for mending of the new wyndow before the Organs	iij d.
It' payed to Hew Davas Smyth for yron warke & for making of a Casme[nt] in the same wyndow	ij s. iij d.
It' payed for glasyng of the same wyndow	xviij s.
It' payed to the same Glasyer for sowdering of the gutter	viij d.
It' payed to a Tyler for mending of the cape wyndow in saynt Johns Chauncell	iiij d. ob.
It' payed for ij^o bushelles of lyme	ij d.
It' payed to a plommer for sowdering of the church gutter at a nother tyme	xx d.
It' payed to Hew Smyth for colys to the same	j d.

It' payed to Harry Water Sexten for his Salary at Mychaelmas — xxvj s. viij d.

It' payed to the Officiall for smoke farthynges — iij s. vj d. ob.

It' payed Thomas Quedmanton for mending of the Clok — iiij s.

It' payed to Richard [blank] Clerke in ernyst at entryng of his service — j d.

It' payed for a bell rope — xxj d.

It' payed for a pyn to the candilstyk be fore Mr Cleche[1] — j d.

It' payed for making of a stole of purpell velvet of the gyft of Mr Smyth[2] — viij d.

It' payed for a pownde of sysis at Alhalowtide — viij d.

It' payed for making of the rode light agayn the same tyde — xv d.

It' payed for half a pownde of sysis agayn Crystmas — iiij d.

It' paied for making of the rode light agayn the same tyme — ix d.

It' payed for a quartern of sysis for the holy bow at the same tyme — ij d.

It' payed for iij li. of candyll at the same tyme — iij d.

It' payed to a laborer for paving of the aleys aboute the church yerd — iiij s. viij d.

It' payed for iij lode of erthe — xviij d.

It' payed to Harry Water Sexten for his salary at Cristmas — xxvj s. viij d.

It' payed for vj quarters of lyme — vij s. iiij d.

It' payed for ij crestes & a bushell of lyme — ij d.

It' paied for mending of the gutter — xij d.

It' payed for a pownde & an halfe of ensens for the quere — xxj d.

It' payed for a pece of lyne[3] — iiij d.

It' payed for girdylles for awbys & for curteyn ringes — iiij d.

It' payed for nayles & rak hokes — xj d.

It' payed for making clene of the church gutter — iiij d.

S[um]ma ix li. viij s. iij d. ob.

[p95] It' payed to Harry Horethorn for a daye & an halfe warking in the organ loft — viij d.

It' payed for a punchon of viij fote longe fyve ynchis brode & iiij ynchys thyck — vj d.

It' payed for xxx fote of borde — x d.

It' payed for a ladder — vj d.

It' paied for an horse hyde — xxij d.

It' payed for turnyng of the claper of the iiij[th] bell — vj d.

1. The meaning is unclear. Richard Cleche, draper, was four times Warden of the Gild Merchant or Mayor between 1487 and 1506, a member of the Mass of Jesus gild in 1493 and donor of plate to the parish. He was buried in 1525-6 but not in the church. See accounts page 160.

2. For more on Richard Smyth see Appendix 2.

3. This was probably linen.

It' paied for yre warke to the gate	ij d.
It' payed for a claps to the cofers in the rode loft	iij d.
It' payed for a barell for to cary water & lyme to the making of the church yerd wall	v d.
It' payed for yre warke to make fast the wyndows of the organs	j d.
It' payed for ij bawdryckes to ij° bells	viij d.
It' payed for a bawdryk to the grete bell	vj d.
It' payed for a pyn to the bawdryk of the iiijth bell	j d.
It' payed for wyne to the clarkes on palme sonday	iiij d.
It' payed to William longe {for} Under Sexten for his yeres wages	v s.
It' paied for keping of thobite for the benefactors of the church	iij s. vj d.
It' payed to Harry Water Sexten for setting on of the paras of the childern awbys v tymes	xv d.
It' paied to the same Harry for setting on of <the paras of> iiij Awbys for the pristes	ij d.
It' payed for mending of a surplice	viij d.
It' payed for the mending of ij Copys	ij d.
It' payed for reborde to one of the Copys	j d.
It' payed for pynnys to pyn <on> the awter clothis	j d. ob.
It' payed for for setting on of a frontell upon an Awter cloth & iiij^{or} Amys	ob.
It' payed for mendyng of the vayle cloth in the quere for lent	ij d.
It' payed for settyng up of the frame for the sepulcre lyght	iiij d.
It' payed for carying away of j lode of muk out of the church	ij d.
It' payed for making of xiiij li. wex to the pascall & the fonte taper	vij d.
It' payed to William Trew for quyte rent of the tenementes of the church for a yer endyd at our lady day thAnnunciacion	iij s. vj d.
It' payed for writing of the accompte	ij s.
It' payed for making clene of the grete candylstykkes agayn Cristmas	viij d.
It' payed for bering of Sir Thomas grete antiphoner to & fro the church at all dyvyne service to William Longe for the yer	viij d.
It' payed for a quartern {of} & viij li. of wex bought at London	xv s.

It' payed for an holy bussh agayn Chrismas	ij d.
It' payed for wasshyng of the Churche gere	iij s. iiij d.

S[um]ma {xlj s. vij d.} xliiij s. xj d.

S[um]ma to[ta]lis xiiij li. {ij d.} iiij s. vj d.

Et sic habet in Superplug' {xlij s. vij d.} xlv s. xj d.[1]

Dismissus est ab officio procurator Simon Lambe & in loco suo electus est Rogerus Bryce

1513-14
[p96] Comptus off Richard Barnys and Roger Bryce Proctors off the Church off Seynt Laurens in Redyng from the Fest off thannunciacion off oure ladye in the yere off oure lord. M. CCCCC xiiji unto the Same Fest off our ladye next Comyng 1514[2]

[In a different hand] Anno v° H viij

In primis the seid proctures have Receyvyd att Ester for the pascall	xl s. viij d.
It' Rec' off the wyfes For the gatheryng at hocktyde	xxix s. viij d.
It' Rec' off the men For the gatheryng at hocktyde	vij s.
It' Rec' off Richard Turnor for ij° lode of flyntes	xij s.
It' Rec' off John Kentes wyfe that was found in the Church	j d.
It' Rec' off the yong men For ther gatheryng at Wytsontyde	x s. xj d.
It' Rec' for the Tree that stode in the mercat place	iiij d.
It' Rec' of Sir John Tendall & off Roger Bryce that was found in the Church	j d. ob.
It' Rec' of John Appowell in yernest for the stabull in the gutter lane	j d.
It' Rec' For the Roode light {At hr} <on> all halou day	x s. xj d. ob.
It' Rec' For the Roode light on Crystmas day	x s. vj d.
It' Rec' off Master Carpenter for a C of Bryckes	vj d.
It' Rec' off Master Barton for a C & di' of Bryckes	ix d.
It' Rec' off Richard Turnor for di' of C of Bryckes	iij d.
It' Rec' off John Barfote for ij C off Bryckes	xij d.
It' Rec' off Nicholas hyde warden off the masse of {joh}	xxxiij s.

1. The word *superplus* or *surplusagium* means excess of expenditure over income i.e. deficit. The correct amount the churchwardens were in deficit was only £1 14s 10d since they had underestimated their income. See above.

2. The writer originally put the starting date as MCCCCCxiij (1513) but then added another 'i' making the date 1514 which was incorrect. The end-date of 1514 in the right-hand margin is correct.

Jh[es]u toward the Sextens Wages For a yere Endyd at Crystmas	iiij d.
It' Rec' off John Barfote warden off the masse off our lady toward the Sextens wages For a yere endyd the same Fest	xxxiij s. iiij d.

S[um]ma ix li. vj d.

For Rentes dew at myhelmas anno quinto R[egni] Regis H viij

It' Rec' off Robert Cokseter For a tenement in the north syde of the new Strete for a yere	x s.
It' Rec' off Wylliam Carpenter for a tenement in the south syde off the same strete for a yer	xij s.
It' Rec' off Willyam Long for a tenement in the same syde off the strete by the yer	xij s.
It' Rec' off Thomas Dodson for a tenement in the north syde of the same strete for a yer	vj s. viij d.
It' Rec' off Thomas Raynold For a stabull in the gutter lane for a yere	vij s.
It' Rec' off Thomas Everard For a gardeyn plott in the same lane for a yere	iiij d.
It' Rec' off Thomas Slythurst for ij° gardeyns in the south syde off the luckmer lane by yer	ij s. viij d.
It' Rec' off William Hunt Joyner for quyte Rent of the howes that he inhabitith in the hygh strete per annum	xiij d. ob.
It' Rec' off Isabel Hart for the quyte Rent of the tenement off William Justice that she inhabitith in yn the mercat place by the yere	xij d.
It' Rec' off Roger Johnson Coryar[1] for a ten[emen]t in the Est syde of the mercat place by the yer	x s.
It' Rec' off John Wylder off the Thele for a di' an acre of mede lying by langney by yer	xiij d.

S[um]ma iij li. iij s. xd. ob.

[p 97] For the grete bell & gravys	
It' Rec' For the grete bell at the berying of Alysaunder Wyld	xij d.
It' Rec' at the month mynd of the same alysaunder	xij d.
It' Rec' For the great bell of Richard Turnor for his fathers mynd	xij d.

S[um]ma iij s.

---

1. A coryar or currier dressed leather.

For Seates

It' Rec' off John a gate For hys wyffes seate	vj d.
It' Rec' off John Whelar For hys wyffes seate	vj d.
It' Rec' off Olyver grete For hys wyffes seate	vj d.
It' Rec' of John Johnson For hys moder & hys wyfes seates	xij d.
It' Rec' of Richard Saunder For hys wyffes seate	vj d.

S[um]ma ij s. viij d.[1]

S[um]ma de omnibus receptis xij li. x s. ob.

Expenses

In primis payd For nayles to the Sepulcre & to the Font	ij d.
It' payd For Whypp Cordes to hang the Sepulcre Cloth with the Curteyns	j d.
It' payd to harry horthorne for ij peces to hang the sepulcre cloth on	ij d.
It' payd to Nicholas hyde for ij° bushelles of Colys to make the halowyd fyre on Ester yeve	ij d.
It' payd for watchyng of the Sepulcre	viij d.
It' payd for a li. of Encence	xij d.
It' payd for mendyng of the {Canapye} Frame for the Canapye to hugh Smyth	j d.
It' payd for mendyng of the lockes off the greate Cofer {that} brought from Master Clechis	j d.
It' payd to Symon lombe for the dettes of the Church	xlv s. xj d.
It' payd to a mynstrell on our dedicacion day	v d.
It' payd for ij quarter of stone lyme	ij s. iiij d.
It' payd for a Surplyce for the paryssh prest	vij s. iiij d.
It' payd for mendyng of the style in the church yard	iiij d.
It' payd for mendyng of the grete bell whele & for makyng the scaffold before the Roode	vj d.
It' payd to Suffringan to make upp his payment	x d. ob.
It' payd to Nicholas hyde for nayles to the vestre	v d.
It' payd for iiij lode of sond	ij s.
It' payd for ij C of Bryckes	xij d.
It' payd to Thomas Nicols & hys Felow with ther servants for iij deyes & di' in making hygh awter & pavyng	v s. v d.
It' payd for mendyng off a Surplyce	j d. ob.
It' payd to hugh Smyth for Clammys to the vestre of Iron	v d.
It' payd for ij° quarter & di' of {lyme} stone lyme	ij s. ix d.

1. The total should be 3s and the total income £12 10s 4½d.

It' payd to Robert Hawtrell for Removyng of the front of the hygh auter & settyng upp of the same in Seynt Johns Chauncell & for traunslasyng[1] of setes ther	xiiij s.
It' payd to Rychard Turner toward the white auter Clothis over & besyde as it is knowen to the paryssh	x s. ij d.
[p 98] It' payd Hugh Smyth for a key & a {locke} stapull to the locke on the procession dore	ij d.
It' payd to a laborer for iiij dayes at Removyng of the hygh awter & seynt Johns awter	xvj d.
It' payd to William More of Caversham for di' a M[l] off Bryckes	ij s. vj d.
It' payd for ij li. of Sowder & for mendyng of the gutter	xiij d.
It' payd to Troll for makyng of Seynt Johns awter	xvj d.
It' payd for a kyltherkyn of bere a genst wytsontyde	xvj d.
It' payd for a dosen of good ale & iij galans of peny ale to Richard Turner	xx d.
It' payd for Cariage of the tre at Witsontyde	vj d.
It' payd for makyng of the font taper that was broken	j d.
It' payd for mendyng of the grete bell whele	iiij d.
It' payd for ij° Skynnes of parchment for wrytyng of the fest of Jh[es]u	v d.
It' payd to ij° Carpenters for makyng of a pale at the stabull in the gutter lane for iiij daies	iiij d.
It' payd to Richard yeve for a post & a pece to make Rayles to the same pale	iiij d.
It' for ij° postes for the same pale	vj d.
It' payd for a C of nayles for the same pale	vj d.
It' payd for a Rope for the Clocke weyng xvij li. di'	ij s. ij d.
It' payd for mendyng of the Cape wyndow in seynt Johns Chancell & mendyng of the gutter	xij d.
[A pointing finger in the margin by the next two entries]	
It' payd for a galon of ale for the Ryngers at the gettyng of Turwyn[2]	ij d.
It' payd for a galon of ale for the Ryngers at the deth of the kyng of Scottes	ij d.
It' payd for a lytle Rope for the watch of the Clocke wayng viij li.	xij d.
It' payd for a Rope for the iiij[th] bell waying xv li.	xxj d.
It' payd for a Rope for the iij[de] bell waying xij li.	xviij d.
It' payd for smoke farthynges to the officiall	iij s. vj d. ob.
It' payd for mendyng of the gutter of the tenement in the mercat place in the which roger Coryar dwellith	ij s. viij d.

1. Moving.
2. This refers to the taking of Tournai by Henry VIII's army in 1513. The entry below refers to the Battle of Flodden in which James IV of Scotland was killed.

It' payd for xx^{ti} fote of bourd for the same gutter	v d.
It' payd for di' a C of lathis & a pecke of tyle pynnes	iiij d.
It' payd for iij C of lath nayles	iiij d. ob.
It' payd for tylyng of the same howse	xj d.
It' payd for mendyng of the bawdryke of the grete bell	viij d.
It' payd for makyng of the bokyll for the same bawdryke & mending of the laten pax	j d. ob.
It' payd for ij C of tyles to John Skynner	xij d.
It' payd to a tyler & hys man for ij° dayes werk uppon the tenement in the gutter lane	xxj d.
It' payd for henges of the dore & mendyng of the locke of the same tenement	iiij d.
It' payd to harry horthorne for an evys bourd to the same hows	ij d.
It' payd to Richard Turner for di' a C of tyles	iij d.
It' payd for a galon of ale to harry horthorne & his men at the havyng the Cofer in to the steple	ij d.
It' payd for di' a li. of frankencence a genst Crystmas	vj d.
It' payd for iij li. of talow Candyll	iij d.
It' payd for a li. of syses a genst Cristmas {to the vycar}	viij d.
It' payd to William Edmondes for makyng a lettre to barkbye	j d.
It' payd for mendyng of a surplice & settyng on the porels of albes	xvj d.
It' payd for wasshyng of the Church gere	iij s. iiij d.
[p 99] It' payd to hugh Smyth For mendyng of the Clocke & for yrons to hang the Curteyns on at high auter	iij d.
It' payd for the Cope Chest <& for caryage of the same Chest>	x s. x d.
It' payd for makyng of the Roode lygh[t] a genst all Haloutyde	xv d.
It' payd for makyng of the Rode lyght a Cristmas	ix d.
It' payd to harry water Sexten for his hole yeres wages endyd at Cristmas	v li. vj s. viij d.
It' payed for making of a bawdrycke for the iij ^{de} bell	vij d.
It' payd to William long for his yeres wages endyd at Cristmas	v s.
It' payd for holy a genst Crystmas	j d.
It' payd for makyng clene of the ij° grete Canstyckes in the quyre	viij d.
It' payd for mendyng of the polley of the Clocke	ij d.
{It payd for a lode of thornes to the tenement that long} dwellyth in	{xij d.}
It' payd for Reparacions done to the same tenement	xiij d.
It' payd for Caryage of Sir Thomas grete boke to & fro the Church	viij d.

It' payd to Mr pouncer for ij C of pament & for cariage of the same pament	iij s. ij d.
It' payd to a laborer for iij dayes & di' at the besynes in brekyng of the awter in seynt Johns Chauncell	xiiij d.
It' payd to Troll & his servantes for iij dayes werk in makyng of the awter in seynt Johns Chauncell with pavyng in bothe Chauncelles & other werkes per	iij s. iiij d.
It' payd for nayles for Closyng up the dore in seynt Johns Chauncell	ob.
It' payd to William Trew for quyte rentes of the tenementes longyng to the Church <endid a mychelmas>	iij s. vj d.
It' payd to Symon Alsey for mendyng of the bere with stuffe to therto belongyng	iij s. iiij d.
It' payd for makyng of iij° stolys & for grene buckeram to lyne them with	xvj d.
It' payd for a quart of basterd for the Clarkes on palme sonday	iiij d.
It' payd for kepyng of the obytt for the benefactoris of the Church	iij s. vj d.
It' payd for makyng Clene of the basyn for the pascall & the ij grete Candstykes in the quere a genst Ester	x d.
It' payd for a polley to hang the pascall & for mendyng the polley that the Sacrament hangith on	viij d.
It' payd for Cord for the same polley	v d.
It' payd for makyng of the pascall & the font taper	vij d.
It' payd for Caryage of a lode of mucke from the Church	ij d.
It' payd for makyng of this accompt	ij s.
It' payd to harry horthorne for settyng upp of the frame a boute the Sepulcre & for Closyng of the dore in {to} seynt Johns Chauncell to the quyre	vj d.
It' payd to the paynter for whytyng of the parclose	xvj d.
It' payd for ale at Removyng of the sepulcre to the carpenters	iij d. ob.

S[um]ma[1]

S[um]ma totalis xiiij li. xiiij s. vj d. ob.

Et sic habet in superplug' xliiij s. vj d. {ob.} dew to the seid barnys the which Richard Barnys have ben dismyssed & in his place electe John Kent

---

1. This seems to be an error. There is no sub-total needed since expenses are not sub-divided.

1514-15

[*p 100*] **Comptus of Roger Bryce and John Kent proctors
of the Churche of Seynt laurence in Redyng from the
fest of thannunciacion of our lady in the yere of our lord
god M^l CCCCCX iiij unto the same fest of our lady next
commyng 1515** [*In another hand*] <Anno vj° h viij>

Receytes

In primis the seid proctors have receyvyd at Ester for the pascall	xxxix s. viij d.
It' rec' of the wyves for the gatheryng at hocktyde	xxij s.
It' rec' of the men for gatheryng at hocktyde	iiij s. viij d.
It' rec' of yong men for gatheryng on feyr day	ix s. ij d.
It' rec' of Elizabeth mackeney for a seate	viij d.
It' rec' of the bequest of Nicholas bereman	xx d.
It' rec' for the Rode lyght on all halou day	xj s.
It' rec' of Thomas beckford for a seate for his wyfe	viij d.
It' rec' for the Rode lyght on Crystmas day	xv s. xj d.
It' rec' of the wardens of the masse of Jh[es]u to ward the Sextens wages for a yere endyd at Crystmas	xxxiij s. iiij d.
It' rec' of the wardens of the masse of our lady toward the Sextens wages for a yere endyd at Crystmas	xxxiij s. iiij d.

S[um]ma viij li. xij s. j d.

For rentes dew at the fest of Seynt Michaell tharc' anno
r[egni] r[egis] H viij^i vj°

It' rec' of Robert Cockseter for a tenement in the north syde of the New strete for a yere	x s.
It' rec' of William Carpenter for a tenement in the south syde of same strete for a yere	xij s.
It' rec' of William long for a tenement in the same syde of the strete for a yere	xij s.
It' rec' of Thomas Dodson for a tenement in the north side of the New strete for a yere	vj s. viij d.
It' rec' for a stable in the gutter lane for a yere	vij s.
It' rec' of Thomas Carpenter for a gardyn plot in the same lane	iiij d.
It' rec' of Thomas Slythurst for ij° gardyns in lurkmer lane by the yere	ij s. viij d.
It' rec' of [*blank*] Hunt Wydow for quyte rent of the hows that she inhabitithe in the hygh strete	xiij d. ob.
It' rec' of William Justice for his tenement in the mercat place in the hold of Robert Avenante	xij d.

It' rec' of Roger Johnson Coryar for a tenement in the mercat   x s.
place for a yere

It' rec' of John Wylder of the thele for di' acre of mede lying   xiij d.
by langney for a yere

S[um]ma iij li. iij s. x d. ob.

For the greate bell & gravys

It' Rec' for the greate bell at the burying of Conys wyfe   xij d.

It' rec' for the grave of John Roke   vj s. viij d.

It' rec' in ernest for a terment[1]   j d.

It' rec' for the grave of Roger bryce   vj s. viij d.

It' rec' for the grave of william faryngton   vj s. viij d.

It' rec' for the grave of william leyceter   vj s. viij d.

It' rec' for the greate bell at the burying of {roger Bryce}   xij d.
<faryngton>

S[um]ma xxviij s. ix d.

S[um]ma de omnibus rec' xiij li. iiij s. viij d. ob.

[*p 101*]   Expenses

In primis payd to Richard Barnys for the Church Dett as it   xliiij s. vj d.
apperith in the fote of the last accompte

It' paid for spyke nayles   ob.

It' payd for mendyng of the bell whel   vij d. ob.

It' paid to a laborer   ij d.

It' payd for a li. of frankencence   x d.

It' payd for paper   ob.

It' paid for watchyng of the Sepulcre   viij d.

It' payd for ij bz of Colis & for ale   iiij d.

It' payd for scowryng of Canstickes & pascall basyn   x d.

It' payd to a taberer for iij days   xij d.

{It' payd for his mete & drynke}   [*blank*]

It' payd to dawncers & for belles   xij d.

It' payd for mendyng of a surplice   ij d.

It' payd for a locke to the font   ij d.

It' payd for a key for an almary in the quere & for ij° ies for   iiij s.
the Curteyne wyres

It' payd for nayles & Racke hokes   v d.

It' payd to a suffryngan for halowyng of the high awter   vj s. viij d.
seynt Johns awter & a Superaltare[2]

---

1. The word is written with a tild as for 'tenement' above but obviously refers to an interment.
2. A superaltar was a portable consecrated stone containing relics. It could be placed on an unconsecrated table on which a priest could then say Mass.

It' payd for Colys at the same tyme	j d.
It' payd for mendyng of the chalice for the hygh awter & mendyng of a sencer	iiij s.
It' payd to John knyght for makyng crossis to the hygh awter & other service	viij d.
It' payd to ryngers on holy Thursday	ij d.
It' payd for a clampe of Iron to mend the bere	ij d.
It' payd for mendyng of an awter Cloth	iij d.
It' payd for payntes & pynnes on Corpus Chr[ist]i day	j d. ob.
It' payd for mendyng of a towell & surplice	iiij d.
It' payd to Mr Egerley as yt apperyth by {th} a byll	x s. vj d.
It' payd for v li. of sowder after vj d. the li. & werkmanshypp	ij s. viij d.
It' payd for warkemanshypp of viij li. di' of sowder	xvj d.
It' payd for woode	iiij d.
It' payd for livereys	iij d.
It' payd for half a hors hyde	x d.
It' payd for mendyng of the bawdryckes of all the belles	ij s.
It' payd for bromys	j d.
It' payd for a quarter of wex & the Caryage	xj s. x d.
It' payd for mendyng of the lanterne	iij d.
It' payd for mendyng of grownde pynnyng of the postes under the organs	ij d.
It' payd to Richard Turner[1] for a Cros	iij s.
It' payd for Caryage of a lode of mucke	ij d.
It' payd for strenges for the chyldern amys	ob.
It' payd for makyng of the roode lyght a genst all Haloutyde	xv d.
[p 102] It' payd for a new whele for a second bell	v s. iiij d.
It' payd to the regestre for smoke ferthynges	iiij s. vj d. ob.
It' payd for carying of the patron of the greate bell clapper to handley	j d.
It' payd towardes the Curteynes in the quere	iiij s. iiij d.
It' payd for makyng of a lytle bere	iij s. iiij d.
It' payd for a Rope to the ij^de bell	xviij d.
It' payd for hangyng of the clapper of the greate bell	ij d.
It' payd for a new clapper to the greate bell waying vj^xx vj li. after iij d. a li.	xxxj s. vj d.
It' payd for mendyng of the ij^de bell whele	vj d.
It' payd for mendyng of a surplice	ij d.
It' payd for a new showle	vj d.
It' payd for mendyng of the glas wyndows	vj s.
It' payd for scowryng of ij° Canstyckes a genst Crystmas	viij d.
It' payd for clensyng of the gutter	iiij d.

1. For more about Richard Turner see Appendix 2.

It' payd for beryng of Sir Thomas boke to & fro the church for a yere	viij d.
It' payd for mendyng of the grete bell whele & the rope	viij d.
It' payd for holy & Ivye	ij d.
It' payd to long for kepyng of the Clocke	vj s. viij d.
It' payd to long for wages	v s.
It' payd for a rope weying xiij li. at j d. ob. a li.	xix d.
It' payd for iij li. of Candylles {at ij° ty}	iij d.
It' payd for makyng of the roode lyght a genst Cristmas	vij d. ob.
It' payd for Racke holys pynnes & poyntes	j d. ob.
It' payd for mendyng of iij surplices	iiij d.
It' payd for xij fadom[1] of rope for the greate bell	vj d.
It' payd for wasshyng of the church gere for a yere	iij s. iiij d.
It' payd for wafers	ob.
It' payd for kepyng of the obyte	iiij d.
It' payd for ij elles iij quarter of Canvas for the hygh awter	xj d.
It' payd for nayles	j d.
It' payd for a showle	j d. ob.
It' payd to Nicholas wood sexten for a yere salary endyd at thannunciacion last	vj li. vj s. viij d.
It' payd to William Trew for quyte rentes of the tenementes belongyng to the church at the fest of Seynt Michaell tharchangell last past for a yere	iij s. vj d.
It' payd for a quart of basterd for the clarkes on palm Sonday	iiij d. & ale ob.
It' payd for makyng of the pascall & the font taper	vj d.
It' payd payd for ij torchis weyng xxvij li. at iiij d. a li.	ix s.
It' payd for a man & a hors to london for a wryt for barkebye	iiij s. ij d.
It' payd to harry horthorne for certeyn thynges done	xx d.
It' payd for makyng of this accompte	ij s.

S[um]ma totalis xv li. ix s. iij d. ob.

Et sic habet in superpleg' xliiij s. vij d.

And so have ben dismyssed roger Bryce & in his place
electe John Barfote

---

1. Probably a fathom, equal to six feet in length.

1515-16

[*p 103*] **Comptus of John Kent & John Barfote proctors of the Church of Saynt laurence in Redyng from the fest of thannunciacion of our lady in the yere of our lord god a M^l D xv unto the same fest next folowyng**

[*In the right-hand margin in the same hand and ink.*] **1516**
[*In another hand and ink in small letters*] <anno vij & viij >

Receytes

In primis the seid proctors have receyvyd at Ester for the pascall	xlj s. xj d.
It' Rec' of the wyves for the gatheryng at hocktyde	xxij s.
It' Rec' of the men for the gatheryng at hocktyde	viij s. vj d.
It' Rec' of the yong men for the gatheryng on Saynt phillip & Jacobs day	vj s. iiij d. ob.
It' Rec' of the yong men for the kyng play	xliij s. xj d.
It' Rec' of Mr Cleche	iiij d.
It' Rec' for the Roode {lyde} <light> on all halou day	xiiij s.
It' Rec' for the Roode lyght on Cristmas day	xiiij s. iij d.
It' Rec' of the bequest of William white	iij s. iiij d.
It' Rec' of wardens of the masse of Jh[es]u toward the Sextens wages for di' yere endyd at thannunciacion of our lady	xvj s. viij d.
It' Rec' of the wardens of the masse of our lady toward the Sextens wages for iij quarter endyd at thannunciacion of our lady	xxv s.

S[um]ma ix li. xvj s. <iij d.> ob.

Rentes dew at the fest of Saynt Michaell tharch[a]ngell
Anno vij^o

In primis of Robert Cockseter for a tenement in the North Syde of the New strete for a yere	x s.
It' of William Carpenter for a tenement in the south syde of the same strete for a yere	xij s.
It' of william long for a tenement in the same syde for a yere	xij s.
It' of Richard baldyng for a tenement in the north syde of the New strete for a yere	vj s. viij d.
It' of John appowell for a stable in the gutter lane for a yere	vij s.
It' of Thomas Carpenter for a gardyn plott in the same lane	iiij d.
It' of Thomas Slythurst for ij gardeyns in the lurkemer lane per annum <to be paid at midsomer and Crystmas>	ij s. viij d.
It' of [*blank*] hunt widow for quyte rent of the tenement that she inhabitith in the hygh street	xiij d. ob.
It' of william Justice for this tenement in the mercat place in the hold of Robert Avennat	xij d.

It' of Roger Johnson Coriar for a tenement in the mercat place by the yere — x s.

It' of John wylder of the thele for di' an acre of mede lying by langney for a yere — xiij d.

S[um]ma iij li. iij s. x d. ob.

[*p 104*]   For the grete bell & gravys

It' Rec' for the grete bell at the burying of Richard Turners wife	xij d.
It' Rec' for the grave of the same Richard Turners wyfe	vj s. viij d.
It' Rec' for the Coveryng of the same grave	vj d.
It' Rec' for the grete bell at the buryeng of William lendall	xij d.
It' Rec' for the grave of the same William & the Coveryng of the same[1]	vij s. ij d.
It' Rec' for the grete bell at the buryeng of philipp Rysby his wife	xij d.
It' Rec' for the same philipp for his wyfes grave	vj s. viij d.
It' Rec' for the Coveryng of the same grave	vj d.
It' Rec' for the grete bell at the buryeng of Isabell Hart[2]	xij d.
It' Rec' for the grave of the same Isabell	vj s. viij d.
It' Rec' for Coveryng of the same grave	vj d.
It' Rec' of Mr Wattes for hys wyves grave	vj s. viij d.
It' Rec' for the grete bell for the same	xij d.
It' Rec' for Coveryng of the same grave	vj d.
It' Rec' for Mr whites grave	vj s. viij d.
It' Rec' for the grete bell for the same	xij d.
It' Rec' for the Coveryng of the same grave	vj d.
It' Rec' for the grave of Cristian wilcox[3]	vj s. viij d.
It' Rec' for the grete bell for the same	xij d.
It' Rec' for Coveryng of the same grave	vj d.
It' Rec' for the Coveryng of John Rokes grave	vj d.
It' Rec' for movyng of the Setes at the makyng of the same grave	xij d.
It' Rec' of Richard a man for his wyfes grave	vj s. viij d.
It' Rec' for Coveryng of the same grave	vj d.
It' Rec' for the grete bell	xij d.
It' Rec' for the Coveryng of the grave of Roger Bryce	vj d.
It' Rec' for settyng of the seates over the same grave	xij d.

---

1. In his will made 4 May 1515, William Lendall asked to be buried in St Laurence's church. TNA Will of William Lendall, PROB 11/18/12.
2. In her will Isabel Hart or Hurt or Hert 1515 bequeathed twenty pence to both parish gilds and asked to be buried in the church. BRO Will of Isabel Hert, D/A1/1/23.
3. In her will made 20 April 1515, Christian Wilcox bequeathed a silver goblet with a cover to make a chalice for the Mass of Jesus and 13s 4d to Our Lady Mass. TNA Will of Christian Wilcox, PROB 11/18/8.

It' Rec' for the bequest of Richard wryght baker	iij s. iiij d.
It' Rec' of dyvers persons toward the makyng of the dore out of the quere	ix s.

S[um]ma iiij li. {xvij s}. vijj d.

For setys

It' Rec' of William Edmondes for his wyfes sete	vj d.
It' Rec' of Richard Turner for his wyfes sete	vj d.
It' Rec' of Richard a man for his wyfes sete	vj d.
It' Rec' of John lambe for his wifes sete	vj d.
[*In the margin by the next three entries*] beneth the font	
It' Rec' of John partryche for his wyfes sete	{vj d.}iiij d.
It' Rec' of Agnes Byrd for her sete	iiij d.
It' Rec' of Agnes Ivye for her sete	iiij d.
It' Rec' of Robert dwyte{s} for his wifes sete	vj d.
[*p 105*] It Rec' of [*blank*] Johnson for his wyfes sete	vj d.
It' Rec' of Agnes wattis wever for her sete	vj d.
It' Rec' of william lendall for his wyfes sete	vj d.
It' Rec' of [*blank*] osteler	j d.
It' Rec' of Henry Heyre for his wyfes sete	vj d.
[*In the margin by the next entry*] beneth the font	
It' Rec' of william Cone for his wyfes sete	iiij d.
It' Rec' of william way for his wyfes sete	vj d.
It' Rec' of Charles Myller for his wyfes sete	vj d.
[*In the margin by the next entry*] beneth the font	
It' Rec' of Thomas underwode sadeler for his wifes sete	iiij d.

S[um]ma vij s. iij d.

S[um]ma de omnibus rec' xvij li. vij s. xj d.

Expenses

In primis payd to John Kent for the Churche dett as it apperyth in the fote of the last accompte	xliiij s. vij d. ob.
It' payd for the helyng of iiij gravys	xiiij d.
It' payd for Coles & Ale	iiij d.
It' payd for takkes & Racke hokes	ij d.
It' payd for grete nayles	j d.
It' payd for franckencens j li.	x d.
It' payd for wacchyng of the sepulcre	viij d.
It' payd for movyng & setting upp ij° setes next the font	ij s.
[*p 106*] It payd for beryng & tryeng of the stones from the quere doore	iij d.
It' payd for mendyng of the bawdryck for the iiij[th] bell	x d.
It' payd for Ryngers on holy Thursday	ij d.

It' payd for a new bawdryck for the litle bell	vj d.
It' payd for makyng of the Cope gyvyn by Mr vicar	x s.
It' payd for the Orpherey to the same Cope	xx s.
{It payd for mendyng of the grete organs	xiij s. iiij d.}
It' payd for expens to barkebye at the same tyme	vj s. viij d.
It' payd for a pece of waynscote for mendyng of the stoppe	ij d.
of the same organs	

[*A pointing finger in the margin.*]

It' payd for nayles to Caynes pageant in the mercat place[1]	iij d.
It' payd for a lock to the Cope Chest	iij s. iiij d.
It' payd for mendyng of awbys & surplyces	iiij d.
It' payd for tapys for the Chylderne	iij d.
It' payd for ij° Crewatts	vij d.
It' payd for new castyng of a C vij li. of metall at j d. ob. a li.	xxj s. iij d. ob.
& xviij li. of new metall at iiij d. a li. for the lytell bell & for	
hangyng of the same bell in the steple v d.	
It' payd for makyng of the ij^{de} bell whele	iiij s.
It' payd for mendyng of the bawdryck for the same bell	viij d.
It' payd for mendyng of the bawdryck for the iij^{de} bell	x d.
It' payd for Coveryng of iiij gravys	xiij d.
It' payd for a li of Syses at Haloutyde	vij d.
It' payd for makyng of the Rode lyght a genst the same tyme	xv d.
It' payd for makyng of the grete bell whele	vj s. viij d.
It' payd for makyng of a bawdryck for the same bell	ij s. iiij d.
It' payd for mendyng of the claper to the iiijth bell	iiij d.
It' payd for a Rope to the lytle bell	vj d.
It' payd to the subsydye[2]	xij d.
It' payd for mendyng & settyng on of the patenes uppon	vj d.
uppon [*sic*] the childrens aubis	
It' payd for makyng of the Rode lyght a genst Cristmas	vij d. ob.
It' payd for iij li. of Candylles	iij d. ob.
It' payd for makyng of the dore in to the quere out of Saynt	xiiij d.
Johns chauncell	
It' payd for Canvas & bokeram & for mendyng of a Cope	vj d.
It' payd for scowryng of the Canstickes a genst Cristmas	viij d.
It' payd for settyng upp of the frame about the sepulcre at ij°	xvj d.
tymes	
[*p 107*] It payd for a di' li. of syses	iiij d.
It' payd for a quarter of frankencens	iij d.
It' payd for v Ropys weyeng iiij^{xx} li. at j d q' a li.[3]	viij s. iiij d.
It' payd for mendyng of the glas wyndows	ij s.

1. This was probably a play based on the biblical story of Cain and Abel.
2. This was a graduated tax on income from land of twenty shillings a year or more. M. Jurowski, C. L. Smith and D. Crook, *Lay Taxes in England and Wales, 1188-1688* (1998), 133.
3. The price per pound was a penny and a farthing, a quarter of a penny. A farthing is written as q'.

It' payd for iij lodes of yerth for the tenementes belongyng to the Church	xv d.
It' payd for lyme & sond	xvij d.
It' payd for helyng of iij gravys & mendyng of other thynges	xv d.
It' payd for nayles at dyvers tymes	j d.
It' payd for wasshyng of the Church gere for a yere	iij s. iiij d.
It' payd for makyng of the pascall & the font taper	vij d.
It' payd for a quarte of bastard for the Clarkes	iiij d.
It' payd for kepyng of the Clock to long	viij s. viij d.
It' payd to long for his wages	v s.
It' payd to long for beryng of Sir Thomas boke to & from the church for a yere	viij d.
It' payd to long for Clensyng of the gutter	iiij d.
It' payd for kepyng of the obyte	iiij s. iiij d.
It' payd for the quyte rentes of the tenementes belongyng to the church for a yere endyd at the fest of Saynt Michaell tharchangell last past	iij s. vj d.
It' payd to the regestre for smoke farthynges	iij s. vj d. ob.
It' payd for scowryng of the Canstickes & the pascall bassen	x d.
It' payd to william Mylward Sexton for {a y} iij quarter wages endyd at the fest of thannunciacion of our lady	iiij li.
It' payd for makyng of this accompte	ij s.
It' payd for mendyng the gape wyndow	viij d.
It' payd for pynnes & payntes	ij d.
It' payd for makyng of the dore out of the quere	xviij s.

S[um]ma de omnibus expens xiiij li. iij s. ix d.[1]
[*In the margin*] 14 17s. 1d. ob.

And so owyng iij li. iiij s. ij d.

{And so remayneth clere to the Churche}

Ther of the seid accomptant axeth to be allowed for a quarter rent of the tenement in the north side of the new strete	xx d.

And so remayneth clere to the Church at this accompte
iij li. ij s. vj d

And at this accompte hath ben dysmyssed the seid John kent & <in> hys rome electe John vansbye Unde Super Robertum Barkeby[2]	xiij s. iiij d.

---

1. This total is correct.
2. Robert Barkby owed the churchwardens 13s 4d which would be deducted from the balance.

[*p 108*] [*in a later hand*]
    Ordinances concerning the Ringing of Kelsall[1]
Hit is Covenantyd & aggreyd by the assent & consent of all
the parysshe that what person wyll have the greate bell of
the gyfte of harry kelsall to be rong at the knyll or any other
terment or obyte, All such persons to pay for the same bell
so Ryngyng at every tyme xiij d. to the churchwardens for
the use of the same church, And to every person that wyll
<have> hym tylled to paye iiij d. to the seid wardens, And
that the seid bell be rong or tylled for no person but he pay
as ys a bove expressed,
Provyded all way that the seid bell to be rong or tylled at all
tymes for the obite or myndes of the seid harry kelsall <to
be kepte>, And also {of } at the obites & myndes to be kept
for Mr Thomas Justice vicar of the parisshe church of saynt
laurence with out paying any money ther for, but to have the
seid bell rong & tylled for the seid ij° persons at all tymes
free,

                    [*In a later hand*] seat rent
Also hit is aggreyd that all women that shall take any seate
in the seid churche to pay for the same seate vj d. exepte in
the myddle range & the north range be neth the font, the
which shall pay but iiij d. & that every woman to take her
place every day as they cummyth <to churche> exepte such
as have ben Mayors wyfes,

1. For more about Henry Kelsall see Appendix 2.

25 March to 29 September 1516

[*p 109*] **Comptus of John Barfote & John Vansbye[1]
proctors of the churche of Saynt Laurence in Redyng
from the fest of thannunciacion of our lady in the yere of
our lord a M[l] D xvj & in the vij[th] yere of the Regne of
kyng henry the viij[th] unto the fest of Saynt Michaell
tharchangell then next followyng that ys to wytt for di' a
yere And the seid wardens have Receyvyd the rentes of
all the tenementes for iij quarters endyd at the fest of the
Nativite of Saynt John Bapt'[2] & so remayneth in the
tenantes handes at the seid fest of Saynt Michaell to be
gatheryd & recyvyd for a quarter endyd at the same fest
And also the seid wardens have payed all officers wages
& other charges due at the seid fest of Saynt Mychaell**

Receytes

Inprimis the seid wardens have ben charges with tharrerages	xlix s. ij d.
of the last accompte over & besyde xiij s. iiij d. uppon	
barkebye whiche ys discharged	
Of the pascall money at Ester	xlj s. jd. ob.
Of the men & women for the gatheryng at hocktyde	xxv s. v d.
Of the yong men for the kyng play at wytsontyde with a	xxxj s.
quarter of malt gyven by Roger Johnson preysed at iiij s.	
Of the tree sold in the mercat place	iij d.
Of the parisshe for the rood lyght at haloutyde	xiij s. iij d.
Of the wardens of Jh[e]s[u] masse toward the sextons wages	xvj s. viij d.
for di' a yere endyd at the fest of Saynt Michaell anno viij	
Of the wardens of our lady masse toward the sextons wages	xvj s. viij d.
for di' a yere endyd at the same fest	

S[um]ma ix li. xiij s. vj d. ob.

Rentes

Of Robert Cockseter for a ten[emen]t in the north syde of	vij s. vj d.
the new strete for iij quarters endyd at the fest of the	
Nativite of saynt John Baptist last before the date of this	
accompte after	
x s. a yere	
[*p 110*] Of William Carpenter for a tenement in the south	ix s.
syde of the same strete for iij quarters endyd at the same fest	
after xij s. a yere	

1. An alternative reading is Vausbye, 'n' and 'u' being difficult to distinguish in this script.
2. The feast of St John the Baptist, 24 June, was one of the quarter days. Rents were due on at Michaelmas, 29 September, so in this half year's accounts three-quarters of the rent, not due until 29 September 1516, had already been paid.

Of William long for a tenement in the same syde for iij q[u]arters endyd at the same fest after xij s. a yere	ix s.
Of Richard baldyng for a tenement in the north syde of the same strete for iij quarters endyd at the same fest after vj s. viij d. a yere	v s.
Of John a ppowell for a stable in the gutter lane for iij quarters endyd at the same fest after viij s. by the yere	v s. iij d.
Of Thomas Carpenter for a gardeyn in the same lane for iij quarters endyd at the same fest after iiij d. a yere	iij d.
Of Thomas Slythurst for ij gardeyns in lurkemer lane for di' a yere endyd at the same fest after ij s. viij d. a yere	xvj d.
Of Roger Johnson Coryer for a tenement in the mercat place for iij quarters endyd at the same fest after x s. a yere	vij s. vj d.

S[um]ma xliiij s. x d.

And remaynyng not receyvyd for asmoche as it is payable at Michelmas onlye to be receyvyd by the next wardens this parcelles followyng

Of John wylder of the thele for di' acre of mede lying by langney for a yere endyd at the fest of saynt Michaell anno viij°	xiij d.
Of William Justice for his tenement in the hold of Robert Avenant for a yere endyd at the same fest	xij d.
Of [blank] hunt wydowe for the tenement that she inhabitith in the high strete for a yere endyd at the same fest	xiiij d. ob.

[p 111] The grete bell & gravys	
For tyllyng of the grete bell at the terment of Nicholus kent	iiij d.
For tyllyng of the grete bell of Mr pownsar[1]	iiij d.
For tyllyng of the grete bell of Mr Trewe	iiij d.
For tyllyng of the grete bell of Mr Carpenter	iiij d.
For tyllyng of the grete bell of phillipp Risbye	iiij d.
For Ryngyng of the grete bell at the buryeng of william Staunford	xij d.
For the grave of the same william	vj s. viij d.
For tyllyng of the grete bell at his month mynde	iiij d.

S[um]ma ix s. viij d.

Seates

Of william Clarke of Chabley for his wifes sete	vj d.
Of John wynet for his wyfes sete	vj d.

1. In his will made 28 June 1517, John Pownsar, draper bequeathed 6s 8d to be paid to Jesus Mass by his wife, also a member of the gild, and 6s 8d to Our Lady Mass. Kerry, *A History*, 173-4.

Of John baghurste for his wifes sete	vj d.
Of harry wynet for his wyfes sete	vj d.
Of Nic' vans for his wyfes sete	vj d.
Of John Johnson for a rerage of his moder & wyfes sete	iiij d.

S[um]ma ij s. x d.

S[um]ma de omnibus rec' xij li. x s. x d. ob.

Expenses

Inprimis payd to harry water for a reward for his service	iij s. iiij d.
Payd for ij bz of colis	ij d.
Payd for a li. of frankencens	xij d.
Payd for watchyng of the sepulcre	viij d.
Paid for drynk at the same tyme	ij d.
[*p 112*] Paid for scouryng of the Canstikes & the pascall basyn	x d.
Paid for carying of a lode of muck fro the churche	ij d.
Paid for nayles	{ob.} <j d.>
Paid for helyng of Mr whites grave & tylyng uppon the churche	xj d.
Paid for di' a C of tyles at the same tyme	iiij d.
Paid for ij baner poles	xxj d.
Payd for mending of a Canstick stondyng a fore saynt Thomas Awter	x d.
Payd for mendyng of the gutter to harry glasyer	ij s. j d.
Payd for ij torchis waying xxxviij li. at iiij d. a li.	xij s. viij d.
Paid for mendyng of the procession wey	x d.
Paid to a mason for mendyng of harvys well	vj d.
Paid to david Tailor for mendyng of a Cope of Crymson velvet	viij d.
Paid to the officiall for smoke ferthynges	iij s. vj d. ob.
Paid to william Myllyng sexten for di' yere wages endid at Michelmas anno viij°	liij s. iiij d.
Paid for M^l of tyle v s. payd for ij quarter di' of lyme at xiiij d. a quarter ij s. xj d.	vij s. xj d.
Paid to long for his wages after v s. a yere for iij quarters endid at Michelmas	iij s. ix d.
paid to long for kepyng the Clock after vj s. viij d. a yere for iij quarters endid at the same fest	v s.
paid to long for beryng of Sir Thomas boke to & fro the church for iij quarters at the same fest	vj d.
paid to long for clensing of the gutter after iiij d. a yere for iij quarter endid ut supra	iij d.
paid for a lode of sond vj d. paid for tyle pynnes ij d.	viij d.

paid to Thomas Nicols for werkyng at longes hows & busses hows	v s. x d.
paid for bourdes for the louer iiij d. paid for a gutter tile & a crest j d.	v d.
Paid for a Courbe for harvys well	v s.
Paid for a bawdryke for the iiij[th] bell	x d.
Paid for settyng upp the table in our lady chancell & other werkes ther	vij d.
Paid for makyng the rode light a genst haloutyde	xv d.
Paid for a li. of sises a genst the same tyme	viij d. ob.
Paid for mendyng of the whelis of the belles	viij d.
Paid for makyng of the iiij[th] bell clapper weying lxj li. at ij d. ob. a li. xij s. viij d. ob. wher of ther was delyvered an old clapper weying lx li. at ob. a li & so payd[1]	x s. ij d. ob.
Paid for quyte rentes of all the tenementes for a yere endyd at Mich' anno viij°	iij s. vj d
Paid to the kynges paynter for a reward for seyng the tabernacle	vj s. viij d.
Paid for makyng of this accompte	ij s.

S[um]ma de omnibus expenses vj li. xix s. xj d.

Remaynyng of this accompte v li. x s. xj d. ob.

And at the same accompte have ben continewed the seid Wardens till the next yere, And thaccomptes to be made all wey uppon the day of Saynt Symond & Jude from hensforthe[2]

[*In the margin by the next entry*] a
Remembre the salt with the Cover gyven by william Staunford[3]

---

1. Part of the cost of the clapper, 12s 8½d, was offset by trading an old one valued at 2s 6d.
2. The feast of SS Simon and Jude was 28 October. The accounting year still ran from one Michaelmas to the next but presumably the accounts were to be presented to the parish meeting on 28 October.
3. For more about William Staunford or Stamford see Appendix 2.

1516-17

[*p 113*] **Thaccompt of John Barfote & John Vansbye <agayn> Wardens of the church of saynt laurence in Redyng from the feast of saynt Michaell tharchangell in the yere of our lord M^l D xvj & the viijth yere of the regne of kyng henry the viij unto the same fest then next followyng anno ix° that is to wit for one hole yere, And so remayneth in the tenantes hondes at the seid fest of saynt Michaell to be gatheryd & receyved for a quarter endid at the seid fest, And also the seid Wardens have payde all officers wages & other charges due at Michelmas anno ix°**

[*In the margin in a later hand, incorrectly*] 1517 and 1518.[1]

[R]eceites[2]

In primis the seid wardens have ben charged with the arrerages of the late accompte as apperith in the fote of the same	v li. x s. xj d. ob.
It' of the parissh for the roode lyght at Cristmas	xiij s. ij d.
It' of the pascall money at Ester	xlj s. x d.
It' of the men & women for gatheryng at hock[3]	xxviij s.
It' of the yong men for the gatheryng at the kyng play	xxiij s.
It' of the tree of the kyng play late standyng in the mercat place	xij d.
It' of Nic' hyde warden of the masse of Jhesus toward the sextens wages for a yere endid at Mi[c]helmas anno ix°	xxxiij s. iiij d.
It' of the wardens of our lady masse toward the sextens wages for a yere endyd at Mi[c]helmas anno ix°	xxxiij s. iiij d.
It' of Nic' hyde for a parclose late stondyng in saynt John Chauncell	vj s. viij d.

S[um]ma {ix} xiiij li. xj s. iij d. ob.

[Re]ntes

[*All the entries in this section are preceded by*] a

It' of Robert Cokseter for a tenement in the north syde of the new strete for a yere endyd at Mydsomer anno ix°	x s.
It' of Richard Baldyng for a tenement in the same strete for a {tenement}<yere> endyd at the same fest	vj s. viij d.
It' of William Carpenter for a tenement in the south side of the same strete for a yere endyd at the same fest	xij s.

---

1. The dates in the preamble are correct.
2. The first letter 'R' was lost when the pages were trimmed, probably at an earlier rebinding. It will be replaced at all similar places without comment.
3. This should read 'hocktide'.

It' of William lasham for a tenement in the same strete late in the hold of william long for a yere endyd at the same fest	xij s.
It' of John a ppowell for a stable in the gutter lane for a yere endyd at the same fest	vij s.
It' of Thomas Carpenter for a gardeyn in the same lane for a yere enyd at the same fest	iiij d.
[*p 114*] It' of Thomas Slithurst for ij° gardeyns in lurkmer lane for a yere endyd at the same fest	ij s. viij d.
It' of Roger Johnson Corior for a tenement in the mercat place for a yere endyd at the same fest	x s.
It' of John wylder of the thele for di' an acre of mede lyeng by langney for a yere endyd at Mi[c]helmas anno viij° for asmoch as It is payable but onys a yere	xiij d.
It' of william Justice for his tenement in the hold of Robert Avenant for a yere endyd at the seid fest of saynt Michaell anno viij°	xij d.
It' of Johanne Hunt widowe for her tenement in the high strete for a yere endyd at mi[c]helmas anno viij°	xiij d. ob.

S[um]ma iij li. iij s. x d. ob.

Grete bell & Gravis

In primis for ryngyng of the grete bell for the knyll of Raphe white of Okyngham[1]	xij d.
It' for tillyng of the bell at the terment of Richard Tyrnors wif	iiij d.
It' for ryngyng of the grete bell for the knyll of Christofer spakemans wif	xij d.
It' for the grave of the same wif	vj s. viij d.
It' for the Coveryng of the same grave	vj d.
It' for ryngyng of the grete bell at her moneth mynde	xij d.
It' for ryngyng of the greate bell for the knyll of John pownsar	xij d.
It' for the grave of the same John pownsar	vj s. viij d.
It' for Coveryng of the same grave	{vj d.} xij d.
It' for ryngyng of the grete bell at his moneth mynde	xij d.
It' for tylling of the grete bell at the terment of william staunford	iiij d.
It' for tylling of the grete bell at the terment of John Roke	iiij d.
It' for ryngyng of the grete bell for the knyll of william laward	xij d.
It' for the grave of the same william	vj s. viij d.
It' for Coveryng of his grave	vj d.

1. Okingham or Wokingham is a small town about seven miles south-east of Reading.

It' for tylling of the grete bell at the knyll of whit the   xij d.
belfownders wif
It' for the grave of the same wif   vj s. viij d.
It' for Coveryng of the same grave   vj d.
It' for tyllyng of the grete bell at the terment of Nic' kent   iiij d.

S[um]ma xxxvij s. vj d.

[*p 115*]   [S]eatis
In primis of phillipp visbye for his wifes seate   vj d.
It' of the goldsmyth for his wifes seate   vj d.
It' of John Bleke for his wifes seate   vj d.

S[um]ma xviij d.

S[um]ma de omnibus recept' ix li. xv s. ij d.

Expens
In primis paid for lyne to the high awter   ij d.
It' paid for reryng of the table at the high awter   iiij d.
It' paid for mendyng of the parysshe prestes surplice at ij°   iij d.
tymes
It' paid for mendyng of a vestement   vj d.
It' paid for mendyng of the bawdrick of the iiij^th bell   viij d.
It' paid for mendyng of the iij^de bell whele   ix d.
It' paid for {mend}makyng of the roode light a genst   vij d. ob.
Cristmas
It' paid for di' a li. of sises a genst Cristmas   iiij d.
It' paid for iij li. of Candilles a genst the same tyme   iij d. ob.
It' paid for mendyng of ij° vestymentes   vj d.
It' paid for for rebond to the same vestementes   iij d.
It' paid for half a hide of white lether   xiiij d.
It' paid for makyng of a bawderick to the grete bell   ix d.
It' paid for a quarte of bastard for the clarkes uppon palme   iiij d.
sonday
It' paid for the obite for the benefactors of the churche   v s.
It' paid for xiiij li. of wax for the church   viiij s. iiij d.
It' paid for payntes & nayles for the Canapye   j d. ob.
It' payd for makyng of the pascall taper & the font taper   vij d.
It' paid for mendyng of the church yard stile & mendyng of   xij d.
a ladder
It' payd for mendyng of the hond bell   vj d.
It' paid for a li. di' of Frankensence   xviij d.
It' paid for mendyng of the shippes & sensers of silver   v s.
It' paid for mendyng of an awbe   ij d.
[*p 116*] It' paid for settyng upp of a beame at our lady awter   ij d.

It' paid for makyng of the almery for bokes with all maner of stuff to the same — xij s. x d. ob.

It' paid for makyng of the lofte for the sepulcre light — lj s. ij d.

It' paid for mendyng of the beame for saynt Clementes light[1] — viij d.

It' paid to a glasyer for mendyng of the wyndows — xiij d.

It' paid for mendynge of the best Crosse — xiiij d.

It' paid for mendyng of the Canapye — vj d.

It' paid for mendyng of the cansticles of sylver — iij s. iiij d.

It' paid for a gowne of cane color damaske wher of made ij° Copis of the procuryng of Richard Turner & Ric' Barnys — xx s.

It' paid for bokeram rebond & Canvas for the same ij Copis & a nother cope made of an Awter cloth of red tissue of the gift of John pownsar & a nother cope<made> of an Awter cloth of whit Tissue of the gifte of the parisshe — xiiij s.

It' paid for makyng of the same iiij Copis — xj s.

It' paid to William Edmondes for sortyng of evydences of the church[2] — iiij d.

It' payd for makyng clene of the church at ij° tymes with cariage iij° lode of muck — ij s.

It' paid for mendyng of a Cope & a Chesible — x d.

It' paid for makyng of ix new seates in the south syde of the church — iij li.

It' paid for Coveryng of pownsars grave whites wifes grave Christofer spakman wifes grave & for mendyng of other thynges in the church — xxij d.

It' paid for nayles at dyverce tymes — xvij d. ob.

It' paid for sope for wasshyng of the Corporasses for a yere — ij d.

It' paid for wacchyng of the sepulcre — viij d.

It' paid for colis — ij d.

It' paid for scouryng of the pascall basyn & the Canstickes — x d.

It' paid to the officiall for smoke farthynges — iij s. vj d. ob.

It' paid for mendyng of an Orforey to a Cope — iiij d.

It' paid for ij° bell ropes — ij s. vj d.

It' paid for wasshyng of the church stuffe with settyng on the paroures for ij° yeres endyd at Mi[c]helmas anno ix° — vj s. viij d.

It' paid for certayne Iron werkes & lockes that is to witt for mendyng of the clock iij s. iiij d. xiij^{xx} braddes xij d. ij° lockes for the boke Almery[3] xij d. ij° payr of gyemows x d. & ij° Irons for saynt Thomas Awter ij d. — vj s. iiij d.

It' paid to harry horthorne for mendyng & dressyng of the old setis sett in the north side of the church with stuff for the same — xij s. ij d.

---

1. This would have ben placed at St Clement's altar. The altar was sold in 1549. See below.
2. William Edmonds was the abbey's steward and seems to have had some legal training. The 'evydences' were the parish's deeds, leases and other important documents. See Appendix 2.
3. This was a chest in which to keep service books.

[*p 117*] It paid to william myllyng sexten for one quarter endyd at Crismas xxvj s. viij d. & for iij quarters endid at Mihelmas anno ix° after xxx s. a quarter	v li. xvj s. viij d.
It' paid to long under sexten for his half yeres wages endyd at thannunciacion of our lady ij s. vj d. & to Ric' Andrew for a quarter endid at Mihelmas anno ix° xv d.	iij s. ix d.
It' paid to the same sextens for kepyng of the clock ut supra	v s.
It' paid to the same sextens for clensyng of the gutter ut supra	iij d.
It' paid to John knyght for mending certayne thinges in the churche	ij s.
It' paid for a lode of Tyles	v s.
It' paid for the quite rents for all the tenementes belongyng to the churche for a yere endyd at Mihelmas anno ix	iij s. vj d.
It' payde to William Edmondes for iij^e dayes besynes in taking of the Inventory & for regestryng the same[1]	ij s.
It' paid for making of this accompte & writyng of the same	ij s.

S[um]ma payd & expendid ix li. viij s.

Sic deb' vij s. ij d. unde super

John white for his wifes grave	vj s. viij d.
It' for Coveryng of the same grave	vj d.
It' for the grete bell ryngyng at the buryeng	xij d.
It' for the greate[2] ryngyng at the buryeng of william laward	xij d.
It' for Coveryng of the grave of the same william	vj d.

Et sic in superplus ij s. vj d.

At this acc' have ben dismyssed the seid John Barfote & in his place electe Thomas Everard

---

1. This refers to the inventory of church goods made in 1517. 'Regestryng' may refer to making a fair copy which at some date was bound in with the accounts.
2. The word 'bell' has been omitted.

1517-18

[*p 118*] **Thaccomptes of John Vansbye & Thomas Everard wardens of the churche of Saynte laurence in Redyng from the Fest of Saynt Michaell tharchangell in the yere of our lord anno M^l C xvij & the ixth yere of the regne of kyng henry the viijth unto the same Fest then next followyng that is to witt for one hole yere endid at Mi[c]helmas anno x^o And so remayneth in the tenantes hondes to be gatherid & received for a quarter endid at Mich' anno x^o And also the seid wardens have payed all officers wages & other charges due at the seid fest of Saynt Mich' anno x^o**

Arr'

In primis the seid wardens have ben charged with tharrerages of the last acc' as apperithe in the fote of the same accompte	nihil quia in superpl'
It' of John white for his wifes grave	vj s. viij d.
It' for the grete bell ryngyng at her buryeng	xij d.

S[um]ma vij s. viij d.

Rec'

[*In the margin by the next entry*] a

It' for the rode light at all haloutide	xiiij s. iij d.
It' for the rode light at Cristmas	xiij s. vj d.
It' for the pascall money at Ester	xlij s. ix d. ob.
It' for the gatheryng of men & women at hock	xxvij s.
It' of the yong men for the gatheryng with the king play	xxv s. v d.
It' of the wardens of the masse of Jh[esu]s toward the sextens wages for a yere endid at Michelmas anno x^o	xxxiij s. iiij d.
It' of the wardens of the masse of our ladye toward the sextens wages for a yere ended at the same fest	xxxiij s. iiij d.

S[um]ma ix li. xvij s. iij d.

Rentes

[*In the margin by the next entry*] a

It' of John Barfote for a tenement in the North side of the New strete in the hold of Robert Coxseter for a yere endid at Midsomer anno xj^o	x s.
It' of John Burre^1 for a tenement in the same strete for a yere endid ut supra	vj s. viij d.

---

1. On p. 112 of the accounts, the name is written Busse.

It' of Thomas harvie for a tenement in the same strete for a yere endid ut supra	xij s.
It' of william lasseham for a tenement in the same strete late in the hold of william long for a yere endid at the same fest	xij s.
It' of John Appowell for a Stable in the gutter lane for a yere endid ut supra	vij s.
It' of thomas Carpenter for a gardeyn in the same lane for a yere ut supra	iiij d.
It' of Thomas Slithurst for ij⁰ gardeyns in lurkmerlane for a yere endid ut supra	ij s. viij d.
It' of Roger Johnson Coriour for a tenement in the mercat place for a yere ut supra	x s.
[*p 119*] It' of John wilder of theThele for di' acre of mede lyingby langney for a yere endid at Mi[c]helmas anno x⁰ for asmuche as it is paialle[1] but ons a yere	xiij d.
It' of william Justic for a tenement in the hold of Robert Avenant for a yere ut supra	xij d.
It' of Johanne hunt Widowe for her tenement in the high strete for a yere endid at Mi[c]helmas anno x⁰	xiij d. ob.

S[um]ma iij s. x d. ob.

The grete bell

In primis of John white for tillyng of the greate bell at his wifes yeres mynd	iiij d.
It' for ryngyng the knyll of John pertriche	xij d.
It' for tyllyng at the moneth mynd of the same John	iiij d.
It' for ryngyng the knyll of Thomas pichar	ij s.
It' for tyllyng at a terment holden by william wattis	iiij d.
It' for tyllyng at a terment holden by Thomas Everard	iiij d.
It' for tyllyng at a terment holden for John wilcox	iiij d.
It' for tyllyng at a terment holden by Richard Cleche	iiij d.
It' for tyllyng at a terment holden for Alice Sharpe	iiij d.
It' for tyllyng at a terment holden by Richard a Man	iiij d.
It' for tyllyng at a terment holden by Christofer Spakeman	iiij d.
It' Ryngyng at a terment holden for John pownsar	xij d.
It' Ryngyng at the knyll for John Molners Fleccher	xij d.
It' for tyllyng at the moneth mynde of the same John	iiij d.
It' for Ryngyng the knyll of the wif of Robert Dodson dyer	xij d.
It' for tyllyng at the moneth mynde of the same wife	iiij d.
It' for tyllyng at a terment holden by Robert Blake	iiij d.
It' for Ryngyng the knyll {of} for the wif of william kene	xij d.
It' for Ryngyng the knyll {of} for the wif of John lambe	xij d.
It' for Ryngyng at her moneth mynde	xij d.

---

1. This should read 'payable'.

It' for Ryngyng the knyll of John lambe	xij d.
It' for Ryngyng at his monethe mynde	xij d.
It' for Ryngyng the knyll for william Trew	xij d.
It' for tyllyng at a terment holden for william Staunford	iiij d.
It' for tyllyng at a terment holden for william laward	iiij d.

S[um]ma xvj s. viij d.

[*p 120*]   Gravis[1]
[*In the margin by the next entry*] a

In primis for the grave of John pertriche	vj s. viij d.
It' for Coveryng of the same grave	vj d.
It' for the grave of John Molyns	vj s. viij d.
It' for Coveryng the same grave	vj d.
It' for the grave of the wif of Robert Dodson	vj s. viij d.
It' for Coveryng of the same grave	vj d.
It' for the grave of the wif of William kene	vj s. viij d.
It' for Coveryng of the same	vj d.
It' for the grave of the wif of John lambe	vj s. viij d.
It' for Coveryng of the same	vj d.
It' for the grave of John lambe	vj s. viij d.
It' for Coveryng of the same grave	vj d.
It' for the grave of John Eton	vj s. viij d.
It' for Coveryng of the same grave	vj d.
It' for the grave of William Trewe Junior	vj s. viij d.
It' for Coveryng of the same grave	vj d.
It' of Richard Goodyere for a child buried with dodsons wif	iij s. iiij d.

[*In the right-hand margin by the next entry in a later hand,
very heavily deleted* {of Henry Kelsalls bequest The great
bell}
In the left-hand margin is a pointing hand.]

It' for the grave of Rand' kelsalles moder	vj s. viij d.
It' for coveryng of the same	vj d.

S[um]ma iij li. vij s. x d.

Seates

It' of John Avenant for his wifes sete	vj d.
It' of Culverhous for his wifes sete beneth font	iiij d.
It' of Charles Miller for his wifes sete	vj d.
It' of John Russell for his wifes sete	vj d.
It' of James Jackson for his wifes sete	vj d.
It' of william Johnson for his wifes sete	vj d.

1. The binding shows through here. It seems to be a page with a Collect from the Book of
Common Prayer with woodcuts or engravings.

It' of william Tomson for his wifes sete	vj d.
It' of John whyttyngham for his wifes sete	vj d.
It' of Robert Rawlens for his wifes sete	vj d.
It' of Robert Browne for his wifes sete	vj d.
It' of Stevyn Thorpe for his wifes sete	vj d.
It' of John Fleccher for his wifes sete	vj d.
It' of Thomas gile for his wifes sete beneth font	{vj d.} iiij d.
It' of John Flowre for his wifes sete	vj d.
It' of william Myllyng for his wifes sete	vj d.
It' of henry horthorne Junior for his wifes sete	vj d.
It' of Henry More for his wifes sete beneth font	iiij d.

S[um]ma viij s.

S[um]ma tot' xvij li. xiiij s. ij d.

[*p 121*] Expenses	
In primis payd to John Barfote that the church was indettid as apperith in the fote of the last accompte	ij s. vj d.
It' for Coveryng of lawardes grave & ground pynnyng of a sete	vij d.
It' for a cord for the clock	iij d.
It' for settyng on the fote of the holy water pott	ij d.
It' for makyng of the rode light a genst all haloutide	xv d.
It' for a li. of sises a genst the same tyme	viij d.
It' for a payr of henges for the tenement in the hold of John Burre & di' C of peny naile	vj d.
It' for makyng of the rode light a genst Cristmas	vij d. ob.
It' for di' li. of sises a genst the same tyme	iiij d.
It' for iij li. of Candilles	iij d. ob.
It' for a pax	xvj d.
It' for leying of a stone & mendyng of other fawtes	viij d.
It' for lyme & sand for the same	iiij d.
It' paid to Richard Turner for a grayle in prent over & beside v s. gyven by Thomas white of london[1]	v s. iiij d.
It' payd for a lock	iiij d.
It' paid for a lode of erthe to the hous in the hold of Thomas harvye	vj d.
It' paid for reparacon of the gutter	ij s.
It' paid for dressyng of the lawnde for the canopie	ij d. ob.
It' for makyng of a whele for a bell & mendyng of the bere	xxij d.
It' for keping of the obite for the b[e]n[e]factors	v s.

1. A printed service book was still unusual enough to require comment. Thomas White was probably Sir Thomas White, a Reading-born London merchant who founded St John's College, Oxford. He endowed two scholarships to the college for Reading boys, one awarded to William Laud. D. Phillips, *The Story of Reading* (Newbury, 1980), 46.

It' for a li. of Frankencence	x d.
It' for dressyng of the lawnd a bout the pix	iiij d.
It' for nayles & coles	ij d.
It' for cariage of a lode of dust	ij d.
It' for wacchyng of the sepulcre	viij d.
It' for scouryng of the pascall basyn & the canstikks	x d.
It' for wasshyng of the walles in the churche with ij d. in sise	iiij s. ij d.
It' for a quarter of pamentes	v d.
[p 122] It' payd for makyng of Irons for the high awter & mendyng of Irons for the rode lofte	xx d.
It' for carying of robell out of the churche	ij d. ob.
It' for a yerd & di' of blew bokeram	viij d.
It' for mendyng of iiij copis	viij d.
It' for rebond for the same	v d.
It' for mendyng of an awter cloth & rebond for the same	xvj d.
It' for mendyng of the awbes & mendyng of iiij surplices	viij d.
It' for a key & settyng on a lock at the hous that burre holdeth	ij d.
It' for a quarter of pamentes	v d.
It' for iiij ropis	iij s. viij d.
It' for a yerd & di' of bokeram with j d. in Crewle	vij d.
It' paid to the officiall for smoke ferthynges	iij s. vj d. ob.
It' for cariage of a lode of robell	ij d.
It' for wasshyng of the churche gere	iij s. iiij d.
It' for Coveryng of iiij gravys	xvj d.
It' for pamentes	x d.
[In the left-hand margin by the next entry] wages	
It' paid to william myllyng sexten for iij quarter endid at midsomer v li. & for a quarter endid at mi[c]helmas anno x° <v s.> for asmuche as the same william departid out of service the morow after saynt laurence day[1]	v li. v s.
It' payd to Stevyn Thorpe for the tenement in the new strete for iij quarters rent endid at mi[c]helmas anno x° ix s. and for di' yere endid at the same fest toward his wages vj s. viij d.	xv s. viij d.
It' payd to Richard Andrews for his wages for a yere endid at Mi[c]helmas anno x°	x s.
It' paid to the same Richard for kepyng of the Clock	vj s. viij d.
It' paid to the same Richard for clensyng of the gutter	iiij d.
It' paid for quite rentes of all the tenements for a yere endid at Mich' anno x°	iij s. vj d.

S[um]ma paid & expendid ix li. xviij d.

---

1. The feast of St Laurence was on 10 August.

So remaynyng of this accompte made on the day of the fest
of Saynt Symon & Jude vij li. xvj s. ij d.

At this accompte hath ben dismissed John vansbye and in
his place electe william Edmunde

1518-19

[*p 123*] **Thaccomptes of Thomas Everard & william
Edmunde Wardens of the churche of saynt laurence in
Redyng from the Feste of saynt Michaell tharchaungell
in the yere off our lord a M C xviij & the xth yere of the
regne of kyng henry the viijth unto the same Fest then
next followyng that is to witt for one hole yere endyd in
the xjth yere of the regne of the seid kyng And so
remaynyng in the tenauntes hondes to be gathered &
receyved for a quarter rent & {endyd} at the seid Fest of
Saynt Michaell anno xj^o And also the seid Wardens have
paid all officers wages & other charges dew at the seid
Fest of Saynt Michaell anno xj**
[*In the right-hand margin in a sixteenth-century hand*]
{1518 1520} [*and in a modern hand*] <1519 and 1520>.[1]

Arr'

In primis the seid wardens have ben charged with the
arrearages of the last accomptes as apperith in the Fote of
the same accomptes

vij li. xvj s.
ij d.

S[um]ma vij li. xvj s. ij d.

[R]ec'

Item for the rode light at all haloutide	xij s. v d. ob.
Item for the rode light at Cristmas	xiiij s.
It' for pascall money at Ester	xl s. v d.
It' for hockmoney gatherid by men & women	xxxij s.
It' for wost[2] off torches	iij d.
It' for old tymbre sold at certayne tymes	iij s. ob.
It' for iij bourdes	viij d.
It' of Ric' Goodyere in parte of payment of xxxiij s. iiij d. for a salt gyven by william Stamford[3]	vj s. viij d.
It' for a lode of stonys	viij d.
It' for di' C ridge tyle - lx brod tiles	ij s. viij d.

1. The original text is correct. These are the accounts for 1518-19.
2. This was meant to be 'waste'.
3. Elsewhere his name is written as Staunford. See accounts p. 114. The balance was paid the next year. See accounts p. 129.

It' for a qu' of sleyght lyne[1]	x d.
It' off {or} the gifte of Mr barton toward the makyng of vestr'	xl s.
It' of the gifte of Mr Wattes for the same	xl s.
It' of Mr Cleche for the same	x s.
It' of Mr Cleche for an old table sold	vj s. viij d.
It' for ropis endes	iiij d.
It' of the Wardens of Jh[esu]s toward the sextons wages	xxxiij s. iiij d.
It' of the Wardens of our lady toward the sextens wages for a yere	xxxiij s. iiij d.

S[um]ma xiij li. xvij s. iiij d.

[*one word missing*] heving to[ward] the repar[acio]ns of the [chur]ch[2]

Item gyven by diverce persons toward the reparacion of the church gatherid every Sonday after the new yeres day unto the Sonday after Michelmas day which amounteth to the sum of as it apperith by a boke of ther names.	xxj li. ij s. j d.

[*p 124*] Rentes	
In primis of John Barfote For the tenement in the north syde of the newe strete in the hold of Robert Coxseter for a yere endid at Midsomer anno xj°	x s.
It' of thomas Harvy for a tenement in the same strete for a yere endyd at the same Feste	vj s. viij d.
It' of Stevyn Thorpe for a tenement in the same strete for a yere endyd at the same Feste xij s. nihil rec' for why allowyd toward his wages	nihil
It' of william lesseham for a tenement in the same strete late in the hold of William longe for a yere endid at the same Fest	xij s.
It' of John appowell for a stable in the gutter lane for a yere endid at the same Fest	vij s.
It' off thomas Carpenter for a gardeyn in the same lane For a yere endid at the same Feste	iiij d.
It' of Thomas Slithurst for {t} ij° gardeyns in lurkemer lane For a yere endid at the same Feste	ij s. viij d.
It' of Roger Johnson Coriour for a tenement in the mercat place for a yere endid at the same fest	x s.

---

1. This is slaked lime.
2. This is written in the margin in a different hand along with a pointing finger. Some letters were lost when the page was cropped. The book referred to has not survived.

It' of John wilder of the thele for {a} di' acre of mede lying by langney for a yere endid at Michellmas anno x° for asmucheas it is payable but ons in the yere — xiij d.

It' of William Justice for his tenement in the hold of Robert avenant for a yere endid at the seid Feste of saynt Michaell anno x° — xij d.

It' of Johanne hunt widow for her tenement in the hygh street for a yere endid at the seid Fest of saynt Michaell anno x° — xiij d. ob.

S[um]ma lj s. x d.

The grete bell

It' for ryngyng the grete bell at william Trewis moneth mynd — xij d.

Item for ryngyng at the mynd of kenys wife — xij d.

It' for tyllyng the grete bell at a terment holden by Mr Wattes — iiij d.

It' for tyllyng at a terment holden by John kent — iiij d.

It' for tyllyng at a terment holden by Thomas everard — iiij d.

It' for tyllyng at Wylcox terment — iiij d.

It' for tyllyng at a terment holden by Richard a Man — iiij d.

It' for the knyll of Robert Blakes wyff — xij d.

It' for ryngyng at her monthe mynde — xij d.

It' for tyllyng at a terment for John pownsar — iiij d.

It' for tyllyng at a terment holden by Symon lambe — iiij d.

It' for tyllyng at a terment holden by Robart Dodson — iiij d.

It' for tyllyng at a terment holden For William Trewe — iiij d.

[p 125] It' for tyllyng at a terment holden by William kene — iiij d.

It' for tyllyng at a terment holden for William Staunford — iiij d.

It' for tyllyng at a terment holden by my lord of Enseham[1] — iiij d.

It' for tyllyng at a terment holden by John kent — iiij d.

S[um]ma viij s. iiij d.

gravis

It' of Robert Blake For his wifes grave — vj s. viij d.

It' for Coveryng of the same grave — vj d.

S[um]ma vij s. ij d.

1. This could refer to the Abbot of Eynsham but no connection with Reading has been traced. The entry does not imply that the 'lord of Ensham' did anything more than pay for the burial.

Setis

It' of John knyght for his wyfes Sete	vj d.
It' of phellipp wynger for his \<wyfes\> sete	vj d.
Of Johanne Curtes for the chaunge of a sete	iiij d.
It' of Robert Dodson dyer for his wyfes sete	vj d.

S[um]ma xxij d.

S[um]ma tot' xlvj li. iiij s. ix d.

Expens

In primis paid for v^M CCCC of Breke	xxvij s.
It' paid for xx^{ti} qu[a]rter of lyme viij d a qua' to Mr barton	xiij s. iiij d.
It' paid for cariage of the same from Shiplake iiij d. a qua'	xx d.
It' for xix qua' & vj bz of lyme at xvj d. a quarter	xxvj s. iiij d.
It' for iij qua' di' of lyme at xiiij d. a quarter	iiij s.
It' for xij bz of stone lyme	xxiij d.
It' gyven by mr wattes v bz of lyme	
It' for Cariage of robell	iij s.
It' paid to Troll for werkmanship at dyverce tymes	liij s. iiij d.
It' for cariage of {robell} vj lodes of sand	j s.
It' paid to John knyght for certayne besynesse	ij d.
It' paid for cariage of ix lodes of sand	iij s.
It' for xviij li of yron for the wyndows at ij d. a li. S[um]ma	iij s.
It' paid for iij^M of tiles	xv s.
It' paid for nailes of dyveres sortes	xv s. j d. ob.
It' paid for tile pynnes	ix d.
It' paid for viij^C lathes at v d. a C	iij s. iiij d.
It' iiij^C lathes at iiij d. ob. a C	xviij d.
[p 126] paid to Richard Turner for iiij lodes of stones	vj d.
It' for a lode of Erthe	iiij d.
It' for v lode off sand carieng	xx d.
It' for vj lodes of stonys	iiij s.
It' paid for gutters & Crestes	vj s.
It' paid to Waterman for pargettyng & other we[r]kes	xij s. iiij d.
It' to a laborer iij^e dayes	x d.
It' to Troll for selyng mendyng of the Amners hows for	iij s. iiij d.
mendyng of the arche & mendyng of the wyndows[1]	
It' paid fawlyng of Juystes	xxij d.
It' for caryng of robell out of the churche	viij d.
It' gyven to the Carpenters servantes	ij d.
It' for caryng of tymbre to the church	j d.
It' for colour for the beme	j d.

---

1. A house for which the churchwardens paid quit rent to the almoner of the abbey.

[*The next six entries are bracketed together in another hand*] Rate of wages

It' paid Hawtrell for xj dayes vj d. a day	v s. vj d.
It' paid for his man xlj dayes v d. a day	xvij s. j d.
It' for a nother man xj dayes iiij d. a day	iij s. viij d.
It' paid Hawtrell for v dayes v [d.] a day	ij s. j d.
It' paid to a Joynour for xiij dayes at vj d. a day	vj s. vj d.
It' paid for xiiij days to a Joynour at v d. a day	v s.
It' paid hughe Smythe for barris for the wyndows xliij li. price the li. j d. ob.	v s. iiij d.
It' for a dogg of Iron[1]	vj d.
It' paid to the glasier for glasying of the wyndows & the fire	iij s. vj d.
It' paid for glasyng lxxxij fotes at v d. a fote	xxxiiij s. ij d.
It' for glasyng of the vestrie	x d.
It' for ij lockes a bold & ij staples	xx d.
It' ij payr of henges	xiiij d.
It' ij payr of gyemows	xij d.
It' gyven by william[2] toward the glas wyndows vij li. of lede	
It' For makyng cleyn of the lofte	ij d.
It' gyven by Nicholas hyde a pece of Tymbre of xl fote	[*blank*]
It' payd to Myller the Joynour in parte of payment iiij li. vj s. viij d. for makyng of the parclose in the newe chapell	xxvj s. viij d.
It' paid to harry horthorne for tymbre werkmanshyp & for bowdryng of men as apperith by his billes	vij li. iiij d.
It' paid for glewyng of sertayne lose peces of the tables	xij d.
It' for a lock to the west dore	v d.
It' for thred For settyng on the awbes	ob.
It' paid to a Syngyng man for a reward	ij s.
[*In the left-hand margin*] wages	
It' paid to william myllyng Sexten in contentacion of his wages	xj s. viij d.
It' for makyng cleyn of the roufe of the churche	iiij d.
It' paid to John knyght for makyng clene of the rode lofte	vj s. viij d.
[*p 127*] Item paid for helyng of iiij gravis with lyme & sand	xix d.
Item paid for cariage of the tabernacles by the barge[3]	vj s.
It' paid to Cone for settyng upp the tabernacles	ij s. vj d.
It' paid for makyng of a scafold	ij d.
It' paid for iiij clammes of Iron for the tabernacles	viij d.
It' paid for iiij clammys of Iron for the gret table	viij d.
It' paid for ij clammys set in the wyndow in saynt Johnns chauncell	iiij d.
It' for makyng clene of the canstikes in the rode loft	iiij d.

1. A fire dog which supported burning wood in a hearth..
2. No surname is given.
3. Barges could bring goods from London via the Thames and the Kennet right to the Town Wharf, a short distance from the church.

It' for a bell rope for the fore bell	xiiij d.
It' for a lode of erth to the tenement in the hold of Roger Coriour	vj d.
Itm for mendyng of the wyndows in the highe chauncell	xij d.
It' for mendyng of a Surplice	iij d.
It' for mendyng of the awter clothes	ij s.
It' paid For wasshyng & dressyng of the halpas with the xij Apposteles[1]	xiij s. iiij d.
It' paid For mendyng of the grete bell clapper	v s. iiij d.
It' for glew & nayles for the tabernacles	x d.
It' paid for wyer for the xij Appostels	viij d.
It' paid for caryng of a lode of duste	ij d.
It' paid for v li. of wax for the rode light a ganst haloutide viij d. a li.	iij s. iiij d.
It' for makyng of the old wax	xiij d. ob.
It' for iiij li. of wax for the rode light a genst cristmas	iij s.
It' for makyng of xj li. of old wax	v d. ob.
It' for makyng of the pascall & the font taper	viij d.
It' for ij li. of wax for the same	xvj d.
It' for payng & enbrowdreyng of the auter clothe of white & Rede	xx s. viij d.
It' for rebond & bokeram for the cope of whyte damaske	iij s. viij d.
It' for iij yerdes of saten of Cipers[2] to make a cirten before the xij appostles	xxj d.
It' for rebond & bokeram for iij^e moses[3]	vij d.
It' for a new deske in the quere	v s. iiij d.
It' for a li. of frankencence	xij d.
It' for coveryng of a grave	vj d.
It' for colis	ij d. ob.
It' for wacchyng of the sepuclere	viij d.
It' for nailes	j d. ob.
It' for makyng clene of the sepulcre & other thynges & havyng a way the robell	ij s.
It' for makyng of an auter in the vestrie	vj d.
It' for mendyng of the iiij^th bell whele	ij s. ij d.
It' for clensyng of a draught in the tenement of Roger coriour	iij s. viij d.
It' {for} to the officiall for smoke farthynges	iij s. vj d. ob.
It' paid for takyng downe of the table of the highe awter & lettyng upp of the same & for makyng of the halpas & for a pece of Tymbre	iiij s.

---

1. Twelve statues of the apostles probably formed part of a reredos on an elevated platform (a halpace) behind the High Altar. The wire was to hold a curtain.
2. A valuable fabric brought from Cyprus called 'satin of cypres'.
3. This may refer to three effigies of prophets or more probably three men playing that role in the Palm Sunday service. See Introduction.

It' for ij men werkyng in the churche a day	xij d.
It' for tymbre occupied in the procession wey	xvj d.
It' for liiij^C xxij li. of led at v s. iiij d. the C	xiiij li. viij s.
[*p 128*] It' payd to the plummer for Castynge & leying of the same led on parte of payment of xxvij s.	xviij s.
It' payd for cariage of the same led out of the Abbey[1]	ix d.
It' paid for a newe deske	vj s.
[*In the left-hand margin*] wages	
It' paid to Stephyn Thorpe toward his wages for a yere endid at Michelmas anno xj^o	xiij s. iiij d.
It' paid to pynder for a quarter service	xiij s. iiij d.
It' paid to Richard Andrews under sexten for a yere endid at Michelmas anno xj^o	xij s.
It' paid for scouryng of the Canstickes & pascall basyn	x d.
It' payd for makyng & regestryng of this accompte	ij s.

S[um]ma tot' xlvj li. xviij s. viij d.

Et sic in superpl' xiiij s. j d.

And at this accompte hath ben dismyssed the seid Thomas Everard & in his place chosen William knyght

1519-20

Thaccomptes of William Edmunde & William knyght Wardens of the parisshe churche of Saynt laurence in Redyng from the Fest of saynt Michaell tharchangell in the yere of our lord anno M^l D xix & the xjth yere of the regne of kyng henry the viijth unto the same Fest then next followyng 1520
[*In the right-hand margin in sixteenth century hand*]
{1519 to} 1520 1521[2]

Arr'

In primis the seid wardens have ben charged with tharr' of the last accompte as apperith in the Fote of the same accompte nihil quia in superpl'

Rec'

It' Rec' for the roode light at all haloutyde	xiij s. v d.
It' for the roode light at Cristmas	xj s.

1. The amount of lead is prodigious, 5422 lbs. The sum paid did not include the cost of the 22lbs, about 10d. It would have been very convenient to have used the abbey's wharf which was on the northern bank of the Kennet and bring the cargo through the abbey precinct, adjoining the church.

2. The marginal comment is an error; the accounts are definitely for 1519-1520.

It' for an old table sold	xiij s. iiij d.
It' for xx C of old ledd sold at iiij s. x d. the C	iiij li. xvj s. viij d.
It' for an old Chest sold	iiij s.
It' for the pascall money at Ester	xliij s. iiij d.
It' for hokmoney gatheryd by men & women	xxv s. ob.
It' for CCC xx li. of new ledd at v s. x d. the C	xviij s. vj d.[1]
It' for a Cofre Sold	iij s. iiij d.

[p 129] It' of White for xij C iiij qua' of old led at iiij s. x d. the C[2]	iij li. xix d. ob.
It' of Richard Turner for C C di' v li.[3] of new led at v s. x d. the C	xiiij s. xj d.
It' of the gatheryng at the kyng play	xxiiij s.
[A pointing finger in the margin by the next entry.]	
It' of Segemond the organmaker for the grete organs C C di' of led	nihil
It' for tile sherdes sold	vj d.
It' for old tymber sold	x d.
Rec' of Goodyere for a salt of sylver gyven by William Staunford in full payment of xxxiij s. iiij d.	xxvj s. viij d.
It' of dyverce persons gyven toward the reparacion of the Churche	v li.
It' of the wardens of Jh[esu]s toward the sextens wages for a yere	xxxiij s. iiij d.
It' of the wardens of our lady toward the sextens wages for a yere	xxxiij s. iiij d.
It' for iij q[u]arter and v li. of led	iiij s. v d.
It' of Mr Barton toward the raparacion of the quere	vj s. viij d.
It' of Richard <Turner> toward the same	vj s. viij d.
It' of Symon lambe toward the same	vj s. viij d.
It' of Sir John Richmand toward the same	iij s. iiij d.

[In the left-hand marginin very small writing] {8 li.[?9 d.]}]
S[um]ma xxvij li xj s. vij d.

Rentes

It' of John Barfote for a tenement in the new strete in the hold of Robert Coxseter for a yere endid at Midsomer anno xij°	x s.
It' of Thomas Harvy for a tenement in the same strete for a yere ut supra	vj s. viij d.

---

1. The correct total is 18s 8d.
2. The top part of C and part of superscript abbreviation for quarter on first line were removed when the page was trimmed. This total is correct.
3. 255 lbs in Roman nunerals i.e. 100+100+half a hundred (50) + 5. The cost is rounded up to the nearest penny.

It' of Henry Moore for a tenement in the same strete for a yere ut supra	xij s.
It' of William Lasseham for a tenement in the same strete for a yere ut supra	xij s.
It' of John Appowell for a stable in the Gutter lane for a yere ut supra	vij s.
It' of Thomas Carpenter for a gardeyn in the same lane	iiij d.
It' of Thomas Slithurst for ij° Gardeyns in the Lurkemer lane ut supra	ij s. viij d.
It' of Roger Johnson Curiour for a tenement in the Mercat place ut supra	x s.
It' of John Wilder of the Thele for di' acre of medow etc	xiij d.
It' of William Justice for a tenement in the hold of Robert Avenant	xij d.
It' of Johanne Hunt widowe for her tenement in the high strete	xiij d. ob.

S[um]ma iij li. iij s. x d. ob.

Grete bell

It' for tillyng the grete bell at terment of William Trew[1]	iiij d.
It' for tillyng at the terment holden by Mr Wattes	iiij d.
It' for Ryngyng at the terment of my lord Abbott[2]	xij d.
It' for Ryngyng at the knyll of Thomas Barbour	xij d.
It' for Ryngyng at the moneth mynde	xij d.
It' for tyllyng at terment for Mr pownsar	iiij d.
[p 130] It' for tyllyng at a terment holden by Thom[a]s Everard[3]	iiij d.
It' for tillyng at a terment holden for Staunford	iiij d.
It' Ryngyng the knyll of Wrightes wif	xij d.
It' Ryngyng the knyll for Sir John Richemond	xij d.
It' tyllyng at the month mynde	iiij d.
It' Ryngyng at the knyll for Kentes wif	xij d.
It' tyllyng at the monthes mynde	iiij d.
It' Ryngyng at the knyll for Mr Carpenter	xij d.
It' Ryngyng at the moneth mynde	xij d.
It' tyllyng at a terment for John lambe	iiij d.

S[um]ma x s. viij d.

1. William Trew, yeoman, was one of the ten members of the Jesus Mass gild named in Henry Kelsall's will, 1493. Kerry, *A History*, 169.
2. Abbot John Thorne III died 1519. B. R. Kemp, *Reading Abbey: an introduction to the history of the abbey* (Reading Museum and Art Gallery, 1968), 53. He was buried in the abbey.
3. Some letters were lost when the page was cropped destroying the superscript 'a' in Thomas and partially removing the abbreviation for 'er' in Everard. For more about him see Appendix 2.

Gravis

It' for the g[r]ave of Johanne Derlyng	vj s. viij d.
It' for the Coveryng of the same	vj d.
It' for the grave of Thomas Barbour	vj s. viij d.
It' for the Coveryng of the same	vj d.
It' for the grave of kentes wif	vj s. viij d.
It' for Coveryng of a grave in Saynt Johns Chancell broken for sir John Richemond	xij d.
It' for the grave of Mr Carpenter	vj s. viij d.
It' for the Coveryng of the same	vj d.

S[um]ma xxix s. ij d.

Setes

It' of Richard Birt for his wifes sete	vj d.
It' of John Skynner for his doughters seate	vj d.

S[um]ma xij d.

S[um]ma tot' xxxij li. {xvj s.} xvj s. iij d.

Expenses

In primis paid Thomas Everard for the churche dett	xiiij s. j d.
It' paid for makyng of iij[e] new Copis of the gifte of my lord[1] with rebond canvas & werkemanshipp	xvj s. iij d.
It' paid sir Thomas halle for a reward beside his wages	iij s. iiij d.
It' paid for makyng of the roode light with a li. of sises a genst allhalouday	xvj d.
It' paid Harry Horthorne for removyng a sete in Saynt Johns Chauncell	viij d.
It' paid Troll for removyng of the steppis in the quere growndpynnyng the setes in Saynt Johns Chauncell & for lyme therto	ij s. x d.
[p 131] It' paid for v li. of wax at x d. a li.	iiij s. ij d.
It' paid for Colis occupied in the vestrye	iiij d.
It' paid for makyng the rode light a genst Cristmas with di' a li. of sises	x d.
It' paid for Candilles	iij d.
It' paid for xxviij pamentes	xiiij d.
It' paid Harry Glasyer for mendyng of the wyndows in the churche	ij s. ij d.

lviij s. iiij d.

---

1. It appears that either Abbot John or the newly elected Abbot Thomas gave the fabric only.

It' paid William More the Tiler for x quarter of lyme v M^l of Tiles & iiij ^{M} of Brekes[1]

It' paid Hugh Smyth for diverce Iron werk for the churche	xij d.
It' paid for nayles of Dyverce sortes	xj d.
It' paid John paynter in ernest of xiiij li. xiij s. iiij d. for gildyng of the ij^o Tabernacles in the quere with all nessessaries therto	xx s.
It' paid for ij^o dosen of Thredden poyntes for the Canapie	ij d.
It' paid for the obite for the benef[ac]torum[2] of the churche	v s. iiij d.
It' paid Troll for Coveryng ij^o Gravis with a bz of stone lyme	viij d.
It' paid for wacchyng of the sepulcre	viij d.
It' paid for Colis	j d.
It' paid for makyng and settyng on the Orferis on the best paned Cope	xij d.
It' paid for makyng of the pascall & the font taper	vij d.

[*A pointing finger in margin by the next entry.*]

It' paid to yong Slithurst for a reward for playing uppon the organs	xx d.
It' paid Thomas Taberer for the kyng play at Witsontide	x s.
It' paid for his mete & drynk at Thomas Barbours	ij s. iiij d.
It' paid for lyvereis for this yere & the Last yere	viij d.
It' paid Troll for ij^o Tilers iij^e days at vij d. a day	iiij s. viij d.
It' paid for ij^o laborers iiij dayes at v d. a day	iij s. iiij d.
It' paid for a new bawderik to the greate bell	ij s. vj d.
It' paid for mendyng of a surplice	vij d.
It' paid for ix lodes of sand at iij d. a lode	ij s. iij d.
It' paid ij^o Tilers v dayes & one tiler ij dayes at vij d. a day	vij s.
It' paid a laborer iiij days & di' & ij laborers v dayes at v d. a day	vj s.
It' paid for cariage of iij^e lodes of Robell	vj d.
It' paid for ij qua' of stone lyme	ij s. viij d.
It' paid a Tiler & his man iij days xij d. a day a laborer di' a day ij d. & for leyng of a stone in the churche viij d.	iij s. x d.
It' paid for ij lodes of sand	vj d.
It' paid ij^o Tilers iij days & di' at vij d. a day	iiij s. j d.
It' paid iij^e laborers iij days & di' at v d. a day	iiij s. iiij d. ob.
It' paid ij^o Tilers vj days at vij d. a day	vij s.
It' paid iij^e laborers iiij days at v d. a day	v s.
[*p 132*] It' paid to a laborer ij days[3]	x d.

---

1. This appears to refer to the William More of Caversham who had previously supplied the parish with bricks. See above p. 97. The quantities suggest a substantial brickfield in Caversham.
2. The scribe used a Latin word meaning 'of the benefactors', instead of simply 'benefactors'.
3. The tops of the letters of this entry were lost when the page was cropped.

It' paid a Tiler vj days at vij d. a day ij laborers vj days   ix s. iij d.[1]
v d. a day

It' paid ij° laborers a day   ix d.

It' paid for iij pekkes of Tile pynnes[2]   vj d.

It' paid for iiij ^M of Tiles   xx s.

It' paid a Tyler vj dayes vij d. a day ij laborers vj days & di'   viij s. vj d.[3]

It' paid for ij qua' of stone lyme   ij s. viij d.

It' paid to White for iij C of latthes at v d. a C   xv d.

It' paid for ij M of Tiles   x s.

It' paid to ij° Tilers vj days at vij d. a day & ij° laborers vj   xij s. x d.
days & one laborer ij° days

[in the margin in a different hand] a new lofte   x s.

It' paid Miller the Carvar in parte of iij li. rest[4] of makyng of
the new lofte

It' paid Henry Horthorne for plankyng the gutter nayles   xvj s. x d.
bourdes & warkmanshipp

It' paid for iij M^l of Tiles   xv s.

It' paid ij° tilers iiij days vij d. a day & ij° laborers iiij days   ix s. viij d.[5]
v d. a day

It' paid to the plummer for the rest of castyng & leyng of the   ix s.
gutter of led

It' paid for a M^l di' of Tiles   vij s. vj d.

It' paid for a lode of sand   iij d.

It' paid ij° Tilers ij dayes & iij laborers ij° days   iiij s. x d.

It' paid ij° Tilers a day iij laborers a day   ij s. v d.

It' paid for xiij C of lathe nayle   xij d.

It' paid for clensyng of Saynt Johns Chauncell & the loftes   xiiij d.

It' paid for vj C of lathes   ij s. vj d.

It' paid for mendyng of a surplice   vj d.

It' paid a Tiler & his man a day   xij d.

It' paid Wheler for Crestes & gutters   v s.

It' paid for mendyng of the Clock   iij s. iiij d.

It' paid for pavyng in the mercat place be fore the tenement   v s.
in the hold of Roger Coriour

It' paid to Pastelar & his man for iiij days & di'   iiij s.

It' paid to Pasteler & his man   iij s. iiij d.

It' paid for a M^l of lathe nayle   x d.

It' paid to the offic' for Smoke Ferthynges   iij s. vj d. ob.

---

1. The total is wrong; it should be 8s 6d. The confusion may have arisen because the same
workmen were being paid for similar but different lengths of time.
2. A peck was a quarte of a bushel.
3. This total is wrong. It should be 8s 11d.
4. The balance of his payment.
5. The total should be eight shillings.

Wages

It' paid to Stephyn Thorpe for his wages	xiij s. iiij d.
It' paid to the same Stephyn for a tenement in the hold of Henry Moore graunted hym toward his wages for a yere	xij s.
It' paid Richard Andrews under sexten for his wages for a yere	xij s.
It' paid for scouryng of the Canstikkes for a yere	x d.
It' paid for wasshyng of the churche gere	iij s. iiij d.
It' paid for a bell rope	xl d.
It' paid a key for the hall dore of the tenement in the hold of Harry More	vj d.
It' paid Harry Horthorne for plankes bourdes nayles & werkmanshipp uppon the gutter betwene the Chauncelles wherof the Amner must pay one half[1]	ix s. ij d.
[*p 133*] It' paid to Harry Horthorne for plonkyng of the gutter betwene the tenement in the hold of Roger Coriour & the tenement of Jh[esu]s in the mercat place[2] for the half ther of as apperithe by a bill	iij s.
It' paid to the plummer for leying half the gutter	iijs. iiij d.
It' paid for xiiij li. of wax at x d. a li.	xj s. viij d.
It' paid for a li. di' of Frankencence	xviij d.
It' paid for nayles of dyverce sortes	xvij s. x d.
It' paid for tile pynnes	v s. v d.
It' paid for vj C of latthes at v d. a C	ij s. vj d.
It' paid for ij payr of Gymews for the organs	v d.
It' paid for frenge for the high awter Clothe of whit & grene	ij s.
It' paid for di' a li. of Crewle Frenge	xij d.
It' paid for xix C lathes at v d. a C	vij s. xj d.
It' paid for rebond for the new awter Clothe of white	vj d.
It' paid for Canvas for Coveryng of Saynt Michaell	iij d.
It' paid for cariage of the Image from Maynard of london	iiij d.
It' paid to the plummer for leying of the Amners parte of the gutter betwene the Chauncelles	ij s.
It' paid for xxiiij C of long lathes at vij d. the hundred	xiiij s.
It' paid for nayles of dyverce sortes	iiij s. viij d. ob.
It' paid Troll in parte of payment of xxiij s. iiij d. for selyng of the quere tylyng of the dormentes over the new wyndows for makyng of his skaffold & for all necessaries to the mason belongyng	xvj s. viij d.

---

1. As rector of the parish, the abbey was responsible for the upkeep of the chancel. It seems the chancel was a charge on the almoner's income from some town properties though this is not specifically stated in the schedule of abbey possessions in 1539-40 printed in J. B. Hurry, *Reading Abbey* (1901), 88-91.

2. A property owned by the Jesus gild. Apparently the cost of repairs was shared.

It' paid for Iron Barres for the wyndows weyng xxix li. at   iij s. vj d. ob.[1]
j d. ob. a li.

It' paid Whit for Glasse in parte of payment for glasse for   xviij s.
the quere   viij d.

It' paid for pavyng of a grave in Saynt Johns Chauncell   iiij d.

It' paid to Stephyn for arrerage for the tenement in the new   iij s.
strete

It' paid for iij M[l] of latthe nayles a[t] x d. a M[l]   ij s. vj d.

It' paid for makyng & regestryng of this accompte   ij s.

S[um]ma tot' xxvij li. xiij s. vij d.

Sic debet v li. ij s. viij d.

At this accompte hath ben dismyssed William Edmunde and
in his place chosen Richard Turner

[*In the margin before the next three entries*] nihil

Uppon[2] phillipp Risby graunted toward the reparacion of the   iij s. iiij d.
Chauncell

Uppon Richard yeve for the same   iij s. iiij d.

Uppon David Williams for the same   xij d.
sol'

Uppon Henry More for di' yeres rent of the tenement in the   vj s.
New strete[3]

---

1. The total should be 3s 7½d.
2. This is the English form of *super* used on p. 93 of the accounts. It means sums owing.
3. 'Sol' written in left-hand margin by this entry indicating that the debt was later paid.

1520-21

[*p 134*] Thaccomptes of William Knyght & Richard Turner Wardens of the church of Saynt laurence in Redyng From the Fest of Saynt Michaell tharchangell in the yere of oure lord anno M[l] D xx[ti] & the xij[th] yere of the regne off kyng Henry the viij[th] unto the Same Fest then next Followyng

[*In left-hand margin in a modern hand*] 1521
[*and in a sixteenth-century hand*]1522

Arr'

In Primis the seid wardens have ben charged with	v li. ij s.
tharrerages of the last accompte as apperith in the fote of the	viij d.
same accompte	
It' uppon Harry More for di' yeres rent of the tenement in	vj s.
the south side of the New strete	

S[um]ma v li. viij s. viij d.

Rec'

It' Rec' For the rode lyght at all halloutyde	xiiij s. ij d.
It' Rec' for the Rode lyght at Cristomas	xiij s.
It' Rec' of Mr Vicar toward the reparacion of the churche[1]	iiij s. viij d.
It' Rec' For the pascall money at Ester	xlvj s. viij d.
It' Rec' of Mr Amner toward the charges of the rouges	xxvj s.
castyng of the quere	viij d.
It' Rec' of a certayn persone toward the charges of the	vj s. viij d.
rouges castyng of the churche by the procuryng of Ric'	
Turner	
It' Rec' For Hokmoney gatherid by the women clere	xxxj s. vj d.
It' Rec' For Hokmoney gatherid by the men clere	vj s. vj d. ob.
It' Rec' of the gatheryng of the kyng play at witsontide clere	xvj s.
It' Rec' of the bequest of Mr Trew	xx s.
It' Rec' of the wardens of Jh[esu]s toward the Sextens	xxxiij s.
Wages for a yere endid at Mich' anno xiij°	iiij d.
It' Rec' of the Wardens of oure lady toward the Sextens	xxxiij s.
wagys for a yere endid ut supra	iiij d.
It' Rec' for refuse latthis sold	ij s.
It' Rec' of the bequest of Mr Carpenter[2]	vj s. viij d.

1. The vicar was Richard Bedowe.
2. Thomas Carpenter was four times Mayor of Reading between 1504 and 1510. In his will made 20 August 1520, he bequeathed 6s 8d to the repair of the church, ten shillings to Our Lady Mass and asked to be buried in the church where the brethren of Jesus Mass thought convenient. Richard Abyndon, parish clerk, was a witness. TNA Will of Thomas Carpenter, PROB 11/20/3.

It' Rec' of the bequest of Mr Justice	xx s.
It' Rec' of the bequest of Raphe White	iij s. iiij d.

S[um]ma xiiij li. iiij s. vj d. ob.

[*This entry is written in larger letters*]
S[um]ma xix li. xiij s. ij d. ob.

[*p 135*] Rentes	
It' Rec' of John Barfote for a tenement in the north side of the New strete in the hold of Robert Coxseter for a yere endyd at Midsomer anno xiij°	x s.
It' of Thomas Harvey for a tenement in the same strete for a yere endid at the same Fest	vj s. viij d.
It' of Harry More for a tenement in the same strete For a yere endid at the same Fest	xij s.
It' of William Lasscham for a tenement in the same strete for a yere endid at the same Fest	xij s.
It' of John Appowell For a stable in the gutter lane for a yere endid at the same Fest	vij s.
It' of Margeret Carpenter widow For a gardeyn in the same lane for a yere ut supra	iiij d.
It' of Thomas Slithurst for ij° gardeyns in Lurkemer lane for a yere ut supra	ij s. viij d.
It' of Roger Johnson Coriour for a tenement in the mercat place for Di' yere endid at Cristmas	v s.
It' of John wilder of the Thele for half an acre of mede lying by langney for a yere endyd at Mich' anno xij° for asmuche as it is paiable but ons a yere	xiij d.
It' of William Justice for a tenement in the hold of Robert Avenant For a yere endid at Mich' anno xij°	xij d.
It' of Johanne Hunt widowe For a tenement in the high strete For a yere endid at Mich' anno xij°	xiij d. ob.

S[um]ma lviij s. x d. ob.

Grete bell[1]

It' For tyllyng at the terment holden by Mr Everard	iiij d.
It' For tyllyng at the terment of Mr Pownsar	iiij d.
It' For tyllyng at the terment {of} holden by John Kent	iiij d.
It' For tyllyng at the terment holden by Symon lambe	iiij d.

---

1. According to a parish agreement of 1515-16, the wardens charged twelve pennies for ringing a knell, probably a passing bell, but only four pennies when the ringers tolled the bell summoning people to a funeral or a month's mind (accounts p. 108).

It' For tyllyng at the terment holden For sir John Richemond	iiij d.
It' For tyllyng at the terment holden by Robert Dodson dyer	iiij d.
It' For Ryngyng at the knyll of the wif of Roger Johnson	xij d.
It' For Ryngyng at the knyll of William Kene	xij d.
It' For Ryngyng at the knyll of William Trew	xij d.
It' For Ryngyng at the terment holden For Mr payn	xij d.
It' For tyllyng for the terment holden For stanford	iiij d.
It' For Ryngyng at the month mynde of William Trew	xij d.
It' For tyllyng at the month mynde of Roger Johnson	iiij d.
It' For tyllyng at the terment holden by Richard Turner	iiij d.
It' For tyllyng at the terment holden by Mr wattes	iiij d.
It' For Ryngyng at the knyll For John Glymyn	xij d.
It' For Ryngyng at the knyll of William Traunder the kynges servant	xij d.

S[um]ma x s. iiij d.

[*p 136*] Gravis	
It' for the grave of the wif of Roger Johnson	vj s. viij d.
It' for the Coveryng of the same grave	vj d.
It' for the grave of William Trewe[1]	vj s. viij d.
It' for the Coveryng of the same grave	x d.

S[um]ma xiiij s. viij d.

Setis

[*In the margin before the next six entries*] a	
It' of Richard Clark for his wifes sete	iiij d.
It' of my lord for his moder sete	iiij d.
It' of William Buryton for his wifes sete	vj d.
It' of Thomas Balsar for his wifes sete	iiij d.
It' of Nicholas Hide for a rome for his doughter in the void sete behynde his wif	iiij d.
It' of Mistres Bridges for a sete	vj d.

S[um]ma ij s. iiij d.

S[um]ma tot' de omnibus rec' xxiij li. xix s. v d.

Expenses

In primis payd for makyng of the rode light a genst allhaloutide with a li. of sises	xviij d.

---

1. William Trewe was one of ten members of the gild of the Mass of Jesus named in Henry Kelsall's will 1493. Kerry, *A History*, 169.

It' paid to Miller the Carvar in parte of l s. rest for makyng of the new lofte[1]	vj s. viij d.
It' paid to Pasteler the Carpenter for makyng of certayn besynes in the churche	ij s. x d.
It' paid to Troll for Coveryng of gravis & for tilyng of the skelyng in the procession wey	xviij d.
It' paid for cariage of Rubell out of the procession wey	iij d.
It' paid for makyng of the rode light a genst Cristmas with di' li. of sises	viij d.
It' paid for mendyng of surplices belongyng to the churche	viij d.
It' paid to John Knyght for certayne besynesse in the churche	iij d.
It' paid for nayles & tile pynnes	j d. ob.
It' paid for Evisbourd	iiij d.
It' paid for mendyng of the cloth be fore Saynt Clement	iiij d.
It' paid for emendyng of the gutter over the vestrie	iij d.
It' paid to a mason for roughcastyng of the churche	xiij s. iiij d.

[*The total of the expenses on this page is written in Arabic numerals at the bottom right hand side.*]

28s 8d ob.

[*p 137*] It' paid to the same Mason for Whityng of the Chauncell	xij d.
It' paid for Gravell occupied in Rough castyng of the Churche	xx d.
It' paid to a laborer for siftyng of gravell	iiij d.
It' paid for iiij quarters of stone lyme for the same	v s. iiij d.
It' paid for reparacions & emendyng of other necessaries in the churche	ij s. vij d.
It' paid for reparacion of the porche of the churche	ij s. x d.
It' paid for a fire pan[2]	xvj d.
It' paid for hangyng of the Canapie	iiij d.
It' paid for di' a li. of Frankencence	vj d.
It' paid for rebond & for mendyng of the Sepulcre Cloth	iij d.
It' paid for the obite for the benefactoris of the churche	vj s. viij d.
It' paid for lent clothis for the high awter & Saynt Thomas awter	vj s. ij d.

[*A pointing finger in margin.*]

It' paid to the clokmaker for a new Clok in parte of payment of v li.	xl s.
It' paid for emendyng of the glasse wyndows	ij s.
It' paid to Hugh Smyth for certayne besynes in the Churche	vj d.
It' paid for Wax and for makyng of the rode light the pascall & the font taper	x s. vij d.

1. The payment of 6s 8d to Miller is the remainder (rest) of his fee of fifty shillings.
2. This was possibly to hold the charcoal in the censer.

It' paid for emendyng of the rectors stolis	ij s.
It' paid for emendyg of a vestment	iiij d.
It' paid to Wheler for tils & lyme	xj s.
It' paid for cariage of a lode of muck	ij d.
It' paid for bourdes for makyng of the pentice over the Image of Saynt laurence & for settyng upp the same Image without the churche at thest end of the quere[1]	iiij s. ij d.
It' paid for emendyng of surplices	v d. ob.
It' paid for a Bawdrik for a bell	x d.
It' paid for a hose cloth gyven to the overseer of My lord Cardynalles werkes to licence Chayney the mason to cum from thens[2]	iiij s. iiij d.
It' paid for tiles nayles & Cord	iij d. ob.
It' paid for lyngyng of stolis	ij d.
It' paid for emendyng of the Canstik of silver	ij d.
It' paid to Harry Wier for charges in goyng for a prest	xv d.
[A pointing finger in margin]	
It' paid to John knyght for Coveryng of the rode lofte & the Images	xiiij d.
It' paid for charges in Ridyng for Chayney the Mason	iij s. iiij d.
It' paid for a new Bere	xj s. iiij d. ob.
It' paid for cariage of Robell out of the churche	xij d.
It' paid for a surplice for the parisshe prest	viij s.
It' paid for bell ropis	iiij s. iiij d.
[p 138] It' paid to the officiall for smoke ferthynges	iij s. vj d. ob.
It' paid to Harry Cobbe in parte of vj s. for takyng downe of the bracis of the beamys & for settyng upp of vj new corsis	iij s.
It' paid to white the Belfownder for arrerages of the glasse for the <new> wyndows in the quere in full payment for the same wyndows	xiij s. iiij d.
It' paid for nailes & oker for the churche	ij s. vij d.

Wages

It' paid to Emery the sexten for his wages for half a yere endid at the Fest of saynt Michaell tharchangell anno xiij°	v marcs
It' paid to Steven Thorpe toward his wages for a yere endid at the same fest	xxvj s. viij d.
It' paid to Richard Andrews undersexten toward his wages for a yere endid at the same Fest	xij s.
It' paid for the scouryng of the Canstikes for a yere	x d.
It' paid for wasshyng of the stuff belongyng to the churche for a yere	iij s. iiij d.

1. This statue was erected outside (without) the church, on the east wall facing the abbey.
2. This was probably Thomas Wolsey's palace at Hampton Court which was constructed between 1515 and 1526. It is less than thirty miles from Reading. S. Thurley, *The Royal Palaces of Tudor England* (Newhaven and London, 1993), 41-3.

It' paid for a frame to sett on the Clock	ij s. vj d.
It' paid to Segemond the organmaker for transposyng of the grete organs as apperithe by a bill therof made	vj li. xx d.
It' paid for di' li. of Frankencence	vj d.
It' paid for half yeris rent for the tenement in the hold of Emery	viij s.
It' paid for makyng of the Accompte	ij s.

S[um]ma tot' paid & expendid xxj li. xj s. vj d. ob.

Sic debet xlvij s. x d. ob.

Wher of uppon William Edmunde for half yeres rent of the tenement in the hold of Harry More	vj s.

So rest Clere uppon this Accompte xlj s. x d. ob.

[The next two entries are bracketed and totalled together]

It' uppon Mr Thomas Justice for the grave of Mistres Smyth his moder vj s. viij d.	vij s. ij d.
It' for Coveryng the same grave vj d.	

At this Accompte hath ben dismyssed William Knyght & <in> his place chosen Robert Blake

1521-22

[*p 139*] Thacc' of Richard Turner & Robert Blake Wardens of the churche of Saynt laurence in Redyng from the Fest of Saynt Michaell tharchangell in the yere of our lord anno M^l D xxj & the xiijth yere of the regne of kyng Henry the viijth unto the same Fest then next followyng, that is to witt for one yere endid at Mich' anno M^l D xxij° & the xiiijth yer of the regne of the seid king

[In the right-hand margin in a sixteenth-century hand] 1522 and 1523[1]

Arr'

In primis the seid acc' have ben charged with tharr' of the last acc' as apperith in the fote of the same accompte	xlj s. x d. ob.
It' of William Edmundes for tharr' of the tenement in the hold of Harry More	vj s.

S[um]ma xlvij s. x d. ob.

---

1. This contradicts the correct dates in the preamble which are clearly dated 1521-1522 both by calendar and regnal years.

Receites

Rec' for the rode light at allhaloutid	xvij s.
Rec' for the rode light at Cristmas	xvj s. ix d.
Rec' for the pascall money at Estur	xlj s. iij d.
Rec' of the women for gatheryng on hockmonday a bove all charges	xviij s. v d.
Rec' of the men for the gatheryng on hoktewisday a bove all charges	vj s. vj d.
Rec' of the wardens of Jh[esu]s toward the sextens wages for a yere endid at Mich' anno xiiij°	xxxiij s. iiij d.
Rec' of the wardens of our lady toward the sextens wages for a yendid[1] at Mich' anno xiiij°	xxxiij s. iiij d.
Rec' for led of the old font sold {for}	vij s.

S[um]ma viij li. xiij s. vij d.

Rentes

Rec' of John Barfote for a tenement in the north side of the new strete in the hold of Robert Coxsetur for a yere endid at Midsomer anno xiiij°	x s.
Rec' of Thomas Harvie for a tenement in the same strete for a yere ut supra	vj s. viij d.
Rec' of Harry More for a tenement in the same strete for half yere endid at Cristmas	vj s.
Rec' of William lasseham for a tenement in the same strete for a yere endid at Midsomer	xij s.
Rec' of John Appowell for a stable in the gutter lane for a yere endid ut supra	vij s.
Rec' of Margaret Carpenter for a gardeyn in the same lane for a yere ut supra	iiij d.
Rec' of Thomas {Carpenter} Slithurst for ij° gardeyns in lurkmerlane for a yere ut supra	ij s. viij d.
Rec' of John Fletchar for a shopp in the Mercat place for iij° quarters endid ut supra	v s.
Rec' of the same Flecchar for the tenement ther for vij wekes aftur j d. a weke	vij d.
Rec' of John wilder of the Thele for di' acre of medowe lying by langley for a yere endid at mich' anno xiij° for asmuche as it is payable but ons {in} in the yere	xiij d.

1. Year ended.

Rec' of William Justice for a tenement in the hold of Robert Avenant for a yere endid at mich' anno xiij°	xij d.
Rec' of Johanne Hunt for a tenement in the high strete for a yere endid at Mich' anno xiij°	xiij d. ob.

S[um]ma liij s. v d.[1]

[p 140]   Grete bell

Rec' for Ryngyng of the knyll of Thomas Wattes	xij d.
Rec' for Ryngyng of the knyll of Mistres Smythe	xij d.
Rec' for Ryngyng at her month mynde	xij d.
Rec' for Ryngyng at her xij Month Mynde	xij d.
Rec' for tillyng at a terment holden by Mr Everard	iiij d.
Rec' for tyllyng at the mynde of willyam trew	iiij d.
Rec' for tillyng at the terment of John wylcox	iiij d.
Rec' for tyllyng at the terment of John Turnner	iiij d.
Rec' for tyllyng at the terment for benit	iiij d.
Rec' for tyllyng at the terment of Stamford	iiij d.

S[um]ma vj s.

Graves

Rec' for the grave of the wyffes of John bukworth	vj s. viij d.
Rec' for Coveryng of the same grave	[blank]
Rec' for the grave of Mistres Smyth	vj s. viij d.
Rec' for coveryng of the same grave	vj d.
Rec' for the grave of Henry Horthorn	vj s. viij d.
Rec' for coveryng of the same grave	viij d.
Rec' for the grave of willyam lasseham[2]	vj s. viij d.
Rec' for Coveryng of the same grave	viij d.
Rec' for the grave of the wyfe of Nyc' Kene	vj s. viij d.
Rec' for Coveryng of the same grave	viij d.
Rec' for the grave of thomas wattes	vj s. viij d.
Rec' for Coveryng of the same	vj d.

S[um]ma l s. ij d.[3]

Seyttes

Rec' of Rychard saunders for his[4] wyffes sete	vj d.
Rec' of thomas waker for his wyffes sete	vj d.
Rec' of Margaret staunton	iiij d.

---

1. This total should be 53s 5$\frac{1}{2}$ d.
2. For more information about William Lasseham see Appendix 2.
3. The total is incorrect. It shoud be forty-three shillings.
4. The scribe has used the conventional abbreviation for 'es' in all the following entries; they have been transcribed as 'is'.

Rec' of Ryc' gardyner	iiij d.
Rec' of Mr wattes	vj d.
Rec' of Nyc' Kene	iiij d.
Rec' of William underwode for his wyffes sete	iiij d.
Rec' of Roger Coryar for his wyffes sete	vj d.
Rec' of wyers wyff for her sete	iiij d.
Rec' of Robert Ellys for his wyffes sete	vj d.
Rec' of phyllyp Rysby for his mothers sete	vj d.
Rec' of henry Corrour for his wyffes sete	vj d.
Rec' of Robert Blake for his wyffes sete	vj d.
Rec' of William Corkyngton for his wyffes sete	vj d.
Rec' of Robert Oyle for his wyffes sete	iiij d.
Rec' of Ryc' Cavye for his wyffes sete	iiij d.
Rec' of Randall laurenc for his wyffes sete	iiij d.
Rec' of humfrey sexton for his wyffes sete	iiij d.
Rec' of Thomas Grey for his wyffes sete	iiij d.
[*p 141*] Rec' of William turner for his wyffes sete	iiij d.
Rec' of Roger Johnson for his wyffes sete	vj d.
Rec' of Mistres Dawson	v d.
Rec' of Ryc' goldsmyth for his wyffes sete	ij d.
Rec' of James pewterer for his wyffes sete	vj d.
Rec' of John Rycardes for his wyffes sete	iiij d.
Rec' of Christofer Johnson for his wyffes sete	iiij d.
Rec' of Johanne Rumsey wydow for a sete	iiij d.
Rec' of hugh Joynour for his wyffes sete	iiij d.
Rec' of Ryc' Adderton for his wyffes sete	iiij d.
Rec' of edward phylyppes for his wyffes sete	iiij d.
Rec' of Aleyn Chawndler for his wyffes sete	iiij d.
Rec' of John a morpud for his wyffes sete	vj d.
Rec' of willyam Fayrechyld for his wyffes sete	vj d.
Rec' of wayter hethcobe for his wyffes sete	iiij d.

S[um]ma xiij s. iij d.[1]

S[um]ma totalis de omnibus Recept' xvij li. iiij s. iiij d. ob.[2]

Exspenses or paymenttes

In primis payd to the cloke makear in {full} \<parte> payment of {v li.} \<vj li. x s.> For the new cloke & the dyall	iij li.
It' for makeyng of j li. of syses a genst all haloutyde	j d.
It' payd for the tymber & sawyng of viij Corbettes for the new arches[3]	viij d.

---

1. The correct total is 13s 5d.
2. The total income corrected was £16 17s 2d. The corrected annual surplus was 4s 5$\frac{1}{2}$ d.
3. See Introduction for a discussion of improvements to the church at this date.

It' payd for tymber for the dyall	iiij d.
It' payd for makeyng of ij bawdrykes	xj d.
It' payd to iiij laborares for besynes done yn the chyrch when the new arches were mayd	iiij s. xj d.
It' payd to thre tyllers & theyr laborers for whyttyng the church & tylleyng ther[1] the pynnacle dyd breke & payveyng certon places yn the chyrch	ix s.
It' payd for settyng the olde seattes with the new seattes be foore our ladye	v s. vj d.
It' payd for tymber for the cloke hows	ij s.
It' payd for layyng of a new rafter brokyn with the pynnacle	xij d.
It' payd for mendyng of ij bell roopes	iij d.
It' payd to iiij laborers for makeyng clene the chyrche agenst Crystmas	iij s. v d.
It' payd for makeyng of xj tapers agenst Crystmas	xvj d. ob.
It' payd for tryyng of the rode lyght & makyng of lynkes	iiij d.
[*p 142*] It' payd to henry hoorethorne for the wyndow yn the sowth syde of the chyrch next the stepyll be sydes that he have gyven[2]	vij s. iiij d.
It' payd to willyam Justyce for di' yeres rent of the ten[emen]t that emery dwellyth yn	viij s.
It' payd for makeyng of the cawssye at the qwere dore	viij d.
It' payd for iij pecces of Tymber to hold yn the cawssye	xij d.
It' payd for makeyng clene the gutter & haveyng down the pynnacle that Fell ther yn	ij d.
It' payd yn reward to a syngyng man	xx d.
It' payd for iij loodes of erth & sond for the cloke hows	xviij d.
It' payd for Caryeg of Rubell from the qwere dore	x d.
It' payd for makeyng of ij staf torches for the hygh awter with wyke & ij stavys of vyrre for the same	xiij d.
It' payd to troll & hes man & a laborer workyng opon the cloke hows & paveyng yn the north range	xxiij d.
It' payd for bordyng of the olde seattes where the old font stode & for makeyng of a seat at the west doore	xviij d.
It' payd for naylles for the seattes	xvij d.
It' payd for the bordes of all the olde seattes	ij s.
It' payd for the obyte holden the morrow after palme Sondey for the benefactours of the chyrch	vj s. iiij d.
It' payd for makeyng of the Cover for the Fonte	xij d.
It' payd for yorn worke for the same	x d.
It' payd to Mr Everod for bordes for the cover of the fonte & for di' M[l] tyles occupyde over the new wyndow	[*blank*]
It' payd for j li. of Frankencens	xij d.

1. Where.
2. The scribe has omitted 'been'. The entry should read 'that he hath been gyven'.

It' payd for a surplesse for thomas balsere — iij s. iiij d.

It' payd John paynter for payntyng of sent leonard left by the wyffes unpayntyd — xx d.

It' payd to John paynter for payntyng the lent awter cloth & the Judas — xij d.

It' payd to Segesmond by thadvyse of the parysh for transposyng & new castyng the fore fronte of the organs & settyng yn the new stope — xiij s. iiij d.

It' payd for a bz of Colis & takkys — j d. ob.

It' payd for watchyng of the sepulcre — viij d.

It' payd for scouryng of the Canstykes agenst Crysmas — x d.

It' payd for makeyng the pascall & font taper — vij d.

It' payd for a bell roope to the iiij^th bell — ij s. iij d.

It' for lyme & sande — xviij d.

[*p 143*]It' payd for half a hyde of whytlether — xiiij d.

It' payd for glayssyng the new wyndow next the stepoll conten' xlij footes & di' at iiij d. ob. the foote — xvj s.[1]

It' payd for glassyng the stepoll wyndow over the dyall with parte of old glas & parte new — vij s. vj d.

It' payd for yorn bars for the same wyndows Conteynyng xxxiiij li. & di' at ob. q' the j li. — ij s. ij d.[2]

It' payd for washyng the stuff belongyng to the chyrch — iij s. iiij d.

It' payd to the offyc' for smoke Farthynges — iij s. vj d. ob.

It' payd to Ryc' Cavy for makeyng the clapper of the grete bell contenyng v^xx xix li. at ob. the j li. — [*blank*][3]

It' payd to John barfote for a new pryntyd legend be sydes the rest therof by hym gyven to the chyrch — iij s. iiij d.

Item payd for a M^l of pavyng tyles ledeyd for the church after xxiij s. ix d. the M^l as many as shall suffyce for the church — xx s.[4]

It' payd for nayles to bord the olde seates & for other reparacions yn the church — xviij d.

It' payd for vj bz of lyme — vj d.

It' payd for half a bz of tyle pynes occupyed over the wyndow — ij d. ob.

It' payd for whypcord — ob.

It' payd for cloth to enlenght the lent awter cloth — iij d.

It' payd to Ryc' Andrews for a brush — iij d.

It' payd for mendyng of the gret bell bawdryke & for emendyng of ij bell roopes — iiij d.

It' payd for iij sloppys for the chyrch — vj s.

---

1. This total has been rounded up to the next shilling; the actual cost was 15s 11¼d.
2. This total has been rounded to the nearest penny. Ob. q' means ½ d + ¼d =¾d.
3. The total is 5s 11½ d.
4. The cost indicates that only 842 tiles were purchased. They appear to have been glazed ('ledyd').

It' payd for lyme & sand for growndpynyng the new seattes	xviij d.
It' payd for makyng of this accompte	ij s.

Wayges

It' payd to thomas balsar for his half yere wages Endyd at Michaelmes anno xiiij°	iij li.
It' payd to Stevyn Thorpe for his wages for a yere Endyd at Mychaelmas anno ut supra	xxvj s. viij d.
It' payd to Ryc' Andrew for his yeres wayges endyd ut supra	xij s.
It' payd to thomas balsar yn reward for his attendaunce be fore he enteryd yn to his servys	iij s. iiij d.
It' payd to Ric' Turner for arrerages to hym dew	x s.

S[um]ma totalis de omnibus expenses atque solucionibus
xvj li. xij s. xj d. ob.

Sic deb' xij s. iiij d. At this acc' hath ben dismissed Richard
Turner & in his place chosen David Williams

{M[emoran]d[um]} that Mr vicar owt to the churche in wax	[blank]}

1522-3

[p 144]¹ **Thacc' of Robert Blake & Davyd Willyams
wardens of the chyrche of sent lawrence in Redyng
Frome the Fest of Saynt Mychaell tharchangell, In the
yere of our lorde anno M¹ vᶜ & xxij & the xiiij^th yere of
the regne of kynge henry the viij^th unto the same Fest
then next folloyng, That ys to wyt for one yere endyd at
Mich' anno M¹ ccccc° xxiij° & the xv^th yere of the Regne
of the sayde kyng**

[In the left hand margin in a sixteenth century hand] {1524}
[and in a modern hand] 1522 1523 {and 1524}

Arr'

In primis the sayd accounte hathe ben charged with the arr' of the laste accounte as dothe appere yn the fote of the same	xij s. iiij d.

Receptes

Rec' for the roode lyght at allhalloutyde	xvj s.
Rec' for the roode lyght at crystmas	xviij s. iiijd.
Rec' for paschall money at easter	xlj s.
Rec' of the women & men at hoketyd clere	xxij s.
Rec' of the wardens of Jh[esus] towardes the Sexton wagges for a yere endyd at Mich[aelm]es anno xv° r[egni] r[egis] henrici viij¹	xxxiij s. iiij d.

1. Between pages 144 and 189 the binding made with an English service book shows through.

Rec' of the wardens of our lady towardes the Sexton wagges for a yere endyd at Mich[aelm]es anno xv° r[egni] r[egis] henrici viij[i]	xxxiij s. iiij d.

S[um]ma viij li. xvj s. iiij d.

Rentes by the yere

Rec' of John Barfote for a tenement yn the north syde of the new strete yn the hold of John Swane For a yere endyd at Mydsomer anno xv°	x s.
Rec' of thomas harvy for a tenement yn the same strete endyd ut supra	vj s. viij d.
Rec' of harry More for a tenement yn the same strete for iij quarters endyd at Mich[aelm]es anno xv°	nihil
Rec' of lessham wyff for a tenement yn the same strete for a yere endyd at Mydsomer	xij s.
Rec' of John appowell for a stabull yn gutter layne fore a yere endyd ut supra	vij s.
Rec' of Margyt Carpenter For a garden yn gutter layn for a yere endyd ut supra	iiij d.
Rec' of thomas Slythrust for ij gardens yn lyrkemer layn for a yere endyd ut supra	ij s. viij d.
Rec' of John Fletcher For a Shope yn the Market place for a quarter & di' endyd [blank]	ij s. viij d.
Rec' of John wylder of thele for di' acre meddow lyyng by {langley} langney for a yere endyd at Mich[aelm]es anno xiiij° payable but ons a yere	xiij d.
Rec' of willyam Justice for a tenement yn the hold of Robert Avenant for a yere endyd at Mich[aelm]es ut supra	xij d.
Rec' of Johanne hunte for a tenement yn the hygh strete for a yere endyd ut supra	xiij d. ob.

S[um]ma xliiij s. vj d. ob.

[p 145] Greate Bell	
Rec' for the knyll of the vycar of hakfeld[1]	xij d.
Rec' for the knyll of Mistres Dabscourt	xij d.
Rec' for the knyll of Davye Joons	xij d.
Rec' for the knyll of thomas Tayller	xij d.
Rec' for the knyll of John Whyttyngham	xij d.
Rec' for the knyll of Mistres vyncent	xij d.
Rec' for the knyll of John wynyet	xij d.

---

1. Probably Heckfield, Hampshire, about eight miles south of Reading. The connection with St Laurence's parish is uncertain.

Rec' for the knyll of John boyers wyff	xij d.
Rec' for Ryngyng at the monthes mynd of Mistres vyncent	xij d.
Rec' for Ryngyng at the monthes mynd of John wynet	xij d.
Rec' for tyllyng at the terment of John wylkox	iiij d.
Rec' for tyllyng at the terment of willyam whyt	iiij d.
Rec' for tyllyng at the terment of John pownsir	iiij d.
Rec' for tyllyng at the terment of thomas Carpenter	iiij d.
Rec' for tyllyng at the terment of Thomas wattes	iiij d.
Rec' for tyllyng at the terment of willyam lendall	iiij d.
Rec' for tyllyng at the terment of Mr Trew	iiij d.

S[um]ma xij s. iiij d.

Graves

Rec' for the grave of John boyers wyff	vj s. viij d.
Rec' for Coveryng of the same	vj d.
Rec' for the grave of thomas Tayller	vj s. viij d.
Rec' for Coveryng of the same	viij d.
Rec' for the grave of harry carpenter	vj s. viij d.
Rec' for Coveryng of the same	vj d.
Rec' for the grave of Davye Joons	vj s. viij d.
Rec' for Coveryng of the same	viij d.
Rec' for the grave of Mistres vyncent	vj s. viij d.
Rec' for coveryng of the same	viij d.

S[um]ma xxxvij s. iiij d.

Seattes

Rec' of gowghes wyff for her seate	vj d.
Rec' of [?Innpardes] wyff For her seate	iiij d.
Rec' of Ric' sperepoyntes wyff for her seate	iiij d.
Rec' of James bluettes wyff for her seate	vj d.
Rec' of John webbes wyff for her seate	iiij d.
Rec' of Robert Medwyns wyff for her seate	iiij d.
Rec' of Ryc' Bassettes wyff for her seate	vj d.
Rec' of Thomas pesse wyff for her seate	iiij d.
Rec' of John Sheppardes wyff for her seate	iiij d.
Rec' of water Cutler wyff for her seate	iiij d.
[*p 146*] Rec' of Ric' {Ellys} <elms> wyff for her[1] seate	iij d.
Rec' of eadward shoveleres wyff for her seate	iiij d.
Rec' of John goldynges wyff for her seate	iiij d.
Rec' of thomas brygges wyff for her seate	iiij d.
Rec' of thomas haylles wyff for her seate	iiij d.
Rec' of edward aynsworth wyff for her seate	iiij d.

---

1. The writer mistakenly added a superfluous tild signifying 'er'. This has been omitted.

Rec' of Robert gregorys wyff for her seate	iiij d.
Rec' of John Bukes wyff for her seate	vj d.
Rec' of thomas Davys wyff for her seate	iiij d.
Rec' of thomas Sowthes wyff for her seate	vj d.
Rec' of John Craynes wyff for her seate	iiij d.
Rec' of thomas yonges wyff for her seate	vj d.
Rec' of Christofer butlers wyff for her seate	vj d.
Rec' of Mother Marchall for her seate	iiij d.
Rec' of John Brygges wyff for her seate	vj d.
Rec' of herry Reades wyff for her seate	iiij d.
Rec' of peres hyndes wyff for her seate	vj d.
Rec' of Nyc' keene wyff for her seate	vj d.

S[um]ma x s. xj d.

The new Seattes

Rec' of Mistres Carpenter towardes the makeyng of the new seates	iij s. iiij d.
Rec' of phylype Cappar yn lyke wysse	x s.
Rec' of Ryc' a man yn lyke wysse	x s.
Rec' of thomas tayllar yn lyke maner	x s.
Rec' of willyam Davy yn lyke maner	viij s. viijd.
Rec' of John vansey yn lyke maner	vj s. viij d.
Rec' of Robert Blake yn lyke maner	vj s. viij d.
Rec' of John skynner yn lyke maner	vj s. viij d.
Rec' of Davy wyllyams yn lyke maner	vj s. viij d.
Rec' of Christofer Bocher yn lyke maner	vj s. viij d.
Rec' of John Buke yn lyke maner	v s.
Rec' of Robert elwode yn lyke maner	v s.
Rec' of John Russell yn lyke maner	iij s. iiij d.
Rec' of John Johnson yn lyke maner	iij s. iiij d.
Rec' of willyam pasteler yn lyke maner	iij s. iiij d.
Rec' of willyam eadmondes yn lyke maner	iij s. iiij d.
Rec' of Ryc' Noves yn lyke maner	iij s. iiij d.
Rec' of thomas poynte yn lyke maner	xij d.
Rec' of Nyc' keene yn lyke maner	xx d.
Rec' of wyllyam tomson yn lyke maner	ij s.
[p 147] Rec' of John wynet yn lyke maner	iij s. iiij d.
Rec' of John Nashe yn lyke maner	iij s. iiij d.
Rec' of John Barkear yn lyke maner	iij s. iiij d.
Rec' of thomas Mason yn lyke maner	ij s.
Rec' of John boyer yn lyke maner	iij s. iiij d.
Rec' of willyam Smyth yn lyke maner	xx d.
Rec' of Robert Ellys yn lyke maner	iij s. iiijd.
Rec' of Ryc' Basset yn lyke maner	iij s. iiijd.
Rec' of Mr Cletch yn lyke maner	vj s. viijd.

Rec' of Jenckyn tayller yn lyke maner	iij s. iiijd.
Rec' of Charlles Myller yn lyke maner	iij s. iiijd.
Rec' of Randall kelsall yn lyke maner	iij s. iiijd.
Rec' of Ryc' Chester yn lyke maner	iij s. iiijd.
Rec' of Davy gybbes yn lyke maner	iij s. iiijd.
Rec' of John Andros yn lyke maner	ij s.
Rec' of John a gate yn lyke maner	ij s.
Rec' of Robert Dwyte yn lyke maner	xxij d.
Rec' of willyam wey yn lyke maner	ij s.
Rec' of willyam Coone yn lyke maner	iij s. iiij d.
Rec' of willyam Mavys yn lyke maner	ij s.
Rec' of John hall yn lyke maner	xij d.
Rec' of John Randall yn lyke maner	iiij d.
Rec' of willyam bakear yn lyke maner	xij d.
Rec' of Ryc' goodyere yn lyke maner	xviij d.
Rec' of Ryc' Clarke yn lyke maner	xiiij d.
Rec' of John knyght bocher yn lyke maner	viij d.

S[um]ma viii li. xij s. ij d.[1]

S[um]ma totalis Recept' xxij li. xiij s. vij d. ob.

[p 148] Expenses	
In primis payde to Charlles myller for yron & seycolles[2]	xxj s. iiij d.
It' for j li. of sysses for alhallouday	x d.
It' to Norrys for makeyng of ij bawdrykes	ix d.
It' to spouner for makeyng the roode lyght	vij d.
It' to the same spouner for makeyng of iiij torchettes	xj d.
It' payde for naylles to amende the seattes	viij d.
It' to Henry Cobe for makeyng the seattes	xvj s. viij d.
It' payd for iiij payre of Jymmows for the chyrch wyffes seate	xvj d.
It' payd to John Hogges	xij d.
It' payd to {John} Ryc' Joynner for mendyng of Davy willyams wyffes seate	ij d.
It' payd to the same Ryc' for mendyng of the mens seattes	x d.
It' payd for half j li. & a q[u]arterne of wex	vij d. ob.
It' payd to spouner for makeyng of the roode lyght a genst Crystynmas	ix d.
It' payd for ij torchettes	xiij d.
It' payd to trolle for mendyng iij graves & for lyme therto	xj d.
It' payd to norrys for mendyng the bell roopes	vj d.

1. This list is one of a number made when the churchwardens needed funds for large projects. See a much larger collection for recasting the Harry Bell in 1567.
2. This was sea coal or mined coal as opposed to charcoal. It came via the Thames from London.

Wayges

It' payd to thomas balsar for his q[u]arter wagges endyd at crystynmasse	xxv s.
It' payd to steven thorpe for hes {q[u]arter} <yeres> wayges endyd at Mych[aelm]es	xxvj s. viij d.
It' payd to Ryc' bowrrer of My lord Cardynalles Chappell for a reward[1]	xxv s.
It' payd to Ryc' Andrew for his yeres wayges endyd at Mych[aelm]es	xij s.
It' payd to Hew Smyth for certeyn yron warke yn the chawncell	xxiij d.
It' payd for a pownd & a half of sysses a genst Crystmas	xv d.
It' payd to Robert Smyth for makeyng ij keyes & mendyng the loke	ij s. iiij d.
[p 149] It' payd for a Crosse & payntyng of the same	xvj d.
It' payd for a bell Roope	xvj d.
It' payd for gyldyng of ij kandylstykes	xx s.
It' payd to edward Tayller for mendyng of old vestmentes	xvj d.
It' payd to Symons wyff for ij old surplesses	xij d.
It' payd for skowreyng the kanstykes	x d.
It' payd for mendyng of old albes	iiij d. ob.
It' payd for tallow kandylles agenst Crystmas	iiij d.
It' payd for ij new albes	ix s. xj d.
It' payd to troll & his servant for mendyng the new wyndow	xxij d.
It' payd for vj [C] & an half of lath naylles	vij d.
It' payd to Mr Everard for di' M[l] tyelles	ij s. vj d.
It' payd at the obytte for the benefacturs	v s. vj d.
It' payd to Ryc' andros wyff for mendyng of old albes	vj d.
It' payd for Caryyng of dung from the chyrch	iij d.
It' payd for makeyng of playeres garmentes	vij d.
It' payd for xj li. of wex for the paschall & makeyng therof	ix s. vij d.
It' payd for a quart of bastard	iiij d.
It' payd to willyam wey for Sir willyams hors hyer [2]	v s.
It' payd to Roger Johnson for stevens hores hyere	xvj d.
It' payd to John paynter for makeyng of geyre for the play	iij s. iiij d.
It' payd for watchyng the Sepulcre	viij d.
It' payd for washyng the chyrch geyre	iij s. iiij d.
It' payd for a loode of sond	v d.
It' payd to Norrys for mendyng the greate bell bawdryke	v d.
It' payd to buttes the tyeller	xix s. viij d.

1. He was probably a singer from Wolsey's choir at Hampton Court and so a very competent professional. The parish occasionally employed additional choristers from other places.
2. Sir William was a priest. This and the next entry may be connected with the employment of the singer from Wolsey's chapel. From their juxtaposition with those for Eastertide, it may be that he was hired especially for the services of Holy Week.

It' payd for a torchet	xx d.
It' payd to the Joynner for makeyng the beare	ij s.
It' payd for a roope to the greate bell	vij d.
It' payd for a key to the chyrch doore	vj d.
It' payd to the channoner for mendyng of coops	viij d.
It' payd for v loodes of sond	ij s. j d.
It' payd to Henry Horthorn for mendyng the greate bell	x d.
It' payd to willyam Nycolas & his man for xj days pavyng yn the chyrche	x s. iij d.
[p 150] It' payd for mendyng of a loke & a key	v d.
It' payd to Norrys for mendyng a bawdryke	iiij d.
It' payd for a bell roope	xij d.
It' payd to Ryc' Joynner for mendyng the seattes	iiij d.
It' payd for a mate for the chyld wyffes seate	ix d.
It' payd to willyam Edmondes for qwyte rent[1]	iij s. vj d.
It' payd to thomas reed register for Smok Farthynges	iij s. vj d. ob.
It' payd to Ryc' turner for an albe	iiij s.
It' payd for j li. of Frankensence	xij d.
It' payd for sylk & bukeram to amend the Coops	ij s. iij d.
It' payd to henry Cobe for makeyng the new seattes	iiij li.
It' payd to chenye the mason for makeyng the fonte	xxxj s. viij d.
It' payd to garret for makeyng the Cloke	xxx s. viij d.
It' payd to Mr Everard	vj s. viij d.
It' payd to the plummar for makeyng the fonte & mendyng of the stepull	ix s. x d.
It' payd to John knyght for makeyng clene all the chyrch & the roode lofte	ix s. vj d.
It' payd to buttes for tylle & lyme	ix s. viij d.
It' payd for naylles for the new seattes	iij s. iij d.
It' payd for xij gutter tylles & Ryge tylles	vj d.
It' payd to Mr wattes	ij s.
It' payd to willyam Davy for ij^C lathes	x d.
It' payd for iij^C pavyngtylles	vj s.
It' payd to mayster Hyde for certen necessarys to the chyrch	vij s. xj d.
It' payd for the processe mayd agaynst segemond[2]	viij s. vj d.
It' payd for makeyng of thys accompte	ij s.
< It' payd for careag ij canstyckes from London>	<vj d.>

S[um]ma totalis Solucionum xxiiij li. vij d. ob.

{Et sic debet Compotus xxvij s. vj d.}

1. William Edmundes was under-steward of the abbey, the parish one of its tenants. J. Martin, 'The People of Reading', 333.
2. Segemond had moved and altered the organ (see above pp.138 and 142). His work was obviously unsatisfactory hence a law suit against him.

At this accompte hath ben dismissed Robert Blake & in his place elect & chosen Christofer Butteler.

Et sic in surpl' xxvij s.

1523-4

[*p 151*] **Thacc' of Dave willyams & Christofer Butteler wardens of the church of Saynt laurenc in Redyng From the Feste of Saynt Mychaell tharchaungell in the yere of our lorde M^l ccccc & xxiij$^{t[ie]}$ & in the xv^t yere of the Regne of Kyng Henry the Eyght unto the same Feaste then nexte foloyng That is to wytt for one hole yere endyd at Michaellmas in the yere of our lorde god M^l v^C & xxiiij^t & in the xvj^t yere of the Regne of kyng henry aforeseid**
[*In the left-hand margin in a sixteenth century hand*] {1525}
[*and in a modern hand*] 1523-4

Arr'

In primis the seid accompt' have ben charged with   nihil
tharrearages of the last acc' as it doth appere in the fote of
the same nihil quia in Surpplus

Rec'

Rec' for the Rode lyght at alhallou tyde	xvij s. ix d.
It' Rec' {of} for the Rode lyght uppon Crystmas day	xviij s. ij d.
It' Rec' for paschall money at Easter	xxxix s. ij d.
Rec' at Hoktyde aswell of the women & of the men	xxiij s. viij d.
Rec' of the wardens of Jh[esu]s towardes the sexton wayges	xxxiij s.
for a yere endyd at Michaell' anno xvj° r[egni] r[egis]	iiij d.
henrici octavi	
Rec' of the wardens of our ladye in lyke maner for the	xxxiij s.
sexton	iiij d.

S[um]ma viij li. xv s. v d.

Rentes at Ferm

Rec' of John Barfote for a tenement in the north syde of the	x s.
new strett for a yere endyd at Mydsomer anno xvj°	
Rec' of Thomas Harvye for a tenement in the same strete for	vj s. viij d.
a yere endyd at the same Feaste	
Rec' of Henry More for a tenement in the same strete in	xx s.
parte of payment of vij li.	
Rec' of John Rypley for a tenement in the same strete for a	xij s.
yere endyd at the same Feast	

Rec' of John Ap powell for a stabull in guttur layn for a yere endyd at the same Feaste	vij s.
Rec' of Margarett Carpenter for a garden in guttur layn For a yere endyd at the same Feaste	iiij d.
Rec' of Thomas Slythurst for ij° gardeyns in lyrkmer layn For a yere endyd at the same Feaste	ij s. viij d.
\<It' of John Fletchar for his shopp in the Market place for a yere endyd ut supra	vj s. viij d.\>

Rentes Ass'

Rec' of John wylder of thele for di' acre medow lyyng by langney for a yere endyd at Michaellmas anno xv° payable but ons by yere	xiij d.
Rec' of william Justice for his tenement in the holde of John Barker for a yere endyd at {the same Feaste} \<Michaellmas anno xv°\>	xij d.
Rec' of John Hunte for a tenement in the hyghe strette for a yere endyd at the same Feaste	xiij d. ob.

S[um]ma iij li. viij s. vj d. ob.

[p 152]   Great Bell

Rec' of Mr Ric' Cletch for hys wyffes knyll	xij d.
Rec' for the knyll of a straunger that dyed at the george[1]	xij d.
Rec' of John Johnson for hes wyffes knyll	xij d.
Rec' of Ric' yeve for his wyffes knyll	xij d.
Rec' of John kentt for tyllyng at the yeres mynd of his Frendes	iiij d.
Rec' of Mr wattes for tyllyng at the yeres mynd of his wyff	iiij d.
Rec' of Mr Everrard for tyllyng at the yeres mynd of his wyff	iiij d.
Rec' of Mr Cletch for tyllyng at the yeres month mynde of his wyff	iiij d.
Rec' of John Jonson for tyllyng at the month mynde of his wyff	iiij d.
Rec' of Ric' yeve for tyllyng at the month mynde of hes wyff	iiij d.
Rec' for tyllyng at the yeres mynd of Thomas Tayllour Corveser	iiij d.
Rec' for tyllyng at the yeres mynd of Willyam lendall	iiij d.
Rec' for tyllyng at the yeres mynd of John a Merkbyes wyff	iiij d.

1. The George was an inn which still stands in King Street to the south of the Market Place. It is mentioned in the Gild Accounts 1511-12. Slade, *Gild Accounts* ii. 173 and listed in a survey of 1552. TNA Misc. Bks. Land Rev. vol. 187, f 320v.

Rec' for tyllyng at the yeres mynd of Mr Trew	iiij d.
Rec' for tyllyng at the yeres mynd of Mr pownser	iiij d.
Rec' for tyllyng at the yeres mynd of John wynnett	iiij d.

S[um]ma viij s. viij d.

Graves

Rec' of Mr Cletch for this wyffes grave	vj s. viij d.
Rec' of Ric' yeve for this wyffes grave	vj s. viij d.
Rec' of the manes grave that dyed at the george for Coveryng of the same	vij s. iiij d.

S[um]ma xx s. viij d.

Rec' of Thomas paysse for his wyffes seatt	vj d.
Rec' of Ric' Franleyns wyff for her seatt	vj d.
Rec' of <John> gryffyn skynner for his wyffes seatt	vj d.
Rec' of John kent for his wyffes seatt	vj d.
Rec' of John shaw for his wyffes seatt	vj d.
Rec' of Robert watlyngton for his wyffes seatt	vj d.

S[um]ma iij s.

S[um]ma totalis recept' xiij li. xvj s. iij d. ob.

[p153] Expenses	
In primis payd the surppll' of the last accompte as it doth appere in the Foot of the same acc'	xxvij s.
It' to Sponer for makeyng of xv li. wex for the Rode lyght at allhallou tyde	vij d.
It' for a lantern for vysytacions	viij d.
It' for threde delyvered to Ric' Andrew at ij° tymes	j d. ob.
It' for a bell ropp weyng xiij li.	xvj d.
It' for fower kanstykes with handles	xiiij d.
It' for a lode of sonde	v d.
It' for hemyng & markyng of thre awlter clothes[1]	j d.
It' for ij li. of kandylles	iij d.
It' for makeyng of ij° awlter clothes with garters & velvet	xiiij s.
It' to Thomas nycolles & his man for one day labour with mete & drynk	xj d.
It' for washyng the church gere	iij s. iiij d.
It' for v li. & di' of wex to renew the Rode lyght at Cristmas at viij d. the pownd S[um]ma	iij s. viij d.

---

1. These were probably plain linen cloths. In the inventories most were identified by size only. This entry suggests these were given identifying marks.

It' for a pownd & di' of sysses	xv d.
It' for washyng the Corparasses	ij d.
It' to Butt for di' quarter lyme	vij d.
It' to Thomas Nicolles for mendyng of pavementes	ij d.
It' to william Eadmundes for qwytt rentes	iij s. vj d.
It' for the karyyng of a lood dung from the church	ij d.
It' for iij li. of kandelles at Crystmas	iiij d. ob.
It' for for ij li. pechers for the qwere	iij d.
It' for makeyng the Rode lyght at Crystmas	ix d.
It' to an alabaster man for makeyng clene the table at Saynt Johns awter & other ymages[1]	xvj d.
It' for mendyng the pyx	xiiij d.
It' for a bell rope weyng xiiij li. & di'	xvj d.
It' for viij li. wex & di' for the paschall & font taper at viij d. the pownd	v s. viij d.
It' for makyng the paschall & font taper	vij d.
It' for mendyng of thre syrplesses	ij d.
It' for keppyng the obytt for the benefactoures of the Church	v s. iij d.
It' for a pownd of Franken sens	xij d.
It' for karyeng dust owt of the church	ij d.
It' for karyeng a lode of dung from the church	ij d.

S[um]ma iij li. xvij s. vij d.

[*p 154*] It' payd for a lode sond	iiij d.
It' payd to butt for ij° quarteres of lyme & ij° bz	ij s. viij d.
It' for a bell rope weyng xiiij li.	xvj d.
It' for makeyng thynventorye of all the church goodes & of all the Implementes belongyng to all the awlteres within the church of Saynt laurence in Redyng[2]	iij s. iiij d.
It' for Coveryng the grave at the church dore	vj d.
It' for mendyng the ij° holybrede baskettes	ij d.
It' for bordes & quarteres for the gatte in the processyon way	ij s.
It' for ij° men for a day & di' with their mett & drynk	xiij d.
It' for di' C x d. naylles for the same gatte[3]	v d.
It' for di' C vj d. naylles for the same gate	iij d.
It' to a tyller & hes man for on day labour with mett & drynk	x d.
It' for a C bryk & tylles with v crest tylles	viij d.
It' for a lode of sond	iiij d.
It' to the Regester for smoke Farthynges	iij s. vj d. ob.

1. Employing a worker in alabaster suggests that some at least of the images were made of this.
2. This is the inventory made in 1524. A marginal note in a later hand reads 'anno 1524'.
3. The nails cost ten pennies for a hundred, the size determining the price.

It' for iiij holly water sprynkelles	iiij d.
It' for a lode of sond	iiij d.
It' to sir John smyth for a quarter wages endyd at Crystmas	xxxiij s. iiij d.
It' to the same sir John smyth for a month wages aftur Cristmas	xvj s.
[*In the margin before this entry*] a	
It' to John Darlyngton towardes his wages	xiij s. iiij d.
It' to steven Thorpe for his yeres wages endyd at Michaell'	xxvj s. viijd.
It' to Ric' Andrew for his yeres wages endyd at Michaell'	xij s.
It' to Ric' Barns for kanves bockeram & for makeyng ij° stolles of grene Tyssew	viij d.
It' for bockeram for ij° stolles of purpoll velvet to the vestment of the gyfte of Mr Trew	iiij d.
It' for di' horse hyde to amende bawdrykes	x d.
It' to norrys for mendyng of iiij bawdrykes	xij d.
It' to Hew smyth for mendyng of a bawdryk bocle	j d.
It' for mendyng thre syrpplesses	j d.
It' for skowryng the kanstykes & watchyng the sepu[l]cre	xix d.
It' for v pendentes for the Rode lyghtes	xvj d.
It' to Thomas Raynoldes for makeyng a stole & a vannell[1] of purpoll velvet to the vestment of the gyfte of Mr Trew	iiij d.
It' to Ric' Turnour for ij° sloppes redy made	v s. x d.
It' for makeyng & regesteryng of this acc'	ij s.

S[um]ma vj li. xiij s. vj d. ob.

S[um]ma totalis {Recept'} <Soluc'> x li. xj s. j d. ob.
Et sic re[mane]t in pecunijs numerat' iij li. v s. ij d.

At this acc' was dymyssed Dave willyams & in His Rome
Elect & chosen willyam Davye

---

1. An alternative reading is 'vaunell'. See Glossary.

1524-5

[*p 155*] **Thaccompt of Christofer butteler & William Davye wardens or proctoures of seynt laurence churche in Reding from the Feaste of saynte Michael tharck' in the xvj**^th** yere of kyng Henryes Regne the viij**^th** unto the same Feaste in the xvij**^th** yere of the Regne of the seid kyng**

[*In the left-hand margin in sixteenth-century hand*] {1526} *and in a modern hand* 1524 to 1525.

Arr'

In primis the seid accompte hath ben chargeid with tharrerages of the last acc' as it doth appere in the Fote of the same accompt	iij li. v s. ij d.

Receptes

Rec' for the Rode lyght at alhallou day	xvij s.
Rec' for the Rode lyght at Cristmas	xviij s. iiij d.
Rec' for paschall money at Easter	xls. iij d. ob.
Rec' of men & women at hocktyde	xxv s. vij d. ob.
Rec' of the wardens of Jh[esu]s towardes the sexton wages for a yere endyd at Michaell' anno xvij° r[egni] r[egis] henrici octavi	xxxiij s. iiij d.
Rec' of the wardens of our ladye in lyke maner for the sexton	xxxiij s. iiij d.

S[um]ma xj li. xiiij s. j d.

Rentes at ferme

Rec' of John Barfott for a tenement in the north syde of the new strett in the hold of John swan for a yere endyd at Midsomer anno r[egni] r[egis] h octavi xvij°	x s.
It' of Thomas harvye for a tenement in the same strett pro anno finito ut supra	vj s. viij d.
It' of harry More for a tenement in the same strett in parte of payment of vj li.	xx s.
It' of Joon Rypley for a tenement in the same strett pro anno finito ut supra	xij s.
It' of John Appowell for a stabyll in guttur layn pro anno finito ut supra	iij s. vj d.
It' of Margytt carpenter for a garden in guttur layn pro anno finito ut supra	iiij d.

It' of Thomas slethurst for ij° gardens in lyrkmer layn pro
anno finito ut supra
ij s. viij d.

It' of Ric' Fletchar for his shopp in the markett place pro
anno finito ut supra
vj s. viij d.

S[um]ma iij li. xxij d.

Rentes Assis

Rec' of John wylder of thelle for di' acre medow lyyng by
langney pro anno finito in festo Michaeles anno r[egni]
r[egis] henrici octavi decimo sexto
xiij d.

Rec' of william Justice for his tenement in the hold of John
Barker pro anno finito ut supra
xij d.

It' of Joon hunte for a tenement in the hygh strett pro anno
finito {a} ut supra
xiij d. ob.

S[um]ma iij s. ij d. ob.

Graves

Rec' {of} for the grave of John paynter & coveryng of the
same
vij s. iiij d.

Rec' for the grave of Issabell lessham & for coveryng the
same
vij s. iiij d.

Rec' for the grave of willyam sadler & for coveryng the
same
vij s. iiij d.

Rec' for the grave of Mayster Cletch by his beqweste[1]
x s.

S[um]ma xxxij s.

[The usual heading is missing][2]

[p *156*] Rec' for the knyll of Issabell lessham & for tyllyng
at the month mynd
ij s. iiij d.

Rec' for the knyll of John payntter & for tyllyng at the
month mynd
xvj d.

Rec' for the {ty} knyll of William sadler & for tyllyng at the
month mynd
xvj d.

Rec' for the knyll of Master Ric' Cletch & for tyllyng by all
the month terme
ij s. iiij d.

Rec' for the knyll of Mestres Dawson
xij d.

---

1. In 1524-5 there are three entries regarding Mr Cletch or Mr Richard Cletch – a knell, an over-
generous bequest for a grave and a bequest of twenty shillings, all presumably for the same man.
In 1525-6 there are two more entries which are probably for the same man, late payments for
ringing and tolling at his burial. This is unusual. In 1526-7 tolling for a Mr Cleche, and the
following year tolling at the year's mind of Master Cletche, appear in the accounts. Only one
Richard Cleche appears in other records of the time and so far no will has been traced for him.
See Appendix 2.
2. The usual heading 'Great Bell' for the next entries is missing.

Rec' for tyllyng at the termmente [*sic*] of Master pownser	iiij d.
Rec' of John kente for tyllyng at the termmente [*sic*] of his Frendes	iiij d.
Rec' of Master Everard for tyllyng at the yeres mynd of his Frendes	iiij d.
Rec' of william knyght for tyllyng at the yeres mynd of william lendall	iiij d.
Rec' for tyllyng at the yeres mynd of Master Trew	iiij d.

S[um]ma x s.

[The usual heading is missing]

Rec' of umfrey sexton for his wyffes seatt	iiij d.
Rec' of Thomas Brown in lyke maner	iiij d.
Rec' of John Abryckett in lyke maner	iiij d.
Rec' of John Franklen in lyke maner	iiij d.
Rec' of Gylbert Johnson in lyke maner	iiij d.
Rec' of harre More in lyke maner	iiij d.
Rec' of Nicholus Rysseby in lyke maner	iiij d.
Rec' of Thomas Everard J[u]nior in lyke maner	vj d.
Rec' of william Aves in lyke maner	vj d.
Rec' of william phylyppes in lyke maner	vj d.
Rec' of Thomas Morrys in lyke maner	vj d.
Rec' of Joon wyar in lyke maner	vj d.

S[um]ma iiij s. x d.

Rec' of Ric' Turnour for the hows in the markett place wherin the flecher dwelleth for the tyme of the kyng beyng here	ij s.
Rec' for broke mettell of the graves weyng ix li.	xviij d.
Rec' of Master priour for lyme lent to hym by Dave willyams	iij s. ij d.
Rec' of the bequest of Master Cletch	xx s.
Rec' of John Sadler towardes the new organs	viij d.

S[um]ma xxvij s. iiij d.

S[um]ma tot' Recept' xviij li. xij s. iij d. ob.

[*p 157*] Soluc' et Expens fact' per eundum annum

In primis payd to John darlyngton for his di' yeres wages endyd at thannunciacion of our lady anno xvj° r[egni] r[egis] henrici octavi	l s.
It' payd to the seid John for his di' yeres wages endyd at the Fest of saynt Michaell Tharck' anno xvij° r[egni] r[egis] henrici octa[vi]	liiij s. viij d.
It' payd to steven Thorpp towardes his wages for a yere endyd at the same Fest anno ut supra	xxvj s. viij d.
It' payd to Richard Androw for his yeres wages endyd at the same Fest	xij s.
It' payd for the obytt for all the benefactoures of the church	v s.
It' payd to the regester for smoke Farthynges	iij s. vj d. ob.
It' to willyam Edmondes for qwytt rentes	iij s. vj d.
It' for washyng the church gere by the holle yere	iij s. iiij d.
It' for skowryng the kanstykes & watchyn the sepulcre	xiij d.
It' for makeyng the paschall & Font tapper	vij d.
It' for di' j li. Franken sens	vj d.
It' to sir Ric' Baynton for mendyng the grett organs at ij° tymes	iiij s.
It' to Norrys for mendyng the grett bell bawdryk	ij d.
It' to hewg smyth for iiij wyers for the corteyns of the tabernacles	iiij s.
It' for a bell ropp weyng xiij li.	xvj d.
It' for mendyng the whell of the treble bell	xij d.
It' to John paynters wyff for gyldyng of parte of saynt vyncent Tabernacle	iij s. iiij d.
It' for makeyng the Frame for the aungelles uppon Cristmas day	iiij d.
It' for iiij li. percheres for the antems	v d.
It' for mendyng the lok {n} of the chest in Jh[esu]s pew	iij d.
It' for a quarter of a pownd of Franken sens	iij d.
It' for skowryng the kanstykes when the kyng[1] com to town	v d.
It' for makeyng the rood lyght at ij° tymes	xvij d.
It' to the glasyer	vj s. viij d.
It' for karyeng of iij^e loodes of dung	iiij d.
It' for xiiij li. of wex bowght at viij d. the pownd for the paschall Font taper & to renew the rode lyght	ix s. iiij d.
It' for poyntes for the Canapye & in threde	ij d. ob.
It' for drynk in the roode loft uppon palme sonday	j d.
It' for Robert ellys for ij° pesses bockeram	x s. viij d.
It' for makeyng the same ij° pesses in to iiij curteyns with <lyar rynges>[2] & other necesserres	xx d.

1. The king was Henry VIII. The churchwardens may have expected him to attend Mass in the church though there is no record of a seat for the sovereign until Elizabeth's reign.

2. This was possibly intended for 'wyar rynges' (wire rings).

It' for lyne for the same curteyns	ij d.
It' for iiij sloppes redy made	x s.
It' for lyme & sond & for koveryng of iij^e graves	ix d.

S[um]ma x li. xvij s. vij d.

[p 158]   Reparracions of the north yle

It' for xvj bordes for the seellyng of the Roff	iij s. iiij d.
It' for a C iij d. naylles & a C ij d. naylles	v d.
It' for xx^ti vj d. naylles	j d.
It' for a C iij d. naylles	iij d.
It' for di' C vj d. naylles	iij d.
It' for other naylles	vij d.
It' to henry Currer for vij yerdes batauntes	viij d.
It' for a C borde to seell	ij s. viij d.
It' for workmanshyp of the same	ix s.

S[um]ma xvij s. iij d.

Expenses Organorum

It' payd for karyeng the new organs from the water to the church[1]	xv d.
It' to trooll for growdpynyng the org'	ij d.
It' for tymber & bordes for the same	iij s. ix d.
It' for makeyng the paysses for the organes	j d.
It' to Ric' bodye for workmanshypp	iij s.
It' for cordes & naylles to the organes	j d. ob.
It' for brede & drynk for the organ maker whylles he entewnyd the org'	iiij d.

S[um]ma viij s. viij d. ob.

Reparracions of the chauncell

It' payd for a C & di' lathes	vij d.
It' for lath naylles & other naylles necessarye	xvjj d. [sic]
It' for xij bz here[2]	iiij s.
It' for lyme	xiiij s. viij d.
It' to troll for his labour in seellyng & in reward	xij s.
It' layd owt for gold	xxiij s. iiij d.
It' to the paynter for drawyng & payntyng the enbowyng[3]	xvj s. iij d.

---

1. The organ came from London via the Thames and the Kennet. .
2. Animal hair was used to bind and strengthen the lime mortar.
3. Kerry suggests this was the wooden vaulted roof of the chancel. The two entries below refer to bosses on the roof. Kerry, *A History*, 70.

It' for iij^e knottes in the chauncell   vj d.
It' for the gyldyng of them   ij s.

S[um]ma iij li. xiiij s. ix d.

Reparracions of sir bayntons chamber[1]
It' payd for quarteres eveslath & lyme   vj s. iiij d. ob.
It' for vij^C lathes & ix^C lath naylles   iij s. viij d.
It' for bord naylles, lath naylles, q[u]arters & bordes   iij s. ix d.
It' to the Carpenter ij^o dayes   xij d.
It' to Trooll & his man for workmanshypp   vij s. vj d.
It' for makyng & regestryng of this accompte   ij s.

S[um]ma xxiiij s. iij d. ob.

S[um]ma to[ta]lis soluc' xvij li. ijs. vij d.

Et sic Re[mane]t in pecunijs numeratis xxxix s. viij d. ob.

At this accompt was dyssemyssed Christofer butteler & for
hym elect & chossen willyam paslow

1525-6
[*p 159*] **Thaccompte of william Davye & william paslow
wardens of saynt laurence church in Reding from the
fest of saynt Michaell tharchangell in the xvij^th yere of
the Regne of kyng henry the viij^th unto the same feste in
the xviij^th yere of the Regne of the seid kyng**
[*In the right-hand margin in sixteenth-century hand*] {[*date
illegible*] }
[*and in modern hand*] 1525 to 1526

[*no heading*]
In primis Rec' tharrer' of the last accompt as it doth appere   xxix s.
in the foott of the same   viij d. ob.
It' of henry More in parte of payment of v li. Remaynyng at   xx s.
the last accompte for the tenement in the south syde of the
new strett sold to hym for vij li.
It' Rec' for the Rode lyght uppon Alhallou day   xiij s. vj d.
It' for the Rode lyght uppon Crystmas day   xxj s.
It' at Easter for paschall money   xl s. viij d.
It' of men & women at hocktyde   xxvij s. iiij d.

1. Possibly a curate or gild chaplain with accommodation provided by the parish or gild.

It' of the wardens of Jh[esu]s toward the sexton wages	xxxiij s. iiij d.
It' of our ladye wardens in lyke maner	xxxiiij s. iiij d.

S[um]ma x li. xix s. x d. ob.

Rentes at ferme

It' of John Barfott for the yeres rent of the tenement in the north syde of the new strett in the hold of John swan endyd at mydsomer	x s.
It' of Thomas harvy for a tenement in the same strett for a yere ut supra	vj s. viij d.
It' of John Rypley for a tenement in the same strett for a yere ut supra	xij s.
[*In the margin by this entry*] a	
It' of John Ap powell for a stable in guttur layn for a yere ut supra	iiij s. vj d.
It' of Margrett Carpenter for a garden in guttur layn for a yere ut supra	iiij d.
It' of Thomas Slythurst for ij° gardeyns in lyrkmer layn for a yere ut supra	ij s. viij d.
It' of the Flechers shopp in the markett place for a yere ut supra	vj s. viij d.

S[um]ma xlj s. x d.

Rentes Ass'

It' of John wylder of thell for di' acre medow lyyng by langney for a yere endyd at Michaelmass anno r[egni] r[egis] h. octa[v]i xvij°	xiij d.
It' of william Justice for his tenement in the hold of John Barker for a yere endyd at the same Fest	xij d.
It' of Johan huntt for a tenement in the hygh strett for a yere ut supra	xiiij d. ob.

S[um]ma iij s. ij d. ob.

Graves

It' for the grave of sir John goodgame & Coveryng the same	vij s. iiij d.
It' for the grave of william Fayrchyld & Coveryng the same	vij s. iiij d.
It' for the grave of Robert dodson dyer & Coveryng the same	vij s. iiij d.
It' for the grave of Robert dwyght & Coveryng the same	vij s. iiij d.

It' for the grave of Margarett goodyere & Coveryng the same	vij s. iiij d.
It' gyven to the church by the same Margarett a pott price	ij s. v d.

S[um]ma xxxix s. j d.

[*p 160*]   Knylles

It' for the knyll of sir John goodgame & tyllyng at his monthes mynde	xvj d.
It' for the knyll of william Fayrchyld & tyllyng at his monthes mynde	xvj d.
It' for the knyll of Robert dodson dyer & tyllyng at his monthes mynde	xvj d.
It' for the knyll of Symson wyf & for tyllyng at her monthes mynde	xvj d.
It' for {tyllyng} Ryngyng at the terment of Mr Ric' Cletch	xij d.
It' for Ryngyng at the termente of Issabell lessham	xij d.
It' for tyllyng at the termente of Master pownssir	iiij d.
It' for tyllyng at the termente holdon by Master Everard	iiij d.
It' for tyllyng at the termente holdon by william Knyght	iiij d.
It' for tyllyng at the terment of Master Trew	iiij d.
It' for tyllyng at the termente holdon by John Kent	iiij d.
It' for the knyll & tyllyng at the monthes mynde of Margarett goodyere	xvj d.

S[um]ma x s. iiij d.

Seattes

It' Rec' {for} <of> Robert dwyght thelder for his wyffes seatt	vj d.
It' of Robert Roys for his wyffes seatt	vj d.
It' of Raff gladwyn for his wyffes seatt	vj d.
It' of Ric' wyer for his wyffes seatt	vj d.
It' of John hart for his wyffes seatt	vj d.
It' of Christofer Johnson for his wyffes seatt	vj d.
It' of Robert Johnson for his wyffes seatt	vj d.
It' of Agnes lamberd for her seatt	iiij d.
It' of the gyfte of the vycar of [*blank*]	ij s.

S[um]ma v s. x d.

S[um]ma to[ta]lis Recept' xvj li. ij d.

Exspenses by the same yere done

Exspenses Comen

It' payd to John Darlyngton for his yeres wages endyd at Michaellmas anno r[egni] r[egis] h. octa[v]i xviij°	v li. ix s. iiij d.
It' to Steven Thorpp for his wages for a yere ut supra	xxvj s. viij d.
It' to Ric' Androw for his yeres wages endyd ut supra	xij s.
It' to Nores for his yeres wages endyd ut supra	xx d.
It' for the obytt kept for all the benefactours of the church	vij s. vij d.
It' to the Regester for smoke farthynges	iij s. vj d. ob.
It' to william edmundes for qwytt rentes	iij s. vj d.
It' for washyng the church gere by all the yere	iij s. iiij d.
It' for skowryng the kanstykes & watchyng the sepulcre	xvij d.
It' for makeyng the paschall & font taper	x d.

S[um]ma viij li. ix s. x d. ob.

[*p 161*] It' for j li. of Franken sens	xij d.
It' for xvj li. & di' of wex to renew the Rode lyghtes at Chrystmas & Easter	xj s.
It' for mendyng of bawdrykes at dyvers tymes	xvj d.
It' for ij° bell Roopps weyyng xxvij li. at j d. qua'[1] the pownd s[um]ma	ij s. ix d. ob. qua'
It' for makeyng the Roode lyghtes agaynst Cristmas	x d.
It' payd for iij li. of perchars for antemes	iij d ob. qua'
It' for j li. of sysses for the aungelles at Crystmas	ix d.
It' for sweppyng the Church agaynste the kyng Com to Town	iiij d.
It' for half a hyde of whyttlether	xj d.
It' for Coveryng of Fyve graves lyme sond wormanshypp [*sic*] mette & drynk	ij s. vj d.
It' for makeyng the Roode lyght at hallou tyde	x d.
It' for a Roope to the grett bell	ij s. j d.
It' for a Roope to the sanctus bell	ix d.
It' to John harte for mendyng the hede of saynt John in the best crose the fette of {a} <jj°> sylver sensoures the ende of the sylver shypp & for sylver putto the sensoures	xiiij s. vj d.
It' to John Whytt for bordes to the new seattes in dettyd of old	viij s.
It' for gyldyng of saynt laurence gredyren[2]	viij d.
It' to the brasyer at london for mendyng of a kanstyk	vj s. viij d.
It' in lyne	j d.
It' for a surplese for the parysh preste & for makeyng therof	viij s.
It' for iiij°ʳ sloppes for men	xj s. x d.
It' for ij° sloppes for children	v s. iiij d.

1. 'Qua' is the abbreviated form of 'quarter' of a penny, i.e. a farthing.
2. St Laurence was usually represented with a gridiron on which by tradition he was martyred.

It' for wyne uppon palme sonday	iiij d.
It' to Thomas gryffyn for makeyng ij° deskes & other workmanshypp in the qwere	iij s. ix d.
It' to the glasyer for mendyng the wyndow in the halpace over the vestre	xvj d.
It' to the same glasyer for mendyng all the wyndowes abowt the church	xx s.
It' for Rybons bowght uppon {certen per} dyvers persones	iiij s.
It' for bockerham & sylk	x d.
It' for mendyng of vestmentes & Cooppes	v s. j d. ob.
It' for di' yerd red sarsenett bockerham Frenge & Croyll for the whytt baner with rede Crose & for makeyng the same	v s. ij d. ob.
It' to the paynters wyff dew for gyldyng of saynt laurence	vj s. viij d.
It' to the same wyff in reward by promes	vj s. viij d.
It' for Colles poyntes & oyll	ij d.
It' for Caryege of dung	iiij d.
It' to hewgh Smyth for dyvers Iron workmanshypp	ij s. vij d.
It' to Fynch for half a dayes werk	ij d.
It' for mendyng the church yerd gatte bordes naylles & workmanshypp	xix d. ob.
It' for mendyng the church yerd walle lyme sond bryk & workmanshypp	ij s. viij d.
It' for a foldyng bord to the lytell orgons	viij d.
It' for naylles occupyed at dyvers tymes	viij d.
It' for makeyng & regestryng this acc'	ij s.

S[um]ma vij li. v s. iiij d.

S[um]ma to[ta]lis xv li. xv s. ij d. ob.

Et sic Re[mane]t in stauro[1] iiij s. xj d. ob.

Et super henricum More	iiij li.

Ad hanc computac' dismissus est will[el]mus davye et pro eo electus est Johannes whytt.

[p 162] [*At the top of the page in a later hand*]
          St Matthews day for the accompt
At this accompt it is enacted established & agrede by thassent & concent of all the worshipfulles of this parresh that every church warden of the parysh of saynt laurence in Redyng for the tyme beyng shall from hens Forward ordeyn	vj s. viij d.[2]

1. The literal translation is 'in store', i.e. a credit balance.
2. This amount is written in the right hand margin, bracketed round the whole paragraph.

prepare & yeld upp their accomptes in the presence of the
parysheners assembled & gathered to gether in the seid
parysh <Church> uppon saynt mathewes day in the moneth
of septembre uppon payn & forfeiture of every one
makeyng defawt {of} contrary to this present agrement unto
the behove & use of the seid church[1]

[The rest of this page is blank]

1526-7

[*p163*] **Thacc' of william paslow & John whytt wardens
of saynt laurence Churche in Redyng from the Fest of
saynt Michaell tharchangell in the xviij[th] yere of the
regne of kyng henry the viij[th] unto the same Fest in the
xix[th] yere of the seid kyng that is to wytt fore one hole
yere**
[*In the left-hand margin in a sixteenth-century* hand]
{[*number illegible*]} {<1528>}
[*and in a modern hand*] 1526 & 1527

Arr'

In primis the seid acc' hath ben Charged with tharr' of the last acc' as appereyth in the Foott of the same acc'	iiij s. xjd. ob.

S[um]ma iiij s. xj d. ob.

Receittes

It' Rec' for the roode lyght at all halloutyde	xvj s. ix d. ob.
It' for the rode lyght at Cristmas	xv s. ob.
It' for paschall money at Eastur	xlij s. vj d.
It' of men & women at hocktyde	xxxvij s. iiij d.
It' of the kyng game at Whytsontyde	xlij s. ix d.
It' of Jh[esu]s wardens towards the sextons wages	xxxiij s. iiij d.
It' of our ladyes wardens towardes the sextons wages	xxxiij s. iiij d.

S[um]ma xj li. xiij d.

Rentes at Ferme

It' of John Barfott for the tenement in the north syde of the new strett in the hold of John Swan for a yere endyd at Mydsomer anno r[egni] r[egis] h. viij[i] xix°	x s.
It' of Thomas harvy for a tenement in the same stret for a yere ut supra	vj s. viij d.
It' of henry More In parte of payment of iiij li. remaynyng for his tenement in the same strett	xx s.

---

1. St Matthew's feast day is 21 September.

It' of Joon Rypley for the yeres rent of a tenement in the same strett endyd ut supra	xij s.
It' of John Appowell for the yeres rent of a stable in guttur lane ended ut supra	iij s. vj d.
It' of Margarett Carpenter for the yeres rent of a garden in guttur lane ut supra	iiij d.
It' of Thomas Slethur[st] for the yeres rent of ij^o gardens in lyrkmer lane ut supra	ij s. viij d.
It' for the yeres rent of the Flecheres shopp in the markett place endyd ut supra	vj s. viij d.

S[um]ma iij li. xxij d.

Rentes Ass'

It' of John wylder of thele for di' acre medow lyyng by langley for a yere endyd at Michaell' in the xviij[th] yere of kyng henry the viij[t]	xiij d.
It' of william Justice for his tenement in the hold of John Barker for a yere endyd at the same Fest	xij d.
It' of Joon hunt for a tenement in the hygh strett for a yere endyd ut supra	xiij d. ob.
It' of henry More for the qwytt rent of his hows wherin he dwelleth for iiij[or] yeres endyd at Michaall' in the xix[th] yere of kyng henry the viij[th]	iiij s. iiij d.

S[um]ma vij s. vj d. ob.

M[emoran]d[um] that where the Churche wardens were Chargeyd with the qwytt rentes dew to the Abbot to the s[um]ma of iij s. vj d. by the yere, now they be Charged but with ij s. vj d., In so moche that henry More is & stondes Chargeyd of & for the qwytt rent of his seid hows hym self. Also the same henry knolegeyth hym self [1] to pay to the Churche of saynt laurence yerely for the qwytt rent of the same hows over & besydes the seid qwytt rent {dew to} of xij d. dew to the Abbott yerely j d.

---

1. 'Acknowledges himself' i.e. agrees that he ought to pay.

[p 164]   Graves

Rec' for the grave of Margarett weston & for Coveryng the same	vij s. viij d.
Rec' for the grave of henry Curroures wyff & for Coveryng the same	vij s. iiij d.
Rec' for the grave of Robert lykley & for Coveryng the same	vij s. ij d.

S[um]ma xxij s. ij d.

Grett bell

Rec' for the knyll of Margaret weston	xij d.
Rec' for Ryngyng at the termente of Robert dwyght	xij d.
Rec' for tyllyng at the terment of Margaret goodyere	iiij d.
Rec' for tyllyng at the terment of Robert dodson dyar	iiij d.
Rec' for tyllyng at the terment of william whytt	iiij d.
Rec' for tyllyng at the terment of william Fayrechyld	iiij d.
Rec' for tyllyng at the terment of Ric' Cletche[1]	iiij d.
Rec' for tyllyng at the terment of Master pownser	iiij d.
Rec' for the knyll of henry Curroures wyff	xij d.
Rec' at the terment of Master Trew	iiij d.
Rec' at the terment of william lendall	iiij d.
Rec' at the monthes mynde of henry Curroures wyffe	nihil

S[um]ma v s. viij d.

Seattes

Rec' of John Smyth for his wyffes seatt	vj d.
Rec' of william gauntlett for his wyffes seatt	vj d.
Rec' for removeyng of william dwyghtes wyff [seatt]	vj d.
Rec' of Robert dwyght for his wyffes seatt	vj d.
Rec' of Mawd Marshall for her seatt	vj d.
Rec' of phylypp pygottes for his wyffes seatt	vj d.
Rec' of John darlyyngton for his wyffes seatt	vj d.
Rec' of william Johnson Curriour for his wyffes seatt	vj d.
Rec' of Als kyllynggale for here seat	{vj d.}<iiij d.>
Rec' of Isabell Maschall for her seat	vj d.
Rec' for removeyng of John goldynges wyff [seatt]	vj d.
Rec' for the seatt of Steven bocheres wyff	vj d.
Rec' of John paynter for his wyffes seatt	vj d.

1. This man is not given the title Mr. His relationships to Mr Richaed Cleche (d. 1525-6) is unknown.

Rec' of Peter broune for his wyffes seatt	vj d.
Rec' of Thomas Everard for his wyffes seatt	iiij d.

S[um]ma vij s. ij d.

Rec' for iiij^{xx} & x li. & di' of old brase sold at j d. ob. the pownde	xj s. iiij d.[1]
Rec' of dyvers persones towardes the gyldyng & payntyng of the transfyguracion over the hygh awter as by a byll it doth apere[2]	iiij li. xiij s. j d.

S[um]ma v li. iiij s. v d.

S[um]ma totalis arr' & Recept' xxj li. xiiij s. x d.

[p165]   Exspenses

In primis payd to John darlyngton {for} \<towardes> his yeres wages endyd at Michaelmas anno r[egni] r[egis] henrici octavi xix°	v li. ix s. iiij d.
It' to steven Thorpp towardes his wages for a yere ended ut supra	xxvj s. viij d.
It' to Richard Andrew for his yeres wages ended ut supra	xij s.
It' to norres for iij^e quarteres wages ended at mydsomer	xviij d.
It' for makeyng & regestryng this acc'	ij s.
It' for keppyng the obytt for the benefactoures of the Churche	vij s. ij d.
It' to the regester for smoke Farthynges	iij s. vj d. ob.
[In left-hand margin by the next entry] [q]uit[3] rents	
It' to william Edmondes for qwyt rentes	iij s. vj d.
It' for washyng the Churche gere by all this yere	iij s. iiij d.
It' for skowreyng the Kanstykes & watchyng the sepulcre	xiiij d.
It' for makeyng the paschall & Font taper	vij d.
It' for j li. Frankken sens	xvj d.
It' for xiiij li. wex to renew the roode lyght at Crystmas & Easter	viij s. ij d.
It' for iij^e bell rooppes weyng xxxix li. at j d. qua' the pound s[um]ma	iiij s. j d. qua'
It' for a lyne to tole the grett bell	viij d.
It' for mendyng of bawdrykes at dyvers tymes	xiiij d.
It' for makeyng the rode lyght at all hallow tyde & Crystmas	xviij d. ob.
It' for iij li perchares for antems	iij d.

1. The cost has been rounded up from 11s 3¾d.
2. This painting above the three lancet windows at the east end of the church was discovered in excellent condition in 1848 but was then 'hacked down, at the desire of the then vicar.' Kerry, A History, 71-73. Kerry's italics.
3. The first letter was lost when the page was cropped.

It' for j li. sysses for the angels appon Crystes day	viij d.
It' for iij li. Candels at Crystmas	iij d.
It' to Ric' Barns for iij^e elles of spruce Canvas to lyne an awter cloth	ix d.
It' to the same Ric' for iij^e elles of soulewyche to lyne an other awter cloth	xij d.
It' for makeyng & enlargeyng the same awter Clothes	xij d.
It' to Ric' Barns for iij^e elles Canves to lyne the best awter Cloth	xvj d.
It' to the same Ric' for lynyng & enlargyng the same	n[ihi]l
It' to Thomas Sentmars wyff for makeyng a Frenge to the same	iiij d.
It' for Croyle to the same	vij d. ob.
It' for a bz of Colles	j d.
It' for di' hyde of whytlether	xij d.
It' for a loke for the Churche yerd gate	iiij d.
It' to norres for sweppyng the Churche at all hallou tyde	iiij d.
It' for bockerham & mendyng of an awter Cloth	xvj d.
It' to Nicholus hyde for a slopp syrples of iij^e elles & di' redy made	ij s. iiij d.
It' for iij^e slopes of lockerham	v s.
It' for naylles for bell whelles & for the skaffold	xj d ob.
Itfor ij° bz lyme	iiij d.
It' for ij° shettes of whytt plate	iiij d.
It' for karyyng dust out of the Churche	viij d.
It' for Clossyng of iij^e settes at the one ende	iiij d.

S[um]ma x li. vij s. qua'	
[*p 166*] It' for repareyng the Casses for the sensers	iiij d.
It' to Robert pasteler for makeyng a skaffold & enlargeyng the hygh awter	iij s. ix d.
It' for skowryng the kanstykes a gaynst Crystmas	vj d.
It' to John whytt for viij^t brasses for belles cont' j^C & x li. at iij d. the j li.	xxx s. xj d.
It' to norres for ij° dayes helppyng to ley the seid brasses	viij d.
It' for new burneshyng the Crysmatorye	vj d.
It' to Trole for Coveryng of ij° graves & mendyng pavementes in dyvers within the Churche	xviij d.
It' to dyrek for mendyng saynt vyncentes Tabernacle	viij d.
It' to william Aves for x brode pavementes	v d.
It' to Mr Turner for vj^xx pavementes	ij s. iiij d.
It' for a bz lyme	j d.
It' to trole for iij^e dayes labour & for his man one day	xxij d.
It' for a bord to amend the lytell organs	iij d.
It' to Robert pastler for hangyng the belles aftur the new brassyng	vj d.

It' to norres to help hym	ij d.
It' for Karyyng home of bordes & powlles for the skaffold	ij d.
It' to norres for sweppyng the qwere	iij d.
It' to Hewgh Smyth for mendyng the Clock the lokes to the organs & an Iron sett apon Jh[esu]s pew with dyvers other n[e]cc[ess]aris in the Churche	xviij d.
It' for enlargeyng of a sewtt vestments of whytt bawdkyn	v s.
It' for mendyng of iiij^{or} Cooppes	x d.
It' for iij^e yerdes of bockerham	xv d.
It' for iiij^{or} oz of garnesheyng ryband	iij s. iiij d.
It' for a shypp of Copper	xx d.
It' for a bell Roopp weyng xiij li.	xx d.
It' payd for makeyng the saw pytt	vij d.
It' for the sawyeres for sawyng of certen tymber at dyvers tymes	viij s. vij d.
It' for the Carver in parte of his payment	iij s. iiij d.
It' to the paynteres for payntyng the transfiguracion over the hygh awter	vj li. xiij s. iiij d.

S[um]ma x li. v s. vj d.

S[um]ma to[ta]lis Exspenses et soluc' xxli. xij s. vj d. qua'

Et sic Remanet xxij s. iij d. ob. qua'
Et super Henricum More pro suo tenemento   iij li.

At this accompt is dismissed william paslow & for hym is Chossen John skynner.

1527-8

[*p 167*]**Thaccompt of John whyte & John <red alias>[1]
Skynner wardens of the parysshe of saynte laurence in
Reding From the Fest of saynt Michaell the Archangell
in the xix**[th] **yere of the reygne of kyng henry the viij**[th]
**unto the same Fest then next Foloyng that is to wytt for
one hole yere endid at the seid**[2] **in the xx**[ti] **yere of the seid
kyng**

[*In the left- hand margin in sixteenth-century hand*] {1529}
[*and in modern hand*] 1527 & 1528

Arr'

In primis the seid acc' hath ben charged with arr' of the last acc' as it doth appere in the Foot of the same accompte	xxij s. iij d. ob. qua'

S[um]ma xxij s. iij d. ob. qua'

Receites

It' Rec' for the Rode lyght at halloutyde	xij s. viij d. ob.
It' Rec' for the Rode lyght at Cristmas	xiij s. viij d.
It' Rec' for paschall at Easter	xlij s. vj d. ob.
It' Rec' of men and women at hocktyde	xl s.
It' of the yong men of the kyng game at ij° tymes[3]	vj s. iiij d.
It' of Jh[esu]s wardens towardes the sextons wages	xxxiij s. iiij d.
It' of our ladyes wardens towardes the same	xxxiij s. iiij d.

S[um]ma ix li. xxiij d.

Rentes at Ferme

It' Rec' of John Barfott for the yeres rent of a tenement in the north syde of the new strete in the hold of John swan endyd at Midsomer anno r[egni] r[egis] h. viij xx°	x s.
It' of thomas harvy for the yeres rent of a tenement in the same strete end' ut supra	vj s. viij d.
It' of henry More in parte of payment of iij li. remaynyng for his hows	xx s.
It' of John whyte for the yeres rent of a tenement in the same strete end' ut supra	viij s.
It' of John Ap powell for the yeres rent of a stable in guttur lane end' ut supra	iij s. vj d.
It' of Margaret Carpenter for the yeres rent of a garden in guttur lane ut supra	iiij d.

---

1. The insertion is in a different hand.
2. The word 'feast' has been omitted.
3. Between 1515 and 1520 this event was called the King Play. See Introduction in the section on parish social activities.

It' of Thomas Sletherst for the yeres rent of ij° gardens in   ij s. viij d.
lyrkmerlane ut supra

It' for the yeres rent of the Flechers shopp in the markat   vj s. viij d.
place end' ut supra

S[um]ma lvij s. x d.

Rentes Ass'

It' of John wylder of thele for di' acre medow lyeng by   xiij d.
langley for a yere endyd at Michaellmas in the xix[th] yere of
kyng h. viij[th]

It' of william Justice for his tenement in the hold of John   xij d.
Barker for a yere endyd ut supra

It' of Joon hont for a tenement in the hygh strete by yere   xiij d. ob.
endyd ut supra

It' of henry More for his tenement in the south side of the   j d.
newe strete wherin he dwelleth by yere

S[um]ma iij s. iij d. ob.

[p 168]   Graves

It' Rec' for the grave of John Andrews wyff   vj s. viij d.
It' for Coveryng the same   viij d.
It' for the grave of Thomas Everrard[1]   {viij} vj s. viij d.
It' for layng the stone apon the same   xvj d.
It' for the grave of Nicholus hyde   vj s. viij d.
It' for Coveryng the same   viij d.
It' for the grave of syr william wryght   vj s. viij d.
It' for Coveryng the same   viij d.
It' for the grave of Randall Kelsall   vj s. viij d.
It' for Coveryng the same   viij d.
It' for the grave of henry horethornes wyff   vj s. viij d.
It' for Coveryng the same   viij d.
It' for the grave of william Coon   vj s. viij d.
It' for Coveryng the same   viij d.

S[um]ma lij s.

Grete bell

It' for tollyng at the monthes mynde of Ric' wyers wyff   iiij d.
It' for tollyng at the termement [sic] of Robert Dwyght   iiij d.
It' for tollyng at the termement [sic] of william whyte   iiij d.
It' for the knell of John Androws wyff   xij d.
It' for tollyng at her monthes mynde   iiij d.

---

1. See Appendix 2.

It' for tollyng at the termement [*sic*] of Mr Cleche	iiij d.
It' for the knell of Thomas Everrard	xij d.
It' for tollyng at his monthes mynde	iiij d.
It' for knyll of Nicholus hyde	xij d.
It' for Ryngyng at his monthes mynde	xij d.
It' for the knell of John Cottelar	xij d.
It' for tollyng at his monthes mynde	iiij d.
It' for the knell of Randall Kelsall[1]	nihil
It' for tollyng at his monthes mynde	nihil
It' for the knell of henry horethorns wyff	xij d.
It' for Ryngyng at her monthes mynde	xij d.
It' for the knell of syr william wryght	nihil[2]
It' for tollyng at hes monthes mynde	iiij d.
It' for the knell of william Coon	xij d.
It' for tollyng at the termement [*sic*] of Mr pounser	iiij d.
It' for tollyng at the termement [*sic*] of Mr Trew	iiij d.

S[um]ma xj s. iiij d.

[*p 169*] Seattes	
Rec' of of Abell for his wyffes seate	iiij d.
Rec' of Mr Barton for a seate for his madens	viij d.
Rec' of Mr hyde for his mades seate	iiij d.
Rec' of Mistres Cruce for her seate	vj d.
Rec' for removeyng of hew levers wyff	iiij d.
Rec' of william love for his wyffes seate	vj d.

S[um]ma ij s. viij d.

It' Rec' of the beqwest of Mr hyde[3]	vj s. viij d.

S[um]ma vj s. viij d.

S[um]ma totalis Rec' & Arr' xvj li. xviij s. qua'

1. There was no charge because he belonged to the Kelsall family. See accounts p. 108.
2. His title indicates Sir William was a priest, probably a gild chaplain. This seems to have been the practice with gild priests: knells at burials and interment in church were charged for but not tolling. Two other chaplains, Sir Robert Hethe (1527-8) and Sir William Webbe (1558), were treated in the same way with no mention was made of tolling. Both gilds made substantial contributions to church funds.
3. In his will made 16 October 1527, Nicholas Hyde bequeathed 6s 8d each to both parish gilds and another 6s 8d to the repair of the church. TNA Will of Nicholas Hyde, PROB 11/22/35.

Expenses

In primis payd to John Darlyngton towardes his wages for a yere endyd at Michaelmas in the xx^{ti} yere of the regne of Kyng h. the viijth	v li. ix s. iiij d.
It' to steven thorpp towardes his wages for a yere end' ut supra	xxvj s. viij d.
It' to Edward ham towardes his wages for a yere end' ut supra	vj s. viij d.
It' to Ric' Androws towardes his wages for a yere end' ut supra	xij s.
It' to Norres for blowyng the organs	ij s.
It' for the obyt kept for the benefactours of the churche	v s. viij d.
It' to the Regester for smoke Farthynges	iiij s. vj d. ob.
It' to william Edmondes for qwyte rentes	ij s. vj d.
It' for wasshyng the churche gere by all this yere	iij s. iiij d.
It' for skowryng the kanstykes at ij° tymes	xviij d.
It' for watchyng the sepulcre	viij d.
It' for makeyng the paschall & font taper	vij d.
It' for j li. of Franken sens	xiiij d.
It' for iiij li. wex ageynste halloutyde	ij s. iiij d.
It' for xvj li. wex & di' at v d. ob. the pound	vijs. vij d.[1]
It' for makeyng the rood lyght at ij° tymes	xvj d. ob.
It' for iij li. tallow Kandelles agaynst crystmas	iij d.
It' to Troll for Coveryng of ij° graves	vj d.
It' for lyme & sand for the same	iiij d.
It' for mendyng a claspe of a boke	j d.
It' for Caryeng of Robell out of the churche	vj d.
It' for poyntes for the Kanapye	j d.

S[um]ma ix li. viij s. viij d.

[p 170] It' to ij° Joyners workyng in the churche iiij^e dayes at xv d. by the day	iij s. ix d.
It' for naylles for the same workes	iiij d.
It' for bordes & quarters	viij d.
It' for mendyng the belles	xvj d.
It' for a lok for the lok to the Ambre at thende of the hygh Awter	v d.
It' for henges to the same	iiij d.
It' for a lok to the long Cofer in Jh[esu]s pew	vij d.
It' for a plank to make the desk in the same pew	iiij d.
It' for for j li. syses for the Aungelles	vij d.
It' for a lood of sande	v d.
It' for a bz of lyme	ij d.

---

1. The cost has been rounded up from 7s 6¾d.

It' for a bz of Colles for easter eve	j d.
It' for a lyne to lett the sacrament up & down[1]	j d.
It' for settyng on parrers apon xij albs	iiij d.
It' for makeyng clene of ij° Kanstykes stondyng apon the hygh Awter	j d.
It' for tapes for the amesses	j d.
It' for mendyng the best crose	xvj d.
It' for a Rope for the Clock	xvj d.
It' for for a lyne to tole the grete bell	x d.
It' for iiij°ʳ albs & amesses redy made for chyldren	x s. iij d. ob.
It' for xiiij yerdes & di' carpet at xiij d. the yardes	xv s. ix d.
It' for bryngyng hom therof	j d. ob.
It' for xj elles & iijᵉ quarters of Canvas to lyne the same carpettes	iiij s. v d.
It' for threde for the same	ij d.
It' for for layng in the lynyng	xiiij d.
It' for caryege of a Coope & a vestment from london & agayn	vj d.
It' for di' Mˡ brykes	ij s. vj d.
It' to norres for sweppyng the churche & other Jobbes	xij d.
It' to pastler for workyng apon the churche workes	iiij s.
It' for Coveryng of Thomas Everardes grave <with a stone>	xij d.
It' for Coveryng of ij° other graves	viij d.
It' for makeyng & regesteryng this Accompte	ij s.

S[um]ma lvj s. viij d.

S[um]ma to[ta]lis exspenses xij li. v s. iiij d.

And so thaccomptaunt debet iiij li. xij s. viij d. wherof payd
to our ladyes box that was borowed therof afore iij li. xvij s.
& so re[mane]t clerly to the churche xv s. viij d.

< Et super henricum more	xl s.>

At this Acc' hath ben dysmyssed John Whyte & in his place
chosen Charlles Myller

---

1. The sacrament, a consecrated host, was contained in the pyx which was suspended from the
canopy above the altar.

1528-9

**[*p 171*] Thaccompt of John skynner & Charls Miller
wardens of saynte Laurence churche in Redyng from the
Fest of saynt Michaell the Archangell in the xx^{ti} yere of
the regne of kyng henry the viijth unto the same Fest in
the xxj^{ti} yere of the regne of the seid kyng**
[*In the left hand margin in a sixteenth-century hand*] {1530}
[*and in a modern hand*] 1528 & 1529

Arr'

Fyrst the seid wardens hath bene charged with tharr' of the last accompt as it doth appere in the Foot of the same	xv s. viij d.

S[um]ma xv s. viij d.

Receptes

It' Rec' for the rood lyght uppon allhallou day	xiij s. ix d.
It' Rec' for the rood lyght uppon Cristmas day	xiiij s.
It' Rec' at easter for paschall money	xlj s. j d.
It' Rec' of men & women at hoktyde	xxxiij s. iiij d.
It' of the kyng game at whytsontyde	xx s.
It' Rec' of the wardens of Jh[esu]s towardes the Conductes wages[1]	xxxiij s. iiij d.
It' of our ladyes wardens towardes the Conductes wayges	xxxiij s. iiij d.
It' Rec' for brykes that was lefte the other yere	xx d.
It' of Thomas Mason towardes a new George	ij s.

S[um]ma ix li. xij s. vj d.

Rentes at Ferme

It' Rec' of John Barfott for the yeres rent of a tenement in the north syde of the new strete in the hold of John swan endyd at midsomer anno r[egni] r[egis] h. viij xxj°	x s.
It' of John appowell for the yeres rent of a stable in the guttur lane endyd ut supra	iij s. vj d.
It' of Margaret Carpenter for the yeres rent of a garden in guttur lane end' at the same	iiij d.
It' of Thomas Slyther[2] for the yeres rent of ij° gardens in lyrkmer lane endyd at the same Feste	ij s. viij d.
It' for the yeres rent of the Fletcheres shopp in the Markat place end' at the same Feste	vj s. viij d.
It' of John whyte for the yeres rent of ij° tenementes let to hym by Indenture for a yere endyd at the same Fest	xiij s. iiij d.

---

1. The amounts are the same as the contributions made by the parish gilds towards the sexton's wages. The Latin word '*conductus*' means a hired man.
2. This name is written 'Sletherst' above.

It' of henry more in parte of payment of xl s. remayng for   xx s.
his howse

S[um]ma lvj s. vj d.

Rentes Assis

It' Rec' of John wilder of thele for di' acre of medow lyeng   xiij d.
in langley for a yere endyd at Michelmas anno r[egni]
r[egis] h. viij^i xx^o

It' of william Justice for his tenement in the hold of John   xij d.
Barker for a yere ut supra

It' of Joon Hunt for a tenement in the hygh strete for a yere   xiij d. ob.
ut supra

It' of henry More for his tenement in the south syde of the   j d.
new strete wherin he dwelleth for a yere endyd ut supra
<anno xxj^o r[egni] r[egis] h. viij>

S[um]ma iij s. iij d. ob.

[*p 172*]   Seates

It' Rec' of Nicholus Craynes wyffe for her seat   iiij d.
It' of william Fremans wyffe for her seat   iiij d.
It' of [*blank*] Osbourns wyffe for her seat   vj d.
It' of william whytchurche for his wyffes seat   vj d.
It' of George Cootes for his wyffes seat   vj d.
It' of Thomas patenson for his wyffes seat   vj d.

S[um]ma ij s. viij d.

Graves

It' Rec' for the grave of Thomas symson   vj s. viij d.
& for Coveryng the same   viij d.
It' for the grave of symon lambes wyffe   vj s. viij d.
& for removeing a stone & Kyveryng the same   xij d.
It' for the grave of sir Thomas   vj s. viij d.
& for Coveryng the same   viij d.

S[um]ma xxij s. iiij d.

Grete Bell

It' Rec' for tollyng at the monthes mynde of Robert Dwyght   iiij d.
It' for tollyng at the yeres mynde of John Androwes wyffe   iiij d.
It' for the Knyll of Thomas symson   xij d.
It' for tollyng at his monthes mynde   iiij d.
It' for the {grave} <Knyll> of symon lambes wyfe   xij d.
It' for tollyng at her monthes mynde   iiij d.

It' for tollyng at the yeres mynde of Thomas Everard	iiij d.
It' for tollyng at the yeres mynde of M[as]ter Cletche	iiij d.
It' for tollyng at the yeres mynde of John Kentes Frendes	iiij d.
It' for the Knyll of sir Thomas[1]	xij d.
It' for tollyng at his monthes mynde	iiij d.
It' for ryngyng at the yeres mynde of Nicholus hyde	xij d.
It' for tollyng at the yeres mynde of henry horethorns wyffe	iiij d.
It' for tollyng at the yeres mynde of William Trew	iiij d.
It' for tollyng at the yeres mynde of william Coone	iiij d.
It' for tollyng at the yeres mynde of John pounser	iiij d.

S[um]ma viij s.

S[um]ma totalis Rec' et Arr' xv li. xj d. ob.

[p 173]   Exspenses per eundum annum

Exspenses Comyn

In primis payd to John Darlyngton towardes his wages for a yere endyd at Michelmas anno r[egni] r[egis] h. viij[l] xxj[o]	v li. ix s. iiij d.
It' to steven Thorpp towardes his wages	xxvj s. viij d.
It' to Ric' Androw for his yeres wages endyd ut supra	xij s.
It' to norres for bloyyng the organs	ij s.
It' for the obyt kept for the benefactours of the churche	vs. viij d.
It' to the regester for Smoke Farthinges	iij s. vj d. ob.
It' to william Edmundes for qwyt rentes this yere	ij s. vj d.
It' for wasshyng the churche gere this yere	iij s. iiij d.
It' for watchyng the sepulcre	viij d.
It' for skowreyngthe kanstykes & standardes	xj d.
It' for mendyng the Fyrst bell	iiij d.
It' for di' hyde of lether hongry	xiiij d.
It' for mendydng of iiij[o] bawdrykes	viij d.
It' for voydyng dung from the pale in the processyon way	j d.
It' for naylles for to mend the belles	j d.
It' for makeyng the roode lyght at alhallou tyde	viij d.
It' for makeyng j li. of sysses at the same tyme	j d.
It' for makeyng the rood lyght at Cristmas	x d.
It' for di' a pound of sysses	iij d.
It' for iiij li. of tallow Candelles	v d.
It' for a dore to a sete in the churche	ix d.
It' for the Caryeng of a lood of dowst	ij d.
It' for a Key to the steple dore	ij d.
It' for mendyng of ij[o] Frokes	ij d.

---

1. His title indicates Sir Thomas was a priest, possibly a gild chaplain. Unlike the other chaplains, a charge was made for his knell.

It' for mendyng the glase wyndowes abowt the churche	ij s. vj d.
It' for tak naylles	j d.
It' for mendyng a chales	xij d.
It' for di' onz[1] of silver put therto more	xxij d.
It' for halloyng the seid chales	iiij d.
It' for mendyng an awbe & an awter cloth	ij d.
It' for a lok for the Font	ij d.
It' for {a} the sewte agaynst Garard Mathew	ix s. v d.
It' for quarte of Malmesey apon palme sonday	iiij d.
It' for mendyng the haly water stok at the west dore with stoff therto[2]	xvj d.
[p 174] It' for coveryng of ij° graves & layng a grave stone	x d.
It' for mendyng the dore {in} <of> saynt Johns Chauncell	ij d.
It' for xiiij li. wex for the paschall at vj d. j li. s[um]ma	vij s.
It' for makeyng the paschall & Font taper	vij d.
It' for j li. of Franken sens	xij d.
It' for a boz of Colles[3]	j d.
It' for Caryeng of ij° loodes of dust at Easter	iiij d.
It' for x gaiters of belles for morece dauncers	ij s. iiij d.
It' for mendyng the style at the churche yard & stuff therto	xvj d.
It' for mendyng of a surpples	j d.
It' for mendyng of a sylken stremer	iiij d.
It' for iij[e] boxes for the churche	xx d.
It' to henry horethorn for the pale in the belfray	ij s. vj d.
It' for Coveryng of sir Thomas grave	iiij d.
It' for for a roope for the sanctus bell	xiiij d.
It' for settyng perrers {of} apon childrens albs	iiij d.
It' for Caryeng a lood of dust	ij d.
It' for a roope for the foore bell	xx d.
It' to the qwens amner servantes for that the belles wer not rong at her Comyng in to the town [4]	viij d.
It' for mendyng the bere	ij d.
It' for {lo} slevyng of ii° albs & for ii° Amesses with the makeyng	xxj d.
It' for xiiij elles & di' of holland cloth for the vayle at vj d. ob. the ell s[um]ma[5]	vij s. x d.
It' for for payntyng the same vale	x s.

1. Ounce.
2. This was a lead-lined holy-water stoup. A common devotion was for parishioners to sprinkle water over themselves in the form of a cross as they entered the church. The stoup was sold in 1547-8. See accounts p. 250.
3. This is an alternative form of 'bz', the abbreviation for 'bushel'. See glossary.
4. The queen was Catherine of Aragon. The money was presumably a fine for the slight to the queen's honour and would be given by her almoner to the poor. The parish was probably aware that her status was diminished by Henry's determination to have his marriage annulled.
5. The length of cloth, over forty-two feet, suggests this was the Lenten veil which was stretched across the chancel during Lent.

It' for rynges Lyre & sowyng the same	x d.
It' for staples & wyer for the same	x d.
It' for a lent vestment with a new albe therto	x s. vj d.
It' for turnyng the whyte vestment at the hygh awter with a new crose therto	ij s. viij d.
It' for iij^e yerdes of braunched ffostyan for the mores daunceres	ij s. xj d.
It' for makeyng clene the churche wyndoes & walles	iiij d.
It' for ij^o holly brede basketes	vj d.
It' for enlargeng the awter clothes for the hygh awter with all maner of stuff therto belongyng & workmanshypp as by a byll is appereth	xxij s. ix d.
It' for makeyng & regesteryng this acc'	ij s.

S[um]ma to[ta]lis {recept'}exspenses Et soluc'
xiij li. xv s. viij d. ob.

And s[ic] re[mane]t xxv s. iij d.
Et super henricum More xx s.

At this accompt is dysmyssed John Skynner & for hym elect
Gilbert Jonson

1529-30

[*p 175*] **Thaccomptes of Charls Miller & Gilbert Johnson Wardens of Saynt laurence churche from the Feast of Saynte Michaell tharchaungell in the xxj^{ti} yere of the reygne of kyng henry the viijth unto the same Feast next folloyng**

[*In the left-hand margin in a sixteenth-century hand*] {and [number illegible]}
[*and in a modern hand*] 1529 & 1530

Arr'

First the said warderns hath ben charged with tharrerage of the Last accompte as it doth appere in the Fote of the same accompte	xxv s. iij d.

S[um]ma xxv s. iij d.

Receites Comen

Rec' in gaderyng for the rode lyght uppon allhallou day	xij s.
Rec' in gaderyng for the rode lyght uppon Cristmas day	xij s. viij d.
Rec' at Easter in paschall money	xxxvij s. viij d.
Rec' in gaderyng at hock tyde	xxvj s. viij d.
Rec' of the kynges game at whytsontyde	xxx s.

Rec' of Jh[esu]s wardens towardes the sextones wages	xxxiij s. iiij d.
Rec' of our ladyes wardens towardes the sextones wages	xxxiij s. iiij d.
Rec' for a pece of bell metell broken of the Fyrst bell	xx d.

S[um]ma ix li. vij s. iiij d.

Rentes at Ferme dew at Midsomer

Rec' of John Barfott for the yeres rent of a tenement in the north syde of the new strete in the hold of John Swan endyd at midsomer anno r[egni] r[egis] h. viij^i xxij^o	x s
Rec' of John Appowell for the yeres rent of a stable in guttur lane endyd ut supra	iij s. vj d.
Rec' of Margarett Carpenter for the yeres rent of a garden in guttur lane endyd at the same Feast	iiij d.
Rec' of Thomas slyther for the yeres rent of ij^o gardens in lyrkmer lane endyd at the same Feast	ij s. viij d.
Rec' for the yeres rent of the Flechars shopp in the Markett place endid ut supra	vj s. viij d.
Rec' of John whyte for the yeres rent of ij^o tenementes in the newe stret lett to hym by Indenture & endyd at the same Feast	xiij s. iiij d.
Rec' of henry More in Full payment for his hows	xx s.

S[um]ma lvj s. vj d.

Rentes Ass'

Rec' of John wilder of Thele for di' acre mede lyeng in langley for a yere endyd at Michaelmas anno r[egni] r[egis] h. viij^i xxj^o	xiij d
Rec' of william Justice for his tenement in the hold of John Barcker for a yere endyd at the same Feast	xij d.
Rec' of Joon hunt for the tenement in the high strete for a yere endyd ut supra	xiiij d. ob.
Rec' of henry More for the qwyte rent of his tenement in the south side of the new strete wherin he dwelleth for a yere end' at Mic' anno r[egni] r[egis] h. viij^i xxij^o	j d.

S[um]ma iij s. iij d. ob.
[*The rest of this page is blank.*]

[*p 176*] Seattes	
Rec' of leonard Cox[1] for his wyffes seatt	vj d.
Rec' of henry watford for his wyffes seatt	vj d.

---

1. Leonard Cox, a graduate of Oxford and Cambridge, was appointed master of the grammar school in 1529. M. Naxton, *The History of Reading School* (Reading, 1986), 12-13.

Rec' of Ric' Cunstable for his wyffes seatt	vj d.
Rec' of George Cowper for his wyffes seatt	vj d.
Rec' of Robert Gorgany for his wyffes seat	vj d.
Rec' of William Barbour to my lord Abbott for his wyffes seatt[1]	vj d.
Rec' of [*blank*] Bullok the brasier for his wyffes seat	vj d.
Rec' of Antony lever for his wyffes seat	vj d.
Rec' of henry Cooke for his wyffes seatt	vj d.
Rec' of peter Dun for his wyffes seatt	vj d.
Rec' of Robert phyllpp for his wyffes seatt	vj d.
Rec' of John Androw for his wyffes seatt	vj d.
Rec' of water dye for his wyffes seatt	vj d.
Rec' of John shaa for his wyffes seatt	vj d.
Rec' of henry horethorn for his wyffes seatt	vj d.
Rec' of Thomas perkyns for his wyffes seatt	vj d.

beneth the Font

Rec' of Robert Ellys for his mothers seat	iiij d.
Rec' of Anker Swyfte for his wyffes seatt	iiij d.
Rec' of Margarett Cooke for her seatt	iiij d.

S[um]ma ix s.

Greatt Bell

Rec' for the knyll of Robert Medwyns wyffe	xij d.
Rec' for tollyng at her monthes mynde	iiij d.
Rec' for tollyng at the terment of Mr Ric' Cletche	iiij d.
Rec' for tollyng at the terment of Thomas Everard	iiij d.
Rec' for the knyll of Ric' Chestre	xij d.
Rec' for tollyng at his months mynde	iiij d.
Rec' for the knyll of John Androws wyffe	xij d.
Rec' for tollyng at her monthes mynde	iiij d.
Rec' for the knyll of Nic' eves wyffe	xij d.
Rec' for tollyng at her monthes mynde	iiij d.
Rec' for tollyng at the terment of Mr pounser	iiij d.
Rec' for tollyng at the terment of W. Trew	iiij d.
Rec' for tollyng at the terment Nic' hyde	iiij d.
Rec' for tollyng at the terment of h. horethornes wyffe	iiij d.

S[um]ma vij s. iiij d.

Graves

Rec' for the grave of <Robert> Medwyns wyffe	vj s. viij d.
Rec' for Coveryng the same	viij d.

---

1. 'Barbour' is William's occupation: the abbot's barber

Rec' for the grave of Ric' Chester	vj s. viij d.
Rec' for Coveryng the same	viij d.
Rec' for the grave of John Androws wyffe	vj s. viij d.
Rec' for Coveryng the same <& moveyng a stone>	xij d.
Rec' for the grave of Nic' eves wyffe	vj s. viij d.
Rec' for Coveryng the same	viij d.

S[um]ma xxix s. viij d.

S[um]ma to[ta]lis Rec' et Arr' xv li. xviij s. iiij d. ob.

[*p 177*]   Exspenses et soluc' per eundum annum

Wages dewe at Michaelmas anno r[egni] r[egis] h. viij[i]

First payd to John Darlyngton towardes his wages	v li. ix s. iiij d.
It' to Steven Thorpp towardes his wages	xxvj s. viij d.
It' to Ric' Androw towardes his wages	xij s.
It' to william norres his wages wages for bloyng the organs	iij s. iiij d.

Exspenses Comyn

It' to the regester for smoke Farthynges dew at [*blank*] anno ut supra	iij s. vj d. ob.
It' to william Edmundes for qwyte rentes dew this yere	ij s. vj d.
It' for the obytt kept for the benefactours	v s. ix d.
It' for wasshyng the churche gere this yere	iij s. iiij d.
It' for skowreyng the kanstykes this yere	xxj d.
It' for watchyng the sepulcre	viij d.
It' for j li. of Franken sens	xij d.
It' for makeyng the rodelyght agenst alhallou tyde	viij d.
It' for dim j li. of sysses for the same day	iij d.
It' for makeyng the Rodelyght agenst Cristmas	x d.
It' for j li. syses for the same day	vj d.
It' for viij li. of tallow kandelles	x d.
It' for karyeng of ij° loodes of durst out of the churche	iiij d.
It' for a quart of bastard apon palme sonday	iiij d.
It' for xv li. wex for the paschall & font taper at vj d. the j li. s[um]ma	vij s. vj d.
<It' for makeyng the paschall & font taper	viij d. ob.>
It' for ij° bz of Colles for easter eve	ij d.
It' for Coveryng John Androws wyffes grave & layng a stone	viij d.
It' for settyng on parreres of childerns albs at dyvers tymes	vj d.
It' for lymyng byndyng & for the clapses of the new antiphoner	xx s.
It' for a hart skyn for the same	v s.
It' for mendyng the hengyng of ij° belles	ij s. ij d.

It' for a stok for the thred bell	ix d.
It' to a Carpenter for iiij^{or} dayes at viij d. by the day	ij s. viij d.
It' to a Carpenter for iiij^{or} dayes at vij d. by the day	ij s. iiij d.
It' for mendyng of six slopps	iiij d.
It' for mendyng a sirpples for the parishe prest	iiij d.
Payd for mendyng pavementes in the churche at dyvers tymes & for Coveryng of iij^{e} graves	xj d.
It' for vj bz of stone lyme	xij d.
It' for a lood of sond	v d.
It' for a grounsell for the portche	vj d.
It' for groundpynnyng the same	iiij d.
It' for x Foottes of bordes for the same	iiij d.
It' for naylles to the same	j d.
It' for tymber to amend a pew	ii s. iiij d.
It' for naylles to the same	iij d.
It' to the Carpenter for mendyng the pew & the porche	v s. ij d.
[*p 178*] It' payd for mendyng the Case of the lytell organs in the Chauncell & the belloes of the same at ij^{o} tymes	ij s. vj d.
It' for mendyng the lytell portatysses	xx d.
It' for a quarter of a C of brykes	j d. ob.
It' for a laddar	vj d.
It' for naylles to amend M[as]ter stewardes seat^{1}	vj d.
It' for mendyng a baner cloth	ij d.
It' for a manuell of parchement in 2° fo[li]o	ij s.
It' for di' hyde of whyte lether & iij^{e} womes^{2} for bawdrykes	ij s. ij d.
It' for mendyng of bawdrykes this yere	xvij d.
It' for belles for the mores dauncers	iij s. vj d.
It' for iij^{e} hattes for the Morece dauncers	vj d.
It' for Fyve elles of Canves for a cote for made maryon at iij d. ob. thell	xvij d. ob.
It' for for iij^{e} yerdes of bookerham for the morece dauncers	xij d.
It' for iiij^{or} yerdes of here cloth for the high awter at v d. a yerd s[um]ma	xx d.
It' for makeyng & regesteryng this accomptes	ij s.

S[um]ma to[ta]lis soluc' & Expenses
xij li. ix s. vj d.

And so re[mane]t of this acc' iij li. viij s. x d. ob.

---

1. This was probably the abbey's steward.
2. This was leather made from hide on the underside of the animal.

wherof uppon Ric' Chesters wyffe for Coveryng her husbondes grave	viij d.
And uppon Robert Medwyn for his wyffes grave & Coveryng the same	iij s. iiij d.
It' apon William barbour to the lord abbot for his wyffes seat	vj d.
[In the left-hand margin] sol'	vj d.
It' apon {bullok} <[?robert] michell> the brasyer for his wyffes seat	
It' apon anker swyfte for his wyffes seat	{vj d.}<iiij d.>
It' apon water dye for his wyffes seat	vj d.
It' apon Thomas perkyns for his wyffes seat	vj d.
It' apon antony lever for his wyffes seat	vj d.

S[um]ma vj s. x d.

And so re[mane]t clerely uppon this acc' iij li. ij s. ob.

And so is dysmyssed Charls miller & new elect Robert elles

1530-31

[p 179] **Thaccomptes of Gilbert Jonson & Robert Ellis wardens of saynte laurence churche in Redyng from the Feast of saynt Michaell tharchaungell anno r[egni] r[egis] h. viij° xxij° unto the same Feast then next folloyng**

[In left-hand margin in a sixteenth-century hand] {1532}
[and in a modern hand] 1530-1531

Arr'

First the seid accomptantes hath ben charged with tharrer' of the last acc' as it doth appere in the Fote of the same accomptes	iij li. viij s. x d. ob.

S[um]ma iij li. viij s. x d. ob.

Receytes Comyn

Rec' in gaderyng for the Roode lyght uppon alhallou day anno h. viij[i] xxij°	xij s. xj d.
Rec' in gaderyng for the Roode lyght uppon Cristmas day that yere	xiij s. vij d.
Rec' at Easter in paschall money for that yere	xl s. j d.
[In the margin before the next entry] b	
Rec' of the Kyng game & morece dauncers that yere	xxix s. xj d.
[In the margin before the next entry] a	
Rec' of the men & women in gaderyng at hocktyde that yere	xxvij s. ij d.

Rec' of J[hesu]s wardens towardes the sextons wages for a yere endyd at michaelmas anno h. viij[i] xxiij[o]	xxxiij s. iiij d.
Rec' of our ladyes wardens towardes the sextons wages for a yere endyd at the same Feast	xxxiij s. iiij d.

S[um]ma ix li. x s. iiij d.

Rentes at Ferme dew at Midsomer last past before this accomptes.

Rec' of John Barfott for the yeres rent of a tenement in the north syde of the newe strete for a yere endyd at Mydsomer next before this acc'	x s.
Rec' of John appowell for the yeres rent of a stable in guttur lane end' then	iij s. vj d.
Rec' of Mistres Carpenter for the yeres rent of a garden in guttur lane endyd then	iiij d.
Rec' of Thomas slyther for the yeres rent of ij[o] gardens in lyrkmer lane end' then	ij s. viij d.
Rec' for the yeres rent of the Fletchers shoppe in the markett place endyd then	vj s. viij d.
Rec' of John whyte for the yeres rent of ij[o] tenementes in \<the south syde of\> the newe strete endyd then	xiij s. iiij d.

S[um]ma xxxvj s. vj d.

Rentes ass' dew at Michael' anno xxij[o]

Rec' of John wilder of thele for the yeres rent of half an acre mede lyeng in langley endyd at Michelmas anno r[egni] r[egis] h. xxij[o]	xiij d.
Rec' of william justice for the qwytt rent of his tenement in the Markett place in the tenure of John Barker for a yere endyd at the same Feast	xij d.
Rec' of Johan hunt for the qwytt rent of a tenement in the high strete ended then	xiij d. ob.
Rec' of John whyte for the qwyt rent of his tenement in the new strete late of henry More for a yere endyd at Mic' anno r[egni] r[egis] h. xxiij[o]	

S[um]ma iij s. iij d. ob.

Seattes

Rec' for the seat of Ric' eves wyffe	vj d.
Rec' for the seatt of william kenrykes wyffe	vj d.
Rec' for the seatt of Jenckyn phylypps wyffe	vj d.
Rec' for the seatt of hugh levers wyffe	vj d.
Rec' for the seatt of John byssor wyffe the tayllour	vj d.

Rec' for the seatt of John a markbyes wyffe	vj d.
Rec' for the seatt of Symon lambbs wyffe	vj d.
Rec' for the seatt of william Reynoldes wyffe	vj d.
the midle range afore the font	
Rec' of John Everard for his wyffes seatt	iiij d.
Rec' of william Noves for his wyffes seatt	iiij d.
Rec' for the skeveners {his} wyffe for her seatt	iiij d.
Rec' of william Darlyng for his wyffes seatt	iiij d.

S[um]ma v s. iiij d.

[p 180]	The grett Bell	
Rec' for tollyng at the terment of Mr Ric' Cletche[1]		iiij d.
Rec' for tollyng at the terment of Thomas Everard		iiij d.
Rec' for tollyng at the terment of Symon lambbes wyffe		iiij d.
Rec' for tollyng at the terment of Mr hyde		iiij d.
Rec' for tollyng at the terment of william Trew		iiij d.
Rec' for tollyng at the terment of M[as]ter pownser		iiij d.
Rec' for the knyll of John Russell		xij d.

S[um]ma iij s.

Graves

Rec' for the grave of John Russell & for Coveryng the same	vij s. iiij d.
Rec' for the grave of laurence Malt & for Coveryng the same	vij s. iiij d.
Rec' for the grave of Ric' Foxley & for Coveryng the same	vij s. iiij d.
Rec' of the beqwest of Thomas Overthrow[2]	iiij d.

S[um]ma xxij s. iiij d.

S[um]ma to[ta]lis Recept' et Arr' xvj li. ix s. viij d.

[The next nineteen entries are bracketed together as]
Exspenses Comyn

First payd to John darlyngton towardes his wages for a yere	v li. ix s.
endyd at Michaelmas anno r[egni] r[egis] h. viij[i] xxiij[o]	iiij d.
It' to steven Thorpp towardes his wages for a yere endyd then	xxvj s. viij d.
It' to Ric' andrew towardes his wages for a yere endyd then	xij s.
It' to william norres for bloyng the organs by all that yere	iij s. iiij d.
It' to the regester for smoke Farthynges this yere	iij s. vj d. ob.

---

1. This man's relationship to the Mr Richard Cleche buried in 1525-6 (accounts p. 160) is not known.
2. Thomas Overthrow/Overthrave of Abingdon bequeathed 4d to the high altar of St Laurence and asked to be buried in the churchyard (BRO D/A1/1/161).

It' payd the qwytt rentes dew this yere anno r[egni] r[egis] h. viijⁱ   ij s. vj d.

It' payd for the obytt kept for the benefactours this yere   v s. vj d.

It' for wasshyng the churche gere this yere   iij s. iiij d.

It' for skowreng the kanstykes this yere   xxj d.

It' for watchyng the sepulcre   viij d.

It' for j li. of Franken sence   xij d.

It' for makeyng the rode lyghtes at hallou tyde & for makeyng j li. of sysses   viij d. ob.

It' for makeyng the rode lyghtes at cristmas & for makeyng j li. of sysses   x d.

It' for iij li. of new wex to {re} renew the same lyghtes   xviij d.

It' for xiiij li. of new wex for the paschall font taper & for makeyng therof   vij s. vij d.

It' for ij^o bz of colles for easter eve   ij d.

It' for vj li. of tallow kandelles   ix d.

It' for caryeng out of ij^o loodes of dust   iiij d.

It' for a quart of basterd {for} <uppon> palme sonday   iiij d.

It' to steven thorpp for tetchyng of bargens child this yere   vj s. viij d.

It' for mendyng the stopps of the grete organs   ij d.

It' for iiij^{or} mattes of wyckers for the rectoures   xij d.

It' for mendyng the childrens awbbs   ij d.

It' for setyng on the parreres of the same   vj d.

It' for vj {g} tuckyng gyrdles for the same   iij d.

It' for mendyng the syrples for the parishe perrest   ij d.

It' for for mendyng the glassen wyndoes in the high qwere   iiij d.

It' for naylles to the same   ij d.

S[um]ma paginis ix li. xj s. iij d.

[*p 181*]   Exspenses necessarie

It' payd for xix elles of hollon cloth to make iiij^{or} sloppes at vj d. the ell   ix s. vj d.

It' for makeyng the same sloppes   xviij d.

It' for xvj elles of cloth to make iiij^{or} sloppes at vj d. ob. the ell   viij s. viij d.

It' for makeyng the same slopps   xvj d.

It' for mendyng of vj old slopps   viij d.

It' for makeyng of ij^o old childrens surples   vj d.

It' to hewgh smyth for mendyng a lok & key in the rode loft   iiij d.

It' to the same hewgh for ij^o staples to draw the vale in lent   iij d. ob.

It' for naylles for the glassen wyndose & for the sepulcre   iij d.

It' for mendyng the lantren for visitacions & for new hornes therto   viij d.

It' for mendyng a desk in the qwere   ij d.

It' for a lyne to tole the grete bell   x d.

It' for for mendyng the crose case & for iij^e gemys & naylles to the same	iiij d.
It' for mendyng the gospeller & the Episteler & for sylk for the same	iiij d.
It' for mendyng one of the rectoures stolles	x d.
It' for a new frame for the Canapie	xvj d.
It' for poyntes & naylles for the same	j d. ob.
It' for a lyne to draw the rode cloth uppon palme sonday	ij d.
It' for mendyng the dyall & the kay of the chauncell dore	viij d.
It' for upp trussyng of the forte bell	xij d.
It' for mendyng the rope of the grete bell	ij d.
It' to John hart for mendyng the Copre crose	vij s.
It' for a half hyde of whytlether	xviij d.
It' for makeyng a newe bawdryk	vj d.
It' for a wombb of taned lether	v d.
It' for mendyng of iiij^o old bawdrykes	ix d.
It' to a Carpenter for ijij^{or} dayes workyng uppon the ij^o seates in the bellfray & for his mete & drynk	ij s. iiij d.
It' for naylles for the same seates	iiij d.
It' to M[as]ter Turner for a laddar	xij d.
It' to the {f} Carpenter for ij^o dayes to make a laddar of the may poole & for his mete & drynk	xiiij d.
It' for tymber to make the stepps of the same laddar	ij d.
It' for layng of a grave stone	vj d.
It' for makeyng a skaffold in the roode loft	viij d.
It' for for the swepyng of the rode loft	ij d.
It' to the Carpenter for mendyng ij^o seattes in the churche & mendyng the palle in the procession way & for naylles therto	x d.
It' for di' C of brode paveyng tylles	xviij d.
It' for a quarter of lyme	viij d.
It' for a loode of sond	v d.
It' to william sommer for mendyng the Clok	ij d.
It' for mendyng of dyvers pavementes & for Coveryng of iij^e graves	xvj d.
It' for a gogen & a clam of Iren for the fore bell	xx d.
It' for glassyng the wyndoes at the Clok	xviij d.
It' for newe makeyng of a stole & for Canves & bockerham therto	vj d.
It' for iiij^{or} Cotes for the morece daunceres for a yerd of blew bockerham & for the makeyng of the same	iiij s. j d.
It' for a grosse of belles for the morece daunceres	iij s.

S[um]ma paginis iij li. xxij d.

[*p 182*] It' for makeyng the Iren workes for the fore bell & the grete bell & for C naylles	ij s. viij d.

It' to Ric' Cave for newe mendyng the second bell Clapper &   ij s. viij d.
for turnyng the Eye of the fore bell Clapper
It' to william horethorne for x dayes mendyng the belles at   v s.
vj d. by the day
It' for his borde the same x dayes[1]   ij s. vj d.
It' for his man vij dayes at v d. a day with mete & drynk   ij s. xj d.
It' for for a newe bell whelle for the second bell   v s.
It' to M[as]ter Turner for iiij^or bell stokes   iij s. iiij d.
It' for iij^e newe bell roopes   iiij s. vj d.
It' for makeyng & regesteryng this accomptes   ij s.

S[um]ma paginis xxx s. vij d.

S[um]ma to[ta]lis exspenses & soluc'
xiiij li. iij s. viij d.

And so re[mane]t xlvj s. wherof thacc' axeth all[·2]
[*in the margin before the next entry*] vacat xx d.
First for the Fletchers shopp in the Markett place dew uppon   vj s. viij d.
andrewe pope for the iij^e quarters endyd at our lady day
thannunc' v s. & uppon the Carver for one quarter dewe at
Midsomer xx d. s[um]ma <anno h. viij^i xxiij°>
It' uppon Robert Medwyn{s} for his wyffes grave &   iij s. iiij d.
Coveryng therof
It' uppon Chesters wyffe for Coveryng her husbondes grave   viij d.
[*in the margin before the next entry*] vacat
It' uppon Anker swyffte for his wyffes seat   iiij d.
It' uppon Thomas perkyns for his wyffes seat   vj d.
It' uppon william Cave for the grave of Ric' Foxley & for   vij s. iiij d.
Coveryng therof

S[um]ma allocand' xviij s. x d.

And so re[mane]t clere uppon this accomptes xxvij s. ij d.

And thus is dyscharged Gilbert Jonson & for hym chossen
John Appowell

---

1. It was common practice for workmen to be paid a lesser wage if a meal was provided during the day than when it was not. Here the amount allowed for food, three pence a day, was accounted separately and probably met much of this man's accommodation cost.
2. 'All', short for 'allowance', refers to the following sums which the churchwardens had not received and therefore did not have to account for.

1531-2

[*p183*] [*Three words illegible at the top of the page.*]

Thaccomptes of Robert Ellys & John appowell Wardens of saynt Laurence churche in Redyng from the Feast of saynt Michaell tharchaungell in the xxiij^{ti} yere of the reigne of kyng henry the viijth unto the same Feast then next folloyng.

[*In the left-hand margin in a* sixteenth-*century hand*] {1533}
[*and in a modern hand*] 1531 and 1532

Arr'

First the seid wardens hath ben charged with tharr' of the last accomptes as it doth appere in the Fote of the same accomptes	xxvij s. ij d.
Rec' for iij^c quart[er] dewe for the Flechers shope in the Markett place as it doth appere in the Fote of the last accomptes	v s.
The seid accounttauntes hath also ben charged with other peculyer sumes as it doth appere in the Fote of the seid accomptes s[um]ma	xj s. vj d.

Receites Comen

Rec' in gaderyng uppon alhallou day for the roode lyghtes anno r[egni] r[egis] h. viijⁱ xxiij^o	xij s. v d.
Rec' in gaderyng uppon cristmas day the same yere	xiiij s. v d.
Rec' in pascall money at Easter	xxxviij s. vij d. ob.
Rec' of the men & women in gaderyng at hoktyde the same yere	xxxiiij s. viij d.
Rec' of the yong men gaderyng at whitsontide	x s.
Rec' of Jh[esu]s wardens towardes the sextons wages	xxxiij s. iiij d.
Rec' of our ladyes wardens towardes the same	xxxiij s. iiij d.

S[um]ma viij li. xvj s. ix d. ob.

Rentes at Ferme

Rec' of John Barfott for the yeres rent of a tenement in the North side of the Newe strete for a yere endyd at midsomer next before this accomptes	x s.
Rec' of John apowell for the yeres rent of a stable in guttur lane endyd then	iij s. vj d.
Rec' of Margaret Carpenter for the yeres rent of a garden in guttur lane endyd then	iiij d.
Rec' of agnes slyther for the yeres rent of ij^o gardens in lyrkmer lane endyd then	ij s. viij d.
Rec' of John whyte for the yeres rent of ij^o tenementes in the south side of the newe strete endyd then	xiij s. iiij d.

Rec' for the yeres rent of the Flechers shope in the Markett
place endyd then

       vj s. viij d.

S[um]ma xxxvj s. vj d.

Rentes ass'

Rec' of John wilder of thell for the yeres rent of half an acre
mede lyeng in langley endyd at Michelmas anno r[egni]
r[egis] h. viijⁱ xxiij^o

       xiij d.

Rec' of the heires of william Justice for the tenement in the
Marketplace in the tenure of John Barker for a yere endyd
then

       xij d.

Rec' of Robert hunt for a tenement in the high strete for a
yere endyd then

      xxi d. ob.

Rec' of John white for the yeres rent of a tenement in the
south syde of the new strete late of henry More for a yere
endyd at Mic' anno xxiiij^o

         j d.

S[um]ma iij s. iij d. ob.

Rec' of the wardens of Jh[esu]s Masse towardes the
reparracions of the churche bokes

         xv s.

Rec' of the wardens of our lady masse towardes the same

         xv s.

Rec' & borowed of our ladyes box towardes the reparracions
of the ij^o chauncelles

      vj li. ij s.
        iiij d.

Rec' of the Freres in oxford for the great organs[1]

         x li.

Rec' of the gift of M[as]ter amner towardes the reparracions
of the high chauncell

       vj s. viij d.

S[um]ma xvij li. xix s.

[p 184]   Seates

Rec' of Thomas Turner for his wyffes seat   vj d.

Rec' of Mathew benwell for his wyffes seat   vj d.

Rec' of John Jarard for his wyffes seat   vj d.

Rec' of Robert letsam for his wyffes seat   vj d.

Rec' of Robert Tylby for his wyffes seat   vj d.

Rec' of hugh whyte for his wyffes seat   vj d.

S[um]ma iij s.

Great Bell

Rec' for the knyll of M[as]ter Foster   xij d.

Rec' for the knyll of Christofer butler   xij d.

---

1. There were four priories in Oxford. It is not known to which one this sale refers.

Rec' for ryngyng at his monthes mynde	xij d.
Rec' at the yeres mynde of M[as]ter Cletche	iiij d.
Rec' at the yeres mynde of M[as]ter white	iiij d.
Rec' at the yeres mynde of symon lambes wyffe	iiij d.
Rec' at the yeres mynde of M[as]ter Trew	iiij d.
Rec' {of} at the yeres mynde of M[as]ter pouncer	iiij d.
Rec' at the yeres mynde of M[as]ter hyde	iiij d.

S[um]ma v s.

Graves

Rec' for the grave of Christofer Butler & Coveryng the same	vij s. iiij d.

S[um]ma vij s. iiij d.

Rec' of certen persons towardes the great lygear[2]	xxiiij s.

S[um]ma xxiiij s.

S[um]ma totalis Rec' et arr' xxxij li. xviij s. vij d.

Exspenses Comen

payd to John Darlyngton towardes his wayges for a yere endyd at Michelmas anno r[egni] r[egis] h. viij[i] xxiiij[o]	v li. ix s. iiij d.
payd to steven Thorpp towardes his wayges for a yere endyd then	xxvj s. viij d.
payd to Ric' androw for his wayges for a yere endyd then	xij s.
payd to william Norres his wayges for a yere then	vj s. viij d.
payd to the regester for smoke Farthynges	iij s. vj d. ob.
payd the qwyt rentes dewe this yere	ij s. vj d.
payd for the obyt kept for the benefactours of the churche	v s. viij d.
payd for wasshyng the churche gere this yere	iij s. iiij d.
payd for skowryng the kanstykes this yere	ij s. ij d.
payd for watchyng the sepulcre	viij d.
payd for j li. of Franken sence	xij d.
payd for makeyng the rode lights at alhallou tyde	viij d.
payd for makyng the rode lyghtes at cristmas & for sysses	xj d.
payd for xvij li. of new wex at vj d. the pound	viij s. vj d.
payd for makeyng the pascall & Font taper	vj d.

S[um]ma ix li. iiij s. ij d. ob.

[p 185] payd for ij[o] bz of Colles for fyre on easter eve	ij d.
payd for v li. of tallow kandelles	vij d. ob.
payd for a quart of Basterd uppon palme sonday	iiij d.

---

2. A legendary contained the lessons read at Matins. See below p. 186.

payd for karyeng dust out of the churche	iiij d.
payd for iij^e wombes	xv d.
payd for half a hyde of whitlether	x d.
payd for makeyng ij^o bawdrykes for the fore bell & the second	xij d.
payd for makeyng a bawdryk for the great bell	xij d.
payd to Ric' goldsmyth for makeyng a new desk	xx d.
payd for mendyng of iij^e olde deskes	iiij d.
[*The next four entries are bracketed together*]	
payd for ij^o skynes for the rectoures stolles	xij d.
payd for Nayles to the same	iiij d.
payd for girthwebb & canves to the same	xj d.
payd for makyng the same stoles	xij d.
payd for mendyng of ix albs	vj d.
payd for a thong of lether hongre for the organs	iij d.
payd for ij^o elles of Lokerham & makeyng a childes slopp	xvj d.
payd for mendyng of iiij^{or} Coopes	iiij s.
payd for sylk & bockerham to the same	xiiij d.
payd for iiij^{or} oz of vestment Rybon	iij s. iiij d.
payd for paveyng in the churche to ij^o men on day & a half	xvj d.
payd for iij^o bz of lyme	iij d.
payd for a lood of sand	vj d.
payd for a quarter of a pound of white lyer for the regesters bokes	iij d.
payd for makeyng the foldyng hatche by M[as]ter Justice awter	viij d.
payd for ij^o payre of henges for the same	vj d.
payd for ryngyng of sir george Fostter knyll[1]	vj d.
payd for ryngyng agaynst the kynges cummyng	iij d.
payd for a rope to the iiijth bell	xix d.

The coste of the bokes.

payd for iij^e buk skynes ij^o stag skynes & viij shepe skynes	xviij s. vj d.
payd for xxj^{ti} rede skynes	vij s.
payd for glew	xij d.
payd for small threde & pak threde	ij s. ij d.
payd for a dosyn of parchment skynes	ij s. ij d.
payd for xv vellam skynes	x s.
payd to the Joynner for bordes {& bo} to the bokes	xx d.
payd to the boke bynder for byndyng the bokes	xxiiij s.
payd for byndyng the new grale & lymyng therof	ix s. x d.

---

1. He was lord of the manor of Aldermaston, a village about ten miles south-west of Reading. In 1552 Sir Humphrey Foster owned property in London Street TNA Misc. Bks. Land Rev. Survey of Reading 1552, vol. 187 f 314v.

payd for a buk skyn a shepe skyn & rede skynes	ij s. viij d.
payd for naylles & glew for the saites in Saynt Johns chauncell	iiij s. j d.

S[um]ma paginis v li. x s. iij d. ob.

[p 186] payd to John harte for makeyng & gyldyng the Coper sensures	xlvj s. viij d.
payd to Ric' watlyngton for certen reparracions don in the high chauncell & other places	ix s. vj d.
payd to Thomas Carpenter for transposyng the seates in saynt Johns Chauncell & for other certen thynges	xxvij s. ij d.
payd for bordes & tymber for reparracions of both the chauncelles	xij s. iiij d.
payd to Frere peter wryttyng & notyng the new grale & for the vellam there[1]	xlvj s. viij d.
payd to hugh smyth for mendyng the clok & other thynges	vj d.
payd for vellam for the great leager	iij li. xxiij d.
payd for Florisshyng the same boke with stuff therto belonging[2]	iij li.
	ix s. j d.
payd for makyng & regesteryng this accompte	ij s.

S[um]ma xiij li. xv s. x d.

S[um]ma tot[a]lis exspences xxviij li. x s. iiij d.

Et sic remanet iiij li. viij s. iij d. Unde
Super

Freres <oxon> pro le organs	l s.
Robertum Medwyn	iij s. iiij d.
[In the left-hand margin for the next two entries] sol'	
[and in the right-hand margin for next two entries] licet	
{Uxorem Ric' Chester	viij d.}
{Will[elm]um Cave	vij s.
	iiij d.}

<S[um]ma iij li. viij d.>

Et Super computant' xxvj s. xj d.

And so is dismyssed Robert Ellys & for hym elect Robert watlyngton

---

1. 'Frere' or ' brother' usually refers to mendicant friars. Brother Peter may have belonged to the community of Franciscan friars in New Street.
2. Florisshyng probably means illuminating. This was normally done by an artist, not the writer.

wherof is payd to the handes of Richard Turner in parte of	xxij s.
payment of vj li. ij s. iiij d. boroed of our ladyes box this yere	iiij d.
And delyvered to John appowell the churche warden	iiij s. vj d.[1]

1532-3

[*p 187*] **Thaccomptes of John appowell & Robert watlyngton Wardens of saynt laurence churche in Redyng from the Fest of saynt Michell tharchangell in the xxiiij^{ti} yere of the reigne of kyng henry the viij^{th} unto the same Fest then next folloyng.**
[*in the left-hand margin in a sixteenth-century hand*] {1534}
[*and in modern hand*] 1532-1533

Arr'

First the seid wardens hath ben charged with tharr' of the last accomptes as it doth appere in the fote of the same accomptes	iiij s. vj d.
The seid wardens also hath ben charged with other certen detes as it doth appere in the fote of the seid last accomptes	iij li. xvj d.

S[um]ma iij li. v s. x d.

Receites Comen

Rec' in gaderyng for the rode light apon alhallou day	xiij s. ij d.
Rec' in gaderyng for the rode light apon Cristmas day	xiij s. iiij d.
Rec' at easter in pascall money	xl s. ix d.
Rec' of the men & women at hocktyde	xxx s.
<Rec' of the kyng game at whytsontyde this yere>	<xxxiij s. iij d.>
Rec' of the Jh[esu]s wardens towardes the sextons wages	xxxiij s. iiij d.
Rec' of our ladyes wardens towardes the same	xxxiij s. iiij d.

S[um]ma ix li. xvij s. ij d.

Rentes at Ferme

Rec' of John Barfott for the yeres rent of a tenement in the north side of the new strete for a yere endyd at Midsomer anno xxv° h. viij^i	x s.
Rec' of John appowell for the yeres rent of a stable in guttur lane ended then	iij s. vj d.
Rec' of Margaret Carpenter for the yeres rent of a garden in guttur lane ended then	iiij d.

1. This should be 4s 7d, i.e. the stated final balance of 26s 11d less 22s 4d repaid to Our Lady's box.

Rec' of agnes slyther for the yeres rent of ij° gardens in lyrkmer lane ended then	ij s. viij d.
Rec' of John whyte for the yeres rent of a tenement in the north side of the new strete & a nother in the south side of the same strete endyd then	xiij s. iiij d.
Rec' of John knyght for the yeres rent of the Corner tenement in the Market place endyd at Michelmas anno r[egni] r[egis] h. viijⁱ xxv°	xiij s. iiij d.
Rec' of M[as]ter laborne for a quarter rent of his chamber endyd at Mic' anno ut supra	xx d.

S[um]ma xliiij s. x d.

Rentes ass'

Rec' of John wilder of thele for the yeres rent of half an acre mede lyeng in langley endyd at Michelmas anno r[egni] r[egis] h. viijⁱ xxiiij°	xiij d.
Rec' of the heires of william Justice for the tenement in the Market place in the hold of John Barkar for a yere endyd at the same tyme	xij d.
Rec' of Robert Hunt for the yeres rent of a tenement in the high strete then	xiij d. ob.
Rec' of John white for the yeres rent of a tenement in the south side of the new strete late sold to henry more endyd at Mic' anno xxv°	j d.

S[um]ma iij s. iij d. ob.

Seates

Rec' of peter Rede barbor for his wyffes seat	vj d.
Rec' of henry bruar for his wyffes seat	vj d.
Rec' of John Butler for his wyffes seat	vj d.

S[um]ma xviij d.

[p 188] **The grete bell**	
Rec' for the knyll of agnes vansby	xij d.
Rec' for {to} Ryngyng at her months mynde	xij d.
Rec' for the knyll of agnes coone	xij d.
Rec' for tollyng at her monthes mynde	iiij d.
Rec' for the knyll of phyllyp Ryseby	xij d.
Rec' for Ryngyng at his monthes mynde	xij d.
Rec' for the knyll of Margaret hyde¹	xij d.
Rec' for Ryngyng at her monthes mynde	xij d.

---

1. She was the widow of Nicholas Hyde. See Appendix 2.

Rec' for the knyll of Robert philpp	xij d.
Rec' for Ryngyng at the yeres mynde of Christofer Butteler	xij d.
Rec' for tollyng at the yeres mynde of M[as]ter Ric' Cletche	iiij d.
Rec' for tollyng at the yeres mynde of symon lambs wyffe	iiij d.
Rec' of John Kent for tollyng at the terment of his Frendes	iiij d.
Rec' for tollyng at the terment of M[as]ter Trew	iiij d.
Rec' for tollyng at the terment of M[as]ter powncer	iiij d.

S[um]ma xj s.

Graves

Rec' for the grave of agnes vansby	vj s. viij d.
Rec' for Coveryng the same with a stone	xij d.
Rec' for the grave of agnes Coone	vj s. viij d.
Rec' for Coveryng the same	viij d.
[*In the margin before the next entry*] cc	
Rec' for the grave of Mistres hide	vj s. viij d.
Rec' for Coveryng the same	viij d.
Rec' for the grave of philipp Riseby	vj s. viij d.
Rec' for Coveryng the same with a stone	xij d.
Rec' for a barre of yren valewed at ij s. wherof is spent in the churche workes xvj d. & so remayneth to the churche	viij d.

S[um]ma xxx s. viij d.

S[um]ma totalis recept' & arr' xvij li. xiij s. vij d. ob.

[*no heading*]

payd to John Darlyngton towardes his wages for a yere endyd at Michaelmas anno r[egni] r[egis] h. viij^i xxv^o	v li. ix s. iiij d.
payd to stephyn thorpp towardes his wages for a yerre endyd then	xxvj s. viij d.
payd to Ric' andrew towardes his wages for a yere endyd then	xij s.
payd to william Norres his wages for bloyng thorgans this yere end' then	vj s. viij d.
payd to the regester for smoke farthynges this yere	iij s. vj d. ob.
payd the qwytt rentes dew this yere	ij s. vj d.
payd for the obytt kept for the benefactours this yere	v s. vj d.

S[um]ma viij li. vj s. ij d. ob.

[*p 189*] payd for wasshyng the churche gere this yere	iij s. iiij d.
payd for skowryng the kanstykes this yere	ij s. ij d.
payd for watchyng the sepulcre this yere	viij d.
payd for j li. & a half of {sysses} Franken sence	xviij d.

payd for xiiij li. new wex at vj d. the pound	vij s.
payd for makeyng the roode lightes agenst hallou tyde & Cristmas	xviij d.
payd for vj li. of tallow kandelles	ix d.
It' for a quart of basterd apon palme sonday	iij d.
It' for ij° boshell of colles for fyre on easter eve	ij d.
It' for makyng the paschall & font taper <& j li. of sysses>	viij d.
It' for ij° half hides of whitlether for bawdrykes	ij s. iiij d.
It' for makeyng of iij^e bawdrykes	xviij d.
It' for ij° bell roopes	ij s. {ij} vj d.
It' to the glasyer for mendyng the glassen wyndowes	xxx s.
It' for naylles to the same	j d. ob.
It' for the kareynge of ix lodes dung from the pale in the procession way	xviij d.
It' for the karyege of ij° lodes of dust from the churche	iiij d.
It' to them that fyld the dung cartes	vj d.
It' for half a quarter of stone Lyme	viij d.
It' for brykes	vj d.
It' to the carpenter for mendyng the churche ende over the Rode loft	ij s.
It' for layng the brykes there	ij s.
It' for ij° M^{li} tylles	x s.
It' for for ij° quarters of lyme	ij s. viij d.
It' for ij° lodes of sand	x d.
It' for iiij^{or} Joystes for the churche ende over the Rode loft	xij d.
[*in the margin in a different sixteenth-century hand*] 1534[1]	
It' for ryngyng at the birth of the princes <Elizabeth> [< > *in a different hand*] {<edward mare>}[2]	iiij d.
It' for lockerham for a childes surples	xiiij d. ob.
It' for v d. naylles & other naylles at dyvers tymes	xj d.
It' for naylles for the sepulcre	ob.
It' for mendyng the bell roops	ij d.
It' to edward Jenyns for goyng to bynfeld for a syngyng child[3]	iiij d.
It' for Mendyng the organs	ij s.
It' for mendyng the parishe prestes surples	iij d.
It' for x li. sowder for the gutturs & the belles	iij s. iiij d.
It' for wod to the plommer	ij d.

S[um]ma paginis iiij li. v s. j d. ob.

---

1. The marginal note is incorrect. Elizabeth was born on 7 September 1533 and so within the 1532-3 accounting year.
2. The writer has inserted the names of Elizabeth's siblings, Edward and Mary for reasons unknown. The insertion must be after the birth of Edward in October 1537.
3. Binfield is a village nine miles east of Reading.

[p *190*] It' for settyng on parrours apon the childrens albs & for mendyng the albs at dyvers tymes	x d.
It' for mendyng of iiij^{or} grete kanstykes	ij s. ij d.
It' for ij^o bz of lyme	ij d.
It' for layng a stone apon Mistres vansbyes grave & for mendyng of other paymentes in the churche	x d.
It' for Coveryng of agnes Coones grave	iiij d.
It' for layng a stone on philipp Risebyes grave	viij d.
It' for new makeyng the boltes for the fore bell & for yren therto	xviij d.
It' for new hengyng the fore bell	v s.
It' to a carpenter iij^e dayes at vij d. by the day to heng & trym the same belles	xxj d.
It' for for naylles & workmanshypp in mendyng the selyng in the belfray	ij d. ob.
It' for Coveryng of Mistres hydes grave	vj d.
It' for makeyng a bawdryk for the grete bell	vj d.
It' for makeyng & regesteryng this accomptes	ij s.

S[um]ma xvj s. v d. ob.

S[um]ma tot[a]lis solut' xiij li. vij s. ix d. ob.

Et Sic debet iiij li. v s. xd. Unde
Super

Johannem knyght Capper for iij^e quarters rent of the hows in the Markett place called the Flechers hows	x s.
And the accomptaunt also axeth alloc' of & for the peculyer sumes charged in the begynyng of this accomptes as there it doth appere[1]	iij li. viij d.

Et Sic Re[mane]t of this Accomptes xv s. ij d.

And so is dysmyssed John appowell tayller & for hym new elect Richard Noves

At this day it is aggreid that the Gilt Cupp of the gifte of
Mistres hide alweys to remeayne in the Custody of the
Mayour if the Mayour dwell in the parisshe And if the
Mayour dwell out of the parisshe then to remayne & be in
the Custodye of hym that was last Mayour in the same
parisshe, to thuse declared in the will of the seid Mistres
hide whiche ordre taken by John reade al[ias] Skynner then
Mayour Mr Barton Mr Everard Mr Turnour Mr Vansby

---

1. The debts recorded at the beginning of the year (p.187) were £3 16d, not £3 8d.

{Mr dav[*2 letters illegible*]de?} Mr white & dyverce others of the parisshe.[1]

Mistris hid dissesed in this yere ,1534,[2]

The saide Cuppe was given for the use to be carried before all bryddes that were wedded in Sanct laurence Churche, And nowe is turned, to be occupied there, at all tymes when nede is, to occupie more then one communyon cuppe, at one tyme, to use & occupie it ther, as a communyon cuppe, etc,[3]

1533-4

[*p 191*] **Thaccomtes of Robert watlyngton & Richard Noves wardens of saynt laurence churche in Redyng from the Feast of saynt Michell tharc' in the xxv^{ti} yere of the reigne of kyng henry the viijth unto the same Feast then next Folowyng.**

[*In the right-hand margin in a sixteenth-century hand*] {ended 1447-15} [*and in the left-hand margin*] <1535> [*and in the left-hand margin in a modern hand*] 1533-4

Arr'

First the seid wardens hath ben charged with tharrer' of the last acconmptes as it doth appere in the Fote of the same acomptes	xv s. ij d.
The seid wardens also hath ben charged with other peculyer sumes of dettes as it doth appere also in the Fote of the last accomptes	iij li. viij d.

S[um]ma iij li. xv s. x d.

Receites Comen

First rec' apon all hallou day for the rode lightes anno r[egni] r[egis] h. viij^i xxv^o	xij s. xj d.
Rec' apon cristmas day the same yere for the rode lyghtes	xiij s. ij d.
Rec' in paschall money the same yere	xl s. ij d.
Rec' of men & women at hock tyde the same yere	xxxv s. vij d.

1. The names are those of leading men in the parish headed by the then mayor, who doubtless dominated the discussion. That the mayor had custody of the cup is indicative of his importance in the parish meeting. See Introduction for a discussion of his role there.
2. This agreement is in a different sixteenth-century hand and ink. The next sentence is in yet another hand. The date is incorrect; she died in 1532-3
3. This entry is in another sixteenth-century hand, almost certainly after 1549 because it uses the term 'communion cup' rather than 'chalice'. A note in a modern hand reads, 'Compare this with the writing on p. 311 Anno 1564.'

Rec' of {J} the yong men gatheryd on the Fare day that yere	xix d.
Rec' of the Jh[esu]s wardens towardes the sextons wages end' at Mic' anno xxvj°	xxxiij s. iiij d.
Rec' of our ladyes wardens towardes the sextons wages dew then	xxxiij s. iiij d.

S[um]ma viij li. x s. j d.

Rentes at Ferme

Rec' of John Barfott for the yeres rent of a tenement in the north side of the new strete endyd at Midsomer last before this accomptes	x s.
Rec' of John appowell for the yeres rent of a stable in guttur lane end' then	iij s. vj d.
Rec' of Margaret Carpenter for the yeres rent of a garden in guttur lane end' then	iiij d.
Rec' of agnes slyther for the yeres rent of ij° gardens in lyrkmer lane end' then	ij s. viij d.
Rec' of John white for the yeres rent of ij° tenementes in the south side of the newe strete endyd then	xiij s. iiij d.
Rec' of M[as]ter labourne for one quarter rent of his chamber end' at cristmas	xx d.
Rec' over for the rent of the corner tenement called the Flechars shopp	xviij d.

S[um]ma xxxij s. x d.

Rentes Ass'

Rec' of John wilder of thele for the yeres rent of half an acre mede lyeng in langley endyd at Michaellmas anno h. viijⁱ xxv°	xxiij d.
Rec' of the heires of william Justice for the tenement in the Market place in the hold of John Barker for a yere endyd then	xij d.
Rec' of Robert hunt for the yeres rent of a tenement in the high strete endyd then	xiij d. ob.
Rec' of the tenement in the newe strete late of henry More for a yere endyd at Michaelmas anno r[egni] r[egis] h. viijⁱ xxvj°	j d.

S[um]ma iij s. iij d. ob.

[p 192]	Seates	
Rec' for the seate of Mestres Margaret stonbank		vj d.
Rec' for the seat of John byrdes wyffe		vj d.

Rec' of thomas Tayller for his wyffes seat	vj d.
Rec' of william watlyngton for his wyffes seat	vj d.
Rec' of peter rede for his wyffes seat in the midle range before the Fonte	iiij d.

S[um]ma ij s. iiij d.

Great bell

Rec' for the knyll of Ric' Eve	xij d.
Rec' for tollyng at his months mynd	iiij d.
Rec' for ryngyng at the yeres mynde of agnes vansby	xij d.
Rec' for the knyll of henry Cokes wyffe	xij d.
Rec' for toleyng at the yeres mynde of philipp Rysseby	iiij d.
Rec' for toleyng at the yeres mynde of Symon lames wyffe	iiij d.
Rec' of John Kent for toleyng at the yeres mynde of his frendes	iiij d.
Rec' for toleyng at the yeres mynde of M[as]ter pownser	iiij d.
Rec' for the knyll of blakeman of Tylehurst	xij d.
Rec' for the knyll of sir Robert heth	xij d.
Rec' for ryngyng at his months mynde	xij d.
Rec' for the knyll of Als watlyngton	xij d.
Rec' for ryngyng at her months mynde	xij d.

S[um]ma ix s. viij d.

Graves

Rec' for the grave of Ric' Eve	vj s. viij d.
& for Coveryng the same	viij d.
Rec' for the grave of Als paynter wydow	vj s. viij d.
& for Coveryng the same	viij d.
Rec' for the grave of sir Robert heth	vj s. viij d.
& for Coveryng the same & laying of a stone	xvj d.
Rec' for the grave of Als watlington	vj s. viij d.
& for Coveryng the same	viij d.
Rec' for Coveryng of Ric' chesters grave dew of old	viij d.

S[um]ma xxx s. viij d.

S[um]ma totalis Recept' & Arr' xvj li. iiij s. viij d. ob.

[*p 193*] Exspenses Comen	
payd to John Darlyngton towardes his wages this yere endyd at Michaelmas anno r[egni] r[egis] h. viij¹ xxvj^o	v li. ix s. iiij d.
payd to steven thorpp towardes his wages this yere endyd then	xxvj s. viij d.

payd to Ric' Androw towardes his wages this yere endyd then	xij s.
payd to william Norres his wages this yere endyd then	vj s. viij d.
payd the qwyte rentes dew this yere	ij s. vj d.
payd for the obytt kept for the benefactours of the churche this yere	v s. x d.
payd for wasshyng the churche gere this yere	iiij s. iiij d.
payd for skowryng the kanstykes this yere	ij s.
payd for watchyng the sepulcre	viij d.
payd for a pownd of Franken sense	xij d.
payd for xiiij li. of new wex bought at london	vj s. viij d.
payd for karyeng the same wex from london	j d.
payd for makeyng the rode lightes agenst halloutyde & Cristmas	xviij d.
payd for vij li. of tallow kandles	x d. ob.
payd for quarte of basterd {at} <for> the passion apon palme sonday	iiij d.
payd for ij° busshels of colles for fyre on easter Eve	ij d.
payd for makeyng the pascall font taper & for j li. of sysses	viij d.
payd for half a hide of whitlether	xiiij d.
payd for mendyng of bawdrykes this yere	xij d.
payd for a rope to the great bell	ij s. ij d.
payd for a rope to the treble bell	xix d. ob.
payd for a rope to the sanctus bell	xij d.
payd for karyeng away of ij° lodes of rubell	iiij d.
payd for ij° busshels & an half of sleked lyme	ij d. ob.
payd for ij° lodes of sond	x d.
payd for ryngyng at the kynges commyng to town & other tymes	vj d.
payd for settyng on parrers apon the childrens albs	viij d.
payd for mendyng of one of the rectours stoles	ij d.
payd for mendyng the cover of the font	iij d.
payd for dowles to make viij[th] new slopps	xij s. vij d.
payd for makeyng the same slopes	ij s. iiij d.
payd for a lyne to pull upp the rode cloth	j d. ob.
payd for poyntes for the Canapye	ob.
payde to pastler for settyng the braunche apan the rode loft & layng bordes there	xvj d.
payd for a quartern of bordes	viij d.
payd for cuttyng the iren barre in the rode lofte & for workmanshypp of the same with naylles therto	vj d. ob.

S[um]ma paginis x li. vij s. ix d.

[*p 194*] payd for mendyng the braunche apon the rode lofte	ij d.
payd to pastler the Carpenter for mendyng the fore bell whele & mendyng other fawtes in the same	xvij d. ob.
payd for naylles for the same & for other reparracions	iiij d. ob.
payd for a pece of tymber to make bell wheles	xvj d.
payd for sawyng the same pece	viij d.
payd to a man of Crenden for trussyng & serchyng the belles[1]	xx d.
payd to Norres for his attendance to the same	iiij d.
payd for Coveryng of iij^e graves	xij d.
payd for Coveryng of sir hethes grave with a stone[2]	xij d.
payd to Mr labourne for refourmyng the resurreccion play	viij s. iiij d.
payd for a ryng & a latche with a catche for the chauncell dore	viij d.
payd to the Curyers wyfe for bordyng of a syngyng man	xx d.
payd for makeyng & regesteryng this accomptes	ij s.

S[um]ma xx s. viij d.

S[um]ma totalis exspences xj li. viij s. v d.

[*in the margin before the next entry*] sol'
  Et sic re[mane]t apon this accomptes iiij li. xvj s. iij d. ob.
                    Unde
[*in the margin before the next three entries*] Super
[*and at the beginning of the next two entries*] x

{Rec' over of} william Dave for the grave of Ric' Foxley	vj s. viij d.

[*in the margin before the next entry*] sol'

& for coveryng the same grave	viij d.

  {Et sic re[mane]t apon this accomptes v li. iij s. iij d. ob.
                    Unde}
[*in the margin before the next two entries*] Super

Freres oxon' pro le organs	l s.
Robertum Medwyn Carpenter dew of old	iij s. iiij d.

Et sic re[mane]t xxxv s. vij d. ob.

<Rec'> aftur of william Dave the sumes above	vij s. iiij d.

          Et sic re[mane]t xlij s. xj d. ob.>

Wherof payd to our lady masse in parte of payment of v li. borowyd there[3]	xl s.

1. Probably the village of Long Crendon, South Buckinghamshire.
2. Sir Robert Hethe was buried in church and a stone laid there earlier in the year (accounts p. 192). Why a second attempt at laying a stone was needed is not clear.
3. The churchwardens had borrowed five pounds in addition to a donation of £1 2s 4d from Our

And so re[mane]t clere apon this accomptes ij s. xj d. ob.

And so is dismyssed Robert watlyngton, and Ric' Noves.
And of new chosen william paslow & Robert hodson

1534-5
[*p 195*] **Thaccomptes of william paslow & Robert hodson
wardens of saynt Laurence churche in Redyng from the
Feast of saynt Michaell tharchaungell in the xxvj^{ti} yere of
the reigne of king henry the viijth unto the same Fest then
next Folloyng** [*sic*]{1535}
[*In the left-hand margin in a sixteenth-century hand*] {1536}
[*and in a modern hand*] 1534-5

Arr'
First the seid wardens hath ben charged with tharrerage of   ij s. xj d. ob.
the last accomptes as it doth appere in the Fote of the same
accomptes

S[um]ma ij s. xj d. ob.

Arr'
The seid wardens also hath ben charged with other particuler   l s.
detes that is to witt apon the Freres of Oxon for the organs
& apon Robert Medwyn for parcell of his wyffes grave dew   iij s. iiij d.
for iiij^{or} yeres past

S[um]ma liij s. iiij d.

Receptes Comen
First Rec' in gaderyng in the churche <for the rode lightes>   xj s. iij d. ob.
apon all hallou day this yere
Rec' apon Cristmas day for the same   xiij s. iiij d.
Rec' in paschall money this yere   xxxix s.
Rec' of men & women gaderyd at hocketyde   xxxvij s. iij d. ob.
Rec' of Jh[esu]s wardens towardes the sextons wages for a   xxxiij s.
yere end' at Mic' last before this accomptes   iiij d.
Rec' of our ladyes wardens in lykewysse towardes the   xxxiij s. iiij d.
same

S[um]ma viij li. vij s. vij d.

Lady's gild in 1531-2 for repairs to the chancels (accounts p. 183). They repaid £1 2s 4d the
same year (p. 186) and in 1533-4 another two pounds. Obviously they were not finding
repayment easy.

Rentes at Ferme

Rec' of John Barfott for the yeres rent of a tenement in the north side of the new strete endyd at Midsomer last before this accomptes	x s.
Rec' of John ap powell for the yeres rent of a stable in guttur lane endyd at the same Feast	iij s. vj d.
Rec' of Margaret Carpenter for the yeres rent of a garden in guttur lane endyd then	iiij d.
Rec' of Agnes slythurst for the yeres rent of ij° gardeyns in lyrkmer lane endyd then	ij s. viij d.
Rec' of John white for the yeres rent of ij° tenementes in the south side of the new strete endyd then	xiij s. iiij d.
Rec' for the hyre of the Flechers shopp in the market place this yere	iiij d.

S[um]ma xxx s. ij d.

Rentes Ass'

Rec' of John wilder of thele for the yeres rent of half an acre mede lyeng in Aston Mede endyd at Michelmas anno r[egni] r[egis] h. viij^i xxvj°	xiij d.
Rec' of the heires of william Justice for the tenement in the Markett place in the hold of John Barker for a yere endyd at the same Fest	xij d.
Rec' of Robert hunt for the yeres rent of a tenement in the high strete end' then	xiij d. ob.
Rec' the qwyte rent of the tenement in the south side of the new strete late sold to henry More for a yere endyd at Mic' anno r[egni] r[egis] h. viij^i xxvij°	j d.

S[um]ma iij s. iij d. ob.

[p 196] Seattes	
Rec' of John Byllyngton for his wyffes seate	vj d.
Rec' of Mistres kent & Mistres knyght for a seate	vj d.
Rec' of Thomas skynner for his wyffes seate	vj d.
Rec' of John hychyns for his wyffes seate	vj d.
Rec' of Ric' pynnok for his wyffes seate	vj d.
Rec' of Olyver Southworth for his wyffes seate	vj d.

S[um]ma iij s.

Great bell

Rec' for the knyll of Symon lambb & ryngyng at his monthes mynde	ij s.
Rec' for the knyll of Ric' Barnes & ryngyng at his monthes mynde	ij s.
Rec' for the knyll of M[as]ter Ric' Bedow & ryngyng at his monthes mynde[1]	ij s.
Rec' for tollyng at the monthes mynde of philipp Rysseby	iiij d.
Rec' for tollyng at the yeres mynde of Ric' Eve	iiij d.
Rec' for the knyll of Mistres Carpenter & for tollyng at her monthes mynde	xvj d.
Rec' for the knyll of Thomas Everard servantis Abbatis[2]	xij d.
Rec' for tollyng at the yeres mynde of Mistres vansby	iiij d.
Rec' for tollyng at the yeres mynde of Nicholus hyde	iiij d.
Rec' for tollyng at the yeres mynde of John Andrewes wyffe	iiij d.
Rec' for the knyll of M[as]ter Everard & for ryngyng at his monthes mynde	ij s.
Rec' for the knyll of Nicolus Eve & tollyng at his monthes mynde	xvj d.
Rec' for the knyll of John Andrewes wyffe & tollyng at her monthes mynde	xvj d.
Rec' for tollyng at the yeres mynde of Christofer butteler	iiij d.
Rec' for tollyng at the yeres mynde of Robert watlyngtons wyffe	iiij d.
Rec' for tollyng at the yeres mynde of Sir heth	iiij d.
Rec' for tollyng at the yeres mynde of M[as]t[er] pounser	iiij d.
Rec' for the knyll of M[as]t[er] wattes & ryngyng at his monthes mynde	ij s.

S[um]ma xviiij s.

Graves

Rec' for the grave of Symon lambb & Coveryng the same with a stone	x s.
Rec' for the grave Ric' Barnes & Coveryng the same with a stone	vij s. viij d.
Rec' for the grave of Mistres carpenter & Coveryng the same with a stone	viij s.
Rec' for the grave of Thomas Everard[3]	vj s. viij d.
Rec' for Coveryng of M[as]ter Bedowes grave	xij d.
Rec' for the grave of Nicholus Eve & coveryng the same	vjj s. iiij d.

1. In his will made 15 November 1533 and proved 21 January 1533/4 Richard Bedow, the vicar, bequeathed 40s for repairs to the church. Kerry, *A History*, 175-7. See accounts below.
2. In a different hand in the right-hand margin 'Abbates servant'.
3. In the right-hand margin in a different hand 'Abbates servantes grave'.

Rec' for the grave of John Androwes wyffe & coveryng the same	vij s. iiij d.
Rec' for the grave of M[as]ter wattes & coveryng the same with a stone	vij s. viij d.

S[um]ma lv s. viij d.

Rec' of the gyfte of Ric' Barnes	vj s. viij d.
Rec' of the gyfte of M[as]ter Bedow	xl s.
Rec' of the gyfte of M[as]ter wattes[1]	xx s.
Rec' more & borrowed	v li. vj s. viij d.
<videlicet of Jh[esu]s Masse v markes & of our ladyes masse>	<xl s.>

S[um]ma viij li. xiij s. iiij d.

[*p 197*] Rec' of M[as]ter Everard for vij C tylles to hym sold	iij s. vj d.
Rec' of steven thorpp for v C tylles to hym sold	ij s. vj d.
Rec' of Ric' Androw for old tymber to hym sold	vj d.
Rec' more for half C tyles	iij d.
Rec' for lxxx tyles sold	v d.
Rec' for the old harnes of saynt george sold	vj d.

S[um]ma vij s. viij d.

S[um]ma tot[a]lis recept' & arr' xxv li. xv s.

Exspenses Comen

payd to John Darlyngton towardes his wages dew at Mic' last past	v li. ix s. iiij d.
payd to steven thorpp towardes his wages this yere endyd then	xxvj s. viij d.
payd to the sexton towardes his wages this yere endyd then	xij s.
payd to william Norres his wages for bloyng the organs this yere	vj s. viij d.
payd the qwyte rentes dew this yere	ij s. vj d.
payd for the obytt kept for the benefactours this yere	v s.
payd for wasshyng the churche gere this yere	iij s. iiij d.
payd for skowryng the kanstykes this yere	xx d.
payd for watchyng the sepulcre this yere	viij d.
payd for j li. {of} and di' of Franken sense	ij s.
payd for xiiij li. of new wex at vij d. ob. the pound	viij s. ix d.

---

1. In his will made in July and proved in November 1535, William Wattes made bequests to both parish gilds and gave 20s for repairs to the church. Kerry, *A History*, 177-8.

payd for makeyng the rode lightes agenst halloutyde & Christenmas	xxij d.
payd for ij li. of tallow kandelles	viij d. ob.
payd for a quarte of Basterd for syngyng the passion apon palme sonday	iij d.
payd for ij° bz of Cooles for Fyre on easter Eve	ij d.
payd for makeyng the paschall font taper & j li. of syses	xv d.
payd for halff a hyde of whitlether	x d.
payd for mendyng of bawdrykes & bell roppes at dyvers tymes this yere	xiiij d.
payd for vj busshels & an half of lyme at ij d. the bz	xiij d.
payd for karyeng away on lood of Rubbell	vj d.
payd for settyng on parells apon the albs at dyvers tymes	viij d.
payd for ryngyng at the kynges comyng to town & at his goyng	viij d.
payd for iij[e] bell ropps	v s. iiij d.
payd to Thomas Alyn for playng at the organs vij wekes	ix s.
payd to Thomas skynner for playng at the organs from saynt Thomas day unto candlemas day & for iije wekes aftur	xij s.
It' payd to edward ham in ernest for his service	j d.
payd for iij[e] plankes for seates in the churche	xvj d.
payd for Coveryng the graves of Symon lambb Ric' barnes M[as]t[er] bedow & Mistres Carpenter	iiij s. viij d.
payd for ij° clamps of Iren for the stepp afore the Jh[esu]s awter	iiij d.

S[um]ma xj li. v d. ob.

[p 198] payd for xxx[ti] brykes	iij d. ob.
payd for mendyng of xvij Coopes & the hangynges in the qwere	vj s. viij d.
payd for the mendyng of ij° surplesses & iij[e] sloppes	v d.
payd to a syngyng man that cam from Ryckemansworth[1]	ij s.
payd for mendyng a kanstyk & a holy water stok	viij d.
payd for mendyng the glassen wyndow over the dyall	xiiij d.
payd for mendyng the forth bell clapper	iij s. iiij d.
payd for mendyng the sanctus bell whele	xij d.
payd for C and di' of pavyng tyles	iiij s.
payd for mendyng the organs	ix s.
payd for mendyng the great paxe	j d.
payd for mendyng the lantren for visitacions	vij d.
payd for Fetchyng of bestones sun from hendeley[2]	v d.

---

1. Rickmansworth is a town in Hertfordshire.
2. Henley-on-Thames is a town in south Oxfordshire about eight miles from Reading.

payd for iiij^{or} yerdes of motteley at xiij d the yerd to make a Cote for John Browne that sang the mean[1]	iiij s. iiij d.
payd for lynyng & makeyng the same Cote	xxj d.
payd for poyntes for the Canapie	ob.
payd for an ounces of garnesshyng rybond	xiiij d.
payd to Richard Turnour for his costes & labour when he went to Eaton[2] for a Clerk <at dyvers tymes>	iij s.
payd for [blank] yerdes of rede fustyen inaples[3] at [blank] the yerd & for vj yerdes of grene bockerham at vj d. the yerd	xl s. ij d.
payd for a yerd of rolled bockerham	vj d. ob.
payd for ix elles of hollond to make M[as]ter vicar a surples at ix d. the ell & for makeyng of the same s[um]ma	viij s. ix d.

S[um]ma iiij li. {iiij} <ix> s. v d. ob.

Costes don apon sir Nic' chamber

payd for bordyng the wall there & for naylles thereto	viij d.
payd for Fewtryng the draugght there	xvj d.
payd for a key to the shopp dore[4]	ij d.
payd for brykes to pave the hall	xvij d.
payd for iij^e busshelles of stone lyme	vj d.
payd to the Carpenter for workmanshypp & for tymber	ij s. vj d.

S[um]ma vj s vij d

Charges of Saynt George

First payd for iiij^{or} Caffes skynes <& ij^o horsse skynes>	iiij s. vj d.
payd for makeyng the loft that Saynt George standeth appon	vj d.
payd for ij^o plonkes for the same loft	viij d.
payd for iiij^{or} pesses of Clowt lether	ij s. ij d.
payd for makeyng the yren that the hors resteth apon	vj d.
payd for makeyng of saynt Georges Cote	viij d.
payd to John paynter for his labour	xlv s.
payd for roses belles gyrdle swerd & dager	iij s. iiij d.
payd for settyng on the belles & roses	iij d.

1. The mean was the middle line in polyphony sung by a tenor or alto. Motley was a cloth of
mixed colours, possibly the same as mingled cloth, woven with several coloured yarns.
2. Eton was a collegiate foundation of priests and scholars in Buckinghamshire
3. Probably a corrupt form of inapes or anapes, a cloth originally made in Naples.
4. This suggests the priest's room was behind or above a shop.

payd for naylles necessarie therto   x d. ob.
payd for makeyng & regesteryng this accomptes   ij s.

S[um]ma iij li. v d. ob.

S[um]ma tot[a]lis exspenses & sol'
xviij li. xvj s. xj d. ob.

Et Sic re[mane]t vj li. xviij s. ob. Unde Super ut sequitur
verte folium
[p 199] Super Fratres oxon   l s.
Executores Magistri Ricardi Bedow   xl s.
Robertum Medwyn   iij s. iiij d.

S[um]ma iiij li. xiij s. iiij d.

Et Sic re[mane]t super Computant' xliiij s. viij d. ob. to our
ladies Box for money borowed as is afore
wherof {he} paid {to me} xl s. {& yet he oweth viz iiij s.
viij d. ob.}[1]

And So is dysmyssed william paslow & new elect Richard
{H} Dodgeson

[*In the margin in a later sixteenth- or seventeenth-century
hand.*]   The letting of the halfe Acre of meede[2]
Ad retroscriptum Compot' willelmi paslow & Roberti
hodson tent' in Festo Appostolorum Simonis & Jude anno
r[egni] r[egis] h viij[i] xxvij[o] venit Johannes Blakeman de
hamlet voc' blandes infra parochiam de Tylehurst et cepit de
prefat' procurator' sive gardian' unam di' acr' prati iac' in
quodam prato voc' Aston Mede infra parochiam de
Burghfeld in Com' Berk' Habend' & tenend' sibi & assignat'
suis a Festo sancti Michaelis Archangeli ultimo preterit' ante
dat' prescript' usque ad Finem termini quadriginta annorum
extn' prox' sequenc' & plenar' complend' Reddend' inde
annuatim durant' d[i]c[t]o termino procuratoribus sive
gardian' {dict'} ecclesie sancti laurenc' Rading' pro tempore

1. From the original credit balance of £6 18s 0 ½ d, the churchwardens deducted £4 13s 4d still
not received leaving them £2 4s 8½ d in hand. They paid off another two pounds of the debt to
Our Lady's gild with the rest handed on to the next wardens. It seems they still owed one pound
to the gild.
2. This was a new lease. The previous tenant, John Wilder, is first named in the accounts of
1508/9. The parish had leased the land at the same rent from at least 1498. The parish meeting
was seemingly the time for dealing with important property transactions. The lease is in standard
form for a set time with an entry fine or fee to take on the lease, and a fixed yearly rent. During
the term of the lease, inflation would make the fixed rent very advantageous to the tenant.

existent' tresdecem den' sterling solvend' ad Festum sancti Michaelis Archangeli [?t[ermi]ni] Et dedit pro Fine iij s. iiij d.

[*John Blakeman of the hamlet called Blandes within the parish of Tylehurst came to the accounting of William Paslow and Robert Hodson held on the feast of the apostles Simon and Jude [28th October] in the 27th year of the reign of King Henry VIII [1535] and took from the aforesaid proctors or wardens half an acre of meadow lying in a certain meadow called Aston Mede within the parish of Burghfield in the county of Berkshire. To have and to hold to him and his assignes from the last feast of Saint Michael Archangel before this writing until the end of the term of forty years fully completed paying annually at the feast of Saint Michael Archangel during the said term to the then proctors or wardens of the church of Saint Laurence, Reading thirteen pence sterling.   And he gives 3s 4d as a fine.*]

1535-6

Thaccomptes of Robert hodson & Ric' Dodgeson wardens of saynt laurenc churche in Redyng from the Feast of saynt Michell tharchaungell in the xxvij^{ti} **yere of the reigne of king henry the viij**th **unto the same Feast next followyng. 1536**

[*In the left-hand margin in a sixteenth-century hand*] {1537}
[*and in a modern hand*] 1535 1536

Arr'

First the seid wardens hath ben charged with tharrer' of the last acc' as it doth appere in the fote of the same accomptes S[um]ma iiij s. viij d. ob.	iiij s. viij d. ob.

The seid wardens also hath ben charged with other particler detes as it doth appere also in the fote of the seid accomptes, that is to witt apon the Freres of oxon l s. apon Robert Medwyn in partie of payment for his wyffes grave dew for Fyve yeres past iij s. iiij d. & apon thexecutours of Mayster Bedow xl s. s[um]ma	iiij li. xiij s. iiij d.

S[um]ma iiij li. xiij s. iiij d.

Receites Comen

Rec' in gaderyng for the Rode lyghtes apon alhallou day	x s. v d.
Rec' in gadryng for the rode lyghtes apon Cristmas day	x s. vij d.
Rec' at Easter in paschall money this yere	xxxvij s. x d.

Rec' of the men & women gaderyd at hocketyde this yere	xxxvij s. vj d.
Rec' of Jh[esu]s wardens towardes the sextons wayges for a yere endyd at Michaelmas last before this accomptes	xxxiij s. iiij d.
Rec' of the wardens of our ladye towardes the same	xxxiij s. iiij d.

S[um]ma viij li. iij s.

[p 200]   Rentes at Ferme

Rec' of John Barfott for the yeres rent of a tenement in the North syde of the newe strete endyd at midsomer last before this accomptes	x s.
Rec' of John apowell for the yeres rent of a stable in guttur lane endyd at the same Feast	iij s. vj d.
Rec' of kateryn Carpenter for the yeres rent of a garden in the same lane endyd then	iiij d.
Rec' of agnes slyther for the yeres rent of ij° gardeyns in lyrkmer lane endyd then	ij s. viij d.
Rec' of John white for the yeres rent of ij° tenementes in the south side of the new strete endyd then	xiij s. iiij d.
Rec' of the Flechers shopp in the Markett place this yere	n[ihi]l

S[um]ma xxix s. x d.

Rec' of John Blakemon of blandes for a Fyne of half an acre mede lyeng in aston mede lett to hym for xl^ti yeres	xl d.
Rec' of the beqwest of williyam knyght	vj s. viij d.

S[um]ma x s.

Rentes Ass'

Rec' of John Blakeman of blandes for the yeres rent of half an acre mede lyeng in aston mede within the parishe of Burghfeld for a yere endyd at Michelmas anno r[egni] r[egis] h. viij^i xxvij°	xiij d.
Rec' of the heires of williyam for the tenement in the Markett place in the hold of John Barker for a yere endyd then	xij d.
Rec' of Robert Hunt for the yeres rent of a tenement in the high strete endyd then	xiij d. ob.
Rec' for the yeres rent of the tenement in the south side of the new strete late of Henry More for a yere endyd at Mic' anno r[egni] r[egis] h. viij^i xxviij°	j d.

S[um]ma iij s. iij d. ob.

Seattes

Rec' of James wylde for his wyffes seatt \<the middle range\>	iiij d.
Rec' for the seatt of williyam lyppescoms wyffe	vj d.
Rec' for the seatt of John Chundlers wyffe	vj d.
Rec' for the seatt of Ric' smythes wyffe	vj d.
Rec' for the seatt of John barkers wyffe the yonger	vj d.
Rec' for the seatt of John Browns wyffe the elder	vj d.
Rec' for the seatt of John byllyngtons wyffe	vj d.
Rec' for the seatt of {John} Steven Cawettes wyffe	vj d.
Rec' for the seatt of Henry wattes wyffe	vj d.

S[um]ma iiij s. iiij d.

[p 201]   The great bell

Rec' for ryngyng at the yeres mynde of M[as]ter Richard Bedow	xij d.
Rec' for ryngyng at the yeres mynde of Richard Barns	xij d.
Rec' for ryngyng at the yeres mynde of Symon lambb	xij d.
Rec' for tollyng at the yeres mynde of Nicholus hyde	iiij d.
Rec' for tollyng at the yeres mynde of Thomas Everard	iiij d.
Rec' for tollyng at the yeres mynde of Agnes vansby	iiij d.
Rec' for tollyng at the yeres mynde of Als watlyngton	iiij d.
Rec' for the knyll of williyam knyght	xij d.
Rec' for ryngyng at his monthes mynde	xij d.
Rec' for the knyll of Anne hodson	xij d.
Rec' for ryngyng at her months mynde	xij d.
Rec' for ryngyng at the yeres mynde of williyam wattes	xij d.

S[um]ma ix s. iiij d.

Rec' for the grave of williyam knyght & Coveryng the same with a stone	vij s. viij d.
Rec' for the grave of Anne hodson & for Coveryng the same	vij s. iiij d.

S[um]ma xv s.
S[um]ma tot[a]lis rec' cum arr' xvj li. xij s. x d.

Exspenses Comen

payd to John Darlyngton towardes his wages dew at Michaellmas last past before this accomptes	v li. ix s. iiij d.
payd to steven Thorpp towardes his yeres wages dew then	xxvj s. viij d.
payd to the under sexton towardes his yeres wages dew then	xlvj s. viij d.
payd to williyam Norres for blowyng the organs this yere	vj s. viij d.
payd to the same williyam for lyghtyng the tapers this yere	ij s. iiij d.
payd to Ric' Androw for kepyng the clok one quarter end' at Mic' last	xxd.

payd the qwyte rentes dew this yere	ij s. vj d.
payd for the obytt kept for the benefactours this yere	v s. iiij d.
payd for wasshyng the churche gere this yere	iij s. iiij d.
payd for skowryng the kanstykes this yere	ij s. ij d.
payd for watchyng the sepulcre this yere	viij d.
payd for j li. of Franken sense	xvj d.
payd to the regester for [*blank*][1]	ij s ob.
payd to Robert watlyngton tharrer' of the same for the last yere	ij s ob.
payd for iij li. of new wex for the rode lightes	ij s.
payd for makeyng the rode lightes agenst halloutyde & Cristmas	xvj d. ob.
payd for vij li. of tallow kandles	viij d. ob. qua'
payd for makeyng of iiij li. & an half of syses	iij d. ob.
payd for a quarte of basterd for the passion on palme sonday	iij d.
payd for ij° bz cooles for fyre on easter eve	ij d.
payd for xij li. of wex for the paschall & font taper	vij s.
payd for makeyng the paschall & font taper	xiiij d.
payd for karyeng away ij° loodes of Rubbell	iiij d.

S[um]ma xj li. vj s. j d. ob. qua'

[*p 202*] payd for mendyng of Coopes & vestmentes this yere	ij s.
payd for half a hyde of whitlether	xx d.
payd for mendyng of bawdrykes this yere	iiij d.
payd for a lyne to toll the great bell	viij d.
payd for a lood of sond	vj d.
payd for Coveryng of Fyve graves & mendyng other fautes	iiij s.
payd to hugh smyth for iiij^or gemeys for the bere	ij s. ij d.
payd to the same Hugh for mendyng the rectours stole[2]	ij d.
payd to Ric' Joynner for makeyng a dore to an ambre	iij d.
payd for naylles	j d.
payd to sir labourne for a boke of the resurreccion play for a quare of paper & for byndyng therof	ix s. x d.
payd for takeyng down the braunche in the qwere	iiij d.
payd to Hugh Smyth for settyng upp the same braunche agayn & for mendyng a dore to an aumbrey	viij d.
payd to the same hugh for a loke to the cloke	vj d.
payd to the same hugh for mendyng the clok	iiij d.
payd to sir peter the Frere for mendyng a boke	iiij d.
payd for mendyng the organs	xij d.

1. This payment had previously been recorded as 'smoke farthings' or Peter's Pence. The blank may indicate uncertainty about its designation. A statute of 1534 had forbidden payment to Rome and appropriated it to the crown. *The Tudor Constitution*, ed. G. R. Elton (Cambridge, 1965), 351. No payment appears in the accounts of 1533-4.

2. Probably stool rather than stole. The rectors or cantors sat in front of the choir stalls.

payd for iiij^{or} slopps at ij s. j d. ob. a pece S[um]ma	viij s. vj d.
payd for a new bere & for mendyng the old	v s. vij d.
payd for Fyne Croyll	ij d.
payd for ij° bz of lyme	iiij d.
payd for viij yerdes of narrow lyre	j d.
payd for xij yerdes of brode lyre	vj d.
payd for cloth delyvered to John paynter	iiij d. ob.
payd for xxvj^{ti} pavementes at ob. a pece	xiij d.
payd for makeyng ij° Coopes of Cremysyn saten	iij s. iiij d.
payd for makeyng a Fresse Cote for byestons son	viij d.
payd for makeyng & regesteryng this accomptes	ij s.

S[um]ma xlvij s. v d. ob.

S[um]ma totalis exspenses[1] xiij li. xiij s. vij d. ob.

And so remayneth lix s. ij d. ob. Unde
[*in the margin before the next entry*] Super

[*in margin*] Super Freres Oxon	l s.
Et super Robertum Medwyn	iij s. iiij d.

And so remayneth apon this accompte v s. x d. ob.
And thus dysmyssed Robert Hodson & new chosen Steven
Cawett

---

1. The abbreviation used is that for 'sir'. This has been transcribed as 'ses'.
2. For more about Stephen Cawett or Cawood see Appendix 2.